We Shall Bear Witness

Wisconsin Studies in Autobiography

WILLIAM L. ANDREWS
Series Editor

We Shall Bear Witness

Life Narratives and Human Rights

Edited by

MEG JENSEN

and

MARGARETTA JOLLY

The University of Wisconsin Press

The University of Wisconsin Press
1930 Monroe Street, 3rd Floor
Madison, Wisconsin 53711-2059
uwpress.wisc.edu

3 Henrietta Street
London WC2E 8LU, England
eurospanbookstore.com

Printed in the United States of America

Library of Congress Cataloging-in-Publication Data
We shall bear witness: life narratives and human rights /
edited by Meg Jensen and Margaretta Jolly.
pages   cm — (Wisconsin studies in autobiography)
Includes bibliographical references and index.
ISBN 978-0-299-30014-2 (pbk.: alk. paper)
ISBN 978-0-299-30013-5 (e-book)
1. Human rights.   2. Essays.   3. Human rights in literature.
4. Human rights in art.   5. Human rights—Study and teaching.
I. Jensen, Meg, editor of compilation.   II. Jolly, Margaretta, editor of compilation.
III. Series: Wisconsin studies in autobiography.
JC571.W3   2014
323—dc23
2013043104

We dedicate this volume to the witnesses, survivors, and activists
who have so generously shared their stories in this book, EMIN MILLI,
NAZEEHA SAEED, and HECTOR ARISTIZÁBAL.

And you, my friends who have been called away,
I have been spared to mourn for you and weep,
Not as a frozen willow over your memory,
But to cry to the world the names of those who sleep.

ANNA AKHMATOVA

Stories can conquer fear, you know. They can make the heart larger.

BEN OKRI

It is not the voice that commands the story: it is the ear.

ITALO CALVINO

Contents

Part Three. Representation

Part Four. Justice

Part Five. Learning

Foreword

Life Stories in a Human Rights Context

MARY ROBINSON

Human rights increasingly enter every aspect of the modern world, and the day-to-day lives of people in every country. Milestones have included the adoption of the Convention on the Elimination of Discrimination against Women (CEDAW) in 1979, the Convention on the Rights of the Child in 1989, and the World Conference on Human Rights in Vienna in 1993. But implementation of rights is not without controversy, and neither is it a steady transition.

When I became the United Nations High Commissioner for Human Rights in 1997, I drew attention to the fact that even within the UN itself, in discussions on peacekeeping or development issues, the human rights perspective was often omitted or downplayed at the time. There has been some improvement, but we have still not fully implemented an explicitly rights-based approach to the Millennium Development Goals.

Many say that personal testimonies and life writings about the experience of abuse and struggle play a crucial role in showing not just the human cost but also incredible resilience. It was important to me as high commissioner to travel to the places where violations of human rights were occurring, listen to victims, and try to help amplify their stories as direct witnesses of abuse. I recall vividly sitting in Freetown, Sierra Leone, with three young girls who had been captured together with child soldiers during the fighting in 1999 and had become sex slaves to the boys and men of the rebel group. Their stories were horrific, and told with tears, but the three girls had escaped, and with support from the United Nations Children's Fund (UNICEF) were now in school uniforms and about to sit exams. Somehow, they had the courage to put their lives back together.

The reason I formed Realizing Rights: The Ethical Globalization Initiative was to put more emphasis on economic and social rights and to illustrate how to protect and promote them in practice. Working with my colleagues and our partners in a number of African countries on rights to health and decent work;

on women, peace, and security issues; and on corporate responsibility, I became aware of a new human rights issue. Severe weather shocks were undermining livelihoods, and adversely affecting rights to food, safe water, and health, in countries all over Africa. In Liberia the rainy seasons were no longer predictable, affecting agricultural production. In northern Uganda, instead of seasons the pattern had become long periods of drought, followed by flash flooding, then more drought. In Malawi the incidence of both flooding and severe drought was worse than ever experienced. I realized the injustice of this, given that the whole of Africa is responsible for less than 5 percent of greenhouse gas emissions, and yet the effects of climate change are much more severe there than elsewhere because of already vulnerable conditions.

This led me to link issues of human rights, development, and the negative impacts of climate change and establish the Mary Robinson Foundation— Climate Justice. The UN Human Rights Council has recently adopted a series of resolutions concerning the negative impacts of climate change on the enjoyment of human rights and established a new mandate for an independent expert on human rights and the environment. No doubt this will lead to further rich stories of how economic and social rights in particular are being negatively impacted.

I am therefore delighted to introduce this new collection of essays coedited by Meg Jensen and Margaretta Jolly about life narratives in human rights contexts. It is an original and timely book. It brings together in one volume the views of literary critics interested in the way we write about rights and the resilient writings of those who have themselves suffered abuse. Importantly, it also includes the views of practitioners and policy makers in the field of action. All three together show the political, as well as intellectual, need for ongoing critical, humane conversation in this vital area of study.

Acknowledgments

The editors would like to thank our colleagues and collaborators at the Centre for Life History and Life Writing Research at the University of Sussex, the Centre for Life Narratives and the Helen Bamber Centre at Kingston University, and the Departments of Creative Writing and Human Rights at the University of Minnesota. In particular we acknowledge our debt for the initial vision of these interdisciplinary conversations to Professor Patricia Hampl, Department of English and Creative Writing, University of Minnesota; the writer and broadcaster Annette Kobak, Centre for Life Narratives, Kingston University; and Professor Barbara Frey, director of the Human Rights Program, University of Minnesota. We are also grateful to William Andrews, series editor at the University of Wisconsin Press, for his encouragement in seeing this book join the wonderful Wisconsin Studies in Autobiography. We wish to acknowledge the Staff Development Fund in the School of Humanities at Kingston University for their financial support in the production of this volume, and J. Naomi Linzer Indexing Services for the careful preparation of the index. We are especially grateful for Professor Brian Brivati's numerous, invaluable, and expert contributions to the production of this volume from brainstorming to interviewing to writing and editing. Further thanks are due to Dr. David Rogers, Kirsten Winterman, Professor Vesna Goldsworthy, Professor Sidonie Smith, Professor Kay Schaffer, and Professor Julia Watson for their ongoing support, and to Richard Jolly, June Jolly, and Nick Fairclough, without whose enthusiasm and care this volume would be the poorer.

We Shall Bear Witness

Introduction

Life / Rights Narrative in Action

MARGARETTA JOLLY

The Human Rights Act 1998 (also known as the Act or the HRA) came into force in the United Kingdom in October 2000. . . . The Act sets out the fundamental rights and freedoms that individuals in the UK have access to. They include:

- Right to life
- Freedom from torture and inhuman or degrading treatment
- Right to liberty and security
- Freedom from slavery and forced labor
- Right to a fair trial
- No punishment without law
- Respect for your private and family life, home and correspondence
- Freedom of thought, belief and religion
- Freedom of expression
- Freedom of assembly and association
- Right to marry and start a family
- Protection from discrimination in respect of these rights and freedoms
- Right to peaceful enjoyment of your property
- Right to education
- Right to participate in free elections

UNITED KINGDOM GOVERNMENT CITIZENS' ADVICE PAGE

Sign our petition: no arms for atrocities

Emmanuel Jal was forced to join a militia group, pick up a machine gun and fight in Sudan's bloody civil war when he was just eight years old. Sudan is just one of 19 countries where tens of thousands of children

3

are still forcibly recruited as child soldiers. Their recruitment, abduction and arming would be a lot harder if the arms trade was globally regulated. It's not. But the first global treaty regulating the trade could be created this year.

We need UK leaders to stand up for human rights ahead of international talks on arms regulations. Clegg, Miliband and Hague have already voiced their support for an Arms Trade Treaty that protects human rights, but David Cameron has been notably silent on this issue. We have one chance to get this right.

- Add your name to our petition to David Cameron
- Watch Emmanuel speak about why he's supporting our campaign

AMNESTY INTERNATIONAL HOME PAGE

You might imagine, reading government advice pages like that from the UK cited above, that human rights advance through the civilizations of law—with rights codified; appeals made to courts in response to violations, deprivation, and abuse; and obligations acquired by governments and citizens.[1] This legal approach has an important place. But it is only part of a much wider story. Human rights as an emancipatory tool have also developed at crucial moments in response to people's everyday demands that those around them understand their experiences of injustice. The glimpse that Amnesty International gives us of Emmanuel Jal's childhood in violent Sudan, and his personal appeal for its current campaign, tells us as much about the evolution of human rights as any law.[2]

This book looks at the mobilization of public concern through personal accounts and life story narrations as a frequently neglected dimension of change and delivery. Could black South Africans have overturned apartheid without narrating personal stories of suffering? Could Aboriginal Australians or Argentinian "mothers of the disappeared" have emerged as political subjects without readers, listeners, and cinemagoers, not to mention lawyers and politicians, witnessing their narrations? Could the so-called Arab Spring have happened without digital storytelling in the Facebook revolutions and dissident blogs? The language of life stories continues to inspire movements for reform from Latvia to Burma, from American transsexuals to Tibetan monks.

But public airing of human narratives of suffering and abuse is not all powerful. The eloquent personal petitions from Chinese dissidents have done little to dislodge the Chinese government's position on local democracy. Nor have African Americans' prison memoirs and websites convinced many

Americans that their prison system might involve abuse of rights.[3] The government-run community courts of public truth telling in Rwanda have arguably failed to produce narratives of remorse, truth, or empathy on either side.[4] And Brian Brivati, in this volume, proposes that policy makers observed but were not fully motivated to interpret the digital voices of the Arab/North African revolutions of 2011. How effective are testimonies as tools for enhancing human rights? The very different cases discussed in this book, ranging from survivors of al-Khalifa's Bahrain to those of the European Holocaust and Australia's asylum policy, show that there is no simple answer to this question. Rather, life stories gain political purchase in the context of particular historical conditions and opportunities. These conditions are part of what shapes testifiers' classic journeys from silence to speech gaining a hearer, being actively listened to, finding particular representational forms, and then finding their way to a juridical context.

This is more than a political and legal journey; it is a psychological one. How could it not be? The stories we discuss here are limit cases, sometimes politically strategic but often originally forged out of extreme suffering, often told reluctantly, though sometimes eagerly, in the hope that in doing so the experiences they depict will never be repeated. The powerful effects of this storytelling for the survivor are well known, but this book considers the drawbacks as well as the uses of therapeutic or sentimental frameworks. What is not in doubt, however, is that this element of the testimony requires more than a legal response. Indeed, the life story as a human rights story cries out for emotional recognition and mourning, the compensation of public remembrance and education. Here testimony merges with other aesthetic forms to take the audience far beyond the courtroom. Dramatic art, photography, and creative writing, in other words, open up forms of witnessing that create alternative juridical spaces, rendering judgments without issuing punishments. And in these more complex genres and arenas, they can also do what legal and campaign testimony often cannot, in acknowledging the moral complexities of human rights abuse. Creative play with life stories can show that the world is never neatly divided into perpetrators and victims, that people can change sides as victims find themselves complicit or perpetrators fall from power. Creative imaginations also give the lie to simplistic statements about silence and speech.

The art of life narrative can therefore work as a crucial complement to legal or governmental action, in the way that lobby groups like Amnesty have long understood. Yet it brings its own conditions and contradictions, often promising more than it can deliver. In this volume Gillian Whitlock shows how rights-based storytelling is pressured by global media markets, as well as marked by dynamics of liberal shame. Even in sophisticated genres, such as plays, we find pressure to create what Brian Phillips calls in these pages the "human rights hero": one who smooths out flaws and contradictions. Therefore, we must evolve a cultural politics that can push the limits of testimony even as it endorses testimony's moral aims. At the same time, creative writers and other artists who deal with stories of abuse need to become much savvier about the law, as well as about ethics. For this reason, this book ends with the human rights lawyer Mark Muller's personal account of how he has been influenced by, as well as employed, testimony in his work. We also include a "tool kit" for teaching the human rights narrative. Before we get practical, however, let me outline the key terms of the debate, beginning with the concept of human rights itself.

Still a Revolutionary Idea:
Human Rights since the Enlightenment

Persons in trouble today are quick to wonder about their human rights. Yet these rights are still a remarkable idea, and for many counterintuitive. At heart they pose the interests of the vulnerable or unpopular minority against those of the majority.[5] This was a fundamental challenge to the ancient religious or tribal edicts that sustained moral behavior prior to the codification of human rights in the European and American eighteenth century.[6] Although doing to others as you would be done by has stood throughout history and across all major faiths as perhaps the most fundamental ethical guide, until that period, people acquired rights and responsibilities through belonging to a group, whether it be family, indigenous nation, religion, class, community, or state.[7] But the French Declaration on the Rights of Man and Citizen (1789) and the U.S. Constitution and Bill of Rights (1791) established the principle of individual rights, rights that were described as presocial, natural, inalienable.[8] In principle, therefore, all individuals possessed them, and all groups and nations had to recognize them. Human rights thus presuppose a vision of a universal human subject protected by the universal jurisdiction of the "law of humanity."[9] Everyone can suffer, everyone flourish.

We know, of course, that these founding documents contained scandalous exclusions, most obviously of the rights of slaves and women, exclusions that find their parallel today in the realpolitik of human rights processes. I shall turn to these questions shortly. But human rights first gained international, institutional power in response to the devastation of the world wars, with the League of Nations laying the groundwork for the more comprehensive agreements in the United Nations (UN) in 1948. The Nazi exterminations horrified the world, and, via the trials in Nuremberg and Tokyo, established a transcendent memory of what constitutes "crimes against humanity" that politicians across the spectrum still find hard to touch. Further, governments signed on to ideas of rights that even now are far reaching, going well beyond matters of life and death to argue for rights to food, shelter, and education in what has been conceptualized as a "second generation" of rights that are social as well as the civil rights already imagined in terms of voting power, freedom from state persecution, and the like. These principles were captured in the UN General Assembly's stated wish to engender "the advent of a world in which human beings shall enjoy freedom of speech and belief and freedom from fear and want [which] has been proclaimed as the highest aspiration of the common people."[10] Nations now had to be accountable to internationally agreed on standards of individual protection. Thus, although for many human rights is just a slogan, and their defense is almost always contested, human rights law preserves its extraordinary status, often able to override other laws or law enforcers. It is striking that the Human Rights Act of 1998, which currently governs UK law, specifies that if any of the rights and freedoms cited above are breached, "*you have a right to an effective solution in law, even if the breach was by someone in authority, such as, for example, a police officer.*"[11]

What, then, is the nature of the relationship among testimony, life story, and human rights? Human rights and the public life storytelling are intertwined phenomena, symbiotic outgrowths of Enlightenment legacies beginning with a few poignant tales, such as that of the former slave Olaudah Equiano in the 1760s, growing with ever more personal accounts in the nineteenth and twentieth centuries, and mushrooming in the human rights era of the 1990s. On the one hand, humanist philosophies have provided the grounds that allow new constituencies to speak out. But, just as important, personal narratives have themselves been instrumental in formulating new ideas of rights. Indeed, Richard Rorty has influentially argued that sentimental narratives of suffering have been as important as reason, because their realization depends on the development of empathy and community. In other words, he holds that people are not motivated to care for strangers by logic but because a sense of identification has been stimulated, and narratives are the ideal mechanism though which to do so.[12] Legal humanities scholar Judith Henderson seems to support this by examining instances in which judges have been stimulated by stories of suffering to allow compassion to direct landmark advances in human rights cases.[13] Social movement scholars have also studied the effects of sharing personal narratives, which may be as much about sharing strategic action as mobilization.[14]

For our purposes, however, two recent literary historical studies are particularly pertinent. Lynn Hunt argues that the eighteenth-century novel's innovative prose techniques, imitating nonfictional forms of letters and memoirs, allowed the illusion of access to another's interior life in ways that created the conditions for political identification.[15] Hunt's view of the mutually enabling relationship between the realist novel and equality of the subject has been traced through many other cultural studies of the campaigning role of "true stories."[16] But Joseph Slaughter takes a harder line in *Human Rights, Inc.*[17] Although he, too, argues that the bildungsroman shares the narrative grammar of what the Universal Declaration of Human Rights calls "the free and full development of the human personality," he argues that this historically reflects the movement of the citizen-subject from pure subjection not to freedom but to self-regulation in the modern neocolonial state. Looking back now from the perspective of an emerging but still bitterly contested "third generation" of rights, which includes the right to a healthy environment, communication, and cultural participation, we can see how fragile the concept remains.[18]

Undesirable Side Effects?
The Regime of Human Rights

Slaughter's unsparing analysis of the false promises of the bildungsroman's modeling of the human rights citizen is a clear example of how human rights now exist within a "fallen" grand narrative of humanism. The popular press in England mocks the human rights law that prevented "al-Qaida" cleric Abu Hamza from being extradited for so long and decries "political correctness gone mad" with stories like those covering the serial murderer Peter Sutcliffe, who went to the European Court to demand his right to receive a state pension.[19] Some of these arguments conceal a wish to return to the older law of group security above individual freedom. But others are objecting to a new governmentality in "the human rights regime."[20] On one level, this regime simply reflects the effect of the growth of state bureaucracy, where rights are drained of meaning through Kafkaesque experiences of judicial waiting rooms. On a deeper level, the problem lies in the ideology of individual self-determination at the heart of the idea. Marx declared from the start that only economic autonomy could provide liberation, and this required collective action. Now many more consider human rights to be devalued in an age in which individuals can imagine rights to drive their cars without wearing seat belts, to own assault rifles, to attack women seeking abortions, or simply to consume as much as one can pay for. For such reasons, as legal scholar Mary Ann Glendon argues in *Rights Talk: The Impoverishment of Political Discourse*, human rights in an age of global capitalism, neoimperialism, and an energy crisis may only work with a stronger view of ethical responsibility and reduced individual freedom.[21]

Life stories in this context also reflect contradictions within democracies, where human rights discourses have become entwined with domination and power. Smith and Schaffer show that attention to the social specifics of story-telling reveals how people are *constrained*, as well as liberated, by a language of equal rights.[22] This happens psychologically, as well as in terms of practical recompense or political advancement, for example, in the way Aboriginal Australians could get stuck in the position of the abused child once the "stolen generation" narratives took off or when Korean comfort women ironically find themselves repeating the division between good and bad women as they wait for the state to bestow an apology that will wipe the stain of sexual abuse clean. This is a dynamic not only between state and claimant but equally and more insidiously between storyteller and consumer of those stories, who may often be someone implicated in the oppression of the storyteller. Traumatic stories be-come commodified in alarmingly voyeuristic and regressive ways, although commercial narratives like the "true-story" film *Rabbit-Proof Fence*, about brutally stolen Aboriginal girls escaping their captors, are also important in keeping a human rights agenda in the public eye when local campaigns fail.[23]

These effects suggest instances where human rights narratives awk-wardly depend on a humanitarianism that is less robust than it would like to be. A troubling example comes from cognitive psychologists studying the social psychology of altruism. Participants were given the opportunity to contribute five dollars to Save the Children in three different circumstances: first, an iden-tifiable victim with a life story, an African girl from Mali called "Rokia"; second, statistical victims; and third, an identifiable victim, "Rokia," combined with statistical information.[24] It will probably not surprise you that donors gave the most to the identified individual, Rokia. However the researchers also discovered that combining her story with wider statistical information about poverty in Africa significantly *reduced* donations.[25] Such findings add further caveats to the "sentimentalist thesis," in reminding us of what is popularly termed compas-sion fatigue. Lauren Berlant makes related arguments about compassion itself as a cultural construct now claimed and manipulated by the American New Right, and notably masculinized in the process (President Bush as the new man of feeling).[26]

Life stories as rights stories, then, are no simple and singular thing. They are complex constructions, even when they appear to be simple cries of pain. This book suggests several ways in which we can begin to analyze this construc-tion. The first is to consider the life rights story as a process *told in stages*, stages that are psychological, social, juridical, and also, in a particular sense, literary. What might originally be an appeal smuggled out of prison, thrown desperately at any hoped-for audience, can become a quite different object when managed through a lawyer seeking financial reparations, an advocacy organization, or a forgiving book reading on campus.[27] The second is to consider them also as *conversations*, defined through who listens, how, and for what interest. As the Internet increasingly determines the terms of publication, testimony is "remediated" in unpredictable forms. Both of these deeply mark the sense in which we can describe them as a genre that has become powerful and flexible, but also highly politicized, in modern times.

Defining Life Stories as Rights Stories

What does it take to make a human rights story from a life story? At its most general, it must refer to suffering or deprivation. This may be ill-defined. Molly Andrews, in this volume, discusses the difficulty of articulating the kind and degree of pain usually invoked in this context, building on the insights of trauma studies. It may be that the experiences defy narrative shape. However, what initiates the transformation of story into testimony is the context of claim. This claim may be general, appealing for recognition or empathy, or it may be specific, setting out a crime or abuse, something for which judgment and justice are required. These claims refer back, however unconsciously, to the concept that every human possesses natural rights whose abuse is judiciable. And in this respect, as Wilson and Brown put it, "the key is innocence, not suffering."[28] Human rights stories are therefore also protest stories and often, eventually, involve motifs of restitution and triumph.

The demand for recognition or restitution of the innocent, the second defining feature of the genre, involves a third element: referentiality. Legal contexts require strict distinctions between truth and fiction. For this reason, the more aesthetically pointed term *life narrative* is ironically less amenable to the human rights context than *testimony* or even *life story*, although the terms are often used interchangeably by cultural critics.[29] The *Oxford English Dictionary* defines testimony as "personal or documentary evidence or attestation in support of a fact or statement; hence, any form of evidence or proof." A legal definition of *testimony* requires still more: "the evidence of a witness in court, usually on oath, offered as evidence of the truth of what is stated."[30] The testimony is thus crucially linked to the person who gives it, with all its connotations of presence, face-to-face encounter, authority, and reliability. Introducing the first part of this book, writer Annette Kobak reminds us of the vital importance of the eyewitness to the interface between testimony and human rights. If the state is the source of human rights abuse, the testimony of individual citizens in court or in a memoir or diary may be the only concrete record we have of such a history. However, in just the way in which the legal status of the eyewitness remains uncertain in the face of cognitive tests on consistency and validity of account, the human rights life story is also highly contested.[31]

All life storytelling is mediated and conditioned by the vagaries of memory, particularly when trauma is involved. In the extremely political situation of inflicted suffering and potential reparation, the pressures to shape the story are often as stark as the expectation that they will be only and fully truthful. The heightened clash between these two pressures in global political markets can be identified as one cause of the contemporary phenomenon of the "hoax" testimony, for example, by Arab women supposedly victims of honor crimes—and the gleeful exposure of such testimony too.[32] The Internet's facility as a medium for both testimonial and debunking voices only enhances the "environment of suspicion" about the status of life-story-based "evidence."[33] Indeed, the human rights *report*, as a specific and stylized genre, gains its authority precisely by *avoiding* the life story, drawing on fragments of testimony only when they can corroborate carefully stockpiled statistics.[34]

The first part of this volume offers examples of how first-person human rights life stories emerge and then navigate the expectations of testimony. These include Emin Milli's account of being imprisoned in Azerbaijan, Nazeeha Saeed's experience of police brutality in Bahrain, and Hector Aristizábal's narration (with Diane Lefer) of torture in Colombia. All of them feature the hallmarks of suffering inflicted on someone who we judge and feel to be innocent. At the same time, all of them carefully consider the institutional, ethical, and conceptual pressures at work in the construction of public narratives of atrocity. Aristizábal indeed explicitly rejects his own early testimony, in which he portrays himself as a terrified victim, blindfolded and beaten, in favor of a more empowering memory of his use of cunning and courage to survive. The traumatic nature of many human rights narratives shows just how complex it can be to translate memory into words. But just as salient is the role of the listener, interviewer, publisher, lawyer, or artistic interpreter. Smith and Schaffer describe the human rights life narrative as defined largely by its contexts of reception in the networks and meshworks "linking the United Nations, nation-states, and NGOs, and scattered venues or sites of action."[35] These include charity and arts communities, and, indeed, the university. Aristizábal, for example, very precisely locates his narrative in the context of the Program for Torture Victims in Los Angeles. It is shaped, too, by his training in theater of the oppressed techniques and his studies of ritual. Milli shows us how the digital public worked as a lifeline for him. He makes an inspiring case, as an

activist-blogger, for the power of words but is well aware of the challenges involved in "how to make the story of human rights abuse in our country interesting for the world." Saeed, by contrast, emphasizes the pain not only of abuse
but of having to reproduce it for others far from the scene, including those
reading about it in this book.

The second part of the book therefore focuses on the idea of recognition
as a crucial element of the human rights life story, and one that begins at the
earliest stage of testimony. Eva Hoffman introduces this section as the author
of an acclaimed memoir, *Lost in Translation*, in which she examined her initial
search for a language in which to capture her experiences as an emigrant child
of Holocaust survivors but also the author of *After Such Knowledge*, in which she
found herself facing the further imperative to think about who the memory of
the Holocaust is now for.[36] How can we offer appropriate recognition for their
testimony? How do we recognize contemporary activists and claimants? Gillian
Whitlock explores this question in visual terms, by asking us to consider a photographic installation depicting asylum seekers whose faces have been deliberately
obscured to "protect" their identities, in a context where the Australian state
has seriously wavered over recognizing their humanity. Michio Miyasaka explores the problem of recognition in relation to Japanese people living with
leprosy who were harshly segregated under an isolation law for decades despite
the existence of a medical cure. He asks why it is that their testimonies only became "listenable" in the 1990s despite the fact that patients had been creating a
leprosy literature of suffering, anger, and protest since the 1930s. Finola Farrant
takes the question in a challenging direction by arguing that criminologists
should draw out the life stories of convicted criminals both to respect their
human rights and to humanize the criminal justice system.

Here we come back to the fundamental challenges of human rights life
stories—for in a sense they are pulled in opposite directions by the demands of
each part of their terminology—the codes of claim versus the codes of witness,
the functional and the symbolic.[37] And yet the political or emotional power of
the human rights narrative remains, and indeed, the symbolic register may
ironically be more effective in particular contexts. The Guatemalan indigenous
rights activist Rigoberta Menchú's *testimonio* is a case in point. Although its
empirical truth was much debated, at one point threatening her reputation as a
Nobel peace prize winner, ultimately her story helped her gain an enduring
political platform, including funding for a women's charity, and has been part
of a significant improvement for indigenous people's economic, as well as political, inclusion in Guatemala.[38] We therefore need to appreciate that although

the human rights life story is often used interchangeably with the concept of testimony, they are not synonymous.[39] A life story can expand on the status and kind of truth that the testimony represents. And arguably the consciously arranged life narrative can do this still further, precisely because of elements that in legal contexts may be viewed as fictionalizing. An important forum for this wider form of rights narrative is opening up through a new, "third" generation of rights, centered on group-based concerns about the environment, culture, and heritage, in contrast to the legally based processes of civil and social rights. Mary Robinson's campaign for "climate justice," as described in her foreword in this volume, is a powerful example.

In this light, the third part of this book turns to what happens to experiences of injustice and protest as they are transformed by artists and writers. Memoir, lyrics, poetry, fiction, monuments, film, and other forms enable experience to be heard by a wider audience and for the longer term, and are more likely to challenge stereotypes of victims and perpetrators, whose roles may be less distinct than the law requires. These aesthetic forms of witness offer the space for reflection, analysis, and lyricism in the aftermath of atrocity and the complex relation of these to the past. Patricia Hampl introduces this section by considering the ongoing power of Anne Frank's diary, which continues to perform witness to the Holocaust. The complex history of this work's publication and adaptation and its role in the troubling "Holocaust industry" are unable to overshadow its power. Written outside the worst conditions that constitute the horror of the Shoah, Anne Frank's diary does not testify to the camps but rather about everyday life as a thirteen-year-old in hiding. As countless teachers know, the diary endures because it combines the authenticity of a life story in appalling but also familiarly familial circumstances, told with literary grace and inevitable suspense. These generic features, in the context of the continued moral imperative to remember and repent the European Holocaust, demonstrate how tragic literature can grow from testimonial ingredients. Meg Jensen, Brian Phillips, Katrina Powell, and Alexandra Schultheis Moore also track the potential gains of aesthetic approaches to the documentation of abuse. Phillips compares dramatizations of Martin Luther King Jr.'s life to weigh up their varying successes in avoiding simplistic hagiography, posing important questions of genre as well as ethics in doing so. Powell argues that a reflexive, oral-history-based approach to making a film about a victim of forced migration in Virginia ironically restored not just a sense of identity but a less exploitative relationship to being photographed. Moore examines three acclaimed photographers commissioned by the organization Médecins Sans Frontières (Doctors without

Borders), one of whom also uses graphic novelistic reportage, to explore how they refuse the typically objectifying codes of wartime photojournalism.

In some contexts, the creative reworking of trauma bears distinct advantages for the writer as well as the reader. Meg Jensen's essay frames this section for this reason, discussing how fictional autobiography can add to the juridical potential of life story or testimony by increasing the writer's sense of authority and ability to imagine, with powerful therapeutic consequences. An interesting parallel comes from a collection of stories, not from victims but from contemporary human rights workers themselves, who struggle to explain why they do what they do and talk about what it means to listen to testimonies professionally.[40] Strikingly, these practitioners say that, although they may doubt that they can make any predictable difference, they, too, feel driven to say something "that is true," to testify.[41]

Human Rights Narrative Studies:
An Evolving Field

To date there has been a striking lack of research on the precise relationship between life narrative and human rights, despite the wealth of work on trauma and testimony. However, this volume builds on a few important texts. Our key precursor is Kay Schaffer and Sidonie Smith's *Human Rights and Narrated Lives: The Ethics of Recognition* (2004). Although Smith and Schaffer conclude by paying tribute to "the efficacy of stories . . . framed by faith in international covenants calling for dignity, justice, and freedom," their approach deconstructs the naive but persistent liberal humanist view that literature will save the day as the vehicle for compassion and empathy. Yet, significantly, they insist that life narrative plays a central role in the rights process, a role that incorporates but also goes beyond the particular functions of testimony and witness.

The human rights narrative is, in the broadest sense, fictional to start with, a political fiction of individual personhood that is internalized as the modern state develops. But we hope this book shows that the complex arguments repeatedly staged over the representation of rights claims nevertheless prove that life narrative remains specific and important. We therefore need to think further about how such narratives have both fed and challenged the tradition of sentimental fiction that arose alongside the concept of human rights in the eighteenth century. This volume suggests that there are indeed crucial shared functions between fiction and nonfiction—for example, in the ability of both forms of art to facilitate identification with another's interior life. This may be crucial in overcoming the challenges of audience alienation or compassion fatigue, as the communications departments of rights organizations know well. But there are also differences. As G. Thomas Couser argues, life writing "works on the world in a more direct way" than fiction does, for in life writing "it matters whether a memoirist is confessing, boasting, defending, witnessing, or accusing."[42] The reason for this impact relates to the extra ethical claims that readers will project onto a story they believe to be true.[43] Thus, life narrative, though ontologically often indistinguishable from fiction, can act directly as evidence, teacher, judge, witness, community maker, or, indeed, community breaker.

Here Tristan Anne Borer's edited collection *Media, Mobilization, and Human Rights: Mediating Suffering* (2012) takes the question forward. Borer's book compares the impact of television, print news, and social media on mobilization, taking the coverage of the U.S. humanitarian intervention in Somalia in 1992 as the starting point of a new era in real-time, intimate coverage of abuse and claim. She sadly concludes that, though *initially* greater testimonial content worked to great effect in terms of public horror and then public action, today's hyper-mediation of suffering has weakened its impact.[44] Yet, paradoxically, it is evident that life/rights stories are thriving in new forms, as spectacle, celebrity quest, and online petition, as well as being taken up by increasingly diverse claimants who are discovering the political potential of human rights discourse. Furthermore, there is evidence of a powerful new set of hybrid forms that bring together the visual and verbal and at the same time test the boundaries of the "true" as part of their search for appeal to a jaded yet needy global audience. Michael Galchinsky, contributing to Borer's book, focuses on graphic reportage and novels as emergent and ambiguous forms that may be especially productive in creating "a culture without borders" in this respect.[45] Alexandra Schultheis Moore, in this volume, also concludes that mixing art with the documentary tradition in graphic narrative can refresh and empower the mobilizing appeal, even as she warns that too great an aesthetic appreciation can itself undo political efficacy.

Ultimately, it takes the *longue durée* of centuries to really weigh the special power of testamentary forms of life narrative, as Gillian Whitlock eloquently shows us in looking at its mobilization in the eighteenth century as a political agent. Over this time, it has continually oscillated between being immensely effective and pathetically dependent on the uncertain availability of compassionate readers and witnesses, between authorizing the weak and being appropriated as the covert propaganda of the strong. We need much more work on the specifics of the (auto)biographical novel, the biography and the autobiography, the interview-based photograph, and the documentary or multimedia blog as they impact the public sphere in general and policy makers, judges, and juries in particular. Guarantees of evidentiary truth and the concept of witness are what drive the genres of the human rights report and legal case, fueled by a growing digital public of fact checkers and rights observers. Yet, as Schaffer and Smith explain, "Since personal storytelling involves acts of remembering, of making meaning out of the past, its 'truth' cannot be read as solely or simply factual. There are different registers of truth beyond the factual: psychological, experiential, historical, cultural, communal, and potentially transformative."[46]

We hope that without idealizing either story or human rights, this book offers an interdisciplinary approach that recognizes the uses of life story pragmatically and creatively. The fourth part of the book, then, introduced by Julia Watson as a literary critic exploring practical change, focuses on the complex political contexts in which the human rights life story may gain a material outcome. Kay Schaffer and Sidonie Smith brilliantly assess the shape and outcome of digital lobbying by Chinese petitioners, who scramble the old patterns of testimony as they use social networking, blogs, video, or graffiti art to argue their cases in alternative, networked publics. Brian Brivati assesses policy makers' responses to the Facebook-defined testimonial tactics of ongoing revolutions in North Africa. Mark Muller movingly writes about his personal response to the testimonies of his clients as a barrister and international mediator, and the importance of being there in person, too easily avoided in the digital era. But much contemporary rights practice hears only those activists' voices in ways that are immediately useful, without due regard for what happens *after* the court case, campaign, newspaper article, or film. A life-narrative-based approach to thinking about human rights entails a long-term and multifaceted engagement— a form of conversation that is not unlike the way literary scholars read texts— searching between the lines for gaps and subtexts, and also for tales of resilience, endurance, triumph, and strategy as well as suffering and loss. This approach also entails an interest in creative form, language, visual arts, and sonic and digital play.

This conversation between professionals in the field and humanities scholars, as well as with survivors of abuse, is something we hope will continue inside and outside the academy. For this reason, the fifth part of the book consists of a teaching toolkit that builds on classic elements of the human rights curricula to engage in specific exercises that open up questions of genre and generation, position and perspective that can be adapted to different groups or levels of knowledge, ethics included. We hope that this will allow readers to develop their own juridical responses to complex life/rights narratives, in which narrators may be both victims and informants, both abused and abusers. For the future of human rights will require policy makers who are attuned to the subtle arts and politics of life narrative even as it morphs in the age of e-witnessing and a new generation of rights that may go beyond the human altogether. And it needs everyone, no matter what their job, to take responsibility for how they consume others' pain and confess their own.

NOTES

1. For the full text of the advice page, see the UK government's Equality and Human Rights Commission's website, accessed December 31, 2013, http://www.equalityhuman rights.com/human-rights/what-are-human-rights/the-human-rights-act/.

2. For the full text of the petition, see the Amnesty International UK home page, accessed April 10, 2012, http://www.amnesty.org.uk/.

3. Kay Schaffer and Sidonie Smith, *Human Rights and Narrated Lives: The Ethics of Recognition* (New York: Palgrave Macmillan, 2004).

4. Lars Waldorf, "Remnants and Remains: Narratives of Suffering in Post-Genocide Rwanda's *Gacaca* Courts," in *Humanitarianism and Suffering: The Mobilization of Empathy*, ed. Richard Wilson and Richard D. Brown (Cambridge: Cambridge University Press, 2009).

5. Andrew Clapham, *Human Rights: A Very Short Introduction* (Oxford: Oxford University Press, 2007).

6. It should be said that increasingly scholars are exploring the interconnections between these periods and nonwestern forms of human rights. See Micheline Ishay, *The Human Rights Reader: Major Political Essays, Speeches, and Documents from Ancient Times to the Present*, 2nd ed. (London: Routledge, 2007).

7. Richard Wilson and Richard D. Brown, eds., *Humanitarianism and Suffering: The Mobilization of Empathy* (Cambridge: Cambridge University Press, 2009), 6.

8. There are important precursors, notably John Locke's "Two Treaties on Government," 1680–90.

9. Wilson and Brown, *Humanitarianism and Suffering*, 5.

10. Preamble to the Universal Declaration of Human Rights, United Nations, accessed June 2, 2012, http://www.un.org/en/documents/udhr/.

11. "Human Rights," FindLaw UK, accessed December 31, 2013, http://www.findlaw.co.uk/law/government/civil_rights/8650.html.

12. Richard Rorty, "Human Rights, Rationality, and Sentimentality," in *On Human Rights: The Oxford Amnesty Lectures, 1993*, ed. Stephen Shute and S. L. Hurley (New York: Basic Books, 1993).

13. Lynne N. Henderson, "Legality and Empathy," *Michigan Law Review* 85, no. 7 (1987).

14. Charles Tilly, *Stories, Identities, and Political Change* (Lanham, MD: Rowman & Littlefield, 2002).

15. Lynn Hunt, *Inventing Human Rights: A History* (New York: W. W. Norton, 2007).

16. William Andrews's study of the impact of *The Autobiography of Frederick Douglass* on the abolitionist movement and Lauren Berlant's analysis of the parallel cultivation of a less politically attuned "intimate public" through the reading of *Uncle Tom's Cabin* are important and pioneering examples. William L. Andrews, "Introduction," in Frederick Douglass, *The Oxford Frederick Douglass Reader*, ed. William L. Andrews (New York: Oxford University Press, 1996); Lauren Gail Berlant, *The Female Complaint: The Unfinished Business of Sentimentality in American Culture* (Durham, NC: Duke University Press, 2008).

17. Joseph R. Slaughter, *Human Rights, Inc.: The World Novel, Narrative Form, and International Law* (New York: Fordham University Press, 2007). See also Elizabeth Swanson Goldberg and Alexandra Moore Schultheis's analysis of a range of genres, including poetry, the novel, graphic narrative, autobiography, short story, testimonial, and religious fables, in *Theoretical Perspectives on Human Rights and Literature*, Routledge Interdisciplinary Perspectives on Literature (New York: Routledge, 2011).

18. Karel Vasak, "Inaugural Lecture for the Third Generation of Human Rights: The Right of Solidarity," ed. Tenth Study Session (International Institute of Human Rights, 1979).

19. See the BBC's "Abu Hamza Extradition TimeLine," accessed December 31, 2013, http://www.bbc.co.uk/news/uk-19844349. For an example of a contemptuous popular press story, see Rebecca Camber, "Yorkshire Ripper Claims It Is Human Right to Have a State Pension Despite Being Jailed for Murders of 13 Women," *Daily Mail*, March 11, 2012, accessed November 10, 2012, http://www.dailymail.co.uk/news/article-2113464/Yorkshire-Ripper-claims-human-right-state-pension-despite-jailed-murders-13-women.html.

20. Jack Donnelly, "International Human Rights: A Regime Analysis," *International Organization* 40, no. 3 (1986).

21. Mary Ann Glendon, *Rights Talk: The Impoverishment of Political Discourse* (New York: Free Press, 1991).

22. Schaffer and Smith, *Human Rights and Narrated Lives.*

23. All these case studies are detailed in ibid.

24. Paul Slovic, "If I Look at the Mass I Will Never Act: Psychic Numbing and Genocide," *Judgement and Decision Making* 2, no. 2 (2007): 10.

25. Wilson and Brown, *Humanitarianism and Suffering*, 20.

26. Lauren Gail Berlant, *Compassion: The Culture and Politics of an Emotion* (New York: Routledge, 2004).

27. The health rights organization Asia Catalyst gives a succinct example. It explains, "Our approach to research places the survivor of a rights abuse at the center, focusing on the survivor's needs, and the testimony that brings abuses to life. Based on the testimony our partner groups gather, we help the groups create a rigorously-researched report at international standards, including legal analysis and a pragmatic advocacy

plan." Asia Catalyst, "Annual Report," 2011, 6, accessed November 10, 2012, http://asiacatalyst.org/about/annreport2011df.

28. Wilson and Brown, *Humanitarianism and Suffering*, 21.

29. Sidonie Smith and Julia Watson, for example, define *life narrative* as a general term for "acts of self-presentation of all kinds and in diverse media that take the producer's life as their subject, whether written, performative, visual, filmic, or digital." Sidonie Smith and Julia Watson, *Reading Autobiography: A Guide for Interpreting Life Narratives*, 2nd ed. (Minneapolis: University of Minnesota Press, 2010), 4.

30. Jonathan Law and Elizabeth A. Martin, eds., *A Dictionary of Law*, 7th ed., s. v. "testimony *n.*" (Oxford: Oxford University Press, 2009).

31. David Carson and Ray Bull, *Handbook of Psychology in Legal Contexts*, 2nd ed. (Chichester: Wiley, 2003).

32. Gillian Whitlock, *Soft Weapons: Autobiography in Transit* (Chicago: University of Chicago Press, 2007).

33. Sidonie Smith and Julia Watson, "Witness or False Witness: Metrics of Authenticity, Collective I-Formations, and the Ethic of Verification in First-Person Testimony," *Biography* 35, no. 4 (2012).

34. Ron Dudai, "'Can You Describe This?' Human Rights Reports and What They Tell Us about the Human Rights Movement," in *Humanitarianism and Suffering: The Mobilization of Empathy*, ed. Richard Wilson and Richard D. Brown (Cambridge: Cambridge University Press, 2009).

35. Schaffer and Smith, *Human Rights and Narrated Lives*, 8.

36. Eva Hoffman, *Lost in Translation: A Life in a New Language* (New York: E. P. Dutton, 1989); Eva Hoffman, *After Such Knowledge: A Meditation on the Aftermath of the Holocaust* (London: Vintage, 2005).

37. Shoshana Felman and Dori Laub, *Testimony: Crises of Witnessing in Literature, Psychoanalysis, and History* (New York: Routledge, 1991).

38. Rigoberta Menchú and Elisabeth Burgos-Debray, *I, Rigoberta Menchú: An Indian Woman in Guatemala* (London: Verso, 1984); Rigoberta Menchú and Ann Wright, *Crossing Borders* (New York: Verso, 1998).

39. The Spanish term *testimonio* gained currency as a form that should not be measured by reductively empirical (and notably first world) forms of truth, but rather as motivated by a sincere but symbolic call to action on behalf of a collective that is suffering. Interestingly, the Moroccan 2004 Justice and Reconciliation Commission (Instance Équité et Réconciliation) deliberately selected the term *ifada*, "statement," to characterize the official deposition by a witness to claim indemnity, rather than the word *shahada* or *témoignage* (Arabic and French for *testimony*, respectively). This was because *shahada* was associated with the prison testimonies (in the form of communiqués, letters, prison newspapers, and manuscripts) that political prisoners had smuggled out to supporters, which were in turn associated with symbolic, immeasurable national shame, rather than the specific performances necessary in order to judge a claimant's eligibility for financial reparations. See Susan Slyomovics, "Financial Reparations, Blood Money, and Human

Rights Witness Testimony: Morocco and Algeria," in *Humanitarianism and Suffering: The Mobilization of Empathy*, ed. Richard Wilson and Richard D. Brown (Cambridge: Cambridge University Press, 2009), 280.

40. James Dawes, *That the World May Know: Bearing Witness to Atrocity* (Cambridge, MA: Harvard University Press, 2007).

41. Ibid., 166.

42. G. Thomas Couser, *Memoir: An Introduction* (New York: Oxford University Press, 2011), 176–77.

43. Carol Fleisher Feldman and David A. Kalmar, "Autobiography and Fiction as Modes of Thought," in *Modes of Thought: Explorations in Culture and Cognition*, ed. David R. Olson and Nancy Torrance (Cambridge: Cambridge University Press, 1996).

44. Tristan Anne Borer, ed., *Media, Mobilization, and Human Rights: Mediating Suffering* (New York: Zed, 2012).

45. Michael Galchinsky, "Framing a Rights Ethos: Artistic Media and the Dream of a Culture without Borders," in *Media, Mobilization, and Human Rights: Mediating Suffering*, ed. Tristan Anne Borer (London: Zed, 2012). See also Leigh Gilmore, *The Limits of Autobiography: Trauma and Testimony* (Ithaca, NY: Cornell University Press, 2001).

46. Schaffer and Smith, *Human Rights and Narrated Lives*, 7–8. It is notable that the South African Truth and Reconciliation Commission defined four types of truth in its influential final report: factual or forensic truth, personal narrative truth, social truth, and healing truth. *Final Report of the South African Truth and Reconciliation Commission*, vol. 1 (1998), chapter 5, accessed December 31, 2013, http://www.justice.gov.za/Trc/report/index.htm.

WORKS CITED

Andrews, William L. "Introduction." In Frederick Douglass, *The Oxford Frederick Douglass Reader*, edited by William L. Andrews, 1–20. New York: Oxford University Press, 1996.

Berlant, Lauren Gail. *Compassion: The Culture and Politics of an Emotion*. New York: Routledge, 2004.

———. *The Female Complaint: The Unfinished Business of Sentimentality in American Culture*. Durham, NC: Duke University Press, 2008.

Borer, Tristan Anne, ed. *Media, Mobilization, and Human Rights: Mediating Suffering*. New York: Zed, 2012.

Carson, David, and Ray Bull. *Handbook of Psychology in Legal Contexts*. 2nd ed. Chichester: Wiley, 2003.

Clapham, Andrew. *Human Rights: A Very Short Introduction*. Oxford: Oxford University Press, 2007.

Couser, G. Thomas. *Memoir: An Introduction*. New York: Oxford University Press, 2011.

Dawes, James. *That the World May Know: Bearing Witness to Atrocity*. Cambridge, MA: Harvard University Press, 2007.

Donnelly, Jack. "International Human Rights: A Regime Analysis." *International Organization* 40, no. 3 (1986): 599–642.

Dudai, Ron. "'Can You Describe This?' Human Rights Reports and What They Tell Us about the Human Rights Movement." In *Humanitarianism and Suffering: The Mobilization of Empathy*, edited by Richard Wilson and Richard D. Brown, 1–30. Cambridge: Cambridge University Press, 2009.

Feldman, Carol Fleisher, and David A. Kalmar. "Autobiography and Fiction as Modes of Thought." In *Modes of Thought: Explorations in Culture and Cognition*, edited by David R. Olson and Nancy Torrance, 106–22. Cambridge: Cambridge University Press, 1996.

Felman, Shoshana, and Dori Laub. *Testimony: Crises of Witnessing in Literature, Psychoanalysis, and History*. New York: Routledge, 1991.

Final Report of the South African Truth and Reconciliation Commission, vol. 1. 1998. Available at http://www.justice.gov.za/Trc/report/.

Galchinsky, Michael. "Framing a Rights Ethos: Artistic Media and the Dream of a Culture without Borders." In *Media, Mobilization, and Human Rights: Mediating Suffering*, edited by Tristan Anne Borer, 67–95. London: Zed, 2012.

Gilmore, Leigh. *The Limits of Autobiography: Trauma and Testimony*. Ithaca, NY: Cornell University Press, 2001.

Glendon, Mary Ann. *Rights Talk: The Impoverishment of Political Discourse*. New York: Free Press, 1991.

Goldberg, Elizabeth Swanson, and Alexandra Schultheis Moore. *Theoretical Perspectives on Human Rights and Literature*. Routledge Interdisciplinary Perspectives on Literature. New York: Routledge, 2011.

Henderson, Lynne N. "Legality and Empathy." *Michigan Law Review* 85, no. 7 (1987): 1574–653.

Hoffman, Eva. *After Such Knowledge: A Meditation on the Aftermath of the Holocaust*. London: Vintage, 2005.

——. *Lost in Translation: A Life in a New Language*. New York: E. P. Dutton, 1989.

Hunt, Lynn. *Inventing Human Rights: A History*. New York: W. W. Norton, 2007.

Ishay, Micheline. *The Human Rights Reader: Major Political Essays, Speeches, and Documents from Ancient Times to the Present*. 2nd ed. London: Routledge, 2007.

Law, Jonathan, and Elizabeth A. Martin, eds. *A Dictionary of Law*. 7th ed. Oxford: Oxford University Press, 2009.

Menchú, Rigoberta, and Elisabeth Burgos-Debray. *I, Rigoberta Menchú: An Indian Woman in Guatemala*. London: Verso, 1984.

Menchú, Rigoberta, and Ann Wright. *Crossing Borders*. New York: Verso, 1998.

Rorty, Richard. "Human Rights, Rationality, and Sentimentality." In *On Human Rights: The Oxford Amnesty Lectures, 1993*, edited by Stephen Shute and S. L. Hurley, 167–85. New York: Basic Books, 1993.

Schaffer, Kay, and Sidonie Smith. *Human Rights and Narrated Lives: The Ethics of Recognition*. New York: Palgrave Macmillan, 2004.

Slaughter, Joseph R. *Human Rights, Inc.: The World Novel, Narrative Form, and International Law.* New York: Fordham University Press, 2007.

Slovic, Paul. "If I Look at the Mass I Will Never Act: Psychic Numbing and Genocide." *Judgement and Decision Making* 2, no. 2 (2007): 1–17.

Slyomovics, Susan. "Financial Reparations, Blood Money, and Human Rights Witness Testimony: Morocco and Algeria." In *Humanitarianism and Suffering: The Mobilization of Empathy*, edited by Richard Wilson and Richard D. Brown, 265–84. Cambridge: Cambridge University Press, 2009.

Smith, Sidonie, and Julia Watson. *Reading Autobiography: A Guide for Interpreting Life Narratives.* 2nd ed. Minneapolis: University of Minnesota Press, 2010.

———. "Witness or False Witness: Metrics of Authenticity, Collective I-Formations, and the Ethic of Verification in First-Person Testimony." *Biography* 35, no. 4 (2012): 590–626.

Tilly, Charles. *Stories, Identities, and Political Change.* Lanham, MD: Rowman & Littlefield, 2002.

Vasak, Karel. "Inaugural Lecture for the Third Generation of Human Rights: The Right of Solidarity." Edited by Tenth Study Session. International Institute of Human Rights, 1979.

Waldorf, Lars. "Remnants and Remains: Narratives of Suffering in Post-Genocide Rwanda's *Gacaca* Courts." In *Humanitarianism and Suffering: The Mobilization of Empathy*, edited by Richard Wilson and Richard D. Brown, 285–306. Cambridge: Cambridge University Press, 2009.

Whitlock, Gillian. *Soft Weapons: Autobiography in Transit.* Chicago: University of Chicago Press, 2007.

Wilson, Richard, and Richard D. Brown, eds. *Humanitarianism and Suffering: The Mobilization of Empathy.* Cambridge: Cambridge University Press, 2009.

Part One

Testimony

I-Witness

ANNETTE KOBAK

Transforming traumatic experience into the written word—as testimony, memoir, theater, fiction, or advocacy—can be a complex enterprise, as the writers in this part of the book attest. If the trauma has been caused by an authoritarian state, it can also be a life-threatening one. Three of the writers here—Emin Milli, Nazeeha Saeed, and Hector Aristizábal—not only found their lives in jeopardy after speaking out against a government-imposed story but still live under threat of reprisals. As I write, one of them, Emin Milli, has been imprisoned for a second time, in spite of having the support of democratic organizations outside his country: a graphic example of the perils of individual testimony, even in its near-collegiate new digital form. Silence can be psychologically onerous (as the fourth writer, Molly Andrews, suggests), but it is often existentially the safer option—and any authoritarian government seems to know how to keep it that way.

How did we get to this point—or, rather, back to this point? Wasn't the arbitrary arrest of individuals by an authoritarian power at the core of what the Enlightenment tried to banish? Didn't *lettres* stand up against *lettres de cachet* over two centuries ago, and win? Why does an authoritarian government or dictator still feel threatened by one individual who stands up for seeing things differently, and says so? (Why, in an era of globalized communications, are there still dictators?)

You would think that any fledgling dictator might spot that targeting writers has been self-defeating historically: writers usually win in the long run, even if they sometimes have to die to do so. Napoleon Bonaparte, who created the blueprint for modern totalitarian regimes, recognized this, even at the height of his military power. "Do you know what I marvel at most in the world?" he asked the man he had just appointed head of the University of Paris in 1808. "It's the impotence of force in organizing anything. There are only two powers in the world, the sword and the mind. . . . In the long run, the sword is always beaten by the mind."[1] And in that long run—sitting on Saint Helena, seeing the impotence of force, his half a million troops wiped out in Russia, his vast conquests having reduced France to less territory than it had when he took power—the ex-emperor had reason to brood on his insight, as he ordered thousands of books to fill the empty places of swords and battalions.

What is it, then, that dictators fear in writers? It's obvious, you might say: writers tell the truth, and dictators need to suppress the truth in order to stay in power. Yet this is too sweeping: "writers" are a heterogeneous grouping, and not necessarily more ethical or prophetic or even truthful than the rest of a suppressed population (although the best may be some or all of those things). Indeed, because both fiction and nonfiction—and even "simple" manifestoes— need to manipulate form and language to be effective, being crafty with the truth is part of a writer's job specification. The "truth" is that any "truth" will be manhandled a little by words, just to fit into a sentence or paragraph, and distorted a little just by being seen through one pair of eyes. And who knows, in today's fast-changing, information-loaded world, what the truth of any given situation is, once it's become yesterday's news?

If not truth, perhaps dictators fear the power of a writer's tools of narrative and language? They certainly pay writers the compliment of recognizing their power—a "power of the powerless," in Václav Havel's phrase—by banning and censoring them.[2] (Thirty-nine days after making himself first consul—even before establishing a national bank—Bonaparte cut the number of journals in Paris at a stroke from sixty to thirteen.[3]) The mere existence of narratives other than his own seems to threaten a dictator's need to coerce a population to his will, and by definition, his own narrative is not inclusive of others' points of view, nor attentive to the variety, specificity, and changeability of life—the very territory of writers. Through a narrative of projected or collective grievance, he often seeks to yoke his nation's fortunes to his own destiny as a leader (so far, it's been male dictators exclusively).

A complication here is that it is genuinely part of a leader's job to simplify a story in order to persuade a nation—especially a diverse nation—to cohere. The journey from the nuanced phrase of the *memoirist* Barack Obama as he writes of "that constant, honest portion of myself, a bridge between my future and my past,"[4] to the speech by *President* Barack Obama on Libya sixteen years later, in which he said, "Some nations may be able to turn a blind eye to atrocities in other countries. The United States of America is different,"[5] shows the difficulty even an accomplished writer and democratic leader has in maintaining subtlety and truth in the public arena. President Obama manages— barely—to stay within the bounds of fact while also strategically playing to a home audience by championing America's exceptionalism. Václav Havel had a similar problem, frankly charted, in switching from writing to wielding executive power. Mere government—let alone dictatorship—can be on a collision course with writing, even within one person.

If dictators seek control of the metanarrative, they also seek microcontrol of language. Their propaganda can be astute in appropriating its power, knowing that even a one-word or phrase putdown can silence a voice or blight a life. Napoleon called his enemies intriguers against France (rather than against *him*), and despots routinely label their opponents unpatriotic; Havel, a socialist democrat, bridled at being branded "non-class-conscious," "bourgeois," or "hostile" to his country by what he called a "post-totalitarian system,"[6] as the regime well knew he would. Azerbaijani blogger Emin Milli, in this volume, tells us that his government dismisses Facebook users writing against the regime as "having mental problems"—a maneuver familiar from the Stalin era.

Dictators and totalitarian regimes are inventive, too, in finding verbal bromides to dull a population into accepting concepts that, if honestly named, would announce their intentions too clearly. Hitler's *Drang nach Osten* and *Lebensraum* camouflaged land-grabbing as an irresistible Darwinian force or cozy annexation of living space, just as his "final solution" and "special treatment" of the Jews cloaked his actions as scientific remedies to problems of his own making. Any such linguistic smoke-and-mirrors tactic needs watching, just as George Orwell warned, even in nontotalitarian societies: for "quantitative easing" read "printing money"; for "compromised respiration," read "dead." It was the obfuscating words *extraordinary rendition* that alerted vigilant observers to the West's unlawful, routine, and routinely denied secret transfer and torture of prisoners in the Iraq War and before.[7] And, as Philip Gourevitch and Errol Morris eloquently write, the invention of jargon by the military in any country is not a neutral matter: "The military has its own language, a technocratic pidgin, heavy with acronyms and legalese, which blends euphemism and hyperspecificity in a code that is alien to the untrained ear."[8] The since demoted head of U.S. military detention centers in Iraq, former Brigadier General Janis Karpinski, told them, for example, that she "came to understand that calling someone a security detainee was 'far more than just wordsmithing.' She said, 'It was meant as a convenience to sidestep the law, to sidestep the requirements of the Geneva Conventions.'"[9]

The price of freedom being eternal vigilance, writers' vigilance over their territory of words is inherently likely to put them on a collision course with the censorship and propaganda of dictators, who have their own territories of control.

❦

The ur-liberal Benjamin Constant—a myopic cross between Woody Allen and
Samuel Pepys—was also a clear-sighted and sophisticated philosopher of
freedom, eyewitness for a decade to Bonaparte's usurpation of power. (We in
the West have yet to catch up with him, although the Beijing government is
apparently studying his works for insights on democracy.) Constant foresaw the
intrinsic conflict between the uniformity desired by dictators and the specificity
proper to any life form, pinpointing its modern origins to Bonaparte's introduction of conscription and the police state. In late 1813, as Napoleon's empire
was crumbling, Constant wrote, with startling prescience:

> Variety is organization; uniformity is mechanism. Variety is life; uniformity is
> death. Nowadays conquest has an added disadvantage, which it didn't have in
> antiquity. It pursues the vanquished into the interior of their existence. It mutilates
> them, to reduce them to a uniform proportion. Before, conquerors demanded
> that the representatives of conquered nations appeared on their knees before
> them. Now, it's man's morale they want to bring to its knees. They speak end-
> lessly of the great empire, of the whole nation, abstract notions which have no
> reality . . . they sacrifice real people to an abstract entity; they offer up to the
> people en masse the holocaust of the people in their detail and specificity.[10]

It comes as no surprise that a regime's desire for uniformity is expressed in
uniforms, and the more massed uniforms we see the more we can guess to what
extent a dictator or regime has hijacked a nation's narrative. To see thousands
upon thousands of uniformly dressed people emoting at the words of their
leader—Hitler, Kim Jong-un—tells us how powerful narratives are in program-
ming individuals' real lives, and why dictators should want to usurp them, along
with executive power.

Yet, if words can create spectral divisions, they can also help dispel them, as
Havel's helped to do with the "Iron Curtain." The power of the eyewitness
who will not be brainwashed by an official narrative, however coercive, has
proved impressively potent over the past century. Although that power has often
been bought at high personal cost, it has also sometimes had a gratifyingly long
historical fuse. Havel lived to see his powerlessness transformed into democratic
power; with others it has taken longer. The slow-burn effect of an individual's
eyewitness account is almost miraculously exemplified in the continuing—and
literal—unearthing of the documents, notes, diaries, and photographs that
seventy years ago the historian Emanuel Ringelblum and others buried in milk

cans, tin boxes, and other caches in the Warsaw Ghetto. Ringelblum fell victim to the worst of totalitarian regimes, but his testimony has a gathering life of its own, as he hoped. He intended those first-person, eyewitness voices for action. He intended them for the future, that is, for us.[11]

In 1958, looking back on his time in Auschwitz (and turning it into literature), Primo Levi recalled a fellow inmate admonishing him "that precisely because the Lager was a great machine to reduce us to beasts, we must not become beasts; that even in this place one can survive and therefore one must want to survive, to tell the story, to bear witness."[12] Later, in his own voice— and unconsciously echoing Constant's warning—Levi writes, "If from inside the Lager, a message could have seeped out to free men, it would have been this: take care not to suffer in your own homes what is inflicted on us here."[13]

More recently, the "Arab Spring" has shown us new ways in which first-person testimony can break down propaganda narratives—and even better, bypass them. In 1978 Havel didn't foresee that technology, which he feared as being "out of humanity's control,"[14] would arguably create just what he proposed as an antidote to totalitarian regimes:[15] "parallel structures," which, rather than challenging a regime on its own terms—military, force, propaganda— could "affect the power structure as such indirectly, as part of society as a whole. . . . These structures should naturally arise from *below* as a consequence of authentic social 'self-organization.'"[16] The long-term effects are not yet clear, but the "I" voices of millions of texts have set up the conditions for ways of living that are in accord with people's ability to self-organize and grow, rather than living in fear of *diktats* from above.

Yet without understanding what's at stake in the conflict between word and sword (and to give him credit, Bonaparte saw that clearly), we may find that despotism just adapts the new technologies to its own ends. An irony, too, is that the job description of a new breed of dictator might be the head of a media empire, rather than a geographic one, and so able to co-opt not only the tools of words but the writers themselves into the fold of uniformity. Madame de Staël—Constant's sometime companion and an articulate eyewitness to Bonaparte's creeping despotism, for which he silenced and exiled her—flagged clearly two hundred years ago what the issue was, and still is: "Bonaparte isn't only a man, but a system. . . . For this reason, we need to examine him as a great problem whose solution is vital to thought in any age."[17] The great virtue of eyewitnessing, whatever its inherent limitations, is that it dares to stand against systems and for individual experience. Sometimes the vision of one pair of eyes can even see centuries ahead.

NOTES

1. Henri Guillemin, *Madame de Staël, Benjamin Constant et Napoléon* (Paris: Plon, 1959), 185.

2. Václav Havel, "The Power of the Powerless," trans. Paul Wilson, in *The Power of the Powerless: Citizens against the State in Central-Eastern Europe*, Václav Havel et al., ed. John Keane (London: Hutchinson, 1985). Havel's essay was first distributed in *samizdat* form in 1979.

3. Claude Bellanger, Jacques Godechot, Pierre Guiral, and Fernand Terrou, eds., *Histoire Générale de la Presse Française*, vol. 1 (Paris: Presses Universitaires de France, 1969), 550–55.

4. Barack Obama, *Dreams from My Father* (Edinburgh: Canongate, 2008), 105.

5. Barack Obama, speech delivered at the National Defence University in Washington, DC, March 28, 2011; see http://blogs.wsj.com/washwire/2011/03/28/text-of-obamas-address-on-libya/.

6. Havel, "The Power of the Powerless," 35.

7. See particularly Ian Cobain, *Cruel Britannia: A Secret History of Torture* (London: Portobello Books, 2012).

8. Philip Gourevitch and Errol Morris, *Standard Operating Procedure: A War Story* (New York: Penguin, 2008), 32.

9. Ibid.

10. Benjamin Constant, "De l'uniformité," in *De l'esprit de Conquête et de l'usurpation* (1814) (Paris: Flammarion, 1925), 123 (my translation).

11. For more on Emanuel Ringelblum, see http://www.yadvashem.org/yv/en/exhibitions/ringelbum/ringelblum.asp, accessed January 8, 2014.

12. Primo Levi, *If This Is a Man* (London: Penguin 1979), 47 (originally published in Italian in 1958).

13. Ibid., 61.

14. Havel, "The Power of the Powerless," 89.

15. Václav Benda proposed this same antidote in 1978 in "The Parallel Polis," published in the Palach Press *Bulletin* of 1979.

16. Havel, "The Power of the Powerless," 83, 93.

17. Madame de Staël, *Considérations sur la Revolution Française*, ed. Jacques Godechot (Paris: Tallandier, 1983), 353 (my translation).

WORKS CITED

Bellanger, Claude, Jacques Godechot, Pierre Guiral, and Fernand Terrou, eds. *Histoire Générale de la Presse Française*. Vol. 1. Paris: Presses Universitaires de France, 1969.

Cobain, Ian. *Cruel Britannia: A Secret History of Torture.* London: Portobello Books, 2012.

Constant, Benjamin. "De l'uniformité." In *De l'esprit de Conquête et de l'usurpation* (1814). Paris: Flammarion, 1925.

Gourevitch, Philip, and Errol Morris. *Standard Operating Procedure: A War Story.* New York: Penguin, 2008.

Guillemin, Henri. *Madame de Staël, Benjamin Constant et Napoléon.* Paris: Plon, 1959.

Havel, Václav. "The Power of the Powerless." Reprinted in *The Power of the Powerless: Citizens against the State in Central-Eastern Europe*, Václav Havel et al., edited by John Keane, 23–96. London: Hutchinson, 1985.

Levi, Primo. *If This Is a Man.* London: Penguin, 1979. Originally published in Italian in 1958.

Obama, Barack. *Dreams from My Father.* Edinburgh: Canongate, 2008.

Staël, Madame de. *Considérations sur la Revolution Française.* Edited by Jacques Godechot. Paris: Tallandier, 1983.

Beyond Narrative

The Shape of Traumatic Testimony

MOLLY ANDREWS

Abraham Lewin's diary, posthumously published as *Cups of Tears*, documents daily life in the Warsaw Ghetto. In these pages, he reflects on both the impossibility and the necessity of expressing his thoughts and feelings. For instance, he describes the day his wife, along with many others, was transported to Treblinka: "Eclipse of the sun, universal blackness. My Luba was taken away." He is a committed diarist who, nonetheless, doubts what is to be gained by capturing in words the horror that surrounds him.

> But perhaps because the disaster is so great there is nothing to be gained by expressing in words everything that we feel. Only if we were capable of tearing out by the force of our pent-up anguish the greatest of all mountains, a Mount Everest, and with all our hatred and strength hurling it down on the heads of the German murderers of our young and old—this would be the only fitting reaction on our part. Words are beyond us now.
>
> Our hearts are empty and made of stone.[1]

Commenting on this passage, Annette Wieviorka writes, "The victims are certainly beyond words, and yet, dispossessed of everything, words are all they have left. Words which will be the sole trace of an existence conceived not as that of an individual but as that of a people."[2] This essay concerns itself generally with trauma testimony and the narrative challenges it poses. However, it is important to note that each trauma—while sharing some characteristics with other trauma events—is unique, both in terms of the way an individual experiences it and, critically, as a historical event. In using examples from the Holocaust, South Africa, and the 9/11 terrorist attacks, I wish to highlight certain features of traumatic testimonies, while at the same time respecting the important differences between these "limit events."

Geoffrey Hartman speaks of the injunction felt by many survivors of trauma, sometimes following decades of silence: "Thou shalt tell."[3] But tell what, and to whom? Can anyone who was not there understand that ultimately the experiences defy understanding? Despite their deep and lingering anguish, many survivors of trauma do feel compelled to tell their stories, not because they believe that in so doing they will experience relief but rather because not to do so is to betray those who cannot do so.

Oftentimes survivors of trauma articulate their experiences in ways we who are on the "outside" are unable to accept, and so we begin a project to redeem the stories that we are told. This reshaping of blank spaces is carried out in a number of ways, which I will crudely outline here. The journey of redemption begins even before the transmission of the story, when we tell ourselves that the process of telling will itself be a healing one—a journey from suffering to recovery. We encourage a traditional emplotment—what happened where, and when, to whom, and what followed after this—and even when this is not offered, we reorganize what we have heard to fit such a mold. We regard those who tell us their stories as somehow special, often overidentifying with them (and thus appropriating their subject positions as our own), while at the same time presenting them as heroes. We are prone to overinterpret both what we are told and what we are not told. And we refuse to accept that we can neither understand nor represent that which has been told to us, for in many ways the experiences themselves cannot be understood or represented.

Personal Pain and Social Suffering: Does Life Storytelling Heal?

I have written elsewhere about the "myth of healing," which researchers often use to soothe our worries about the potentially detrimental effects of the work we undertake, particularly with vulnerable and/or wounded others.[4] Building on the cornerstone of western psychology, we argue that it is not only good for scholarly purposes that those who have endured suffering should talk about it. Yes, it is important to document their experiences—for historical and/or scholarly purposes—but it is also good, we persuade ourselves, for them to talk to others (which may or may not include us). This overly simplistic model has come under criticism from a number of different angles, two of which I will address here: (1) it misconstrues the boundaries of the scholarly project, and (2) it conflates individual pain and the suffering of the community.

The South African oral historian Sean Field has argued that "oral historians should not cast themselves as 'healers.' . . . Oral history will neither heal nor cure but offers subtle support to interviewees' efforts to recompose their sense of self and regenerate agency."[5] There has been much discussion of the potential healing effects of giving testimony to the Truth and Reconciliation Commission (TRC);[6] however, many of the witnesses who came before the commission did not have this experience, and some even underwent a retraumatization. At the same time, there is no evidence to suggest that the majority of people agreed to give testimony in order to unburden themselves. While this may have been a motivation for some, there were other concrete and practical reasons to testify, including the perceived possibility of reparations for loss, acquiring new information about the fate of absent loved ones, and contributing to the larger project of rebuilding the broken nation. Even those who were retraumatized by giving testimony did not necessarily regret their decision to participate, as their contribution may have achieved other ends at the same time that it caused them anguish.

The TRC was not established as a mechanism to provide individual therapy; indeed, this was not part of its mandate. Rather, the Promotion of National Unity and Reconciliation Act, which established the TRC, refers to the desired goal of the "restoration of human and civil dignity."[7] This is a critically different, possibly conflicting pursuit to personal healing. Politically, the TRC was established as a forum for reconciling the factions of a radically divided country. The healing, if there was to be any, was for the country, not the individual. But this distinction was not always clear. Thus, while the TRC banner, which was in full view much of the time, read "The TRC: Healing the Nation," Desmond Tutu voiced a slightly different message at the first victim hearing.

> We pray that all those people who have been injured in either body or spirit may receive healing through the work of this commission. . . . We are charged to unearth the truth about our dark past. To lay the ghosts of that past, so that they will not return to haunt us and that we will hereby contribute to the healing of a traumatized and wounded people. For all of us in South Africa are a wounded people.[8]

The country needs to be healed, and it requires the participation of its people in order to "unearth the truth" in order to "lay the ghosts of the past." In Tutu's statement, there is an assumed compatibility between the dual goals of realizing individual and communal healing.

However, in her work on the Naxalbari movement in Bengal, Srila Roy has argued that personal pain, when articulated in public testimony, is transformed into "social suffering"; individuals become emblematic of individuals of a kind, and the particularities of their stories—the aspects that make them *their* stories—are lost.

> In the transformation of personal pain into social suffering, the witness is transposed from one that embodies personal trauma to a metaphor of collective violence and suffering . . . [and] personal pain can be silenced in the transformation into collective suffering. . . . [T]he very structure of testimony, as a genre, conditions the public articulation of pain in ways that seriously compromise a representation of the individual subject in pain. . . . [T]he act of testimony gives voice to the silence of pain in the public domain, it forecloses the possibility of listening to and of acknowledging personal pain. . . . Testimony is, in the final instance, a speech act that draws its meaning from a collective, plural "us" rather than the "I" who is in pain.[9]

Roy's argument, and one that seems to be upheld by many in South Africa, is that testifying in public about private pain might ultimately lead to a silencing of the individual sufferer, even though at the same time it might serve to further other, desirable ends, such as establishing a common ground of truth for the rebuilding of shattered communities.

Jean Améry is one of several well-known writers who survived the Holocaust, only to take his own life years later.[10] Before his death, he recorded feeling little comfort from the years that separated him from Auschwitz, Buchenwald, and Bergen-Belsen, where he had been an inmate: "No remembering has become a mere memory. . . . Nothing has healed. . . . Where is it decreed that enlightenment must be free of emotion."[11] Time does not heal all wounds; on the contrary, as Lawrence Langer warns, "[W]e must learn to suspect the effect as well as the intent of bracing pieties like 'redeeming' and 'salvation' when they are used to shape our understanding of the ordeal of former victims of Nazi oppression."[12] While time and narrative are always intricately bound to one another—and if, what, and how trauma is narrated will be influenced in part by the distance of time from the event—time alone neither creates nor erases the narrative impulse of trauma survivors.

Life and Narrative

Jerome Bruner argues that narrative is the only means we have for describing "lived time": "[A]rt imitates life . . . life imitates art. Narrative imitates life, life imitates narrative."[13] Narratives structure our experience, and they are the means by which we organize our memories. It has become commonplace to say that we are the stories we tell, indeed the stories we live. Our stories are our identity, and without them we lose our compass. Yet it is precisely this conventional configuration, this "natural condition of narrative," that eludes so many survivors of trauma when they attempt to give an account of what they have endured. There is pressure to provide a certain kind of narrative, the story of their lived experience, and this emplotment "transforms a succession of events into one meaningful whole."[14] But as philosopher Paul Ricoeur describes it, "I see in the plots we invent the privileged means by which we re-configure our confused, unformed, and at the limit mute temporal experience."[15] Similarly, literary critic Frank Kermode argues, "In 'making sense' of the world we . . . feel a need to experience that concordance of beginning, middle and end which is the essence of our explanatory fictions."[16] Such fictions "degenerate" into "myths" whenever we ascribe their narrative properties to the real.[17] And what happens when no sense can be made of them?

Ricoeur devotes a significant amount of attention to considering the narrative potential of "untold stories." He comments, "We tell stories because in the last analysis human lives need and merit being narrated. This remark takes on its full force when we refer to the necessity to save the history of the defeated and the lost. The whole history of suffering cries out for vengeance and calls for narrative."[18] And yet to narrate suffering can prove impossible for some. Christopher Colvin has argued, "Stories framed as stories of 'trauma' are always already implicated in some way in a specific perspective on psychological suffering and recovery."[19] The very setup of the TRC in which witnesses gave their testimony imposed on their narratives a premature closure (an "ending"), which, however hoped for, was not for them a reality. Colvin provides the example of Mbuyiselo Coquorha, who endured torture and multiple forms of deprivation under apartheid. A crucial component of Coquorha's testimony was his insistence that the effects of this treatment were ongoing. "This is what they have done to me, and I still cannot eat. I am still sick. What will happen to me? I ask you, what will become of me?" he asked the commissioners. As Colvin comments: "[T]he historical moment is not, for him, a new one in any tangible way. He still suffers physically and psychologically from his torture. He still lives in poverty and fears for his life. He still has not been able to recover from a past (and a present) that keeps him too thin, too medicated, too hungry, and too vulnerable. Storytelling here is not redemptive exercise."[20] Some of those who gave testimony before the TRC participated in other, nonofficial, community-based storytelling ventures. Here the focus was not on the therapeutic effects of telling trauma. Rather "crafting the history of the struggle means writing a history about a struggle that is not over. Time has passed but the suffering and the struggling continues."[21] The benefit that is derived from such communal storytelling is one of bonding. As people listen to the stories of others, they can recognize some elements of their own experience. They know that if and when they come to tell their stories, others, in turn, will recognize themselves. This mirroring between self and other functions as connective tissue between traumatized individuals and their communities.

Narratives and Traumatic Testimony

Traumatic testimony is marked by what is not there: coherence, structure, meaning, comprehensibility. The stories of victims of trauma can only be told in narrative form, and, as argued earlier, that very form lends the testimony a framework of meaning that it lacks. Jenny Edkins and others have argued that the very concept of time—which lies at the heart of narrative construction—is different in the articulation of trauma. She distinguishes between "trauma time" and "linear time"—the latter variously referred to as "narrative time"— which, she says, has "beginnings, middles, and ends."[22] Linear time is central to the workings of the nation-state, and even though many of us assume that it is "real," "it is a notion that exists because we all work, in and through our everyday practices, to bring it into being. . . . [T]he production and reproduction of linear time [takes] place by people assuming that such a form of times does exist, and specifically that it exists as an empty, homogenous medium in which events take place."[23] But not only does trauma time not conform to this construction; when it is forced to do so, something crucial is lost—or, stated differently, something fundamentally extrinsic is added. One of the most important implications of this rescripting of traumatic memory into linear time is that memory can be depoliticized.[24] Evidence for this argument can be found in the transcripts of the TRC. Zannie Bock and Nosisi Mpolweni-Zantsi have written thoughtfully about the process by which the words of those who gave testimony before the TRC became transformed into the transcripts that now appear on its website.[25]

Before turning to look at this work, it is important to highlight the extraordinarily difficult task with which the translators were confronted. Prior to 1994, there were two official languages in South Africa, English and Afrikaans. However, in the country's new constitution, eleven languages are officially recognized. Contained within the mandate of the TRC was the stipulation that when at all possible, witnesses should be able to speak in their native tongues. Although there had never been a professional class of interpreters prior to 1994—there was perceived to be no need for such skills as all were assumed to speak either English or Afrikaans—in 1994 all that changed rather dramatically. Not only were interpreters needed, but they were needed immediately, and for very intensive work. In the end, twenty-three people were trained for ten working days, and it was this group of men and women that performed the simultaneous translation of 57,008 hours of non-English-language testimony into English.

Some of the most memorable images of the proceedings of the TRC that were flashed around the world were those of interpreters crying as they performed their duties.[26] It was they who had the impossible job of translating that which could not be communicated. In Edkins's words, "What we can say no longer makes sense, what we want to say, we can't. There are no words for it. That is the dilemma survivors face."[27] Testifiers struggle to put their experiences into words, and interpreters struggle to put these often ruptured and chaotic expressions into another language. As Nancy Huston writes, "There are some things which cannot be translated."[28] The result was that often the original testimony was cleaned up, and in some cases information was added. A close comparison of the recordings and the official transcripts of the hearings shows that sometimes the original testimony differs significantly from its subsequent representation.

In one example, a Mrs. Mhlawuli describes the burial of her husband, whose hand had been chopped off. He was buried without this hand, and in her testimony—translated from Xhosa into English—she says, "We buried him without his right wrist—right arm or whatever—hand actually. We don't know what they did with the hand." This appeared in the official transcripts as "They chopped off his right hand, just below the wrist. I don't know what they did with that hand."[29] When the testimony was "cleaned up," some of the most vital information in it was erased. Not only does the actual testimony reflect more accurately the emotional rupture experienced by the narrator, but, critically, the revised version omits the information that Mrs. Mhlawuli's husband was buried without his hand. This information is culturally significant, for Xhosa people buried without all their body parts cannot rest in peace.[30]

There are other examples in which the "incoherence" of an original statement is cleaned up, thereby no longer communicating the utter rupture experienced by the speaker. In Mrs. Calata's testimony, for instance, in which she recounts a story in which her children see a picture in the newspaper of their father's friend's burned-out car, the English translation of the Xhosa reads, "If Mathew's car is burnt what happened to them [her husband and his friend]? Hey! No! I became anxious and the situation changed immediately."[31] The official, published version of the transcript, however, omits her exclamation of

"Hey! No!" At this point in the hearings, Mrs. Calata became so distressed that Archbishop Tutu decided to adjourn the meeting. However, the deep level of her anguish, as represented by her self-interruptions and exclamations, is not in evidence in the official transcript. Yet these very utterances are an important component of the testimony, as they contribute to our understanding of how the horrific events being described impacted the person who was left behind, struggling to create a narrative.

Language and the "Confusion of Tongues"

Ricoeur describes narrative as a "semantic innovation" that opens us to "the kingdom of the 'as if.'"[32] While narrative might indeed enhance our ability to imagine other possibilities, to envision the "as if," it may be deficient as a tool for capturing the experience of lived human trauma. Elie Wiesel describes his feelings while trying to write about the Holocaust: "[W]ords seem too inconspicuous, worn out, inadequate, anemic, I wanted them burning. Where can one find a novel language, a primal language."[33] Langer makes a similar point: "The universe of dying that was Auschwitz yearns for a language purified from the taint of normality."[34]

But how are trauma survivors to find such a language? Of course the task is impossible. If one is to speak, if one is to offer witness to the things one has known and seen, then one must resort to language, all the while accepting that there cannot but be a chasm between "that world" and "this." Langer terms this "a confusion of tongues," which marks "the clash between the assumptions and vocabulary of the present world of the survivor and interviewer and the word-breaking realities of the concentration camp survivors."[35]

Language is inextricably linked to social structure and power; what words mean, how they are used, the blank spaces that exist between and beyond words, all these issues emerge as key considerations in the current discussion. Edkins writes that "the language we speak is part of the social order, and when the order falls apart around our ears, so does the language."[36] And yet it is not sufficient to state, as many have, that the horrors of the Holocaust (or other "limit events") are simply too terrible for words, and therefore must be left unsaid, and thus unheard. Too often we have heard that those who survive trauma are left speechless; they do not wish to talk about what they have endured, and this remains forever within them as a black hole of suffering. While this may be true for some (and one must avoid retreating into generalizations about "all survivors of trauma"), for many others it is simply not the case. Many survivors of trauma emerge from these experiences wanting to talk about what they very often describe as "unsayable" or "unimaginable." Despite the content of what they say, what is crucial is that they do say it—that is, if there is someone in place to hear it. As Edkins comments, the terms *unsayable* and *unimaginable* have "often served as excuses for neither imagining it nor speaking about it."[37] This is not a sufficient moral response. The claim that those who survived the concentration camps were unwilling or unable to talk about their suffering must be evaluated in light of fact that immediately following the war there was a flurry of testimony published by those who had been to hell and were crawling their way back. However, people did not want to read these accounts. As Wieviorka comments: "Publishers are not philanthropists; they want their books to sell. A successful book often leads to the publication of other books on the same theme. It is the absence of this market of buyers and readers—indicating the indifference of public opinion once the initial shock had passed—which partly explains why the stream of testimonies came to an end."[38] We in the safe outside world told ourselves that the victims of the camps could not speak. But many of those who survived tried to speak; when they found they were not listened to, they stopped speaking.

One of the most thoughtful treatments of the paradox of language in the context of trauma testimony is that of Giorgio Agamben. Following Michel Foucault, he asks, "What happens in the living individual when he occupies the 'vacant place' of the subject. . . . How can a subject give an account of its own ruin?"[39] And yet give an account the survivor must, all the while recognizing that anything that will be said, indeed that can be said, will be an empty container for that which has happened. The significance of such testimony lies not in what is said, but simply that something is said. The fact that the testimony exists is what is critical. He writes, "The subject of enunciation . . . maintains itself not in a content of meaning but in an event of language."[40] Testimony, he tells us, is that which lies "between the inside and the outside of langue, between the sayable and the unsayable in every language—that is, between a potentiality of speech and its existence, between a possibility and an impossibility of speech."[41]

The distinction Agamben makes between the content of meaning and the event of language is a crucial one. The content of meaning of much trauma testimony is, in fact, that there is a void; those who give witness to trauma, and we who are their audience, are, in Maurice Blanchott's words, "guardians of an absent meaning."[42] But the event of language, the fact of the testimony itself, is what is vital, not so much because of the historical information that such testimony conveys (though this is important too) but more because of the depths of darkness that it begins to make visible to those who were not there, "the psychological and emotional milieu of the struggle for survival, not only then but also now."[43]

Limit events pose a challenge to narrative, because they lie beyond language, and possibly beyond representation. Just as these events demand a new language, so, too, they demand a new method of representation; and yet we have not proven ourselves equal to the task, despite the fact that more than half a century has passed since the end of World War II. What might this new representation look like? And might new forms of narrative be useful tools in this most challenging pursuit? Jens Brockmeier's work with twenty-six written personal narratives provided by eyewitnesses of the attacks on the World Trade Center—collected as part of the "9/11 National Memory Survey on the Terrorist Attacks"—offers one attempt to deal with the problem of how people talk about elusive experiences. These accounts, Brockmeier summarizes, speak to "the experience of the limits . . . not only . . . of language but also the limits of experience itself." Echoing the work of Hartman, Dominick LaCapra, and others who have written on the crisis of representation (in relation to the Holocaust), Brockmeier's work on the Twin Towers testimony provides evidence for the claim that at the core of traumatic experience is "its failure to be represented in any common forms or modes or representation." Brockmeier recounts work with "antirealist, experimental, and formally innovative types of narrative," which he characterizes as "non-Aristotelian forms of broken narrative [that] do not claim to represent the original trauma."[44] According to Erika Apfelbaum, such forms might hold more promise for "communicating with others about events that demand witness but defy narrative expression."[45] Brockmeier describes traumatic experience as "a break not just with a particular form of representation but with the very possibility of representation at all. . . . The traumatic gap between language and experience does not just reflect a rupture with the way the world is depicted but with the existential basics of human meaning making."[46] The question of adequate representation, to which there remains no definitive answer, remains at the heart of scholarship on trauma testimony. In the words of Saul Friedlander, notwithstanding a fifty-year accumulation of factual knowledge, "We have faced surplus meaning or blankness, with little interpretive or representational advance."[47]

The Search for Heroic Meanings

The problem of representation poses a key challenge for those who listen to traumatic testimony. Because we believe in the power of stories, and because we are creatures who are forever engaged in creating and deciphering meaning

in our world, we cannot accept what we are told time and time again: there is
no meaning in these stories. There are no heroes. There are no lessons. All this
suffering did not resolve itself in a better world. And yet if we cannot accept
this—and there is much evidence that we do not—then we have not learned
the very first lesson about listening to trauma. For ourselves, we want these
painful narratives to signify something, and we re-create those who offer their
testimony in another image, one that effectively makes further telling more
difficult. Those who emerge from the ruins cannot be who we want them to be,
who we need them to be. We persist in our efforts nonetheless, as too much is at
stake.

Langer tells the story of Magda F., who survived the Holocaust, although
her husband, parents, brother, three sisters, and all their children did not.
Another brother and sister had immigrated to the United States in the 1920s,
where she joined them at the end of the war. They wanted to hear what had
happened, and yet she found herself painfully unable to communicate anything
they could understand. "Nobody, but nobody fully understands us. You can't.
No [matter] how much sympathy you give me when I'm talking here." She
says that she hopes they will never be able to understand "because to understand, you have to go through with it, and I hope nobody in the world comes to
this again, [so] that they *should* understand us. . . . nobody, nobody, nobody."[48]
Here her testimony breaks off. Magda's efforts to communicate what she has
seen are persistent, even while she believes that these attempts will always be
thwarted by the limitations of imagining things of which we have no experience. Hartman writes poignantly about our inability to listen to the void.

> [W]e who were not there always look for something the survivors cannot offer
> us . . . it is our search for meaning which is disclosed, as if we had to be com-
> forted for what they suffered. . . . If we learn anything here it is about life when
> the search for meaning had to be suspended: we are made to focus on what it
> was like to exist under conditions in which moral choice was systematically dis-
> abled by the persecutors and heroism was rarely possible.[49]

As the founder of the Fortunuff Video Archive for Holocaust Testimonies at
Yale University, Hartman knows of what he speaks. Having overseen the collection of over four thousand testimonies of Holocaust survivors, he warns against
the "search for heroic meanings" in which interviewers overidentify with the
witness. This inclination is, he says, "far from innocent" as it effectively eradi-
cates the message of the narratives at the same time that it strips witnesses of their
agency. Rather than experiencing any kind of empowerment from giving testimony, witnesses are instead confined by their listeners to perpetual victimhood.
Removing the weight of the heroic genre, space is created for a different kind

of narrative, one that documents the pain of speaking the unspeakable. As Hartman puts it: "[T]he strength required to face a past like that radiates visibly off the screen and becomes a vital fact . . . [but] breaking the silence is, for those who endured so dehumanizing an assault, an affirmative step, in part because of their very willingness to use ordinary words whose adequacy and inadequacy must both be respected."[50]

Conclusion

In this essay, I have explored some difficulties associated with telling and listening to traumatic testimony. My own entry into this discussion is as one who is interested in political narratives: how the very stories that individuals tell about their own lives function as a point for viewing the wider social context. Personal narratives have the potential to act as a bridge between private and public worlds. In the case of trauma testimony, this is perhaps the most one can hope for. There may be no promise that telling leads to healing, but the very act of speech—no matter how garbled or seemingly nonsensical—can begin the process of reconnecting one to the world of the living. Hannah Arendt has written:

> A life without speech and without action . . . is literally dead to the world; it has ceased to be a human life because it is no longer lived among men. With word and deed we insert ourselves into the human world, and this insertion is like a second birth, in which we confirm and take upon ourselves the naked fact of our original physical appearance. . . . [The impulse to do this] springs from the beginning which came into the world when we were born and to which we respond by beginning something new on our own initiative.[51]

Traumatic testimonies might not provide listeners with a beginning, middle, and end, but they have the potential to assist individuals in moving "beyond the self into what Buber calls the essential-we relationship, so opening oneself up to the stories of others and thereby seeing that one is not alone in one's pain."[52] Here, then, lies the potential gift of narrative: the knowledge that we are not alone.

NOTES

A longer version of this essay appeared originally under the same title in *Beyond Narrative Coherence*, ed. Matti Hyvärinen, Lars-Christer Hydén, Lars-Christer, Marja

Saarenheimo, and Maria Tamboukou (Amsterdam: John Benjamins, 2010), 147–66. It has been reprinted with permission of the publishers.

1. Annette Wieviorka, "On Testimony," in *Holocaust Remembrance: The Shapes of Memory*, ed. Geoffrey Hartman (Oxford: Blackwell, 1994), 24–25.

2. Ibid., 25.

3. Geoffrey Hartman, *The Longest Shadow: In the Aftermath of the Holocaust* (Bloomington: Indiana University Press, 1996), 13.

4. Molly Andrews, *Shaping History: Narratives of Political Change* (Cambridge: Cambridge University Press, 2007).

5. Sean Field "Beyond 'Healing': Trauma, Oral History, and Regeneration," *Oral History* 34, no. 1 (2006): 31.

6. See, for instance, the account of Pumla Gobodo-Madikizela, one of the commissioners of the TRC, in Chris Van de Merwe and Pumla Gobodo-Madikizela, *Narrating Our Healing: Perspectives on Working through Trauma* (Cambridge: Cambridge Scholars Publishing, 2007).

7. Quoted in Field, "Beyond 'Healing,'" 32.

8. Ibid.

9. Srila Roy, "Of Testimony: The Pain of Speaking and the Speaking of Pain" (unpublished paper, 2006), 10.

10. Included in this group are such renowned figures as the Romanian French poet Paul Celan, the Polish writer Tadeusz Borowski, and the Italian writer and chemist Primo Levi (though whether or not Levi's death was accidental is still debated). When Levi heard of Améry's suicide in 1978, he commented that the latter's last book on the death camps should be seen as "the bitterest of suicide notes." Quoted in Diego Gambetta, "Primo Levi's Last Moments: A New Look at the Italian Author's Tragic Death Twelve Years Ago," *Boston Review of Books*, Summer 1999, accessed January 7, 2014, http://bostonreview.net/BR24.3/gambetta.html. When Levi's close friend Ferdinando Camon heard the news of Levi's own death (in 1987), he commented, "This suicide must be backdated to 1945. It did not happen then because Primo wanted (and had to) write. Now, having completed his work (*The Drowned and the Saved* was the end of the cycle) he could kill himself. And he did" (quoted in ibid.).

11. Quoted in Hartman, *The Longest Shadow*, 137.

12. Lawrence Langer, *Holocaust Testimony: The Ruins of Memory* (New Haven, CT: Yale University Press, 1991), 2.

13. Jerome Bruner, "Life as Narrative," *Social Research* 54, no. 1 (Spring 1987): 12–13.

14. Paul Ricoeur, *Time and Narrative* (Chicago: University of Chicago Press, 1984), 67.

15. Ibid., xi.

16. Frank Kermode, *The Sense of an Ending* (Oxford: Oxford University Press, 1968), 35–36.

17. Ibid., 39.

18. Ricoeur, *Time and Narrative*, 75.

19. Christopher Colvin, "'Brothers and Sisters, Do Not Be Afraid of Me': Trauma, History, and the Therapeutic Imagination in the New South Africa," in *Contested Pasts: The Politics of Memory*, ed. Katherine Hodgkin and Susannah Radstone (London: Routledge, 2003), 155.

20. Ibid., 163–64.

21. Ibid., 165.

22. Edkins's use of the term *narrative time* is very different from Ricoeur's theory on the relationship between time and narrative, to which he dedicated three volumes. See Jenny Edkins, *Trauma and the Memory of Politics* (Cambridge: Cambridge University Press, 2003). The important point here, however, is that trauma time is characterized by imprisonment in a forever present.

23. Ibid., xiv–xv.

24. Ibid., 52.

25. Zannie Bock and Nosisi Mpolweni-Zantsi, "Translation and the Media: Translation and Interpretation," in *Truth and Reconciliation in South Africa: Ten Years On*, ed. Charles Villa-Vicencio and Fanie DuToit (Cape Town: David Philip Publishers, 2006).

26. For a discussion on the instantaneous accessibility of images of trauma across the globe, see Susan Sontag, *Regarding the Pain of Others* (New York: Picador, 2003).

27. Edkins, *Trauma and the Memory of Politics*, 8.

28. Quoted in Erika Apfelbaum, "The Dread: An Essay on Communication across Cultural Boundaries," *International Journal of Critical Psychology* 4 (2001): 19–34.

29. Quoted in Bock and Mpolweni-Zantsi, "Translation and the Media," 107–8.

30. Ibid., 108.

31. Ibid., 105.

32. Ricoeur, *Time and Narrative*, 64.

33. Quoted in Apfelbaum, "The Dread," 26.

34. Langer, *Holocaust Testimony*, 93.

35. Quoted in Hartman, *The Longest Shadow*, 140.

36. Edkins, *Trauma and the Memory of Politics*, 8.

37. Ibid., 2.

38. Wieviorka, "On Testimony," 26–27.

39. Giorgio Agamben, *Remnants of Auschwitz: The Witness and the Archive* (New York: Zone Books, 1999), 142.

40. Ibid.

41. Ibid., 145.

42. Quoted in Geoffrey Hartman, ed., *Holocaust Remembrance: The Shapes of Memory* (Oxford: Blackwell, 1994), 5.

43. Hartman, *The Longest Shadow*, 142.

44. Jens Brockmeier, "Language, Experience, and the 'Traumatic Gap,'" in *Health, Illness, and Culture: Broken Narratives*, ed. Lars-Christer Hydén and Jens Brockmeier (London: Routledge, 2008), 29.

45. Apfelbaum, "The Dread," 20.

46. Brockmeier, "Language, Experience, and the 'Traumatic Gap,'" 33–34.

47. Quoted in Hartman, *The Longest Shadow*, 10.

48. Langer, *Holocaust Testimony*, xiv.

49. Hartman, *Holocaust Remembrance*, 133–34.

50. Hartman, *The Longest Shadow*, 142–43, 145.

51. Hannah Arendt, *The Human Condition* (Chicago: University of Chicago Press, 1958), 176–77.

52. Michael Jackson, *The Politics of Storytelling: Violence, Transgression, and Intersubjectivity* (Copenhagen: Museum Tusculanum Press, 2006), 59.

WORKS CITED

Agamben, Giorgio. *Remnants of Auschwitz: The Witness and the Archive*. New York: Zone Books, 1999.

Andrews, Molly. *Shaping History: Narratives of Political Change*. Cambridge: Cambridge University Press, 2007.

Apfelbaum, Erika. "The Dread: An Essay on Communication across Cultural Boundaries." *International Journal of Critical Psychology* 4 (2001): 19–35.

Arendt, Hannah. *The Human Condition*. Chicago: University of Chicago Press, 1958.

Bock, Zanni, and Nosisi Mpolweni-Zantsi. "Translation and the Media: Translation and Interpretation." In *Truth and Reconciliation in South Africa: Ten Years On*, edited by Charles Villa-Vicencio and Fanie DuToit, 101–18. Cape Town: David Philip Publishers, 2006.

Brockmeier, Jens. "Language, Experience, and the 'Traumatic Gap.'" In *Health, Illness, and Culture: Broken Narratives*, edited by Lars-Christer Hydén and Jens Brockmeier, 16–35. London: Routledge, 2008.

Bruner, Jerome. "Life as Narrative." *Social Research* 54, no. 1 (1987): 11–32.

Colvin, Christopher. "'Brothers and Sisters, Do Not Be Afraid of Me': Trauma, History, and the Therapeutic Imagination in the New South Africa." In *Contested Pasts: The Politics of Memory*, edited by Katherine Hodgkin and Susannah Radstone, 153–68. London: Routledge, 2003.

Edkins, Jenny. *Trauma and the Memory of Politics*. Cambridge: Cambridge University Press, 2003.

Field, Sean. "Beyond 'Healing': Trauma, Oral History, and Regeneration." *Oral History* 34, no. 1 (2006): 31–42.

Gambetta, Diego. "Primo Levi's Last Moments: A New Look at the Italian Author's Tragic Death Twelve Years Ago." *Boston Review of Books*, Summer 1999. Accessed January 7, 2014. http://bostonreview.net/BR24.3/gambetta.html.

Hartman, Geoffrey, ed. *Holocaust Remembrance: The Shapes of Memory*. Oxford: Blackwell, 1994.

————. *The Longest Shadow: In the Aftermath of the Holocaust*. Bloomington: Indiana University Press, 1996.

Jackson, Michael. *The Politics of Storytelling: Violence, Transgression, and Intersubjectivity*. Copenhagen: Museum Tusculanum Press, 2002.

Kermode, Frank. *The Sense of an Ending*. Oxford: Oxford University Press, 1968.

Langer, Lawrence. *Holocaust Testimony: The Ruins of Memory*. New Haven, CT: Yale University Press, 1991.

Ricoeur, Paul. *Time and Narrative*. Chicago: University of Chicago Press, 1984.

Roy, Srila. "Of Testimony: The Pain of Speaking and the Speaking of Pain." Unpublished paper, 2006. Copy in author's possession.

Sontag, Susan. *Regarding the Pain of Others*. New York: Picador, 2003.

Van de Merwe, Chris, and Pumla Gobodo-Madikizela. *Narrating Our Healing: Perspectives on Working through Trauma*. Cambridge: Cambridge Scholars Publishing, 2007.

Wieviorka, Annette. "On Testimony." In *Holocaust Remembrance: The Shapes of Memory*, edited by Geoffrey Hartman, 23–32. Oxford: Blackwell, 1994.

The Golden Cage

The Story of an Activist

EMIN MILLI

In 2009 Emin Milli was imprisoned in Azerbaijan for two and a half years for his critical views about the government. He was conditionally released in November 2010, after serving sixteen months of his sentence, in part due to strong international pressure.

How do societies start to change? By the power of words and by the power of human stories. You get inspired by a story, and then another story, until all these ideas build up to shape your mind and your character. I don't believe in this ethos of heroism. I don't think that people just suddenly decide they are going to act; it all builds up slowly until they have to. Most people in closed systems are actually unaware dissidents.

In 2005 I was very soft on criticizing our system, the hard-line opposition never even considered me as part of the opposition, and I didn't consider myself as opposing the system or the government. Instead I thought of myself as a campaigner, striving for Azerbaijan to become a republic of the Internet and for Azerbaijani students to be funded by the state to study in the best universities abroad: it is amazing that parts of this are now happening. While my friends and I have been successful in convincing the government that this is the right thing to do, they have done these things in a corrupt way, without accountability and without vision. We have freedom of expression, but no freedom after expression, online or offline. Bloggers, activists, and journalists are routinely jailed for expressing themselves. Students are sent to study abroad only if they take the oath of loyalty to the regime and stay loyal till the end, online and offline. That is the golden rule: you must obey.

My friend Adnan and I were the first victims of Internet freedom in my country; the government used us to scare the new generation, the middle classes, and society at large. They picked us to use as symbols. They punished us and then let everyone else watch, exactly how it happened in Eastern Europe in the 1970s and 1980s: they used our case to successfully scare a whole society. Our system is not like the Stalinist or Mao or Pol Pot systems; there are no mass killings.

It is a real challenge to make the story of human rights abuse in our country interesting for the world. It's a challenge because people are not really interested. Last night, as I watched the trailer for *Enemies of the People*, the story of two million people killed by the Pol Pot regime, I wondered how my story could possibly seem interesting by contrast.[1] At the beginning of the twentieth century we had a detention center in Azerbaijan, in the capital of Baku where Stalin was kept. Now *that's* an interesting story. It was a horrible place that was eventually torn down. In its place we now have an excellent detention center: I call it the Golden Cage. When I was being held in my room at this new center, representatives from the Council of Europe would enter and say, "Wow, what a nice cage." They would ask me, "Do you have any complaints about the conditions of your detention?" They would look at me as if to say, what is the problem? On our planet there are so many worse places to be.

In these circumstances, you become a tool of a system. You help those in power show the world how "good" and "tolerant" that system is as they maintain a controlled level of violence or human rights abuse so that when Western politicians compare it with other systems they think this one is not so bad. In my cell I was reading an article about Václav Havel's friend who was put in jail in the 1980s. His friend had severe breathing problems, but he was placed in a cell with several inmates who were all heavy smokers. The request to put him in a nonsmoking cell was ignored by the administration of the jail. Havel asked an American friend to call the editor of a US magazine or newspaper and write about his friend to raise awareness and to pressure the authorities to move him to another cell. The editor responded that the story wasn't interesting enough to be published, but they should call again if the prisoner died.

The story of Azerbaijan is not so interesting for the world. Many stories are not reported. There are thousands of instances of human rights abuse, torture, and lack of freedom of expression and freedom of assembly in my country, and yet, because the system controls the whole of society, little is reported. When protests were declared in Azerbaijan and several hundred people took to the streets, the government, rather than explicitly preventing journalists from Al Jazeera or the *New York Times* from reporting on them, simply created bureaucratic problems with travel visas, delaying their entry. By the time journalists were allowed in after a few months, there was no longer anything to write about and no protests to watch.

I am glad that my story caught a bit of attention from the international media. It was unprecedented for Azerbaijan back then. After being in solitary confinement I was moved somewhere in the south of Azerbaijan, in the middle of nowhere. It was very hot, and I was living in a barracks with about one hundred other people, all of them heavy smokers except me, and, just like Havel's friend, I, too, have breathing problems. It is what happened next that made my story interesting to the world. I was conditionally released after a huge campaign, the peak of which was Barack Obama personally raising the case at the United Nations (UN) to our president Aliyev, demanding the release of Adnan and me. I even ended up reading about myself in WikiLeaks. I felt as if I were in a movie, in the middle of everything, trying to absorb what had happened and how my story had become so important. I couldn't decide whether it was worse to have a regime in which millions of people are killed or one in which nobody protests because they are too scared, a system so sophisticated that no one sees anything wrong with it. Visitors to Azerbaijan from the United Kingdom, United States, and other European countries come and see the development of the cities, the restaurants and the bridges; the Discovery Channel made a film about the Flame Towers in Baku, an architectural masterpiece, but it did not see the smaller, "uninteresting" stories of oppression and human rights abuses. This is how I came to the whole idea of writing about these "uninteresting" stories—making them into something people would care about, making them interesting.

After being imprisoned and conditionally released I was not allowed to travel. At the same time, I was invited to numerous conferences, World Press Freedom Day, and the UN Human Rights Council, and rather than say nothing I started, from my kitchen, to participate in such conferences via Skype. This would have been impossible for dissidents in the 1970s or 1980s; in cases such as mine social media matters and may become a very powerful tool in the struggle for freedom, especially in some closed societies.

My first trip since I was imprisoned was to the United Kingdom, to be a John Smith Memorial Trust fellow. The trust director phoned me and told me that the government of Azerbaijan would let me come eventually, if I just kept trying. I didn't think it would be possible, but he said I needed to try. So I went to the airport, checked in, handed over my luggage, and got to passport control. It was there that I was stopped by an official. She looked at my documents and called over her colleague. Then she said to him, "I have number 5 here." He turned to me and announced, "I am sorry, you cannot travel." Instead of going home, I reclaimed my luggage and went to the beach. I ordered some tea and while looking out across the beach started to write a short story—I called it

"My Name is Number 5." I turned my experience into a story and then put it onto my blog. In just one night, two thousand people read it. The next day I went to the airport and tried to pass the border again. In fact it took two more attempts before I was allowed to go to the United Kingdom. But I got there: the director of the trust had been right.

The idea of being reduced to a number resonates with many stories across the world. I remembered myself in jail, being given a number; people in concentration camps having numbers; systems reducing people to numbers. And so, after all this, it seems we should discuss the importance of words, and their power over numbers. In our country, we have a really pessimistic mood; most people don't believe in change. I do. One friend, a philosopher, published an article several months ago claiming that words are dead in Azerbaijan. This article was painful for me to read because I don't believe that words are dead. They may seem dead at the moment as a result of the successful tactics that have been used to buy or break or scare and silence intellectuals, writers, and the great majority of our society. But I have decided for myself that I don't believe that words are dead. I believe that words are incredibly powerful. I found out from friends that some people in the government are really interested in what I am going to write in my book; they want to know what it is going to be about. Here I am, a little, small man, writing some book about an uninteresting story, about me not having enough air, my country not having enough air or freedom, and yet some very important people in my country are interested, and they want to know what I am going to write. This is why I absolutely believe that words are powerful, but only if the people who say those words mean them and can stand behind them. Societies have been changed by the power of words and I believe that powerful words are continuing to change our society every day. This is why I will not remain outside my country, although many of my friends ask me to do so and tell me to write my book in safety. They don't understand why I need to be at home, why I need to put myself at risk. Although I respect and understand people who put safety first, I cannot; after seeing so many injustices—though they may only be minor ones and not like those in Egypt and other countries—I must stay. For some reason, my story has become interesting in some small way for the world, and this is a chance. Now that I have brought this story of violation to the world, it's no longer just about me; I am responsible for others with stories like mine.

Two years or so ago, there was an article about my story, about me being in jail, my life after jail, and the social and economic consequences for someone who speaks out in a country like Azerbaijan. This article was on the front page of the *New York Times*. I never imagined that this could happen; to my knowledge no article about Azerbaijan had ever been on the front page of the *New York Times* since war broke out with Armenia at the beginning of the 1990s. Yes, wars are important, but it is important that the media document, and people in the free world have access to, smaller stories also. This is one of the ways in which change can happen: people in countries like mine can ask, *What is it about that person or that person's story that causes it to get so much attention?* This leads to questions about the importance of human rights, and in turn inspires people, changes perceptions and minds, and creates the foundation for change. As others have said, there are many elements in geopolitics and so on, but unless you get people talking and thinking it is really difficult to start change, and it's very important to start.

On January 26, 2013, Emin Milli was arrested at a demonstration in Baku. He was released two weeks later and continues to be an advocate for freedom of expression and assembly and for greater democratic accountability.

NOTES

This essay was transcribed and edited by Kirsten Winterman.

   1. *Enemies of the People: A Personal Journey to the Heart of the Killing Fields*, written and directed by Rob Lemkin and Thet Sambath (London: Old Street Films, 2009).

The Price of Words

NAZEEHA SAEED

My father always wanted me to be a teacher, an artist, or a musician, but my fate brought me to another adventure, and with a different type of life.

I was only eighteen years old when I started working in journalism. My father was worried for me: he knew that this is a troublesome profession. Nevertheless, my determination alongside his pride in my eventual accomplishments made him stop asking me to change my career.

He passed away before he could see how words became a weapon in the hands and on the tongue of his daughter, putting her at risk many times.

When calls began for a Day of Rage in Bahrain on February 14, 2011, following the success of the Tunisian and Egyptian revolutions, which overthrew the heads of regimes in those countries, I did not pay much attention to them. I had witnessed the Bahraini uprising in the 1990s when I was a teenager and believed that, despite the number of deaths and the suffering of large numbers of Bahraini families in that period, change would only take place in my country when the authorities wanted it to happen.

But February 14 did not pass quietly. At 7:00 p.m. the first deaths were officially announced, and a revolution was launched.

Since I work as a correspondent for Monte Carlo Doualiya Radio and France 24 TV, I covered the event, attempting to simulate journalists who covered the Tunisian and Egyptian revolutions, journalists who, unlike me, have long experience in covering conflicts and troubled areas.

By dawn on the morning of February 17, 2011, Bahrain's modern history was on a new trajectory; with a new curve in the power relationship between the Al Khalifa and the Bahraini people, the security forces attacked protesters in the Pearl Roundabout at three in the morning. I had been asleep for only an hour when I chose to go to the Salmaniya Medical Complex, to which the dead and wounded would be transferred, in order to cover the unfolding events.

53

What I saw in the hospital was more than any Bahraini girl like me could bear. As a journalist, I was used to covering press conferences, interviews, and in the worst cases demonstrations and traffic accidents, but what I saw in the Salmaniya Medical Complex was beyond my, or any Bahraini's, comprehension: two dead people and dozens injured, with shock covering the faces of people, who kept repeating, "The army killed the demonstrators." For the first time we saw army tanks and armored vehicles in the streets.

Because I work for well-respected and long-established media organizations, I must cover my stories objectively and neutrally. That day I had to gather my strength and break the news as I saw it, regardless of my feelings of shock, sadness, and anger.

I'm not a member of the opposition, nor of any political organization, even though I grew up in a house filled with politics and politics was involved in many aspects of our daily lives. Nevertheless, it was my humanitarian upbringing rather than any particular political beliefs that moved me on that day, and led me toward denouncing what was happening.

At 7:00 a.m. I decided to leave the hospital and go home, as fatigue was beating me down. I drove my car toward the Pearl Roundabout, where I got stuck in an unavoidable traffic jam: the streets leading to the roundabout were said to have been closed by security forces and the army. I remained stuck in my car; traffic was moving very slowly, and cars were being forced to move to the right or left rather than proceeding straight on, as that was the road the police had shut down. During the frustrating wait, I could see, in my rearview mirror, that in the distance individuals were walking between cars, heading toward the place where the police were gathered. My heart started to beat fast; I was trapped in my car between the protesters and the police. Soon the trouble began: demonstrators threw stones toward the police, and the police responded with tear gas and rubber bullets. I was scared. I lowered my head but kept peeking up to see what was happening around me, as demonstrators tried to reach the police and shots prevented them. Two shots hit my car. I kept my head down, fearing that one of the shots would penetrate the glass. I was looking at the mirror and through the glass, and did not dare take any photos. I was shivering in fear. I'm in the line of fire, and the cars are moving slowly due to the closure of the street and the heavy morning traffic. Most of the people around me, I thought, did not know that Bahrain was witnessing another event. They had probably left home as usual that morning to go to work and school, without knowing what was happening outside their houses.

A bullet pierced the windshield of the car in front of me, and I saw its glass crumbling. I thought of the kind of horror the woman who was driving the car was experiencing and decided I must find a way out of this situation as soon as possible.

But I was still stuck. I raised my head again, and this time I saw an old man in a light blue *thobe* and white *ghutra* (the Bahraini traditional clothing). He was facing two policemen on the sidewalk, next to the traffic light where the police had closed the road. As I watched, a policeman, wearing his white helmet, lifted his arm and pointed it at the old man's head. He shot the old man, shattering his head.

The next day I would be thirty years old, and destiny chose that I would turn thirty burdened with the memory of an old man's head exploding twenty meters from my eyes. I was not aware of what was happening around me now; it was not a movie, not a nightmare, but a real incident that happened in front of me. I screamed my throat out; unconsciously, I was screaming and shaking. I lowered my head at times and looked out of the window at other times. The old man fell to the ground, and the murderer policeman pulled one of his team-mates with him and returned to where the rest of the police were standing.

In cold blood, the policeman had blown the man's head off and left. I did not believe what I saw. I am in shock to this day. There was a body on the ground, with half a head, surrounded by brain crumbs blown by the barrel of a gun shot less than one meter away.

I was in such shock that at first I did not notice that there was also a young man on the same sidewalk lying on the ground. My terror increased. I was screaming on my own in the car. I thought of getting out of the car, doing something, finding a way to get to them and taking the bodies to a morgue or hospital, but my legs would not carry me; fear was stronger, shock was stronger, and sadness was stronger.

Now cars started to move, and I drove behind them. I passed the body of the old man lying on the ground. After I turned right, and it was almost 8:00 a.m., I wrote on my Twitter account what I had just seen, "near the Gofool traffic light, policeman directs his weapon to an old man's head and explodes it in front of me."

Following my tweet, I got calls from the channel and the radio station that I worked for, from friends and colleagues, and from all over the world, but I wasn't really aware of what was going on around me. Somehow I managed to get home, although I was unable to sleep. I kept shivering for hours and hours before getting busy with work again. News of the death of two more men during clashes near the Pearl Roundabout came to me; those were two more bodies that I saw before I left the ghastly street.

I left home at noon to return to the Salmaniya Medical Complex to keep track of events, and I remained working there during the following days and weeks.

The demonstrations continued at the Pearl Roundabout until March 16, when security forces and the Bahraini army, followed by troops from Saudi Arabia and the United Arab Emirates—this time represented by the Peninsula Shield Forces—surprised the sit-in with an attack. During the following days, a National Safety state was announced, and so began a period of retaliation, harassment, dismissal, torture, and murder.

I did not stop working during that period. Just like many other Bahrainis, I was horrified by these events, but as I had also witnessed that inhuman scene at the roundabout, I was now being asked to recount what I had seen. I was contacted by members of a committee formed by the king to investigate the killings. They were asking for my testimony, but that was not all they wanted. In the same period, doctors, teachers, politicians, athletes, parliamentarians, and journalists were all being arrested, so I suspected that I, too, might be in danger. I had been trained through my work with France 24 TV for two years and with Radio Monte Carlo for more than eight years to be objective and impartial in my reporting, so I knew that I had not adopted the view of events that the regime wanted journalists to use.

And it was not only me that was in fear. Everyone felt like they would be the next victim, as campaigns were launched targeting those who did not agree with the regime's account of events, whether they expressed those dissenting opinions in public or via social media. Some were targeted because of their religion, or their political history. It was difficult to sleep at night, and any signal, accident, or surprise would lead to fear of arrest, torture, and possibly murder.

In April 2011 the situation grew worse as a campaign of arresting journalists, many of whom were my colleagues, began. I tried to prepare myself and my family for such an event, but in reality there was nothing that could have prepared me for that day, nor for the horror, fear, and panic that the security forces were spreading.

On May 22, while I was wearing casual clothing, attending a commercial press conference at one of the telecommunications companies as a correspondent for a weekly economic newspaper, I received a telephone call. A young woman on the other end asked me if I were Nazeeha Saeed. When I replied, she told me to come to the West Riffa police station. I asked her to call me later because I was about to enter the press conference. She responded firmly that there was no need to call back and I that had to go to the police station immediately.

The call ended. I couldn't hear or see what was around me. I stayed at the press conference, not grasping a single word that was said. When the conference ended, I headed home, where I made a number of calls to colleagues telling them what had happened. As we were all threatened with arrest, detention, and sacking, we had recently gotten used to exchanging news with each other in this way.

At home I changed my clothes and put on a formal suit. I hugged my mother, saying good-bye, and drove to the police station. Conflicting ideas kept going around my head. Am I ever going to go back home? Perhaps a quick investigation and I will leave . . . or not? Some people had never returned from their visits to the police, dead bodies not charged with any crime. I called Monte Carlo Doualiya Radio and France 24 TV and told them that I had been summoned to the police station and I thought the investigation would be about news reports I had communicated through their stations. They showed their full support and cooperation and waited for another call from me to update them.

But that did not happen. There was no call of comfort.

I arrived at the Riffa police station, where I was welcomed by policewomen in the women's section of the station. I was asked to wait on a chair in a large room with a number of offices, because the officer was busy. A few women wearing white nurses' uniforms were sitting on the floor, and others were wearing the green cloak of assistant nurses. Their faces were turned to the wall. The scene was disgusting. Shortly afterward, one of them was led into an office, and soon I heard her screams as the officer demanded that the nurse confess. Through the glass door, I then saw a policewoman hitting the nurse and pulling her veil, shouting, "You demand the fall of the regime, and now you will pay the price."

With each blow and each of the nurse's screams of pain, my eyes spun around the room, searching for stability. I think I was jumping out of my chair every time I heard her screams.

The policewomen near me noticed the fear in my face and decided to transfer me to another room. It was then that Officer Sarah Al Mousa entered the room. As our eyes met, I smiled despite my fear, and she said to her colleagues mockingly, "What's wrong with her? Why is she smiling?" I was horror-struck. I was transferred again, which felt a little reassuring. I waited in that room for a while before I was taken by a male officer to another room, where he started to bombard me with accusations and threats. He wanted me to confess that I was part of the media team in a terrorist organization that intended to overthrow the regime but had failed. He also accused me of working for the Iranian and Lebanese channels Al Aalam and Al-Manar, of participating in the unauthorized demonstrations that had taken place in the Pearl Roundabout area, and of shouting slogans meant to overthrow the regime. When he left, he handed me over to a female officer for further questioning and threatened that if I didn't confess he would hire the special forces and army to make me confess.

I denied all charges against me, and I started to tell the officer the details of the work that I had been doing when the protesters were in the Pearl Roundabout earlier that year. I told her how I conduct my work with radio and television, but she didn't like my answers.

She moved me to another room so she could record my testimony, and a policewoman there mocked the formality of my clothes and the size of my body. At first I did not pay any attention to what she was saying as I didn't understand that she was speaking to me: why would she say such terrible things to a person she had never even seen before?

Officer Sarah Al Mousa came into the room, and demanded that I answer her questions, "without lying," as she said. Then came the first slap, then another slap, then she pulled me by my hair and used the dirtiest of words against me. She pulled me up and threw me on the ground and, along with four or five other policewomen, started kicking, punching, and insulting me.

I still did not grasp what was happening. I remember that I started to taste the blood in my mouth. One of the policewomen, overweight and with a face full of makeup, took off my shoe and put it in my mouth. She told me to press on it with my teeth, and said that the shoe was cleaner than my lying tongue. She rejoiced to see me like this, and she asked me to walk into another room where other detainees were standing with their faces to the wall, with one shoe on my foot and another in my mouth.

I stayed there standing for some time until I was allowed to remove the shoe. Then I was blindfolded, and slaps, insults, and vulgar talk continued.

After a while (time began passing very slowly as I did not know when this nightmare would end) I was taken outside the arrest room and asked to sit backward on a chair. Sarah Al Mousa then began to hit me with a plastic hose. I had seen it in her hand when she first came into the room. She hit me on my back, my feet, my head, and demanded that I admit that I was working for Iranian and Lebanese channels and that I had called for the overthrow of the regime.

I denied these charges, and the beating continued.

It stopped for some time, then I was back to standing in the cold, filthy room with the other detainees, and then returned to the other room to receive more torture and interrogation.

In that room every time the door opened the detainees got scared: beating and insults came when that door opened. One of these times, a policewoman approached me and touched my arm with a sharp machine that caused me an electric shock. Each time she did so, she laughed and I was hit with a shock. This happened several times, the electric shock followed by her laughter, and because I was wearing a short-sleeved blouse I could see the burn forming on my arms.

I was asked to imitate the donkey's walk, and then an overweight police-woman sat on my back so I dropped to the ground. Then I was asked to mimic the sound of the donkey. An officer took off the jacket I was wearing, because she said it was protecting me from the blows, and I stayed in my light shirt in the extremely cold room. Al Mousa brought a plastic bottle to my mouth and asked me to drink from it. Another voice in the room said it was "urine," so I pushed it with my hand to reject it. Al Mousa then poured it on my hair and clothes, and pulled me by my hair angrily to the toilet. She shoved my head into the toilet, flushing it and saying that "this water was purer" than me.

The amount of insults and filthy talk I was exposed to through this day was more than I could absorb. In one of the beating sessions the officer pulled me up by my hair, and as she did so the blindfold fell and I saw a male officer in the room, the same officer who had threatened me when I first entered the police station.

Another male officer stepped on my feet with his shoes while he was scream-ing at me, "Why did you say that the police killed a protester?" I told him that I was there, that this is what I saw. He said, "Even if you were there, do you say such a thing to tarnish the reputation of Bahrain?" I was speechless, because this was obviously not the reason I reported what I had seen.

After a number of beatings, they allowed me and some other detainees to sit on the ground and removed the blindfolds. I do not know what time it was, but it felt as if I had been there for a lifetime. I didn't talk; I was waiting to awaken from this terrible dream.

They allowed us finally to go to the bathroom, and brought us some food, but none of us had the appetite. Then a policewoman brought papers for each of us and asked us to sign them and place our fingerprints on them as well. We did so without reading what they said.

The officers then started the process of transferring us to the women's prison, but first the woman officer who had questioned me asked to see the effects of the beatings on our bodies. Until then I had not paid attention to my physical scars as I was completely focused on the ultimate goal, which was to get out of this place as soon as I could. As the officer revealed parts of our bodies, I saw the bruises and injuries to the nurses after their severe beatings. I could not control myself, and I started to cry. She checked me and said that I should not have full "meals" like the rest.

The head of the police station asked to see me. When I was transferred to his office I realized that it was now after 2:00 a.m. When he welcomed me, I started to cry, and he told me that he had not known I was at the station. Apparently, I was being released as a result of the considerable pressure on the Bahraini regime exercised by my colleagues at the television channel as they had not heard from me in thirteen hours. The head of the station ordered that I be given my confiscated belongings back and allowed to contact my mother to tell her I was well. Then I was allowed to leave.

I did not feel the pain in my body; my legs were flying off the ground with joy to leave this place. I got into my car and drove away from the station, but when I got home, I could not get out of the car. My legs weren't strong enough to lift my tired, aching body.

It has hurt terribly to write and remember these things. It does not get easier. I tell my story here, and elsewhere, for the same reason that I remain a journalist, for the same reason I remain in Bahrain, despite offers of asylum — my continuing sense of justice. In uprisings in other Arab countries over the last two years, shoes have been thrown at the faces of dictators, war criminals, state media representatives. Shoes represent uncleanliness. But who was unclean when a shoe was forced into my mouth? My witnessing, of the death of another and my own subsequent abuse for saying so, must be used by an international community, and with the help of the law, to create a better Bahrain, and a better world. But please also remember the cost to the witness of revisiting the terrors of the past: the price of words.

Out of the Inner Wilderness

Torture and Healing

HECTOR ARISTIZÁBAL and DIANE LEFER

In 1982, when I was twenty-two years old, the soldiers came for me.
This is a story of helplessness. It's also a story of agency and of healing.

HECTOR ARISTIZÁBAL

The Narrative of Helplessness

Four a.m. A low-income housing project on the outskirts of Medellín, Colombia. The whole neighborhood shook as military trucks rumbled into the barrio on the hunt for subversives. It was 1982. I was twenty-two years old. We were living under the Estatuto de Seguridad, a repressive law that looked on almost any opposition to the government as communist inspired. It was dangerous to talk politics. Sometimes even more dangerous to create art. Friends of mine from the university had been seized and disappeared only to reappear as cadavers found in a ditch, bodies covered with cuts and burns, toes and fingers broken, tongues missing, eyes gouged out.

It could happen to me. With my theater company, I performed plays that encouraged dissents by poking merciless fun at the military and the rich, at presidents and priests. I'd participated in protests and human rights demonstrations and had organized cultural events that included free and open discussion.

It could happen to my younger brother. It might already have happened. Juan Fernando had left the house two days before to go camping with three other kids. Then my family got word he'd been arrested. My father and I went searching for him and were told he'd been turned over to the army, but we hadn't been able to learn his whereabouts or anything about his case. Did that mean he'd been disappeared? I'd spent a restless night, my sleep troubled by fear for my brother.

Now I was instantly alert. I pulled on a T-shirt and warm-up pants and ran to look out through the blinds. One of the trucks stopped in front of our house directly beneath my window. Should I try to escape? A cold mist made everything indistinct, but by the light of the streetlamp, I could see Juan surrounded by soldiers in the open back of the truck. So at least he was alive, but there was no running for it now. I couldn't try to save myself if the army had my brother.

"Open the door! This is a raid!" A platoon of ten soldiers and a sergeant burst in, pointing their weapons at my terrified parents. My father grabbed our little dog, his beloved Chihuahua, trying to keep her still. "All of you! Sit there!" There was my teenage sister Estela, scared and embarrassed to be seen in the old nightclothes she slept in. There were my brothers—Hernán Darío, who was fighting demons of his own that had nothing to do with politics, and Ignacio, the steady, reliable one who worked as a delivery boy to help support the family.

"You!" One of the soldiers pointed his rifle at me. "What's up there?"

"It's where the boys sleep. Me and my brothers."

I led them up the stairs. They overturned furniture, threw clothes and papers everywhere, tossed my mattress as they ransacked my room. I started to calm down as I watched them search. This meant they weren't after me for anything I'd done. They expected to find something, and I knew they wouldn't. I always cleaned the house when a government crackdown was expected. Pamphlets that criticized the president, leaflets demanding social justice, anything that mentioned trade unions or socialism—including books assigned at school—I'd gotten rid of. That's what I thought, and I was wrong.

When I was fourteen years old, I'd written a letter to Radio Havana Cuba asking for books and magazines about the revolution. I was so proud of that letter, I'd kept a copy for myself. I'd forgotten all about it. Now it was in the hands of the soldiers. And worse. Among my school papers, they found a booklet from the ELN, the Ejército de Liberación Nacional, the second-largest guerrilla group in the country. This little pamphlet could mean a death sentence. It had to be Juan Fernando's. No one else in the family had any interest in the ELN. Was he hiding it? Or had he left it for me to find, a follow-up to our recent disagreement? Then they picked up the photos. As a psychology student, I had been documenting the degrading treatment of mental patients at the charity hospital. According to the sergeant, these wretched-looking human beings were hostages held by the guerrillas.

My mother cried and begged the soldiers to let me go, but I was handcuffed and pushed out to the street. It was August, and a cold gray dawn was breaking. All the world's colors seemed washed out, gone. And it was quiet, abnormally quiet. No shouts, no street vendors, no radios. But hundreds of neighbors had come out of their houses to see what was happening. They watched in silence, and I remember thinking, *witnesses*, hoping that would make a difference, that the army would not be able to just disappear us when so many people had seen us detained.

I was put in the back of the truck with my brother.

"Juan!" Soldiers kicked us and struck us with their rifle butts and told us to shut up, but I had to talk to him. If we couldn't explain away that ELN booklet, one or both of us might die. "I'm going to say you've been in the mental hospital, OK?" We could admit, yeah, he might have picked up some guerrilla propaganda, but he wasn't capable of understanding what it meant. My brother said nothing, but his eyes were full of pain.

We were driven to an army post in another part of town. We entered the compound followed by three more trucks, each carrying one of the boys who'd gone camping with Juan. Soldiers ordered us out and stood us facing a wall. I remember the sun breaking through at last, throwing shadows against the whitewashed adobe, and the brief touches of warmth, now on my shoulders, now my back.

Comunistas! Subversivos! Soldiers ran by in formation, hollering insults: *Hijueputas!* The firing squad stopped and aimed their rifles. Someone shouted, *The one with the red shirt!* Bang! *The one with the long hair!* My heart exploded in my throat. *Long hair* meant me. Bullets slammed into the wall again and again just above my head, but they didn't hit me.

What were they going to do to us? We stood under guard for hours at that wall. The day went on and on, and I shivered in the cold, waiting.

"Don't look!"

But I looked, and saw a short fat man lead my brother's friends away one by one. They were so young, just kids. What would happen to them? At last the soldiers brought them back. "Don't look!" But I saw the boys were soaking wet and trembling. "Shut up! Don't talk!" But there were whispers. *We were tortured. They were tortured. They were tortured.*

The man took Juan Fernando. Minutes went by. Hours. He didn't bring my brother back. Images roared through my mind, mutilated bodies, my brother's face. Torture. When the man came back, he was alone.

The man came for me.

He led me up a hill to a cell at the end of a long one-story building. He blindfolded me. He barked out questions: *Name? Nickname? What organization do you belong to?*

"Sir, I don't belong to any organization."

The blow knocked the wind out of me. The fists slammed into my stomach again. I doubled over, and he kicked me.

"What actions have you planned? Where do you cache your weapons?"

I had no answers for him, and so he beat me. Except for when he knocked me to the ground, I was not permitted to lie down or sit but had to remain standing day and night. When he left, the torture became psychological as I waited with no hope of rescue for his return. The door creaked open. No food. No water. No sleep. More questions for which I had no answers. A second interrogator came to see me. From his way of speaking, this one seemed to be an educated, well-mannered man. He pretended to be my friend. "If you don't give me names," he said in a kind voice, "that man is going to come back. Your brother is already in very bad shape, and if that man comes back, I can't guarantee you will survive." But I had no names to give him.

The torturer called soldiers to help him.

They hold my head underwater, bring me to the verge of drowning again and again. They strip me and attach electrodes to my testicles and send jolts of electricity tearing through my nerves. I scream, but only they can hear me. Then, *el potro*—an ingenious technique that can leave permanent damage but no scars. Soldiers I cannot see cover my hands and lower arms with what feels like a wet sweater. Something is pulled tight, then my arms are jerked behind me, and somehow I'm hanging in space over an abyss of pain, arms wrenched from sockets, my body extended so that the pain is everywhere.

I'm utterly abandoned. The pain disseminates itself to every cell. It extends to the brain and blows out all conscious thought, all sense of self. Was there always a void in the center of me? It's there now. I disintegrate and fall into it.

Days later soldiers drove me around in a small Jeep. One pushed the barrel of his rifle into my mouth. "You're going to die now," he said. "Just like your brother."

Instead, they forced me into an underground passage where I found Juan, alive, and his friends, all of us hidden from view—as we later learned—while a human rights delegation searched for us somewhere above our heads. The ceiling of our dungeon was so low that we had to crawl. The air was hot, thick, and the stench unbearable from human waste and the festering wounds of a black man from Chocó we found chained and shackled there, bleeding to death in the dark. He told us he had no idea why he'd been arrested and tortured. "Worse than a street animal," he said. There was nothing we could do to help him or ease his pain till it turned out another prisoner had bribed a guard for marijuana. "Here, brother." The dying man filled his lungs and began to laugh, and the smoke filled the dark and filthy crawlspace. We all filled our lungs and laughed, and I believe I'll hear our laughter echoing in that cave and in my nightmares for the rest of my life.

It must have been the witnesses and the human rights delegation that saved us. We could have been executed in secret. Instead, we were brought before a judge. Our mental hospital story worked. The ELN booklet was deemed harmless, but my brother went to prison for carrying a subversive weapon—a machete. He went in an idealistic young man. He came out a committed revolutionary, convinced there was no alternative to the armed struggle.

As for me, ten days after my arrest, the army let me go, but the ordeal marked me. It marks me still.

My torturer. I could never forget what he looked like. If I ever found him again, I would have my revenge. Short curly hair, stocky body. The thick eyebrows and a small moustache, broad shoulders, a small but noticeable belly, and penetrating greenish eyes.

My torturer. That's a pronoun I need to lose, and one I hear from so many other survivors—*my* perpetrator, *my* rapist—because, while the state-sponsored violation of a person's body is a very specific assault, it has much in common with other atrocities. When you're in that room, that isolated place where no help can reach you, where you can no longer count on family or friends or human decency, there is one person there with you. He was entirely focused on me, controlling me, watching me, listening to my breath, keeping me alive while holding over me the power of life and death. And I had never in my life paid such close attention to anyone. I was alert to him and to his every response, trying to predict his every move with all my senses until pain overwhelmed everything and I lost my very identity. In that moment of utter surrender, when everyone else had abandoned me, when my own body and mind had betrayed me, only he was there.

For a long time the man who tortured me was a primary figure in my mental life.

I now understand that one of the long-lasting effects of the trauma is to confuse that enforced and claustrophobic connection with intimacy. I need to break that connection and re-create the loving connections in my life. I need to think of that man as *the* torturer, not *my* torturer, and to understand that he belonged to the army, to the system of repression, and not to me.

The Narrative of Agency

What I've told you so far is true, but it's not the whole truth.

There's a slightly different narrative I tell myself. A form of recycling. I look at a dirty experience I instinctively wish to get rid of and instead try to find in it something of value. I will not allow myself to remain obsessed with my weakness. I tell myself, *I survived*. I revisit my wound to remember what made me strong.

So here's the other, equally true, version of my story, the narrative not of my helplessness but of my resistance.

The man blindfolded me. Someone pushed me into a room. About twenty minutes later I heard the lock turn and the door creak open, and I recognized the same smell of tobacco and sweat. Although the man who came to torture me tried to disguise his voice, I realized I was dealing with the same fat man in civilian clothes who had led me up the hill. At that moment, I lost all respect for him. He thought he could hide his identity. He thought I was completely vulnerable and at his mercy, but at that moment I felt superior. I could identify him. That meant I was holding a card he didn't know I had, and that gave me a feeling of power.

It's true the pain was often unbearable. It's also true that I often exaggerated it. I'd done so much physical training as an actor, I could make myself fly back through the room when he hit me. I'd land back against the wall, and get some idea of the dimensions of this terrible space. When they submerged my head, I put on such a great act of drowning that I scared them. I pretended to be more exhausted than I was, falling against the torturer. When he instinctively reached out to catch me, I sighed and pretended to fall asleep in his arms. He didn't like that one bit! Although I could not resist the things they did to me, I refused to be passive. Would my ploys be of any use? I had no idea, but each time I believed I'd outwitted my tormentors I felt stronger.

"Your brother has told us everything," he said. "We know you're an urban guerrilla commander. You're the one who's training those kids."

The son of a bitch had to be lying. Juan Fernando would never have said such a thing. Again, I assured myself I knew more than he did.

"He's crazy," I said. "My brother has been hospitalized." The worst pain was imagining what they might do to him. "Please don't hurt him."

I tried to learn as much about my situation as I could, even when I had no idea how the information might serve me. A loose paving stone in the passageway echoed with a clunk every time the torturer or a guard came within nine or ten steps of the cell. At first the sound made me panic. It meant I was going to be hurt. But then I realized it gave me a warning. I knew when the torturer was coming back. More important, the sound let me know when I was alone and when I was being watched. I counted out the time it took for the guard to make his transit up and down the passage. Then I knew how many minutes I had when I wouldn't be seen. There was something else I could use to my advantage. My hands had been bound behind my back when I was arrested, but after the mug shot, the soldier had handcuffed me in front. That meant I could raise my wrists and push back the blindfold. If I dared.

Clunk. Heart pounding, I waited. Then I slowly raised my wrists, but I didn't have the guts to go further. I counted the minutes. I waited. Clunk. I tried again. Were they watching? I let myself touch the blindfold. I scratched my forehead, waiting to see if anything would happen. I waited. No one hit me. I counted out the time. Clunk. I had to remove the blindfold but—*next time*, I kept telling myself. *I'll do it next time. But they'll catch me*, I thought, and then again promised myself *next time*. It took me what felt like forever, but then I did it. I pushed the blindfold back.

There, through the bars I could see down the hill. There was the wall, and there was Juan Fernando, alive, looking scared. Even at a distance I could sense his tension, but he was alive. He was OK. They had lied to me.

In the story I tell myself now, I saved my brother and he saved me. Every time the torturer entered, all I could talk about was Juan Fernando. *Where is my brother? What are you doing to him? He's fragile. If anything happens to him, our mother will die.* I named people I knew at the mental hospital and claimed they had treated him. By holding onto my love and concern for my brother, I never entirely lost my connection to humanity outside that room. My emotional ties were not completely broken.

Once I finally pushed the blindfold back and got away with it, I did it again and again, but each time the torturer returned I was standing obediently in exactly the same place in the room. Each time I *looked*, my first act was to reassure myself that my brother was still all right. Then I went further. To my surprise, I saw my cell had a toilet. Although I kept complaining of hunger and exhaustion and thirst, when I was unobserved, I was able to drink from the tank. The interrogators had left a pile of evidence in the middle of the room. There was the ELN pamphlet and a photo of one of the mental patients from the hospital in a barred cell—the so-called guerrilla hostage. At the bottom of the pile, there was the only evidence with my name and my handwriting: the copy of the letter to Radio Havana Cuba. I tore it up and flushed it down the toilet. The noise was a risk, but not taking that risk seemed the greater danger.

At the end of ten days, I was released for lack of evidence.

The Acts and Arts of Healing

Besides revising the narrative I tell, I have tried to see the time of my torture as an initiatory ordeal. The initiate is also separated from his accustomed world. He doesn't know where he has been taken. Naked and unprotected, he will face severe trials. He won't know what comes next. He must accept the unknown outcome. Afterward he returns to his society and is celebrated by it.

I am not saying torture *was* an initiation, but that for my own sake, to move past the victim position and claim my own power, I have tried to *resignify* it as such. I had gone through an ordeal—not at the hands of the elders but at the hands of perpetrators. The elders would have taught me to love life and value my culture. Instead, the torturers made me lose faith in life. They made me wish to die to end the pain. They left in me a desire for revenge, fueled by a violent and deadly rage. I had survived, but, unlike the traditional initiate, I wasn't brought back to the community and celebrated. The perpetrators left me in the wilderness, and it was up to me, through my own resources, to find the way home.

But merely returning home is not enough. Like the shaman—though I would not presume to claim that title—the torture survivor has experienced a break with the reality on which most of us rely. His identity has disintegrated. He has descended to hell, but he has also returned, and that means he knows the path. He can go and come back, descend and return. From the terrible depths the shaman brings back medicine and knowledge.

For me this means that to return in the fullest sense I must bring a story back to the world. The private narrative has to be made public. I must speak out against torture; I must bring healing to those who have been to hell and are finding it hard to rediscover the path back to life.

Today approximately half a million torture survivors live in the United States. Many survivors speak reluctantly, if they are able to speak at all. Besides sometimes permanent or chronic physical damage, the psychic disintegration that accompanies torture leaves the survivor on unstable ground. Survivors cope with the symptoms of posttraumatic stress, with impaired memory, anxiety, depression, and difficulties in forming or maintaining relationships. You may know a survivor without being aware of it. You may have a neighbor, friend, partner, teacher, student, patient, client, or colleague who copes silently with torture's long-term effects.

We Latin Americans who survived the horrific repression of the '70s and '80s—often sponsored by the United States and carried out by military officers trained by the US Army at the School of the Americas—have had decades in

Nightwind (detail). Photograph of Hector Aristizábal. Courtesy of Nick T. Spark.

which to process our emotions and learn that breaking the silence is part of healing. The trauma robs you of your community, your language, your relations. All these connections are broken. If we don't reconnect, we replicate the isolation of the torture chamber over and over. We have to find the door and the key to unlock it.

I had spoken out against torture for years, but when, in 2004, photographs surfaced from the hell of the American-run Iraqi prison Abu Ghraib, old feelings of helplessness and rage threatened to overwhelm me. In collaboration with my friends—the writer Diane Lefer, director B.J. Dodge, and musician Enzo Fina, I created *Nightwind*, the autobiographical solo performance about my arrest and torture. With it I've toured the program over thousands of miles through thirty-four countries to mobilize public opinion. Richard Rorty's formulation, as cited by Margaretta Jolly, is an accurate expression of our own experience: audiences identify with my personal story and, in empathizing, come to realizations about torture they did not reach through more objective media reporting.

After a performance, someone always asks how it affects me to relive the trauma. The truth is I'm not sure, although I have many answers. Turning the experience into art, into an aesthetic object, gives me a sense of control and, I hope, creates beauty where once there was only pain. And that very pain empowers me as an activist seeking allies in the struggle against such horrendous practices. Performing has become for me a way to unlock that chamber door. I used to think I needed to unlock it to get out. Now it occurs to me that an open door also serves to invite people in. Torture happens in isolation, in secret. When I bring an audience into the experience with me, not only am I supported by their witnessing, but the space can no longer be a torture chamber. The space itself is transformed.

Does this make me a "human rights hero"? In some eyes, clearly yes. And while the heroic image has been valuable for antitorture advocacy, it also undermines my principal ongoing work, which is to help individuals and communities address and transform their own traumas, whatever they may be. A more complete picture of Hector reveals a man with weaknesses and flaws, a reality I try to make clear in more sustained workshops and events, as well as in my memoir, *The Blessing Next to the Wound*. If the people I encounter feel *I could never be as strong and heroic as he is*, I've failed in what matters to me most: for others to recognize their own heroism and access their own inner strengths.

To help other torture survivors heal, I joined the board of the Program for Torture Victims (PTV), the first program in the United States dedicated to treating survivors suffering the physical and psychological consequences of state-sponsored violence. It got its start in 1980 after two Latin American exiles met in Los Angeles. Dr. José Quiroga, a cardiologist, had been Chilean president Salvador Allende's personal physician before the military coup that cost Allende his life. Ana Deutsch, a psychologist, survived the dirty war in Argentina, escaping to the United States along with her family after the military government threatened to arrest them for their opposition activities. Ana and José knew there were survivors in Los Angeles who weren't getting the care they needed due to poverty or fear or a powerful reluctance to speak of what they had endured. They simply began offering their services, often in their own living rooms, free of charge.

In 1994 PTV gained nonprofit status, and the founders were finally able to seek outside funding, rent offices at Mercado La Paloma, and expand a staff of therapists, social workers, and administrators, as well as a roster of cooperating doctors and immigration asylum attorneys.

Initially most clients came from Latin America. Today, PTV serves people from more than sixty-five countries around the world from Afghanistan to

Zimbabwe. As a board member, I often speak on behalf of PTV while also reaching out to my fellow survivors through the Healing Club. We get together and play theater games. We play soccer. We dance. We have fun, but in service, too, of a serious purpose. When you have a severely traumatized person who can't meet your eye and can't get articulate words out, how will this person be able to go to an asylum hearing and face the immigration judge and answer questions about torture and rape? The games we play are a way to prepare them. I don't do anything threatening. I don't bring up the big issues, at least not at first. There's nothing at stake. We just play and in this way come back into our bodies and reclaim our voices.

I recently worked—or played—with a survivor from Cameroon who arrived in the United States rendered mute. Months later he was able to make a statement to a group of college students. Admittedly, his presentation was brief and he spoke in general terms, offering no personal account. More privately, he told me he loves the United States because in this country everyone gets a fair trial and only terrible criminals go to prison. And "Why doesn't the U.S. care about Cameroon? President Bush invades Iraq to get rid of a dictator. Why won't he invade my country?" This man had suffered horribly for speaking out in a dissenting voice in his homeland. Now, much as I quietly disagreed with his opinions, what mattered to me was that he could express them.

Then there's Meluleki. He's a tall, handsome young man, always clean-cut, and, like many Africans I've met in Los Angeles, he's rather formal. During his first two years in the United States, my friend Meluleki sat in an apartment, doing nothing, just depressed and depressed and waiting and waiting while the government decided whether to grant his application for asylum.

"Go out," I suggested once. "Get a job. Even if it's a crummy job. Just something to do."

"No," he said. "They told me since I ask for asylum I'm not allowed to work. If they catch me working, I don't get it."

So Meluleki waited. No money. Nothing to do. All he had were memories of the life he used to lead and the political violence and torture that made him leave that life behind. I imagine he was like me in that chamber, tormented not just with the pain, not just with the interrogator's questions, but with the bigger questions that never leave you: *Where is everybody? Where is my family, my friends, the country, the values of this society? Why can this happen apparently with such ease? How can people treat other human beings like this? Why doesn't anyone care? Where are the people?*

In Zimbabwe, Meluleki was an actor, which is why his therapist, Ken Louria, wanted us to meet. Now he speaks so softly that the words come out and are swallowed back almost before I can hear what he's said. Someone who doesn't know the consequences of torture might find it hard to believe that this man once projected his strong voice in street theater performances in the open air.

I take him to buy a drum—a djembe drum, a healing drum. We find drums painted in the colors of Africa, another in a multimask design, more adorned with brightly patterned swirls, but the drum Meluleki chooses isn't painted. Instead, it's the grain of the wood and the simplicity of the braided cord around the drum head that give it beauty. The sales clerk comes over to offer help, but for the first time since I've known Meluleki it's clear he needs no help from anyone. As soon as his fingers and palm touch the goatskin, my friend is fully alive.

Over lunch I ask Meluleki about the initiation rites of his tribe.

"The older men of the village initiate you," he explains. "Your uncles, not your father. If something is bothering me or I am in some trouble, I tell my uncle. He may then talk to my father or instruct me to do it, but in our custom, I never go directly to my father."

"Who would be the equivalent of your uncle in Los Angeles?" I ask.

He names his therapist. He names the whole PTV program. "And you," he says, "because you were with me to get this drum."

"When you get your asylum, we should celebrate," I say. "Your uncles should offer you a welcoming ceremony."

He smiles. "That will be good, and I will tell you how."

And so one day in May we sit in a circle in the meeting room downstairs at Mercado La Paloma. The conference table is gone, and the walls are decorated with African fabrics. We are survivors and staff and children and friends. We come from the United States and Sri Lanka, Congo, Guatemala, Eritrea, France, Italy, Palestine, El Salvador, and more. We speak English and Spanish and Shona, Russian, Armenian, and Georgian. Tigrinya, Singhalese, Arabic, Italian, Amharic, and more African languages than I can name.

"I am Hector," I say, moving my arms in a flourish. Everyone repeats, "I am Hector," and the whole circle copies me, waving their arms. "I am Melu," says Meluleki. One by one, we introduce ourselves, a name and gesture, to be imitated and celebrated by all. At last we're back to Meluleki. Now it's his chance to say more than his name, to tell us all exactly how he wants to be known.

He begins to drum. He speaks in remembrance of those who have died in Zimbabwe and then says: "My name is Meluleki. My umbilical cord was buried in the red soils of kwaGodlwayo omnyama . . ." Instantly the Zimbabwean women in the room begin to ululate, galvanizing us all. They join in Meluleki's praise of his people: *umahlaba ayithwale owadeluku biya ngamahlahla wabiya ngamakhand' amadoda.* "This," he says, "is how I praise my chief and identify with the sons and daughters of the soil, the people of my origin, the Ndebele tribe. I remember growing up in the presence of the Fifth Brigade commonly known as the *gukurahundi*, one of the most ruthless armies that has ever existed on this planet. They massacred more than thirty thousand of my beloved brothers and sisters on the instructions of the so-called angel of death, Robert Gabriel Mugabe, who has successfully destroyed my motherland for the past twenty-seven years. I tried with my fellow comrades to voice our concerns through staging theater shows in the schools, crèches, youth centers, and streets of Bulawayo, but the message was too clear to go unheard by the little dogs that he has planted all over. These people visited me without an invitation, and, believe me, it was not a pleasant visit. This is what they did to me."

He doesn't speak now, but his hands fly as he drums, hard and fast, and faster.

"Today I have a scar on my forehead. When I look at the mirror I see a defeated warrior, but it's only for the moment."

Will Mugabe fall at last? Will Meluleki someday return home?

He taps his drum. His fellow countrymen join him as they sing the national anthem: *Mayihlom' ihlasele, nkosi sikelel' izwe lase Zimbabwe.*

We welcome him to the PTV family, first with words. A welcome from his therapist, Ken Louria. A man from Cameroon talks of the support people must give each other: "No matter where you are or how bold, you need someone in front carrying the torch." We welcome him then with our drums. I've got mine. Enzo is playing too, and so is case manager Saba Kidane, who's brought a drum of her own and can't stop smiling as she joins in.

We teach each other songs in our different languages, and when we start to dance, I see an African woman—the one who has sat silent and stiff with tears on her expressionless face—suddenly rise. She's out in front now, leading the dance, swaying and clapping.

"Look, look," says her friend. "This is the first time I see her happy since she arrives in the United States."

Now we have welcomed Meluleki and this woman, too, into the PTV community. It remains to be seen whether they will be welcomed by Los Angeles and into the wider community of the United States.

Where is everybody? We are here.

NOTE

This essay contains material first published in *The Blessing Next to the Wound: A Story of Art, Activism, and Transformation* by Hector Aristizábal and Diane Lefer (Lantern Books, 2010) and is reprinted with the kind permission of the publisher.

Part Two

Recognition

Recognition

EVA HOFFMAN

I come to this project not as a professional historian or theorist but as someone for whom questions of memory and history have been of vital interest—
and, indeed, the note I want to touch on here is the deep interweaving between
the two: between subjectivity and history, individual narrative and collective
memory. My concern with such questions comes, as it clearly does for many of
us, from the very personal seed of family history. I grew up in Poland after
World War II; my parents both survived the Holocaust in what was then the
Polish part of the Ukraine. Their lives were saved by Polish and Ukrainian neighbors who sheltered and hid them at enormous risk, but their entire families were
exterminated. Eventually, I tried to address the long afterlife of this history—
and, by extension, of other atrocities of which we have seen so many since
then—in a book called *After Such Knowledge*. As I studied the various stages of
response to the Shoah, the various forms of understanding and interpretation, I
was also struck by the stages and transformations of personal expression and
testimony, and at every stage by the interbraiding of and interdependence
between personal narratives and historical interpretation—and also between
the teller and the listener, between the giving of testimony and its reception.

To start with myself: my parents' intimate and fragmented stories—speech
under the pressure of trauma is often broken speech—were like potent pellets
of information and early knowledge. My sense of what they had endured meant
that for me the Holocaust was not really history; it was a living, if very dark,
past. My relationship with all the issues raised by it was intense and highly
charged. But in order to understand that event in its historicity, I needed, of
course, to go beyond the family stories—indeed, beyond individual memory—
and to supplement them with a different kind of knowledge. I needed to place
those forms of transmission and knowledge in a broader context, and to study
the structure and the awful dynamics of what had taken place. And so I think it
is with other forms of personal testimony. These are crucial in giving us insight

into the human dimension of collective events. Primo Levi's books are an essential part of our understanding of the Holocaust. And yet these, too, exist in a complex relationship with more public and broader forms of understanding. There are memoirs written before the word *Holocaust* came into use, and others written long after, in which certain formulas of collective understanding become evident. There are stages of memory in which remembering and the telling of stories become automatic and, in a paradoxical way, impersonal.

But in the initial stages of response to the Holocaust, Primo Levi, for example, couldn't find a publisher for his book. Nobody thought his subject was of interest, and this, I believe, added greatly to his sense of isolation. Reflecting on this, and other instances of indifference—indeed, the whole early phenomenon of disavowal, which is also evident in the aftermath of other atrocities (e.g., in Cambodia)—led me to think about another, more affective or ethical kind of dialectic between testimony and reception and the importance of something that may be as fundamental as historical understanding, and may, perhaps, precede it: the processes of acknowledgment and recognition. The injustices attendant on atrocity, and the losses suffered by the victims, cannot be undone. But it seems to me that the one thing we do owe to people whose very identities have been discounted and denigrated is a full recognition of their experience. In other words, the accounts, the testimonies, need to be received and acknowledged.

Recognition can happen in the family or through very personal knowledge of a particular person and particular experiences or in therapy or psychoanalysis and through the weaving of an internal narrative—a story of subjectivity. But I think that just as crucial is the element of a more collective or public recognition, which acknowledges what happened to a group of people—and most often because they belonged to that group. I have talked to Armenians who feel that until the Armenian genocide is named as that and its horror recognized, they will be in the position of Ancient Mariners, burdened with the duty to tell their ancestral story again and again. In a way I think witnesses of terrible events want also to be finally liberated from the obligations of testimony. But that can only happen when that testimony is fully heard and acknowledged. On the other hand, I feel that the force of such procedures as the Truth and Reconciliation Commission in South Africa—for all its flaws—came from the enactment of the processes of recognition, from the victim being able to face the perpetrator and say, this is what happened; this is what I experienced. I will tell my story, and it will be heard. This, I think, has enabled some people to feel that some moral order has been restored: wrongs have been named as wrongs, and their human rights—indeed, their humanity—have been respected and therefore restored.

But this is in the aftermath, and of course it would be so much better if such recognition could be offered before collective violence is unleashed. And so what interests me is whether one can harness the power of testimony, and narrative, to moderate prejudices and antagonisms before they explode in violence and hatred. In a sense such moderation can only happen through political processes. Violence—especially neighborly violence—is often stoked through political and ideological incitement. Conversely, the only hope for quelling prejudices and simmering conflicts is through the inclusion of various groups in the social body, and in according to all of them equal respect and rights. But it would also help if historically hostile groups knew each other's histories—and stories. One wonders if it might be possible to set up truth and reconciliation groups in advance of violence, if the processes of dialogue and recognition could be harnessed before latent (or sometimes fairly obvious) conflicts flare into communal battle and atrocity. So far we are better at dealing with the aftermath of terrible events than at preventing them. But perhaps our painful and lengthening history of crossnational and intranational conflict may lead us to think hard about the possibilities of prevention, and of catching the licking flames of prejudice and hostility before they explode into raging and destructive fires.

Protection

GILLIAN WHITLOCK

The photographs on page 81 of asylum seekers are images from *protection*, an installation by the Australian artists Carl Warner and Ross Gibson, commissioned by the University of Queensland Art Museum as part of *Waiting for Asylum: Figures from an Archive*, a special exhibition held in June 2011 that responded to the asylum seeker archives that are held in the Fryer Library at the university. These archives are collections of letters, gifts, artworks, photographs, cards, and official correspondence around and about the asylum seekers held in detention on the Pacific island of Nauru from 2001 to 2008, when the facility was closed down with the election of the new Rudd government and, for a short time we now know, Australia advanced a more humanitarian policy that ended off-shore detention in these remote camps. These are photographs taken by the asylum seekers in the detention camp on Nauru, some of the 360 photographs in the Fryer archives. For ethical and legal reasons, these photographs cannot be seen in public without masking the identity of the asylum seekers, and in them the mask becomes a commentary as well as a requirement. Hence the irony of the title: *protection*. The mask both responds to ethical requirements that asylum seekers' identity be protected and produces a scar that comments on the defacement and dehumanization of asylum seekers in detention. The censoring mask is both cruel and kind. Applied in a thick, matte impasto of blackboard paint, it intervenes in the smooth surface of the photograph. The idea, Gibson says, is that to remove the mask (and return identity to the asylum seeker) would reveal scouring damage in the aftermath of protection. Scars will remain.[1] In interviews the artist Carl Warner has remarked that it was hard to repeatedly deface the photographs drawn together in *protection* in this way, reflecting on the violence of removing the faces that are such a powerful trigger for humanitarian recognition in response to these images.[2]

These photographs capture refugees who are being "processed," repeatedly giving testimony to experiences of suffering and trauma that struggles to find its

Photographs of asylum seekers in Carl Warner and Ross Gibson's *protection*, 2011, C-type photograph and blackboard paint. Source material courtesy of the Elaine Smith collection, Fryer Library, the University of Queensland. Reproduced courtesy of the artists.

witness. Asylum seekers' testimony appeals both to humanitarianism and to human rights discourse: the seekers elicit compassion, and they claim their rights as individuals. These people speak from the fault lines, a deterritorialized and dislocated space of indeterminate sovereignty, as Suvendrini Perera suggests; refugees mark the boundaries of our citizenship, caught where the principles of security and humanitarianism meet and contest.[3] Erasing the humanity of asylum seekers and denying their rights is a standard protocol in the mass media. These are unwelcome strangers that threaten the body of the nation; they are the abject, border objects that are "ejected beyond the scope of the possible, the tolerable, the thinkable."[4] The photographs they take of themselves are frequently banal, like family snapshots, and they confirm to both the asylum seekers and the activists with whom they correspond that the asylum seekers are in fact "like us." Pictures taken on the beach, in the local supermarket (where some occasionally were allowed to visit), and within the camp itself capture everyday domestic activities. In Australia under the Pacific Solution these people were held in camps located in newly devised territories of exclusion, where their presence marked the boundaries of the nation.[5] Asylum seeker testimony confronts us with difficult questions about the limits of testimony and the absence of witnessing, and it follows from this that they draw attention to the limits of the human in public discourse. The production, circulation, and reception of testimony connects directly to the most fundamental questions of who counts as human, whose lives count as lives, and what makes for a "grievable life." Testimony circulates as a social and political force in the public sphere that commands recognition and ethical response from both institutions and individuals, but there must be an appropriate political, cultural, and social milieu for testimonial agency to occur, for testimony to move and stir its witness into action and appropriate response. To thrive testimony must find recognition from others who will register and witness its truth. Testimony and witnessing move and circulate in the uncertain currencies of what Sara Ahmed calls "affective economies," and if testimony fails to find its witness in this uncertain exchange it remains the sound of one hand clapping: testimony is a speech act that demands recognition and response in terms of social action and social justice. Ahmed emphasizes the social and cultural work of emotions on the move: emotions are not contained in the psychology of the individual but circulate in social and cultural practices, producing the very surfaces and boundaries that enable recognition and response; feelings may stick to some objects, and slide over others.[6] To think of asylum seekers and their testimony in terms of affective economies suggests how the figure of the asylum seeker is located precisely on that boundary where grievable life is subject to negotiation; they occupy the domain of representation where humanization and dehumanization occur ceaselessly.[7] Here, where life is at its most precarious and humanity is at risk, it follows that so, too, is testimony.

Asylum seekers have the nonstatus of people who have not been recognized as refugees; they are in the process of seeking that legal recognition. This depends on the performance in interviews of a narrative that is coded so as to be recognizable according to the conventions of the United Nations Convention Relating to the Status of Refugees—that is to say, a person who has a well-founded fear of persecution for reasons of race, religion, nationality, membership in a particular social group, or political opinion. The mobilization of this convention in specific jurisdictions in the legal and bureaucratic processing of asylum seekers during the refugee determination process creates testimonial occasions where claims to subjective truth and authenticity must be reconciled to the terms and conditions required for creditable claims to refugee status as this is interpreted in narratives of national citizenship and belonging. Asylum seekers who arrive by boat in Australian exclusion zones are required to testify repeatedly in extended protocols of offshore processing, under *protection*. Testimony is elicited and subjected to interrogation variously and repeatedly. There is a biodata interview conducted when they are intercepted at sea, which establishes name, date of birth, and nationality. At the detention center—and detention is mandatory in Australia—asylum seekers go through a screening interview, where an immigration officer determines whether they have a prima facie case for protection. If they pass this screening, they are allowed to lodge an application for protection by filling out a series of documents and then waiting for the primary interview, which determines whether they will be granted a protection visa by the Department of Immigration.[8] Within the refugee determination process, then, asylum seekers are obliged on numerous occasions to testify to their suffering to official witnesses: screening officers, interpreters, assessing officers, lawyers and/or migration agents, doctors, and psychiatrists: "[I]n other words, the refugee determination process depends almost entirely on the ability and willingness of the asylum seeker to perform witness."[9] In the archive these primary interviews and the status determinations that follow are a haunting presence. Within the relative safety of the humanitarian witnessing in their correspondence with activists, asylum seekers testify to the confusion and disorientation produced by this constant work of giving testimony. We also find artifacts of this official process: Department of Immigration and Multicultural and Indigenous Affairs (DIMIA) paperwork such as letters of rejection, requests for further information and documentation, and constant deferrals of decision making.

Citizenship is based on this interrogation, and the asylum seekers must master the codes and conventions of the acceptable narrative in the performance of their testimony. As Mireille Hebing suggests, asylum seekers are required to match their subjective life experiences to the objective parameters of asylum policy in order to achieve credibility within the asylum determination procedure.[10] The gap between those who have passed the credibility test and those who have not is vast, and in Australia it is translated spatially as separation detention, where those with experience of the DIMIA (Department of Immigration & Multicultural & Indigenous Affairs, now Department of Immigration and Border Protection, DIBP) interview are kept apart from new detainees; there must be no rehearsal of the social, cultural, and bureaucratic script that unlocks the door to a protection visa.[11] This must be gained through what is assessed as an authentic performance of suffering and discrimination within the formal criteria.

We now know from the Fryer archives that at the same time asylum seekers held in the Nauru detention center also engaged in ongoing correspondence with activists in Australia in a language that deliberately and consistently deploys and elicits the language of humanitarian compassion and the terms of human rights discourse. Here testimony is given and witnessed in reciprocal exchange — a gifting of narrative and response. Asylum seeker testimony mobilizes painful emotions in its witnesses: shame, guilt, and responsibility. Humanitarian activists speak of their shame variously: in apology, confession, and dissent. In these private letters these deep emotions are felt personally and as a national subject, and in this way the letters become testimony to painful emotions that call on asylum seekers to give witness. As Ahmed argues, shame binds us to others through our testimony to how we have been affected by the failure to give recognition, a failure that must be witnessed: "[T]he relationship to others who witness my shame is anxious; shame both confirms and negates the love that sticks us together."[12] We see, then, that asylum seeker testimony does find its witness, but in these intimate, private networks of humanitarianism, which constitute a counter–public sphere, a space of dissent within the dominant and normative discourses of national interest. What fails to occur is a more expansive public process of mobilizing shame in which the community of the nation accepts responsibility and recognizes the claims to humanity and human rights that asylum seekers make at every opportunity. Public opinion in Australia remains resolutely opposed to more humane procedures for managing asylum seekers, and the rhetoric of these people as threats to national security, border control, and the national interest dominates deliberation on these issues in the public sphere. This failure is inscribed throughout the Fryer archive as the activists openly elicit testimony that they can use in their campaigns on behalf of the asylum seekers: letters are marked as read in public, forwarded to the press, or read aloud in public meetings. There are frequent requests for detainees to produce material suitable for public consumption in Australia in campaigns that appeal for humanitarian empathy in response to their plight, thereby re-framing the dominant discourse.

The processing and detention of asylum seekers that mark the boundaries of Australian citizenship, and the abjection of asylum seekers, secure the national collective. Placed as they are in "borderscapes" where humanitarianism and security meet, it is the national interest and integrity and the dehumanization of asylum seekers that bind a national imaginary in terms of some bodies that belong and other bodies that become contaminated things. To return again to Ahmed's idea of affective economy, hate is economic. It does not reside in a given subject or object; rather it circulates between signifiers in relationships of difference and displacement.[13] The dehumanization of the asylum seeker and his or her construction as a figure of hate is an ongoing process in which the detainee is constructed as a contamination, an intrusion through the constant creation of narratives of crisis and iconic figures—for example, the number of boats, the rapacious people smuggler, or the child at risk. Repeated stereotyping of asylum seekers as figures of abjection occurs in the public sphere: the figure of the asylum seeker stalks the nation and haunts its capacity to secure its borders, its integrity, its identity. This differentiation is incessant, and it is never over: "[I]t awaits others who have not yet arrived."[14] Humanitarian activism and human rights discourse work through testimony to constitute a counter-public discourse that identifies asylum seekers as specific people, with specific histories of suffering and trauma. However, these glimpses of individuals cannot trump the projection of hate, which generates its effects precisely because it is not located in a specific object or figure; it is perpetuated repeatedly in stereo-types, and constantly renewed in narratives of crisis and threat to the integrity of the nation and its citizens and to the authority of the government to control its borders. This is the terrain that the Gibson and Warner artwork *protection* documents.

What do we learn about testimony under these circumstances, when it is such a fragile and tenuous thing? Conventionally testimony is defined as a subset of autobiography, although, as Bella Brodzki remarks in putting this definition forward, testimony to a greater extent than any other kind of autobiographical narrative emerges out of a political context, in response to a particular set of political circumstances and rhetorical conditions.[15] Testimony is a fragile and volatile performative relation between those who testify and those who give witness and the failure to respond to testimony ethically, which Thomas Keenan calls "becoming shameless."[16] Testimony requires its witness, yet political circumstances and rhetorical conditions continuously reshape networks and jurisdictions for testimonial affects.

Testimony travels on the backs of narratives of trauma and suffering, and it is opportunistic. Ahmed's notion of the economy of affect grasps the ways in which testimony is attached to a history of emotions in western modernity. It accrues value and yet is subject to changes in currency and exchange; the value that is attached to people and things is wholly figurative, and it follows from this that we can map the ebb and flow of testimony in terms of cycles, thresholds, and events where emotions of compassion and aversion are a volatile medium. This model shapes a history of testimony by adapting Franco Moretti's "distant reading," which focuses on the relationship between markets and forms, moving beyond the frameworks of national historiography or canonical texts in favor of larger, transnational networks and connections.

The role of the epistolary novel and narrative more generally in shaping imaginative testamentary spaces and the work of emotional training in humanitarian witnessing is now well established,[17] and is a compelling case for the particular role of the bildungsroman in the invention of human rights.[18] However, the role of life narrative, and testimony in particular, in the development of humanitarianism and rights discourse remains largely unobserved, although it was central to the cosmopolitan cultural politics of global modernity. The abolitionists' call for a literature of the world in the nineteenth century invokes not only a transnational formation, world literature, but also what postcolonial criticism might call a worlding of literature—that is, a literature that engages across cultural difference with an ethical awareness of others, an awareness that emerges most acutely in humanitarianism through witnessing narratives of trauma and suffering.[19]

This world literature and worlding of literature are vital to the history of testamentary life narrative in the *longue durée*, that centuries-long perspective Moretti invokes in his essay on literary history, returning to Fernand Braudel's time frames of event, cycle, and *longue durée* to map a cultural geography of the novel. Enlightenment humanism produced collective and overtly political forms of testamentary life narrative, the testimony and memoir. Although testimonial forms are often classified as subtypes or subsets of autobiography proper, both individual and collective forms of autobiographical narrative emerged in copresence and proximity, both associated with debate about the human, human rights, social justice, and civil society, those key concerns in the secular vision of the human promulgated by Enlightenment moral philosophy. Dipesh

Chakrabarty reminds us that this is an ambiguous legacy of European modernity for the colonized, returning to Frantz Fanon's struggle to hold on to the Enlightenment idea of the human as part of a global heritage. As Fanon recognized, the rights of man have been available to the privileged few, despite the cosmopolitan promise of egalitarianism and rights discourse that was fueled by abolitionism. Embedded in the *longue durée* of testimonial narrative are two things: a tradition that empowered subaltern subjects through rights discourse, and a tradition of ethical debate about the limitations of humanitarianism and bearing witness to suffering. These coexist and interact on the page, and throughout the paratexts of testimonial life narrative.

In the *longue durée* of testamentary forms we see the very modern concerns of Enlightenment moral philosophy with the ethics of witnessing and spectatorship, even as the circulation of narratives of suffering produced compassionate recognition across cultures. Testimonial forms appealing to humanitarian sentiment and rights discourse driven by abolitionism were essential to the emotional and political education of modern subjects. Olaudah Equiano's *The Interesting Narrative*, the first autobiographical account by an Afro-British subject, was published in London in 1789, the year of the Declaration of the Rights of Man.[20] *The Interesting Narrative* was (ostensibly) an eyewitness account of the Middle Passage crossing, which the abolition movement required in its campaign to mobilize shame about the Atlantic slave trade. The recent controversy about Equiano's origins is symptomatic of the fragility of the testimonial contract inscribed throughout *The Interesting Narrative* itself, and in Equiano's own anxious shepherding of subsequent editions we see the precarious life of non-European subjects who lay claim to human rights. The mediations of rights discourse and the affective infrastructure secured by humanitarianism are fragile; figures that invoke compassion and empathy—the slave in the case of abolitionism, and the asylum seeker now—also evoke the most profound aversion and contempt. This is the conundrum that haunts the politics of testimony and witness. Testimony bears witness to terrible events; it is the first-person account of collective trauma, suffering, and survival. In testimony the narrator lays claims to truth and authenticity and speaks on behalf of the many who have suffered and cannot speak on their own account. Testimony struggles to bear witness to the unspeakable to spectators who are privileged, and they are likely to be the beneficiaries of exploitation and oppression in other worlds. The addressee, spectator, and witness are all of concern in testimonial discourse. Concerns about spectatorship and bearing witness to the suffering of others arise from the very beginning in Enlightenment theories about the social work of the emotions. After all, Equiano's contemporary Jean-Jacques Rousseau observed that compassion or care for others exists alongside its ostensible opposite, self-love.[21]

An aesthetics grounded in compassion and sympathy is a distinctively modern legacy of the Enlightenment. In his 1759 book *The Theory of Moral Sentiments*, Adam Smith writes about pity, compassion, and the propriety of action to ameliorate suffering.[22] Smithian ethics emphasizes the work of the imagination in provoking feelings of sympathy between the spectator and strangers whose suffering can become real "when we either see it or are made to conceive of it." This ethical humanitarian response to narrative emphasizes the power of benevolence as effective social action, in ways that are specific and individualized. This ethical thinking is a legacy of abolitionism: the power of the first-person narrative to make real the pain of strangers. Equiano's rhetoric repeatedly appeals to the sensibility and sentimentality of the reader, praising men of feeling who respond sympathetically to the suffering of slaves in the West Indies. In testimony the stranger reaches out to others to speak of brutality beyond their understanding so as to elicit benevolent action. In these ways Equiano deliberately appeals to abolitionist discourse so as to elicit an imaginative engagement with horror and suffering, drawing on the liberal discourse of aesthetics and politics.

Theorizing sympathy as a mode of cross-cultural engagement focused on feeling, emotion, and sensibility, developing an intense awareness of the experiences of another, and a distinctively modern notion of the self as socially constituted and mediated through a politics of recognition. Yet concerns about the self-interestedness of benevolence, pity, and compassion, the ethics of spectatorship regarding pain, are there in these beginnings too. Smithian ethics dramatizes the role of the spectator who ultimately remains disinterested. From the outset, humanitarian benevolence raised concerns about the self-interest of the benefactor in this ethical exchange. As Ian Baucom observes, during the nineteenth century romanticism increasingly placed the spectator at the center of the theater of truth: the affective investment in suffering and systemic inequality became preoccupied with the sentimental process of witnessing and spectatorship itself. The liberal, cosmopolitan subjectivity that was evoked became increasingly narcissistic, self-regarding, and aware of itself as a spectator and witness to the sufferings of another.

This approach to life narrative in the *longue durée*, then, emphasizes the power of testamentary forms of life narrative to engage in the global imaginary of liberal western modernity, but the ethics of witnessing and spectatorship have always been problematic. Testimony travels in the volatile networks of suffering and compassion; it is both hostage to history and a marker of the ebb and flow of power and the authority to narrate. Testimony is always on the move, in search of witness and recognition, in a fragile affective economy. The time frames that Moretti invokes take up Braudel's idea of the multiplicity of time in ways that are very useful for mapping a cultural geography of testimonial life narrative. The cycle—temporary structures within the historical flow—grasps the power of testimonial narrative to respond rapidly to opportunity and stage an intervention, so as to project figures that trigger a compassionate response.

The cycle is the time frame I take in my book *Soft Weapons*, a study of how life narrative was transformed in the course of the "war on terror." The subtitle of the book is *Autobiography in Transit*, and it looks at the transformation in markets for narratives that responded to the horror and fascination with Muslim life-worlds that followed the events of 2001. In contemporary mass media there is a transit lane that carries life narratives across cultures, and it is a legacy of that affective economy of global modernity that empowered humanitarianism and rights discourse. Yet as the idea of soft weapons suggests, testimonial life narrative elicits recognition of those who rarely speak of their experiences authoritatively, and it is vulnerable to co-option as propaganda. Given the contradiction of an armed humanitarian intervention that characterized the war on terror, the fact that the cycle of life narratives produced in this period both authorized and questioned humanitarian agency and rights discourse is a sign of the times—a way in which this cycle returns to what I have been suggesting here is a generic characteristic of testimonial life narrative in the *longue durée*. By reading across multiple autobiographical forms and generic frameworks—graphic narratives, blogs, popular biographies, middlebrow memoirs, journalists' accounts, the hoax—I have argued that life narrative now travels globally with unprecedented power and force, and that it requires new kinds of literacy from us as readers and critics—engagements with, for example, autographics and new social media forms. Ongoing remediation is a feature of the testimonial cycle, and a sign of its energy. So, for example, the cycle identified in *Soft Weapons* sustains its energy; Marjane Satrapi's graphic narrative *Persepolis* is remediated as an animated film of the same name; Evan Wright's *Generation Kill* is transformed from memoir into television series; the Norma Khouri hoax testimony to honor killing, *Forbidden Lies / Honor Lost*, becomes a film, *Forbidden Lie$*, in which the producer, Alison Broinowski, reflects autobiographically on spectatorship and her desire to consume the lives of others; and Salam Pax's blog becomes a book, *The Baghdad Blogger*. This remediation is driven by the energy of these narratives as conduits of cross-cultural contact in a cycle in which the mobilization of emotions of various kinds—guilt, shame, responsibility, retribution—complicate spectatorship. Concerns about compassion fatigue, exploitation, and authenticity arise, but we can see this intense self-consciousness about the act of bearing witness as historical and endemic rather than something new. Testimony and witnessing spawn interconnected and dynamic forms of life narrative that can have a short shelf life. The connections between testimony and humanitarianism and rights discourse are exchanges in an affective economy in which value and currency are subject to change.

The energy of the cycle is finite: a flourish of texts in context that brings the familiar into play in new ways. Other life narrative events we might consider in terms of rise and fall in a dynamics of cyclical movement include Truth and Reconciliation Commission narratives in South Africa, the stolen generations narrative in Australia, the residential school narrative in Canada, and versions of Holocaust testimony. The uptake of testimony remains unpredictable and finite. Suffering is not translated into testimony that elicits a cosmopolitan humanitarian response with any reliability or predictability, and the public sphere of national interest remains a critical factor in determining how narratives of suffering and trauma are carried into global networks of human rights activism. This is a dynamic driven by the currents of compassion and aversion that shape relations between those who testify and those who bear witness. As Lauren Berlant argues, the compassionate emotions derive from social training, emerge at historical moments, are shaped by aesthetic conventions, and take place in scenes that are anxious, volatile, surprising, and contradictory.[23]

Then, finally, in Moretti's schema there is the event: the most ephemeral, mercurial opportunity; and individual episodes that Braudel associates with a "breathless rush" of narrative.[24] These are ripples of testimony, the slight disturbance that rises and disperses, leaving few traces. In the context of asylum seeker testimony in Australia, the ruptures that are produced in that narrative of crisis and threat that is attached to the figure of the asylum seeker in the public sphere are in the nature of the event—temporary, ephemeral, breathless. What is the shape of the testimonial event? By happenstance the exhibition of artworks associated with asylum seekers that featured Gibson and Warner's *protection* coincided with an event, a series of occurrences in the Australian public sphere that came together in May and June 2011 to catalyze, briefly, an opening where testimony might enter and find those who bear witness. In the remainder of this essay I want to parse this instance of ephemeral testimonial agency.

Hebing emphasizes the determining function of the social climate and policy environment in the production and circulation of refugee narratives. The first stage of this event is, then, a change in the policy environment, which introduces a period of divisive debate about the offshore processing of asylum seekers in the national public sphere that is concluded, officially at least, with a decision of the High Court of Australia late in August. On May 7, 2011, the Australian prime minister Julia Gillard announced a new policy: the Malaysian solution. Under this proposal, subsequently declared invalid by the High Court of Australia, a fixed quantum of asylum seekers arriving by boat were to be transferred to camps in Malaysia.[25] In return Australia would accept from Malaysia over the next four years four thousand people who had been recognized as legitimate refugees in the course of United Nations High Commissioner for Refugees (UNHCR) processing. Given that Malaysia is not a signatory to the refugee convention, and the UNHCR cannot support this arrangement as children would be involved in this deportation, calls to reopen the detention center at Nauru began to emerge again in response to a perceived crisis in the number of asylum seekers arriving in Australia in 2011.

This change in policy coincided with two graphic documentaries of trauma and suffering that energized the mass media and national debate. The first was *Go Back to Where You Came From*, a confrontational documentary screened nationally in several episodes in June, in which a group of Australian citizens volunteers to retrace the journeys of asylum seekers back to refugee camps in Jordan and Malaysia, and then to the Democratic Republic of Congo (DRC) and Iraq.[26] The second was *A Bloody Business*, screened nationally on May 30, ostensibly not about asylum seekers at all. This documentary used footage filmed by animal rights activists and put on the air shocking sights and sounds of cattle shipped to Indonesia as part of Australia's live export program being brutally abused and tortured in Indonesian slaughterhouses.[27] In footage that was recycled daily by all the country's television channels for weeks afterward, these images and sounds of the gross abuse and suffering of "Australian animals" continued to shock and horrify, to the extent that in June the federal government announced the suspension of the live animal trade to Indonesia until more humane conditions were established in slaughterhouses. With extraordinary affective force these terrible images and the witnessing of pain and suffering that they produced mobilized shame that was registered by individuals and institutions; they produced national culpability and responsibility. The animal became an ethical subject.

This ethical recognition of animal rights and humane responsibility for animal others was almost immediately transferred to the other issue then alive in the mass media: asylum seekers and the heated debate about the Malaysian solution. The transference of humanitarianism and shame from the bodies of live animals (rendered human as "Australian" subjects) to the bodies of asylum seekers (rendered less than human in public discourse) was effected most powerfully in the new social media: the epigrammatic force of the tweet. The economy of tweeting produced a phrase that fused what had previously been two very

Ron Tandberg, "We're Cancelling the Livestock Transport Because of Public Sensitivities," *The Age*, June 2, 2011. Reproduced courtesy of the artist.

different issues into one: "the live export of refugees." A series of powerful cartoons captured the convergence of brutalized humans and animals with visual insight.

It was, then, through testimony of the suffering of animals in the context of debates about public policy that the alterity threshold in perceptions of refugees in the public sphere was challenged and asylum seekers were brought within that category of creatures to which we attach rights and feel obligated: "the circle of the we."[28] This was highly ironic, given that asylum seekers repeatedly testify to their human status even as they are being processed under dehumanizing conditions in the camp. As Thomas Laqueur argues, the divide between neighbor and stranger is vulnerable and our humanitarian responses to testimonial narratives of suffering are unpredictable and mercurial. Yet they can be, I am arguing in this example, triggered in the ephemeral space of the testimonial event. This temporary yet dynamic expansion of moral imagination in response to suffering is precisely the opportunity for testimonial narrative to become viral and engender rare acts of witness and recognition across very different narratives of trauma and suffering. The event is fueled by a finite but passionate sense of moral urgency, produced in this case by a convergence of trauma narratives presented in graphic reality-television broadcasts and transferred via the new collectives produced by social networking that were so vividly alive in contemporaneous events associated with the "Arab Spring" elsewhere.

And so in a third incident of the testimonial event I am mapping here we find another rupture in the framing of asylum seekers as abject in the public sphere of the nation. Laqueur reminds us that in the late eighteenth century when humanitarianism, spectatorship, and rights discourse were emerging in western modernity as a concern for Enlightenment moral philosophy, *human* came to take on new meanings, and so did *death and the dead*. Dying unknown, unmarked, or uncommemorated came to be a sign of abjection, of being non-human (as it is of course for Julia Kristeva). Bringing to public recognition the dead who had been regarded previously as less than fully human, bringing them into the world of the living through mourning and commemoration, is fundamental to humanitarianism and one of the ways it expanded the recognition of precarious life—those to whom the living have ethical obligations. It is, then, not coincidental that at a conjuncture when the bodies of asylum seekers were reframed in the event, there was also a testimony to mourning and an imaginative recuperation of the unmourned bodies of asylum seekers. So a testimony to the dead appeared in a series of brief accounts in the Australian broadsheets in April and May, for example: "The family of a young Afghan asylum-seeker who reportedly hanged himself in Australia's newest detention centre has hit another hurdle in the drawn-out process to repatriate his body."[29] This, too, following Laqueur, is historic: family as the locus of sentiment was crucial to the advent of compassion for the dead in the democratization of the ethical subject late in the eighteenth century.[30]

On March 17, 2011, a twenty-year-old Hazara man called Meqdad Hussain hanged himself at the Scherger detention center on remote Cape York in North Queensland. The corpse was released by the Queensland coroner in May, but it remained in a morgue in Brisbane, unable to be repatriated. His relatives, who had fled persecution in their native Afghanistan to the Pakistani city of Quetta, struggled to have his body repatriated to Pakistan. Pakistani authorities refused to allow the remains into Pakistan because they were unable to accept a deceased person's body without a passport, and as an asylum seeker Hussain had no identity documents. Finally plans were being made to fly Hussain's body to Afghanistan, so his family could cross the border—a hazardous journey—to collect his remains and begin the rituals of cleansing and burial that would release the remains from "no-man's-land." As Laqueur's commentary suggests, by naming Meqdad Hussain and bringing him into view, even briefly in this way, he is brought out of the domain of the abject into the domain of the human in the work of mourning and commemoration. Finally, postmortem, Hussain's body becomes both human and a bearer of rights, and this narrative enters public discourse at a time when the human, the animal, and the dead appear together at the threshold of testimony, located in a shifting and liminal zone that can erupt unpredictably in the uncertain course of the event.

In this ephemeral space of the event asylum seekers testify out of abjection, and their testimony erupts from containment within a counter-public sphere of human rights discourse with extraordinary force. Briefly this impacts thinking about citizenship, obligation, and responsibility in the community of the nation. This returns us to the Warner and Gibson installation *protection*, the exhibition of deliberately defaced photographs that question how we can bear witness in the absence of face, eyes, and names—markers of embodiment privileged by humanitarianism and rights discourse. As it happened these images were released from the archive into public view and the art museum in the context of the event, during which intense moral debate about the suffering of others erupted for a few months in 2011, a temporary yet dramatic opening in the affective economy when asylum seekers were seen as people to whom Australians have ethical obligations. *Protection* responds to that long tradition of humanitarian artwork that demands the "[e]xact, slow, active, engaging seeing" that "is central in the creation of sentiment, in keeping someone else within ethical range."[31] These deliberately defaced photographs question how we can bear witness to asylum seekers. They deflect looking into the face and eyes of the other in neo-Hegelian recognition. Individually and collectively they command "slow looking," "attentive looking," which Laqueur identifies as fundamental to the *seeing* of someone as human in traditions of humanitarian narrative. Reframed in this installation, the photographs produce an insistent regard for the language of hands, dress, and posture, and they require attention to surroundings that are remarkable for their banality and immersion in the everyday. The thick black lines of defacement thread the individual photographs together, and this scarring marks the conditional access of the spectator to these testimonial artifacts. In becoming a work of art in this installation, these photographs demand reflection on spectatorship, bearing witness, and the shifting thresholds of care and

Carl Warner and Ross Gibson's *protection*, 2011, C-type photographs and blackboard paint. Installation view of the exhibition *Waiting for Asylum: Figures from an Archive*, the University of Queensland Art Museum, 2011. Reproduced courtesy of the artists.

indifference that are historical, and deeply embedded in culture and tradition.[32] The ebb and flow of genres of testimony are mapped here as a cultural geography embedded in a *longue durée* that encompasses cycles and events, phases when narratives of suffering erupt from containment in a counter–public sphere of humanitarianism and rights discourse. Testimony does not have a singular form, politics, or ethics; it constitutes different configurations of self, space, and community.[33]

As this case study of asylum seeker narrative suggests, the agency of testimony is contingent; it responds to changing parameters in law and public policy, new technologies and the communities they engender, changing values in the affective economy, eruptions of violence, and negotiations for social justice in global networks of peace and justice. For a brief time, the installation of *protection* in the art museum opened a space that invites us to become the spectator, bearing witness to asylum seekers as embodied subjects transforming spaces of detention for themselves by domesticating the beach and the camp in the banality of the snapshot. They become familiar. It is the thick black impasto that reminds us of the *longue durée* of spectatorship, its ethical constraints, and the changing thresholds of care and indifference.

NOTES

Thanks to my colleagues working in the Fryer archives, Leili Golafshani and Prue Ahrens, for discussions on these artifacts of the Pacific Solution.

1. Gillian Whitlock and Prue Ahrens, *Waiting for Asylum: Figures from an Archive* (Saint Lucia: University of Queensland Art Museum, 2011).

2. Comments by Carl Warner, seminar on *protection*, Fryer Library, June 15, 2011. For further discussion of *protection*, see Prue Ahrens, "Frames of Reference: Reading the Image of the Asylum Seeker in Gibson and Warner's Artwork 'protection'" (paper presented at the International Biography and Autobiography Biennial Conference, Canberra, July 2012).

3. Suvendrini Perera, *Australia and the Insular Imagination: Beaches, Borders, Boats, and Bodies* (London: Palgrave-Macmillan, 2009), 65.

4. Julia Kristeva, *Powers of Horror: An Essay on Abjection* (New York: Columbia University Press, 1982), quoted in Sara Ahmed, *The Cultural Politics of Emotion* (New York: Routledge, 2004), 86.

5. The Pacific Solution is the name given to the Australian government policy of transporting asylum seekers to detention centers on islands in the Pacific Ocean, rather than allowing them access to the mainland.

6. Ahmed, *The Cultural Politics of Emotion*, 64, 9.

7. Judith Butler, *Precarious Life: The Powers of Mourning and Violence* (London: Verso, 2004), 140.

8. On these documents, see Caroline Wake, "Performing Witness: Testimonial Theatre in the Age of Asylum, Australia, 2000–2005" (PhD diss., University of New South Wales, 2010), 88.

9. Ibid.

10. Mireille Hebing, "Refugee Stories in Britain: Narratives of Personal Experiences in a Network of Power Relations" (PhD diss., City University, London, 2009), 207.

11. Wake, "Performing Witness," 97.

12. Ahmed, *The Cultural Politics of Emotion*, 102.

13. Ibid., 42.

14. Ibid., 47.

15. Bella Brodzki, "Testimony," in *Encyclopedia of Life Writing*, ed. Margaretta Jolly (London: Fitzroy Dearborn, 2001), 870.

16. Thomas Keenan, "Mobilizing Shame," In "And Justice for All? The Claims of Human Rights," ed. Ian Balfour and Eduardo Cadava, special issue, *South Atlantic Quarterly* 103, nos. 2–3 (Spring–Summer): 439.

17. Lynn Hunt, *Inventing Human Rights: A History* (New York: W. W. Norton, 2007); Thomas W. Laqueur, "Mourning, Pity, and the Work of Narrative in the Making of 'Humanity,'" in *Humanitarianism and Suffering: The Mobilization of Empathy*, ed. Richard Ashby Wilson and Richard D. Brown (Cambridge: Cambridge University Press, 2009).

18. Joseph R. Slaughter, *Human Rights, Inc.: The World Novel, Narrative Form, and International Law* (New York: Fordham University Press, 2007); James Dawes, *That the World May Know: Bearing Witness to Atrocity* (Cambridge, MA: Harvard University Press, 2007).

19. In June 1840, at a convention organized by the British and Foreign Anti-Slavery Committee in London, the president of the American Anti-Slavery Society, Henry B. Stanton, proposed a resolution that called for a world literature that would be anti-slavery in its principles and sentimental in its address. See Ian Baucom, *Spectres of the Atlantic: Finance Capital, Slavery, and the Philosophy of History* (Durham, NC: Duke University Press, 2005), 210.

20. Olaudah Equiano, *The Interesting Narrative and Other Writings*, ed. Vincent Carretta (New York: Penguin Books, 2003).

21. For discussion of Rousseau's thinking on social emotions, see the comments by Jonathan Marks and Adi Ophir in "Being Human—Who Cares?," seminar presentation at the Institute of Advanced Study, Durham University, March 3, 2009, accessed April 4, 2012, http://www.dur.ac.uk/ias/onbeinghuman/.

22. Adam Smith, *The Theory of Moral Sentiments* (1759; reprint, London: Penguin Books, 2009).

23. Lauren Berlant, ed., *Compassion: The Culture and Politics of an Emotion* (New York: Routledge, 2004), 7.

24. Franco Moretti, *Graphs, Maps, Trees* (London: Verso, 2005), 13.

25. On August 31, 2011, the High Court of Australia imposed permanent injunctions preventing the transfer of asylum seekers to Malaysia. See "The Conversation," accessed January 1, 2014, http://theconversation.edu.au/malaysia-solution-high-court-ruling-explained-3154.

26. See the website of the documentary *Go Back to Where You Came From*, accessed June 4, 2012, http://www.sbs.com.au/goback/.

27. See a description of the documentary *A Bloody Business*, accessed June 4, 2012, http://www.abc.net.au/4corners/content/2011/s3228880.htm.

28. Laqueur, "Mourning, Pity, and the Work of Narrative in the Making of 'Humanity,'" 32.

29. *Weekend Australian*, May 21, 2011, 10.

30. Laqueur, "Mourning, Pity, and the Work of Narrative in the Making of 'Humanity,'" 36. Laqueur's argument is that the ethical category of the human(e) was vastly expanded in the eighteenth century to reach beyond the local community to distant strangers (remote in terms of culture or geography) and across the species boundary.

31. Ibid., 40.

32. See Adi Ophir's commentary on thresholds of care in "Being Human—Who Cares?"

33. Sara Ahmed and Jackie Stacey, "Testimonial Cultures: An Introduction," *Cultural Values* 5, no. 1 (January 2001): 5.

WORKS CITED

Ahmed, Sara. *The Cultural Politics of Emotion*. New York: Routledge, 2004.

Ahmed, Sara, and Jackie Stacey. "Testimonial Cultures: An Introduction." *Cultural Values* 5, no. 1 (January 2001): 1–6.

Ahrens, Prue. "Frames of Reference: Reading the Image of the Asylum Seeker in Gibson and Warner's Artwork 'protection.'" Paper presented at the International Biography and Autobiography Biennial Conference, Canberra, July 2012.

Baucom, Ian. *Spectres of the Atlantic: Finance Capital, Slavery, and the Philosophy of History*. Durham, NC: Duke University Press, 2005.

"Being Human—Who Cares?" Seminar presentation at the Institute of Advanced Study, Durham University, March 3, 2009. Accessed April 4, 2012. http://www .dur.ac.uk/ias/onbeinghuman/.

Berlant, Lauren, ed. *Compassion: The Culture and Politics of an Emotion*. New York: Routledge, 2004.

Brodzki, Bella. "Testimony." In *Encyclopedia of Life Writing*, edited by Margaretta Jolly, 870–71. London: Fitzroy Dearborn, 2001.

Butler, Judith. *Precarious Life: The Powers of Mourning and Violence*. London: Verso, 2004.

Chakrabarty, Dipesh. *Provincialising Europe: Postcolonial Thought and Historical Difference*. Princeton, NJ: Princeton University Press, 2000.

Dawes, James. *That the World May Know: Bearing Witness to Atrocity*. Cambridge, MA: Harvard University Press, 2007.

Equiano, Olaudah. *The Interesting Narrative and Other Writings*. Edited by Vincent Carretta. London, 1789. Reprint, New York: Penguin Books, 2003.

Go Back to Where You Came From. Television documentary, aired June 21–28, 2011. Sydney: SBS1 Australia, 2011.

Hebing, Mireille. "Refugee Stories in Britain: Narratives of Personal Experiences in a Network of Power Relations." PhD diss., City University, London, 2009.

Hunt, Lynn. *Inventing Human Rights: A History*. New York: W. W. Norton, 2007.

Keenan, Thomas. "Mobilizing Shame." In "And Justice for All? The Claims of Human Rights," edited by Ian Balfour and Eduardo Cadava, special issue, *South Atlantic Quarterly* 103, nos. 2–3 (Spring–Summer): 435–50.

Laqueur, Thomas W. "Mourning, Pity, and the Work of Narrative in the Making of 'Humanity.'" In *Humanitarianism and Suffering: The Mobilization of Empathy*, edited by Richard Ashby Wilson and Richard D. Brown, 31–57. Cambridge: Cambridge University Press, 2009.

Moretti, Franco. *Graphs, Maps, Trees*. London: Verso, 2005.

Perera, Suvendrini. *Australia and the Insular Imagination: Beaches, Borders, Boats, and Bodies*. London: Palgrave-Macmillan, 2009.

Slaughter, Joseph R. *Human Rights, Inc.: The World Novel, Narrative Form, and International Law*. New York: Fordham University Press, 2007.

Smith, Adam. *The Theory of Moral Sentiments*. 1759. Reprint, London: Penguin Books, 2009.

Tandberg, Ron. "We're Cancelling the Livestock Transport Because of Public Sensitivities." Cartoon. *The Age*, June 2, 2011.

Wake, Caroline. "Performing Witness: Testimonial Theatre in the Age of Asylum, Australia, 2000–2005." PhD diss., University of New South Wales, 2010.

Whitlock, Gillian. *Soft Weapons: Autobiography in Transit*. Chicago: University of Chicago Press, 2007.

Whitlock, Gillian, and Prue Ahrens. *Waiting for Asylum: Figures from an Archive*. Saint Lucia: University of Queensland Art Museum, 2011. Exhibition catalog.

The Justice of Listening

Japanese Leprosy Segregation

MICHIO MIYASAKA

Human Rights Abuse and Japan's Leprosy Segregation

Human rights related to illness are quite often counterintuitive. There is a need to carefully examine whether the stigmatization of patients in certain contexts constitutes an unjustifiable human rights abuse, or whether some treatments that patients would deem painful or even abusive can be legitimate in such circumstances. People suffering from leprosy—or Hansen's disease—have been stigmatized since ancient times, because, of course, for centuries no cure existed. However, there is insufficient understanding of how this stigma has continued to trample human rights in modern times. With regard to infectious diseases, such as leprosy, tuberculosis, severe acute respiratory syndrome, and influenza, the medical and political debate has continued to focus on the legitimacy of liberty-limiting interventions, especially patient isolation. Although isolating patients with infectious diseases is not universally considered wrongful conduct from a medico-ethical perspective, forced isolation can constitute a human rights abuse when it is excessive and arbitrary.[1] Japan's leprosy control policy exemplifies this type of abuse, but it took several decades and lawsuits against the country before the policy itself was regarded as a human rights abuse.

One way to evaluate human rights abuses surrounding illness focuses on the "lived experiences" of afflicted patients. Lived experiences often include details about the severity of their suffering within a unique set of circumstances to which healthy people are poorly sensitized. This essay will explore how people with leprosy in Japan developed a unique life-story-based literature, which called on empathetic readers and eventually won them major legal "recognition." This story is relatively little known, and thus the first few pages will recount the history of their treatment, including a consideration of the difficult position that medical practitioners and policy makers also faced in managing not only treatment but also public opinion.

Lifetime Isolation

In 2001 the Kumamoto District Court handed down a landmark decision, ruling that the isolation policy and its legal basis, the Leprosy Prevention Law, violated the fundamental human rights guaranteed in the Constitution of Japan. The following year, I made my first visit to the National Leprosarium Kuryu Rakusen-en. This leprosarium is located on a beautiful plateau with quiet, green surroundings. My impression corresponded with the worldview presented in Thomas Mann's *The Magic Mountain.* In Mann's story, the character Hans Castorp visits a tuberculosis sanatorium where his cousin is being treated. This highland sanatorium is extremely different from the outside world. Hans eventually is infected and becomes a resident of the sanatorium. Like many other patients, he is unshaken by his fate and accepts life in the isolated world in which he finds himself. Similarly, the residents I met in the leprosarium also seemed to have accepted the confined lives they had been forced to lead for years.

However, according to the patients' writings, admission to Kuryu Rakusen-en was far from the calm process described in *The Magic Mountain.* Because of the publicity surrounding the Kumamoto ruling, I became aware that a large number of patients' writings and interviews were archived in various forms. Some had been published by major publishing houses, others by each leprosarium or its patients' association (*jichi-kai*) as in-house journals and booklets with small-scale circulation. Trial records and government documents, including patients' testimonies, were also accessible. The majority of the patients' writings and testimonies include sentimental descriptions on a variety of topics, including leaving their families, losing personal relations with friends and colleagues, and giving up their plans for living full and normal lives. As if that were not enough, when leprosy patients experienced forced isolation, they were often treated with hostility. During the first half of the twentieth century, when the majority of patients were detained, they were treated like criminals. For example, one patient describes how, during transportation to the leprosarium, he alighted from the train at a station and awaited a vehicle. While waiting, his attendant drew a chalk circle around him and ordered him not to step outside it. He was not permitted to sit on a station bench or drink water.[2]

From a medical ethics perspective, the isolation of patients is legitimate if their disease is highly infectious, the symptoms are severe, and the disease cannot be prevented or cured. The debate over whether leprosy is an infectious or another type of disease (e.g., a hereditary disease) ended in 1873 with the discovery of *Mycobacterium leprae*. Nineteenth-century doctors became aware that leprosy is not highly infectious or fatal and the symptoms do not worsen in all patients.[3] Leprosy primarily affects the skin, peripheral nerves, eyes, and upper respiratory tract. The physical deformities that occur as a result have spawned dread and horror in most places since ancient times. Nevertheless, the treatment of leprosy with sulfone drugs was established in the 1940s, thereby eliminating the need to isolate patients.

In spite of this, forced isolation of leprosy patients continued in Japan until the end of the twentieth century. Even though leprosy was treatable, the Leprosy Prevention Law, revised in 1953, did not state any clear conditions under which a patient might be released. Therefore, if patients were diagnosed with leprosy, they were isolated in a leprosarium and were not allowed to leave, even after they were cured. The continuation of this isolation policy was linked to Muraiken Undo (literally, the No Leprosy Patients in Our Prefecture Movement). In response to the government's adoption in 1936 of a twenty-year plan for the eradication of leprosy, municipal governments in Japan encouraged citizens to find and report leprosy patients to the authorities.[4] As a result, by 1955, 11,057 people—an estimated 91 percent of all leprosy patients—were admitted to leprosariums. Patients likened this isolation policy to Nazi Germany's policies to eradicate the Jews. They believed that the Japanese government's aim was to solve the problem not by eradicating the disease but by eradicating the *people* with the disease.[5] For them segregation was not only a "forced isolation" but also a "lifetime isolation" that continued even after a patient was cured.

Forced Labor

The greatest difficulties in implementing lifetime isolation for all leprosy patients occurred when patient numbers were the highest. There was no effective treatment for leprosy until the mid-twentieth century; however, the illness was not fatal, and many patients survived until they were middle aged or elderly despite being physically disabled. Thus, the isolation of patients over many years entailed huge financial costs. In the late nineteenth and early twentieth centuries, several countries, India for instance, considered forced isolation, but did not implement it.[6] Along with the morality of respecting patients' rights of self-determination, the cost was prohibitive. However, Japan's policy makers attempted to overcome these financial hurdles by forcing patients to work for low wages. At the National Leprosarium Tama Zensho-en, located in the suburbs of Tokyo, labor for patients began on a voluntary basis, with the leprosarium offering an incentive for them to engage in it. According to a survey conducted at this leprosarium in 1912, the patients admitted to this facility had worked in more than seventy professions, including farming, fishing, commerce, blacksmithing, carpentry, stonemasonry, mechanics, printing, bookstore and restaurant management, and teaching.[7] At Tama Zensho-en, these patients' wages consisted of contributions from the leprosarium's operating costs. Their wages were confiscated by the leprosarium to prevent escape and then exchanged for vouchers that could be used only within the leprosarium. In the 1940s, when Japan was involved in World War II, there was a severe shortage of resources, and patients had to maintain the leprosarium itself, partly by caring for other patients. At the time, at Kuryu Rakusen-en, located in the mountains of Gunma prefecture, the most demanding work was allocated to patients. To save on automobile fuel, patients carried fifteen to forty-five kilograms of charcoal for heating from a village ten kilometers away. Although some patients injured the soles of their feet during this process, they remained oblivious because of their sensory disabilities. A patient wrote that when he took off his boots, the snow became red with blood.[8]

Sterilization and Abortion

The leprosy control policy in Japan differed from those in other countries because of its measures for controlling reproduction among patients. The notion that leprosy patients should not have children was shared to a degree by those involved in patient care at the time. Not only Japanese doctors but also foreign nationals working for the salvation of leprosy patients in Japan held this opinion. The British missionary Hannah Riddell, who opened Kaishun Hospital, a private leprosarium in Kumamoto, believed that men and women should be separated.[9] However, Japan's doctors asserted that physically separating men and women was unrealistic. Instead, doctors in Japan used sterilization and performed vasectomies on male patients. This strategy has often been attributed to eugenics, which had gained popularity in the medical world at the time.[10]

However, doctors believed that sterilization was in the best interest of the patients themselves. In 1915 Kensuke Mitsuda, the director of the National Leprosarium Nagashima Aisen-en, performed the first vasectomy on a male patient at that leprosarium. According to Mitsuda's memoirs, this patient had great respect for Mitsuda. Despite having deformed fingers, the patient had gained admission to Zensho-en by binding a pen to his fist to write the application letter. At the time, he was nearly fifty years old, and he married a woman he fell in love with at the leprosarium. Mitsuda asserted that this patient requested a vasectomy and depicted this situation in an idealized way as love between patients that does not involve children.[11] In his opinion, retaining sexual desire and functions while preventing children from being born was a benefit that doctors should provide to leprosy patients.

This control of reproduction had a serious impact on the lives of many patients. One female patient related her tragic experiences in an interview.[12] She said that she became pregnant prior to her husband undergoing sterilization. When she was seven months pregnant, she was summoned by the leprosarium's doctor. At the time, abortions were legally permitted up to eight months into the pregnancy. She said she wanted to consult her husband first, but the doctor refused to allow her to do so. Following the operation, a nurse showed the woman the live fetus, saying, "What a cute girl—she looks just like you!" The nurse then smothered the fetus's face with a piece of gauze, suffocating her. Several decades later this female patient remained unaware of the reason the doctor and nurse acted in such a manner. And the effect of these policies on reproduction had lifelong ramifications: by the time this woman and other female patients reached old age, it was legal for them to leave the leprosarium, but there were no children or grandchildren to greet them in the outside world, and this discouraged many women from leaving.

Arbitrary Punishment

Leprosy patients voiced their dissatisfaction over their poor treatment to staff. Prior to World War II, however, their complaints were suppressed through physical force. This consisted of punishments extended beyond the rule of law, which were left to the doctors' discretion. Doctors working in leprosariums were agitated about the lack of action taken against disobedient patients by the police. Although they petitioned the government to establish a designated prison for leprosy patients, their request yielded no results. When the Leprosy Prevention Law was revised in 1916, leprosarium directors were granted police authority. Among the various punishments for patients, the most severe was confinement in a *kankinjo* (guardroom) built in each leprosarium and the reduction of meals. In addition doctors set up a special prison at Kuryu Rakusen-en where they could mete out the harshest punishments to patients. While these were officially called *tokubetsu byoshitsu* (literally, "special sickrooms"), in reality they were prisons without heat or light, and from which patients did not easily emerge alive. Many of those imprisoned died in winter, when the snow lay thick on corridors open to the sky between the eight cells of the *tokubetsu byoshitsu*. The room temperature sometimes dropped below negative 3 degrees Fahrenheit. According to records, between 1939 and 1947, ninety-three people were imprisoned. Among them, twenty-two died either during imprisonment or shortly after release.[13]

Tokubetsu byoshitsu have subsequently been discussed as a symbol of human rights abuses by patients seeking changes in the leprosy control policy. None of the survivors of them, however, has spoken about his or her experiences. This is a common phenomenon observed in those who have suffered extreme duress. Survivors of *tokubetsu byoshitsu* left few records and would not discuss their experiences even privately. Only the written testimonies of those who had contact with former prisoners are available. For example, Michita Yamai was a head of workers at a washhouse in Tokyo's Tama Zensho-en.[14] Although the patients worked in boots, many of the boots provided were old and tattered. It was difficult for leprosy patients with sensory disabilities to endure wet feet; therefore, the patients asked that the boots be exchanged for new ones. This request, which was denied, was made to leprosarium officials by Yamai. After the denial of this request, the patients decided to go on strike. Yamai was taken into custody by twenty officials and sent to the *tokubetsu byoshitsu*. Yamai's tearful wife pleaded with the officials for forgiveness; however, they responded by imprisoning his wife as well. Yamai was imprisoned on June 6, 1941, and released on July 18. On his release, he was extremely weak and unable to walk. He died on September 1.

Crying for Human Rights

Patients who had been isolated in leprosariums for extended periods and forced to perform harsh labor began voicing their dissatisfaction. At the time, most patients nationwide were admitted to leprosariums, exceeding their capacity. According to the aforementioned memoirs of Mitsuda, in the National Leprosarium Nagashima Aisei-en in Okayama, approximately 1,200 people had been admitted by 1936. The facility's capacity was only 890 patients.[15] This over-crowding became a causative factor in what was later called the Nagashima Riot. On the morning of August 13, approximately 800 patients abandoned their work and went on strike. Some even broke windows and commenced a hunger strike. The incident was widely reported; as a result, the necessary funds were provided to raise wages and deal with the overcrowding. Although the formation of a patients' association was refused, patients were granted autonomous control over labor and stores. This event was historic in modern Japanese medicine and marked an important achievement: patients had mobilized to assert their rights and, to a certain degree, achieved their goals.

After World War II, with the guarantee of freedom of speech and assembly included in the new Constitution, the patients' rights movements increased and became more organized. Their demands were centered on Promin, a sulfone drug used to treat leprosy. In poverty-stricken postwar Japan, the government attempted to reduce the budget for Promin, but over 140 patients began hunger strikes in their asylums.[16] This drug, developed in a U.S. leprosarium, is highly effective and has been nicknamed the "Miracle of Carville" after a book written by a female patient.[17] Receiving this drug should have allowed patients to obtain freedom from their lives of isolation in leprosariums, but this was not the case. Arguments regarding leprosy drugs between patients and doctors resembled a political, not a medical, dispute. This manifested itself in the offensive and defensive maneuvers surrounding revisions to the Leprosy Prevention Law in 1953. In the Diet, three leprosarium directors testified about the need to maintain (or strengthen) forced isolation. Patients surrounded the Diet building and staged a sit-in, demanding the easing of forced isolation, and some engaged in a hunger strike.[18] The patients presented their case on the basis of scientific evidence. They correctly argued that leprosy is treatable and in fact not even highly infectious. In contrast the doctors' arguments were largely political. Mitsuda gave the following testimony to the Diet: "We must act quickly in admitting the remaining patients, but there are many who refuse. Under the current circumstances, it is not possible to forcibly admit these kinds of people. In this respect, we need to revise the law. If we do not invoke state power in this matter, the situation will remain unchanged for many years to come and infections within households will continue unchecked."[19]

Eventually, the doctors' demands were incorporated in the 1953 revisions to the Leprosy Prevention Law. As before, the law promoted forced isolation, prohibition from leaving leprosariums without permission, and punishments for rebellious patients. The great gap between Japanese and international experts is revealed in records from the Seventh International Leprosy Congress, held in Tokyo in 1962. At this congress, two main points were discussed: (1) common knowledge concerning early detection, early treatment, and ambulatory treatment; and (2) the abolition of laws prescribing forced isolation. A bureaucrat from the Japanese Ministry of Health and Welfare, however, speaking on behalf of the government, stated, "While the peak for infections has passed, there are many patients still at home who have not been admitted who are acting as a source of infection. Therefore, it is desirable for them to be admitted at an early stage."[20]

Writing for Human Rights

People can now learn about the patients' ill-treatment by reading about their experiences in books and court records. But who is the audience for these texts? As Catherine Kohler Riessman states, "events perceived by the speaker as important are selected, organized, connected, and evaluated as meaningful for a particular audience."[21] What types of readers (actual and imagined) have the patients' writings reached? Did a specific audience exist from the outset? Unquestionably, for Japanese leprosy patients, their lived experiences have served to report the realities of human rights abuse. Although survivors of the *tokubetsu byoshitsu* did not record their experiences, many other leprosy patients continued writing in the closed world of the leprosarium. Their activities began during the era of Japanese imperialism, when freedom of speech was not guaranteed. Some accounts were written as diaries and letters in an everyday context; some were written as petitions to leprosarium managers and the government in a legal context, demanding revisions to the law; and others were written as novels or poems in a literary context. Many patients devoted themselves to writing, and some of their works gained professional (and public) estimation that gave rise to a recognized literary genre; nevertheless, the writings left a gap between those who recorded real-life events and those who read about or listened to them.

Leprosy Literature

Even though their voices were silenced by those of powerful doctors and bureaucrats, patients still managed to write about their daily experiences in a range of forms. Despite often being denied a public education, leprosarium patients were taught how to write by volunteers. Thus, they were encouraged to indulge in creative writing. In particular, many engaged in literary writing, which even formed a discrete literary genre called "leprosy literature."[22] Whether explicit or implicit, their literature was thematically based on patients' experience of their illness. These writings included the lived experience of the illness, elucidating many aspects of the patients' lives, such as their lives before and after arriving at the leprosarium, family partings, harsh experiences at the leprosarium, experiences that led to the discovery of joy and love, the deaths of other patients, and the deaths of family members from whom they were separated. All these aspects were depicted with literary passion.

A poem composed in 1941 by an anonymous sixth-grade elementary school student expresses a theme that elicits sympathy: sorrow at being forever separated from family members.

> When it rained
> My mother always
> Roasted beans for me.
>
> I hear the sound of the rain
> Like beans roasting
> And realize my mother is no longer by my side.[23]

How was this poem read? Or, rather, who was the audience? Readers today would probably feel a sense of realism and pity at the way the sound of rain conflates with the sound of beans being roasted by the child's mother. At the time of this poem's composition, outstanding works from among the patients' poems were selected by professional poets who provided the patients with literary guidance. Yuji Kodama, a patient who later became one of the first court plaintiffs to challenge the national government, continued writing poetry for many years. He recalled the first time he met Mitsuo Ohe in 1952. Ohe, a non-patient poet, had singled Kodama out and corresponded with him over several months. During their first meeting, Ohe muttered that he wanted to take Yuji to his home, but it would be difficult.[24] Even though a few readers outside the leprosariums were sympathetic to the patients' plight, their sympathy was based on the assumption that the patients' isolation was unavoidable. Very few readers questioned leprosy's supposed incurability and the patients' need for isolation in leprosariums.

Approximately three months before his death from intestinal tuberculosis in 1939, Kaijin Akashi published *Hakubyo*, one of the most widely read poetry collections in leprosy literature. At the beginning of this collection, which sold 250,000 copies, Akashi wrote, "Leprosy fell upon me like a divine scourge."[25] When his illness became so severe that he was beyond recovery, he viewed it as a "divine revelation." The reasons he gives are as follows:

I was over 30 when I learned to write *tanka* and, as I reflected anew upon myself, other people and the world, I felt in my heart the beauty and the grandeur of existence.[26] In poem after poem, I released years of bitter hardship, sometimes weeping, sometimes dancing for joy as I celebrated that spark of soul incarnate in my body. I gained such insight into the human condition that I became familiar with a love that exists apart from the bonds of flesh.

Only after I lost my sight did a vision of blue mountains and white clouds flare up within me.[27]

Akashi's loneliness, metaphorically represented—"like those luminescent fish dwelling in the sunless depths of the sea, I would not have light until I illuminated myself from within"—resonated particularly among Japanese readers.[28] However, within this expression of autonomy and endeavor to find value within oneself, it seems, readers observed an expression of acceptance of life as a patient forced into isolation. Akashi's graceful, poetic acceptance may have led readers (and some writer-patients) to forget that this harsh isolation was artificial and systematic.

In Tamio Hojo's 1936 novel *Inochi no Shoya* (The First Night of Life), the notion of striving to find values within oneself is depicted from a perspective closer to that of outsiders (nonpatients). This short novel is one of the most widely read works among those written by leprosy patients. Hojo employs a first-person perspective to realistically depict a young male patient (somewhat autobiographically) during his first few days in a leprosarium, when he is treated with indifference by the staff. He closely observes other patients and is shocked at the "faces like rotten pears" of those seriously afflicted with the disease.[29] The young man loses hope and tries, but ultimately fails, to commit suicide. A patient who witnesses his attempt tells him that leprosy patients "are not human. They are life itself." This patient continues, "However, we are phoenixes. When we have new ideas or gain new insights, when we obtain the life of a leper, this is when we are resurrected as humans."[30] In 1936 the novel was published in the influential journal *Bungakkai* and won the journal's prize for newcomers, a stepping-stone to success in Japanese literary society. Hojo took a young nonpatient novelist, Yasunari Kawabata, who won the Nobel Prize for Literature in 1968, as his literary teacher and wrote sixty-six letters to him. Kawabata recognized his talent and sent twenty-four responses, recommending that he read Dostoevsky, Tolstoy, and Goethe.[31]

Hojo's work earned acclaim from influential members of literary circles. As evinced by the fact that Hojo himself hated his works being referred to as "leprosy literature," the works of leprosy patients were ultimately expected to transcend the genre. Hojo's success and reputation illustrate the limits of the

way Japanese society responded to the "life writing" and its representations of
the "lived experiences" of patients. Susan L. Burns has pointed out the gap in
attitudes toward leprosy literature between writers (patients) and readers
(critics). According to a former patient, Hiroshi Shima, one of those who sued
the Japanese government, "writing was the only means to pass beyond the walls
of the leprosarium." In contrast, Otohiko Kaga, a nonpatient novelist, stated
in 2002 that "since it is extraordinarily rich, I thought, isn't this a great gift to
Japanese literature. In 'Hansen disease literature,' there is the style that burst
out of the bodies of those who were sick." Burns questioned Kaga's attitude
because "Here Kaga's concern is not to explain why patients wrote but the
validity of labeling these texts 'leprosy literature' and the significance of this
genre for 'modern Japanese literature.'"[32]

Audiences in Judicial Contexts

With the end of World War II in the 1940s and the appearance of wonder
drugs in the 1950s and 1960s, did approaches to reading 1930s leprosy literature
change? By the end of the 1940s, the effects of the sulfone drug Promin had
been recognized. Patients commenced movements demanding that they receive
the drug in response to revisions made to the Leprosy Prevention Law in 1953,
although they suffered setbacks. One of these was caused by the case of a young
male patient in Kumamoto who was arrested as a suspect in a murder case that
occurred in 1952. The trial was conducted within the leprosarium as a precau-
tion against infection. Although the defendant continued to deny the murder
charge and there was insufficient physical evidence to implicate him, in 1962
he was given a death penalty on the basis of the unreliable testimonies of two
witnesses and the defendant's statement, which the prosecutor is suspected of
having forged.[33] This led to a social movement seeking to ensure the patients'
right to a fair trial. In the 1970s, the therapeutic value of Rifampicin was recognized, and fewer leprosaria doctors kept patients isolated on the grounds of
contagiousness. In the 1980s, the World Health Organization promoted the
use of multidrug therapy. As a result, leprosy became completely curable, and
the isolation of patients was finally recognized as irrational. Over the past few
decades, however, former patients have become increasingly elderly and fragile.
Fujio Ohtani, a former Ministry of Health and Welfare bureaucrat, regretfully
stated that it was difficult to allow old people suffering the aftereffects of leprosy
to leave leprosariums without the provision of social welfare. He thought that
rather than abolishing the segregation policy, ameliorating conditions in

leprosariums would be in their best interest. According to Ohtani, his "misjudgment" may have led to the Leprosy Prevention Law's continuation into the 1990s.[34]

In 1990 an event occurred among lawyers that changed audiences' attitudes toward the writings and testimonies of former patients. A letter received by the Kyushu Federation of Bar Associations from former patient Hiroshi Shima contained the following.

> For the past decade or so, I have been criticizing the inhumanity of Japan's leprosy policies, and have appealed for the abolition of the Leprosy Prevention Law and for revisions to the Eugenic Protection Law [this law approved the use of sterilization and abortions for leprosy patients]. . . . I do not understand how those in legal circles, those who are supposed to have the profoundest of involvements in matters relating to human rights, express no views on this matter and continue to stand by and watch.[35]

Hiroshi Shima's letter prompted the lawyers to visit the leprosarium and collect the testimonies of patients. Although the Leprosy Prevention Law was abolished in the following year, 1991, the lawyers felt that the long-standing failure to take action should be subjected to trials. Shima was motivated to write his letter by one he had received from Noriyasu Akase, a plaintiff in a lawsuit over AIDS, which he had contracted through contaminated blood. In his letter, Akase wrote, "Why don't Hansen's disease patients get angry?"[36] The subsequent AIDS lawsuit focused on the negligence of officials from the Ministry of Health and Welfare and hemophilia specialists who, despite knowing that the blood product imported from the United States was infected with HIV, continued to administer it to patients. Thus, hemophilia patients were driven to take the Japanese government to court. This helped Shima and other former patients decide to highlight their unfair treatment in a judicial context as well.

Therefore, by the later half of the 1990s, patients' stories had been overwhelmingly situated in judicial contexts. When claims were filed for national compensation, many life stories of former patients, in the form of testimonies, were relayed nationwide. In 2001 a landmark decision by the Kumamoto District Court ruled that the isolation policy had violated the fundamental human rights guaranteed in the Constitution of Japan. It held responsible the former Health and Welfare Ministry for failing to seek an early reversal of the 1953 Leprosy Prevention Law, and the Diet for inaction in repealing it, ordering compensation and an apology from the government. Within the context of the court, the patients' testimonies were heard with enthusiasm, leading to the "discovery" of vast quantities of writings from the past. The dominant voices supporting the plaintiffs permeated newspaper and television reporting. Furthermore, as a result of the judgment, a large portion of the Japanese public began reading the writings of former patients.

After the government abandoned an appeal, following which Junichiro Koizumi, the prime minister, met with former patients at his official residence, media attention surrounding the "Hansen's disease problem" began to dwindle. The former patients' judicial victory seemed to signify resolution. In November 2003, however, former patients reemerged in the media spotlight. Inmates of the National Leprosarium Kikuchi Keifu-en were refused a room when they tried to stay at a hotel in Kumamoto prefecture. This incident revealed that the attitudes of the public had changed greatly within a short time. Criticism of the hotel owners dominated until they visited Kikuchi Keifu-en to apologize. The former patients, deeming the hotel owners' explanation of events insufficient, refused to accept the apology. After the refusal was reported, Kikuchi Keifu-en was inundated with letters, faxes, and e-mails that employed vile language to abuse the former patients.[37] According to these anonymous critics, the former patients had won national compensation and now should behave with the modesty befitting weak people who require care. One of the hotel owners stated that as long as discriminatory sentiments exist among people, as hotel owners they had no choice but to refuse certain people.[38] These words thinly veil feelings toward leprosy that have remained unchanged for thousands of years.

Following this incident, my colleagues and I arranged a lecture by Yuji Kodama, a former patient, wherein he stated, "As we were continually subjected to verbal abuse from the staff at the leprosarium, we were used to it. However, this recent incident was tough."[39] He was astonished that so many people outside the leprosarium could adopt such an unsympathetic attitude. Were the audiences of the former patients' testimonies in the 2001 court case and the anonymous critics of 2003 different people? Or had the same audiences assumed a different face?

Concluding Remarks

In this essay, I have argued how, in Japan, liberty-limiting interventions perpetrated on people with leprosy constituted human rights abuse. Only through the patients' writings and testimonies could we feel and know how lifetime isolation traumatized them: They had to give up the lives they expected, planned, and in many cases were actually living. They accepted and endured forced and exploited labor in the leprosariums. They were coerced into sterilization and abortion and the painful memories of these traumas. They had to act submissively, frightened by the arbitrary punishment that had led to twenty-two patients' deaths in the *tokubetsu byoshitsu*.

I have also described how the victims' and perpetrators' stories were interpreted differently, according to context. In the political context, patients likened the isolation policy to Nazi Germany's Final Solution, but the doctors believed isolation was in the best interests of their patients. When the effective drug Promin became available in the 1950s, patients appealed for it on the accurate scientific grounds that leprosy is curable. Yet the doctors testified before the Diet in extremely political ways; they could not justify the legitimacy of isolation scientifically and ignored proven facts. The verbal battle ended with the doctors' triumph. Thereafter, the patients' stories were seldom heard by politicians, lawyers, journalists, academicians, and all others who remained silent or indifferent to the "Hansen's disease problem." Only in the 1990s, when the patients' stories were placed in a judicial context, were they actually heard.

In the literary context, some patients' stories were celebrated as "leprosy literature," and as a great gift to Japanese letters. The stories vividly depicted patients' life experiences. But even leprosy literature did not gain patients a hearing, partly because their stories had to be elaborate works that captured some degree of literary universality: leprosy literature was valued only within a literary context. Readers seldom questioned the assumption that the patients' isolation was unavoidable and unchangeable.

Some argued that the delay in terminating this flawed policy was inertia and that other obstacles had to be overcome first.[40] A better question to ask is whether the delay was ethically acceptable. The Japanese segregation of leprosy patients shows that decades of delay in responding to scientific facts, as well as medico-political regulations, can lead to traumatic human rights abuse. By failing to take prompt action for decades, policy makers ensured that people with leprosy would become old and die—isolated from what they loved and most of what makes life worth living. In conclusion, I invite readers to thoughtfully consider a field that I call the "justice of listening." When people speak to others, should they have the right to choose the context in which their stories are heard? When they are unaware that their stories have been received in a context not in their best interest, should someone else protect them and their stories from harm?

NOTES

I am deeply grateful to Yuji Kodama and Noriko Miyasaka for their support and warm encouragement. I would also like to thank Crimson Interactive Pvt. Ltd. (Ulatus) and Enago (www.enago.jp) for their assistance in manuscript translation and editing, and Japan Society for the Promotion of Science for a grant (KAKENHI grant number 22242001) that made it possible to complete this study.

1. As Christian Enemark and Michael Selgelid remark, ethicists have to consider the possibility of conflict between the promotion of public health and individual rights and that between the protection of national security and individual rights. Christian Enemark and Michael J. Selgelid, "Introduction," in *Ethics and Security Aspects of Infectious Disease Control: Interdisciplinary Perspectives*, ed. Christian Enemark and Michael J. Selgelid (Surrey: Ashgate, 2012).

2. This case is detailed in Kuryu Rakusen-en Kanja Jichikai, *Fusetsu no mon: Kuryu Rakusen-en kanja gojunen-shi* (Gunma: Kuryu Rakusen-en Kanja Jichikai, 1982), 208.

3. Sanjiv Kakar, "Leprosy in British India, 1860–1940: Colonial Politics and Missionary Medicine," *Medical History* 40, no. 2 (1996): 217.

4. Kensuke Mitsuda, *Kaishun byoshitsu: Kyu-rai goju-nen no kiroku* (Tokyo: Asahi Shimbun, 1950), 155–57.

5. In 1977 the nationwide patients' association Zenkankyo published a chronicle of its activities for a quarter century. It states that Japan's leprosy control policy "distinguished people who are necessary to the nation and people who are unnecessary: patients with Hansen's disease were regarded as worthless people, and aimed a fundamental solution." Zenkoku Hansenshi-byo Kanja Kyogikai (Zenkankyo), *Zenkankyo undo-shi: Hansen-shi-byo kanja no tatakai no kiroku* (Tokyo: Ikkosha, 1977), 37–38.

6. Jane Buckingham, *Leprosy in Colonial South India: Medicine and Confinement* (Basingstoke: Palgrave Macmillan, 2001), 157–88.

7. Tama Zensho-en Kanja Jichikai, *Kue Issho: Kanja ga tsuzuru zensho-en no nanaju-nen* (Tokyo: Ikkosha, 1979), 12–32.

8. Kuryu Rakusen-en Kanja Jichikai, *Fusetsu no mon*, 210–12.

9. Takaaki Ikai, *"Sei no kakuri" to kakuri seisaku: Hannah Riddell to Nihon no sentaku* (Kumamoto: Kumamoto Shuppan Bunka Kaikan, 2005).

10. Yutaka Fujino, *"Inochi" no kindaishi: "Minzoku joka" no na no moto ni hakugai sareta Hansenbyo kanja* (Kyoto: Kamogawa Shuppan, 2001).

11. Kensuke Mitsuda, *Aisei-en nikki: Rai to tatakatta rokuju-nen no nikki* (Tokyo: Mainichi Shimbun, 1958), 71–73.

12. Setsuko Horie, *Ningen de atte ningen de nakatta: Hansen-byo to Tamashiro Shige* (Toyama: Katsura Shobo, 2009).

13. Kuryu Rakusen-en Kanja Jichikai, *Fusetsu no mon*, 501–7.

14. Tama Zensho-en Kanja Jichikai, *Kue Issho*, 136–38.

15. Mitsuda, *Aisei-en nikki*, 166–76.

16. See Kuryu Rakusen-en Kanja Jichikai, *Fusetsu no mon*, 271–77; and Zenkoku Hansenshi-byo Kanja Kyogikai, *Zenkankyo Undo-shi*, 34–36.

17. Betty Martin, *Miracle at Carville* (New York: Doubleday, 1950).

18. See Zenkoku Hansenshi-byo Kanja Kyogikai, *Zenkankyo Undo-shi*, 50–56.

19. This testimony is my translation of the official record in *Proceedings of the 12th Kosei Iinkai, House of Councillors, the National Diet of Japan*, vol. 10, November 8, 1951 (in Japanese).

20. Paul Fasal, "The VII International Congress on Leprology," *AMA Archives of Dermatology* 80, no. 1 (1959): 91–92. The bureaucrat's speech is documented in Verification Committee concerning the Hansen's Disease Problem, *Final Report* (Tokyo: Japan Law Foundation, 2005), 622 (in Japanese).

21. Catherine Kohler Riessman, *Narrative Methods for the Human Sciences* (Los Angeles: Sage, 2007), 3.

22. Susan L. Burns, "Making Illness into Identity: Writing 'Leprosy Literature' in Modern Japan," *Japan Review* 16 (2004): 191–211.

23. K. M. [initials of the anonymous author], "Amefuri" [Rainfall], in *Nozomigaoka no kodomo-tachi*, ed. Nagashima Aisen-en Kyoiku-bu (Tokyo: Sangabo, 1941). This is my translation of the full poem republished in Shunsuke Tsurumi, ed., *Hansenbyo bungaku zenshu*, vol. 10 (Tokyo: Koseisha, 2003), 270.

24. Yuji Kodama, *Shiranakatta anata e: Hansen-byo sosho made no nagai tabi* (Tokyo: Poplar-sha, 2001), 67–71.

25. Kaijin Akashi, *Hakubyo* (Tokyo: Kaizo-sha, 1939). Part of his introductory text was anonymously translated in "Illuminating Ourselves," *IDEA* 8, no. 1 (2003): 2.

26. *Tanka* is a genre of Japanese poetry comprising five lines with a pattern of 5-7-5-7-7 syllables in the respective lines.

27. Akashi, "Illuminating Ourselves," 2.

28. Ibid.

29. Tamio Hojo, "Inochi no shoya," *Bungakkai* (February 1936): 65–99.

30. Tamio Hojo, *Inochi no shoya* (Tokyo: Kadokawa Shoten, 1955), 40–41.

31. Kyoji Mitsuoka, "Hojo Tamio no hito to seikatsu," in Hojo, *Inochi no shoya*, 246–54.

32. Burns, "Making Illness into Identity," 199–200.

33. In November 2012, Zenryokyo (the nationwide former patients' association that took over Zenkankyo), Zengenkyo (the council of plaintiffs of the lawsuits against the country), and Kikuchi Keifu-en Nyusho-sha Jichikai (the former patients' association in the National Leprosarium Kikuchi Keifu-en) appealed to the Kumamoto District Public Prosecutors Office for a retrial of his case. This case, known as the "Fujimoto case" or "Kikuchi case," is detailed in Sawako Hirai, "Fujimoto jiken ni tsuite: 'Shinso kyumei' to saishin," *Kyudai-hogaku* 84 (2002): 161–235.

34. Fujio Ohtani, *Rai yobo-ho haishi no rekishi: Ai wa uchikachi joheki kuzure ochinu* (Tokyo: Keiso Shobo, 1996), 250–56.

35. Hansen-byo iken kokubai sosho bengo-dan, *Hirakareta tobira: Hansen-byo saiban wo tatakatta hitotachi* (Tokyo: Kodansha, 2003), 25–50.

36. Ibid.

37. Kikuchi Keifu-en Jichikai, *Kurokawa Onsen Hotel shukuhaku kyohi jiken ni kansuru sabetzu bunsho tsuzuri* (Kumamoto: Kikuchi Keifu-en Jichikai, 2004).

38. Anonymous, "Moto kanja no katagata ni shintsu wo kaketa Maeda soshihainin tono ichimon itto," *Kumamoto Nichinichi Shimbun*, November 20, 2003, 25.

39. Yuji Kodama, personal communication, 2003.

40. Hajime Sato, "Abolition of Leprosy Isolation Policy in Japan: Policy Termination through Leadership," *Policy Studies Journal* 30, no. 1 (2002): 29–46.

WORKS CITED

Akashi, Kaijin. *Hakubyo*. Tokyo: Kaizo-sha, 1939.

———. "Illuminating Ourselves." *IDEA* 8, no. 1 (2003): 2.

Buckingham, Jane. *Leprosy in Colonial South India: Medicine and Confinement*. Basingstoke: Palgrave Macmillan, 2001.

Burns, Susan L. "Making Illness into Identity: Writing 'Leprosy Literature' in Modern Japan." *Japan Review* 16 (2004): 191–211.

Enemark, Christian, and Michael J. Selgelid. "Introduction." In *Ethics and Security Aspects of Infectious Disease Control: Interdisciplinary Perspectives*, edited by Christian Enemark and Michael J. Selgelid. Surrey: Ashgate, 2012. Kindle edition.

Fasal, Paul. "The VII International Congress on Leprology." *AMA Archives of Dermatology* 80, no. 1 (1959): 91–92.

Fujino, Yutaka. *"Inochi" no kindaishi: "Minzoku joka" no na no moto ni hakugai sareta Hansenbyo kanja*. Kyoto: Kamogawa Shuppan, 2001.

Hansen-byo iken kokubai sosho bengo-dan. *Hirakareta tobira: Hansen-byo saiban wo tatakatta hitotachi*. Tokyo: Kodansha, 2003.

Hirai, Sawako. "Fujimoto jiken ni tsuite: 'Shinso kyumei' to saishin." *Kyudai-hogaku* 84 (2002): 161–235.

Hojo, Tamio. *Inochi no shoya*. Tokyo: Kadokawa Shoten, 1955. First published in *Bungakkai* (February 1936): 65–99.

Horie, Setsuko. *Ningen de atte ningen de nakatta: Hansen-byo to Tamashiro Shige*. Toyama: Katsura Shobo, 2009.

Ikai, Takaaki. *"Sei no kakuri" to kakuri seisaku: Hannah Riddell to Nihon no sentaku*. Kumamoto: Kumamoto Shuppan Bunka Kaikan, 2005.

Kakar, Sanjiv. "Leprosy in British India, 1860–1940: Colonial Politics and Missionary Medicine." *Medical History* 40, no. 2 (1996): 215–30.

Kikuchi Keifu-en Jichikai. *Kurokawa Onsen Hotel shukuhaku kyohi jiken ni kansuru sabetzu bunsho tsuzuri*. Kumamoto: Kikuchi Keifu-en Jichikai, 2004.

Kodama, Yuji. *Shiranakatta anata e: Hansen-byo sosho made no nagai tabi*. Tokyo: Poplar-sha, 2001.

K. M. "Amefuri" [Rainfall]. In *Nozomigaoka no kodomo-tachi*, edited by Nagashima Aisen-en Kyoiku-bu. Tokyo: Sangabo, 1941.

Kuryu Rakusen-en Kanja Jichikai. *Fusetsu no mon: Kuryu Rakusen-en kanja gojunen-shi.* Gunma: Kuryu Rakusen-en Kanja Jichikai, 1982.

Martin, Betty. *Miracle at Carville.* New York: Doubleday, 1950.

Mitsuda, Kensuke. *Aisei-en nikki: Rai to tatakatta rokuju-nen no nikki.* Tokyo: Mainichi Shimbun, 1958.

———. *Kaishun byoshitsu: Kyu-rai goju-nen no kiroku.* Tokyo: Asahi Shimbun, 1950.

Mitsuoka, Ryoji. "Hojo Tamio no hito to seikatsu." In Tamio Hojo, *Inochi no shoya,* 246–54. Tokyo: Kadokawa Shoten, 1955.

Ohtani, Fujio. *Rai yobo-ho haishi no rekishi: Ai wa uchikachi joheki kuzure ochinu.* Tokyo: Keiso Shobo, 1996.

Proceedings of the 12th Kosei Iinkai, House of Councillors, the National Diet of Japan. Vol. 10, November 8, 1951. In Japanese.

Riessman, Catherine Kohler. *Narrative Methods for the Human Sciences.* Los Angeles: Sage, 2007.

Sato, Hajime. "Abolition of Leprosy Isolation Policy in Japan: Policy Termination through Leadership." *Policy Studies Journal* 30, no. 1 (2002): 29–46.

Tama Zensho-en Kanja Jichikai. *Kue Issho: Kanja ga tsuzuru zensho-en no nanaju-nen.* Tokyo: Ikkosha, 1979.

Tsurumi, Shunsuke, ed. *Hansenbyo bungaku zenshu.* Vol. 10. Tokyo: Koseisha, 2003.

Verification Committee concerning the Hansen's Disease Problem. *Final Report.* Tokyo: Japan Law Foundation, 2005. In Japanese.

Zenkoku Hansenshi-byo Kanja Kyogikai (Zenkankyo). *Zenkankyo Undo-shi: Hansen-shi-byo kanja no tatakai no kiroku.* Tokyo: Ikkosha, 1977.

Reimagining the Criminal,
Reconfiguring Justice

FINOLA FARRANT

All sorrows can be borne if you put them into a story or tell a story about them.

HANNAH ARENDT, *THE HUMAN CONDITION*

The application of critical analysis to the study of justice and punishment is crucial to understanding, interpreting, and challenging the authoritarianism of state institutions that appear committed to widening the criminal justice net and expanding, exponentially, imprisonment. Indeed, one of the strengths of critical criminology is in the promotion of a criminological imagination that confronts new intellectual and political challenges in what is an increasingly more volatile global situation.[1] There is, therefore, a need to seek alternatives to an increasingly punitive criminal justice agenda, which not only fails to respect human rights but also, at times, actively threatens them. One of the most important facets of a more critically aware criminology is that it falls between theory and politics. It is in this intellectual space that a fruitful, productive, and creative relationship between criminology and human rights can emerge; it is in this space that criminal justice becomes more firmly rooted within social justice.

Despite shared concerns about justice, criminology and human rights have not made natural bedfellows. Criminology's positivist roots, based on pseudo-Darwinian theories of atavism and the "born criminal," have cast a long shadow over the discipline. And within human rights, criminology's engagement with those who have caused harm does not make it an obvious ally. Life story research may, however, offer a methodological bridge between the two disciplines. Life story research can shift easy assumptions that prisoners have foregone their human rights and reveal a far more complex relationship among justice, crime, and punishment. Criminological research that is committed to human rights can help illuminate the exercise of power on lives that have literally been expunged from view. By listening to the life stories of ex-prisoners, theoretical and political analysis about prisons and punishment can help to reveal the microlevel of personal experience and the macrolevel of social and cultural understandings about justice.

Life story research in this context should be about "humanizing the deviant," seeking to turn attention to the taken-for-granted cultural processes involved in the punishment paradigm.[2] Kay Schaffer and Sidonie Smith note, however, that prisoner narratives are frequently confusing as they complicate the roles of "victim" and "perpetrator," a clear demarcation of which is seen as central in human rights.[3] It is "innocent" victims who give moral force to human rights campaigns rather than morally ambiguous offenders.[4] A more nuanced, less didactic understanding of identity may be required if successful challenges to the increasingly punitive criminal justice agenda are to be made. Moreover, the binary distinction of victim/offender is problematic when we listen to the life stories of ex-prisoners as these counternarratives involve more complex identities than analysis through the lens of binary opposites can provide. By incorporating prisoner and ex-prisoner narratives into the wider human rights project a more responsive and effective paradigm of action, based on restoring justice, repairing harm, and making peace, can be achieved.

The use of life story data has, in fact, had a distinguished genealogy within criminology. In seeking to understand the deviant subcultures identified in their mapping of zones within the city of Chicago during the 1920s and 1930s, the Chicago School of Sociology used life histories alongside official statistics and participant observation. Despite this long-standing history, the relationship between criminology and life story methodology has become a rather rocky one. This has culminated in a number of scholars arguing that criminologists have virtually abandoned the approach.[5] Consequently, the voices of those who have been imprisoned are increasingly quiet ones.[6] This is important on at least two counts. First, it comes at a time when mass imprisonment has become a common feature across much of the western world.[7] And with a diminishing number of accounts of prison life, as well as a punitive turn both politically and in the media, public understandings of imprisonment and its effects have become at best partial and at worst highly distorted caricatures. The second issue of interest is that, despite the initial use of life story approaches within the criminological discipline, and in penological research in particular, this eclipse has occurred simultaneously with the concepts of narrative, counternarratives, and life stories becoming more visible in other academic disciplines. The study of narrative and life story has moved beyond the traditional confines of linguistics and language studies and into anthropology, sociology, gender studies, management studies, history, psychology, and law.[8] Such a burgeoning of interest has led to the 1990s being referred to as "the decade of life narratives."[9]

This essay is based on the belief that human rights and criminology have much to offer each other in their common interest in justice. I start by discussing the role life story research plays in the social sciences, and criminology in particular, and consider whether the life stories of ex-prisoners challenge a resurgent positivist outlook. I then present the argument that identity can only be understood through narrative and therefore a life story methodology, with all its complexities and contradictions, is the most appropriate approach for this type of research. As the concept of identity is a key focus of life story research, this is explored by critically evaluating two different ontological positions. Frederick Erikson and Dan P. McAdams argue that life stories aid the construction of a coherent sense of self.[10] On the other hand, Kenneth J. Gergen and Peter T. F. Raggatt offer a position informed by a poststructuralist perspective that views the self as fragmented and even contradictory.[11] I suggest that these distinctions have important consequences. For example, while the former suggests cohesion, the latter allows for a more fluid understanding of identity that might be better suited in considering the thorny issues of "victimization" and "perpetration." Despite these tensions, life story research provides a unique methodological approach that shines a light on our understanding of criminal justice. This essay is therefore about seeking recognition: recognition of the marginalized voices of ex-prisoners; recognition that many western cultures have become overly dependent on incarceration as a form of justice; and, finally, recognition that new ways of conceiving justice can be uncovered if we allow ex-prisoners to speak.[12] In doing this, brief excerpts of two ex-prisoners' stories are analyzed.

Constructing Identity through Stories

Many life story researchers have tended to see identity as an individual achievement.[13] In these understandings, identity is regarded as an integrative function, and therefore the life story or narrative identity serves to make a meaningful, cohesive sense of self. For others, life stories are an expression of different, multiple, and potentially conflicting aspects of the self.[14] These differing ontological positions offer, on the one hand, the idea that a core, integrated sense of self is feasible and indeed desirable in terms of psychological well-being, and can be achieved through narration and storytelling: "narrative is a significant resource for creating our internal, private sense of self."[15] On the other hand, although individuals may derive a sense of purpose and feelings of happiness by integrating the past, present, and future, it is equally the case that life story research can be used without the assumption of a single or definitive identity. Instead a life story can provide "vivid illustrations of oppositional voices in the self through the vehicle of narrative,"[16] "polyphonic versions of possible construction . . . of people's selves and lives."[17]

It was this latter view of contradiction, fragmentation, and conflict that most accurately described the fifteen ex-prisoners' narratives that formed my study on the identity of men who had been in prison. The men's stories did not provide clear or concise answers about offending, incarceration, or life on release. For example, although I did not seek quantitative data, it was apparent that even basic information on which some statistical understanding could be based would be highly problematic. Some of the men could not remember the age they had been when first sent to prison, what type of court had dealt with them, or what offenses they had been charged with. In addition, all the men talked about their initial involvement in crime in relation to the first time they had contact with the criminal justice system as opposed to the first time they had broken the law. This supports the idea put forward by social interactionists that deviancy is not inherent in any act. Instead the focus is on the linguistic tendency of powerful groups and agents to negatively label others as deviant. The self-identity and behavior of individuals is therefore determined or influenced by the terms used to describe or classify them.[18] Part of the story of one man, Charlie, is set out in order to explore the complexity of the victim/offender identity and the impact of being classified as an offender.

Charlie's Story:
Riots and Rethinking Justice

When he was a student, Charlie had attended a demonstration against the British National Party (BNP) in south London.[19] This was an area of significant tension due, in part, to the recent election of a BNP councillor; racist attacks, including the murder of Stephen Lawrence; and the location of a "bookshop" that operated as the BNP's headquarters. There were a number of violent clashes between the police and protesters that day as the march was prevented from passing the bookshop. Charlie had been hit over the head and punched in the stomach by the police. When another police surge took place, he picked up a brick and threw it at the police line.

Although the brick did not hit anyone, a few months later Charlie was at home with his mother and a neighbor watching *Crime Monthly*, a television program that investigates crime, when footage of the demonstration was shown and requests made for information about those who were seen throwing things. One of the images was clearly that of Charlie. He recalled the incident:

> My mum's Irish, and our next-door neighbor was West Indian, so when they saw me on *Crime Monthly* my next-door neighbor went [does West Indian accent], "*Oh god, Charlie boy, you better run boy, run into the country.*" And my mum [does Irish accent], "*Oh bejesus, I told you not to go on that demonstration, but you never listen to me, hail Mary full of grace, the lord is holy. I've spoken to Jesus, and you're not going to prison. Now go to sleep, and we'll talk about it in the morning.*" I was like, oh my god, is this some kind of dark comedy, or is this for real? [20]

Charlie said that he was a peaceful person but the presence of the BNP headquarters in an area of racial tension, hearing Auschwitz survivors talking on the day of the demonstration about the need to fight fascism, and police "brutality" had made him boil over with anger. During the two years he waited before sentencing, Charlie suffered a mental breakdown and was suicidal. He also undertook voluntary work in a home for people with disabilities and met a policewoman who had been paralyzed during a different demonstration:

> That really hit home; it was really powerful. Someone had got a concrete block and smashed it over her spine and left her paralyzed, and she had to use this special machine to communicate. I remember asking [why she had joined the police]. She said she wanted to help people, and I asked her, "Do you hate the people that have done this to you?" and she wrote, "*No, there's too much hate in the world,*" and I never forgot that, that's amazing, to have those feelings, because that's forgiveness, the language of forgiveness, and I thought that's really powerful. And in some ways, you know, ever since then it's helped me to see some sense of humanity around police officers because before then I didn't see any. I saw them as like stormtroopers or racists. I just didn't see any humanity in them because they hadn't shown me any humanity or dignity so I couldn't see any. But when I heard her talk, I thought, bloody hell, for you to be in that space, with what they've done to you, I'd understand if you hated the people that had done that. Sadly now, the thing that makes me sad, I probably wouldn't be allowed to volunteer in some of those places [because of his conviction], and yet the experience made a huge difference to me because then I started to see a sense of humanity, and not see all police officers as violent racists, which I had up to that point, because that's what I saw and witnessed that day.

Charlie received a sixteen-month prison sentence for his involvement in the confrontation. On arriving at the prison, Charlie described the "civic death" of the admissions process.[21] Prison rules were stated and fingerprints and photographs were taken, but the "worst aspect of it was being stripped, having to show them my foreskin; for me it was just abuse."

On reflecting back, well over a decade after his conviction and release, Charlie said that he did not think he should have gone to prison. Having been attacked by the police, he suggested an alternative solution: "I don't look for any of them [the police] to have gone to prison, but I would like to sit down and talk to them, and I think if we lived in a more civilized society we could have sat down and they could have opened up and been slightly honest." Recalling a recent question from somebody about whether he had forgiven himself for what had happened, he said it had never entered his head that he needed to forgive himself; he did not feel bad about the "offense" as no one had been hurt. In fact, rather than prison protecting the public from dangerous and violent offenders, Charlie concluded: "They were sending me into prison for violence. That's what they said, I was a violent man; well, they've sent me in somewhere that is violent. Man, I survived in some ways *by* violence, the thing they were sending me to prison for."

Challenging the Positivist Methodological Paradigm

The advent of the life story approach across multiple disciplines has led to a number of scholars declaring the death of the positivist paradigm.[22] In fact, with an emphasis on quantification, a demand for simplistic answers, and a preoccupation with risk and management, a positivist stance has been particularly resurgent within criminology, while the life story approach, with its concerns about identity and meaning and a commitment to providing space for marginalized voices, has itself become marginalized.[23] Given the dominance of the positivistic paradigm within much criminological research, it is useful to consider what life story approaches have to offer contemporary criminal justice practice.

In their review of the narrative literature Amia Lieblich, Rivka Tuval-Mashiach, and Tamar Zilber argue that narrative research can be classified into three domains.[24] The first is studies in which the narrative is used for the investigation of any research question. For example, it can be used to represent the character or lifestyle of groups that face discrimination and whose voices are seldom heard. A great deal of feminist-informed research falls within this category. The second category includes studies that investigate the narrative itself rather than narrative as a means of studying other questions. This approach is more often found in literature, communications, and linguistics theory, but it can also be found in studies that take the narrative form as the point of analysis. The final category includes those studies whose focus is more on the philosophical importance of the narrative approach: for example, narrative as a mode of human cognition, or narrative as identity.[25] This category is where much criminological research fits.

Writing in 1937, Edwin Sutherland concluded that the most significant difference between professional thieves and white-collar criminals was in their self-conception: "professional thieves, when they speak honestly, admit that they are thieves," Sutherland observed, whereas white-collar criminals "think of themselves as honest men."[26] This is highly pertinent. Studies on the operations of criminal justice institutions are largely studies of the socially excluded. Furthermore, the concept of justice, rather than being equally applied, serves particular values and interests.[27] Not only, as Sutherland asserts, does self-perception have a role to play, but our own understanding of what "crime" is and who "offenders" are is shaped by the workings of the criminal justice system. For me, therefore, life story research with men who have been in prison is not about finding answers to questions such as "How do we reduce the likelihood of offending?" but about structure, power, and discourse. It is about the operation of state power in the form of punitive "justice." If C. Wright Mills's major contribution to radical discourse was in proposing that the sociological imagination lies in analyzing the dynamics between biography and history, it would seem likely that revitalizing criminology's imagination lies in the same direction. As Mills argues: "To *appeal* to the powerful, on the basis of any knowledge we now have, is utopian in the foolish sense of that term. Our relations with them are more likely to be only such relations as they find useful, which is to say that we become technicians accepting their problems and aims, or ideologists promoting their prestige and authority."[28] In the telling of a story, the process of selection, emphasis, and interpretation, and in the creativity of the act of telling, the story shapes and constructs the narrator's personality and reality. Life story narrative is seen as providing an effective means of gaining an understanding of the subjective perspective of self, and an understanding of the lived experience from the view of the person who has experienced it, at a particular moment in time. Rather than regarding life stories as texts of fiction, complete and accurate representations of reality, or a way of understanding dramatic changes in behavior through subjective change in identity or cognitive transformation, they can be regarded as part of a performance.[29] This is a performance from which we can gain insights into the lives of ex-prisoners *and* an understanding of the social and cultural context within which "justice" takes place. Indeed, as Lois Presser explains, concerns about the authenticity of offenders' narratives tell us more about popular cultural tropes that depict offenders as archmanipulators who only tell the "truth" in order to avoid sanctions, whereas such narratives should instead be seen as offering rich insights into human existence and enterprise and can help inform more effective justice interventions.[30]

The narratives of the men involved in the research are vivid accounts that encourage awareness of those human lives that have been subject to the criminal justice system and the sanction of imprisonment. Nevertheless, much criminological research remains "top down" and therefore not only fails to reflect the reality of people's actual experiences but also fails to recognize that marginalized groups can be producers of their own discourse and research and hold the key to potential cultural transformation.

Danny's Story:
Pleasure-Filled but Powerless

Danny's story exemplifies this potential and the need for alternative understandings of justice and punishment. In Danny's story we hear about the sheer joy of raving and "serving up" drugs to fellow clubbers. This chimes with Jack Katz's work on the seductions of crime, which takes as its focus the "often wonderful attractions within the lived experience of criminality" rather than the psychological or social deficits of offenders.[31] The horror of incarceration is, however, also evident in what Danny, has to say.[32]

It is a beautiful, sunny day, and we agree to talk outside, in Danny's garden. With numerous cups of coffee as sustenance we talk all afternoon. Danny is a good-looking, heavily tattooed and pierced ex-raver, and the interview allows him to demonstrate what a fantastic storyteller he is. As with Charlie, he adopts various voices for the tales he tells. Much of his story is told almost as a play with him taking on the characters, including that of his younger self, for which he adopts a high-pitched tone. Danny is currently unemployed and talks at length about the impact of having an ex-prisoner label attached to him, even after a long period of time out of prison, and of the emotional impact of having been incarcerated: "I look back on it, and for sure it was one of the scariest, darkest times of my life." Danny has been in prison once, for offenses related to the supply of class A drugs and fraud, for which he received a three-year sentence at the age of twenty. He was involved in the rave culture of the late 1980s and early 1990s and related that when he was dealing he would look around a club and think, "I'm responsible for everyone loving each other, man." Dealing in ecstasy and cocaine, he had a particular view of his offending that, he argued, did not involve traditional perspectives of himself as a victim or as an offender. He had not been coerced into selling drugs and did not have a substantial drug problem himself. Nor did he believe that his drug dealing caused harm to others; rather it was a service that customers actively sought out.

His words evoked the seductions of what he was doing—enjoying himself, having fun, making money—"a fucking beautiful thing." He went on to say:

> I think the problem is that people in the courts, they're not living in the real world. The problem with drugs is they're so much in everyday use now, recreational, I don't believe that there are pushers at school gates like all the government propaganda used to tell you. Obviously there are deaths in drugs, but that's up the chain, you know. I dunno, it's just a social headache, but I think there should be some change in the law because it's in most walks of life and I just think it's pointless putting little hippy tits like me away. I guess it's another case of crime committed, crime solved, statistic, box ticked. We put this many people in prison this year for drug-related offenses. . . . They talk about overcrowding in prisons, I tell you there's a lot of people who shouldn't be in there, and it's a horrible place.

Danny's story raises, among a myriad of other issues, concerns about youth, subcultures, drug criminalization, pleasure, and the ongoing and long-lasting impact of imprisonment. Moreover, it links, as Mills suggests, the "personal," in the shape of his life story, with the "public" in the shape of drug laws and the enactment of punishment.[33] In Danny's story we can inhabit that theoretical and political territory that is at the microlevel of his personal experience, and the macrolevel of wider social and cultural understandings about criminal and social justice.

Concluding Reflections

Presenting the stories of those who have been excluded and dehumanized by mainstream society has the potential to challenge and transform a range of personal and cultural assumptions. They offer an alternative to the dominant punitive discourse and insight into the operation of power itself. According to H. Porter Abbott, this is because in almost every narrative of interest a conflict of power is at stake.[34] In many societies one of the most extreme operations of state power is embodied in the process of imprisonment and the concomitant loss of liberty. Once at the forefront of narrative and life story research, criminology now has some catching up to do with disciplines that have embraced the opportunities that this methodology has to offer our understanding, not only of individual lives but also of society and culture. A story created, told, revised, and retold allows us to both discover and reveal ourselves. It is in the submerged shadow stories, and the contradictions and complexities within identity, that understandings about the individual and the wider society are revealed.

Criminological analyses have, however, failed to be responsive to the interests and concerns of those on whom the criminal justice system has the most impact. Moreover, due to the very status of being an ex-prisoner, questions are raised about the "truthfulness" of the stories they tell. And the troublesome nature of the ex-prisoner identity is seen to have tested the limits of the human rights paradigm within which criminology should sit.[35] A life story approach to criminological research provides an alternative methodology to what has become a reinvigorated positivistic approach within the discipline, and it simultaneously offers the potential to resist the dominant punitive discourse and broaden the human rights project to incorporate experiences that challenge traditional human rights concepts such as "perpetrator" and "victim." The presentation of counternarratives, stories told by those who have experienced one of the most extreme forms of punishment, illuminates systems of power, and the cultural and historical context that limits particular individual and collective identity possibilities. Charlie's and Danny's stories provide the nexus of these power relations in terms of their personal biographies, Charlie in terms of the devastating mental and emotional impact of being defined as someone in conflict with the state in the form of the police, and Danny in relation to recognition of his lack of power against a state apparatus intent on a war on drugs.

Life stories are a potent vehicle for advancing the human rights of all those affected by harm—whether as victim, offender, or wider community. Based on understandings provided by engagement with life stories, justice can be transformed, and the way contemporary societies view and respond to crime and other harmful behaviors can be challenged. Reducing harm is not about expanding surveillance and control, or accepting an apparently ever-burgeoning prison population. Developing a constructive and progressive alternative to the punishment paradigm requires that victims and offenders come together to discuss what has happened, what harm has resulted, and what should be done to repair that harm in order to prevent further wrongdoing. Such approaches, based on peace as opposed to pain, are slowly emerging in various contexts. On a global scale, we have seen truth and reconciliation commissions in places as diverse as El Salvador, the United States, Morocco, Northern Ireland, the Philippines, and, most famously, South Africa.[36] On a smaller scale, a range of interventions such as victim offender mediation, restorative conferencing, and circles of support and accountability can be found in numerous jurisdictions, including North America; Australia; much of Europe, including Belgium, England, and Wales; New Zealand; and some areas in China. Narrative, then, has the ability to represent the experiences of individuals—both victims and offenders—and to show that we cannot achieve peace until we have listened to the stories of those who have been involved in causing or experiencing harm. Ultimately, narrative is the foundation on which validation, restitution, safety, recognition, and justice can be achieved.

NOTES

1. Elliott Currie, "Preface," in *Critical Criminology: Issues, Debates, Challenges*, edited by Kerry Carrington and Russell Hogg (Cullompton: Willan, 2002), vii–ix.

2. John Muncie and Mike Fitzgerald, "Humanizing the Deviant: Affinity and Affiliation Theories," in *Crime and Society: Readings in History and Theory*, ed. Mike Fitzgerald, Gregor McLennan, and Jennie Pawson (London: Routledge, 1981), 337–58.

3. Kay Schaffer and Sidonie Smith, *Human Rights and Narrated Lives: The Ethics of Recognition* (Basingstoke: Palgrave Macmillan, 2004).

4. A number of stories presented in this volume would fit this criteria.

5. See, for example, Shadd Maruna, "Going Straight: Desistance from Crime and Life Narratives of Reform," in *The Narrative Study of Lives*, ed. Amia Lieblich and Ruthellen Josselson, vol. 5 (London: Sage, 1997), 59–93; Alison Liebling, *Prisons and Their Moral Performance* (Oxford: Clarendon, 2004); and Loïc Wacquant, "The Curious Eclipse of Prison Ethnography in the Age of Mass Incarceration," *Ethnography* 3, no. 4 (2002): 371–98.

6. They are quiet but not completely silent. For examples of more recent criminological life story research, see Ben Crewe, *The Prisoner Society: Power, Adaptation, and Social Life in an English Prison* (Oxford: Oxford University Press, 2009); Ben Crewe and Jamie Bennett; *The Prisoner* (London: Routledge, 2012); Shadd Maruna, *Making Good: How Ex-Convicts Reform and Rebuild Their Lives* (Washington, DC: American Psychological Association, 2001).

7. The United States of America locks up proportionately more of its citizens than any other country in the world, while England and Wales lock up more than most of its western European neighbors.

8. On anthropology, see Holland et al., *Identity and Agency in Cultural Worlds* (Cambridge, MA: Harvard University Press, 1998); and Lewis L. Langness and Gelya Frank, *Lives: An Anthropological Approach to Biography* (Novato, CA: Chandler and Sharp, 1981). On sociology, see Ken Plummer, *Telling Sexual Stories: Power, Change, and Social Worlds* (New York: Routledge, Kegan Paul, 1995). On gender studies, see Selma Leydesdorff, Luisa Passerini, and Paul Thompson, *International Yearbook of Oral History and Life Stories*,

vol. 4, *Gender and Memory* (Oxford: Oxford University Press, 1996). On management, see Mark Learmonth, "Doing Things with Words: The Case of 'Management' and 'Administration,'" *Public Administration* 83, no. 3 (2005): 617–37. On history, see Barbara Allen and Lynwood Montell, *From Memory to History: Using Oral Sources in Local Historical Research* (Nashville, TN: American Association for State and Local History, 1981). On psychology, see Frederick Erickson, "Social Construction of Topical Cohesion in a Conversation," in *Analyzing Discourse: Text and Talk*, ed. Deborah Tannen (Washington, DC: Georgetown University Press, 1982), 43–71; Dan P. McAdams, *Power, Intimacy, and the Life Story: Personological Inquiries into Identity* (New York: Guildford Press, 1985); Dan P. McAdams, *The Stories We Live By: Personal Myths and the Making of the Self* (New York: Guildford Press, 1993); and Dan. P. McAdams, Ruthellen Josselson, and Amia Lieblich, eds., *Identity and Story: Creating Self in Narrative* (Washington, DC: American Psychological Association, 2006). On law, see Anthony G. Amsterdam and Jerome S. Bruner, *Minding the Law* (Cambridge, MA: Harvard University Press, 2000); and Peter Brooks and Paul Gewirtz, eds., *Law's Stories: Narrative and Rhetoric in the Law* (New Haven, CT: Yale University Press, 1996).

9. Schaffer and Smith, *Human Rights and Narrated Lives*, 1.

10. See Erickson, "Social Construction," 43–71; McAdams, *Power, Intimacy, and the Life Story*; and McAdams, *The Stories We Live By*.

11. Kenneth J. Gergen, *The Saturated Self: Dilemmas of Identity in Contemporary Life* (New York: Basic Books, 1991); Peter T. F. Raggatt, "Multiplicity and Conflict in the Dialogical Self: A Life-Narrative Approach," in *Identity and Story: Creating Self in Narrative*, ed. Dan P. McAdams, Ruthellen Josselson, and Amia Lieblich (Washington, DC: American Psychological Association, 2006), 15–35.

12. This essay is focused on ex-prisoners, but the same view is of equal importance with regard to victims.

13. See Erickson, "Social Construction," 43–71; McAdams, *Power, Intimacy, and the Life Story*; and McAdams, *The Stories We Live By*.

14. See Kenneth. J. Gergen and Mary M. Gergen, "Narratives of the Self," in *Studies in Social Identity*, ed. Karl E. Scheibe and Theodore R. Sarbin (New York: Praeger, 1983), 254–73; Gergen, *The Saturated Self*; and Raggatt, "Multiplicity and Conflict," 15–35.

15. Charlotte Linde, *Life Stories: The Creation of Coherence* (Oxford: Oxford University Press, 1993), 3.

16. Raggatt, "Multiplicity and Conflict," 20.

17. Amia Lieblich, Rivka Tuval-Mashiach, and Tamar Zilber, *Narrative Research: Reading, Analysis, and Interpretation* (London: Sage, 1998), 8.

18. Social interactionists have explored these issues. See, for example, Howard Becker, *Outsiders: Studies in the Sociology of Deviance* (London: Free Press, 1963); Erving Goffman, *The Presentation of Self in Everyday Life* (Edinburgh: Social Sciences Research Centre, University of Edinburgh, 1959); Erving Goffman, *Asylums: Essays on the Social Situation of Mental Patients and Other Inmates* (Englewood Cliffs, NJ: Prentice-Hall, 1986); Erving Goffman, *Stigma: Notes on the Management of Spoiled Identity* (Harlow: Prentice-Hall, 1963); George Herbert Mead, *Mind, Self, and Society: From the Standpoint of a Social Behaviorist*

(Chicago: University of Chicago Press, 1934); and Frank Tannenbaum, *Crime and the Community* (New York: Columbia University Press, 1938).

19. The BNP is a far right political party in the United Kingdom. It has a fascist ideology and is best known for its discriminatory views on "race."

20. All the quotations in this section are from the life story interview conducted with Charlie in August 2011.

21. Goffman, *Asylums*.

22. Jerome S. Bruner, *Acts of Meaning* (Cambridge, MA: Harvard University Press, 1990); Theodore R. Sarbin, ed., *Narrative Psychology: The Storied Nature of Human Conduct* (New York: Praeger, 1990).

23. See Maruna, "Going Straight," 59–93; and Liebling, *Prisons and Their Moral Performance*.

24. Lieblich, Tuval-Mashiach, and Zilber, *Narrative Research*.

25. On cognition, see Bruner, *Acts of Meaning*. On identity, see McAdams, *Power, Intimacy and the Life Story*; McAdams, *The Stories We Live By*; McAdams, Josselson, and Lieblich, *Identity and Story*; and Anthony Giddens, *Modernity and Self-Identity: Self and Society in the Modern Age* (Stanford, CA: Stanford University Press, 1991).

26. Edwin Sutherland, *The Professional Thief* (Chicago: University of Chicago Press, 1937), 267.

27. Finola Farrant, "Gender, 'Race,' and the Criminal Justice Process," in *Race and Criminal Justice*, edited by Hindpal Singh-Bhui (London: Sage, 2009), 122–36.

28. C. Wright Mills, *The Sociological Imagination* (Oxford: Oxford University Press, 2000), 193.

29. On fictional texts, see Jacques Lacan, *The Seminar of Jacques Lacan*, book 2, *The Ego in Freud's Theory and in the Technique of Psychoanalysis, 1954–1955* (New York: W. W. Norton, 1991). On representations of reality, see Robert Atkinson, *The Life Story Interview* (London: Sage, 1998). On subjective change, see Maruna et al., "Looking-Glass Identity Transformation: Pygmalion and Golem in the Rehabilitation Process," in *How Offenders Transform Their Lives*, ed. B. M. Veysey, J. Christian, and D. J. Martinez (Cullompton: Willan, 2009), 30–55.

30. Lois Presser, "The Narratives of Offenders," *Theoretical Criminology* 13, no. 2 (2009): 177–200.

31. Jack Katz, *Seductions of Crime: Moral and Sensual Attractions in Doing Evil* (New York: Basic Books, 1988), 4.

32. All the quotations in this section are from the life story interview conducted with Danny in August 2011.

33. Mills, *The Sociological Imagination*.

34. H. Porter Abbott, *The Cambridge Introduction to Narrative* (Cambridge: Cambridge University Press, 2008).

35. Schaffer and Smith, *Human Rights and Narrated Lives*.

36. See Gerry Johnstone and Daniel W. Van Ness, *Handbook of Restorative Justice* (Cullompton: Willan, 2007), for discussion of the various locations where restorative justice can be found.

WORKS CITED

Allen, Barbara, and Lynwood Montell. *From Memory to History: Using Oral Sources in Local Historical Research*. Nashville, TN: American Association for State and Local History, 1981.

Amsterdam, Anthony G., and Jerome S. Bruner. *Minding the Law*. Cambridge, MA: Harvard University Press, 2000.

Arendt, Hannah. *The Human Condition*. Chicago: University of Chicago Press, 1958.

Atkinson, Robert. *The Life Story Interview*. London: Sage, 1998.

Becker, Howard. *Outsiders: Studies in the Sociology of Deviance*. London: Free Press, 1963.

Brooks, Peter, and Paul Gewirtz, eds. *Law's Stories: Narrative and Rhetoric in the Law*. New Haven, CT: Yale University Press, 1996.

Bruner, Jerome S. *Acts of Meaning*. Cambridge, MA: Harvard University Press, 1990.

Crewe, Ben. *The Prisoner Society: Power, Adaptation, and Social Life in an English Prison*. Oxford: Oxford University Press, 2009.

Crewe, Ben, and Jamie Bennett, eds. *The Prisoner*. London: Routledge, 2012.

Currie, Elliott. "Preface." In *Critical Criminology: Issues, Debates, Challenges*, edited by Kerry Carrington and Russell Hogg, vii–ix. Cullompton: Willan, 2002.

Erickson, Frederick. "Social Construction of Topical Cohesion in a Conversation." In *Analyzing Discourse: Text and Talk*, edited by Deborah Tannen, 43–70. Washington, DC: Georgetown University Press, 1982.

Farrant, Finola. "Gender, 'Race,' and the Criminal Justice Process." In *Race and Criminal Justice*, edited by Hindpal Singh-Bhui, 122–36. London: Sage, 2009.

Gergen, Kenneth J. *The Saturated Self: Dilemmas of Identity in Contemporary Life*. New York: Basic Books, 1991.

Gergen, Kenneth J., and Mary M. Gergen. "Narratives of the Self." In *Studies in Social Identity*, edited by Karl E. Scheibe and Theodore R. Sarbin, 254–73. New York: Praeger, 1989.

Giddens, Anthony. *Modernity and Self-Identity: Self and Society in the Modern Age*. Stanford, CA: Stanford University Press, 1991.

Goffman, Erving. *Asylums: Essays on the Social Situation of Mental Patients and Other Inmates*. 1968. Reprint, Englewood Cliffs, NJ: Prentice-Hall, 1986.

———. *The Presentation of Self in Everyday Life*. Edinburgh: Social Sciences Research Centre, University of Edinburgh, 1959.

———. *Stigma: Notes on the Management of Spoiled Identity*. Harlow: Prentice-Hall, 1963.

Holland, Dorothy C., William Lachicotte, Deborah Skinner, and Carole Cain. *Identity and Agency in Cultural Worlds*. Cambridge, MA: Harvard University Press, 1998.

Johnstone, Gerry, and Daniel W. Van Ness. *Handbook of Restorative Justice*. Cullompton: Willan, 2007.

Katz, Jack. *Seductions of Crime: Moral and Sensual Attractions in Doing Evil*. New York: Basic Books, 1988.

Lacan, Jacques. *The Seminar of Jacques Lacan.* Book 2, *The Ego in Freud's Theory and in the Technique of Psychoanalysis, 1954–1955.* New York: W. W. Norton, 1991.

Langness, Lewis L., and Gelya Frank. *Lives: An Anthropological Approach to Biography.* Novato, CA: Chandler and Sharp, 1981.

Learmonth, Mark. "Doing Things with Words: The Case of 'Management' and 'Administration.'" *Public Administration* 83, no. 3 (2005): 617–37.

Leydesdorff, Selma, Luisa Passerini, and Paul Thompson. *International Yearbook of Oral History and Life Stories.* Vol. 4, *Gender and Memory.* Oxford: Oxford University Press, 1996.

Lieblich, Amia, Rivka Tuval-Mashiach, and Tamar Zilber. *Narrative Research: Reading, Analysis, and Interpretation.* London: Sage, 1998.

Liebling, Alison. *Prisons and Their Moral Performance.* Oxford: Clarendon, 2004.

Linde, Charlotte. *Life Stories: The Creation of Coherence.* Oxford: Oxford University Press, 1993.

Maruna, Shadd. "Going Straight: Desistance from Crime and Life Narratives of Reform." In *The Narrative Study of Lives,* vol. 5, edited by Amia Lieblich and Ruthellen Josselson, 59–93. London: Sage, 1997.

———. *Making Good: How Ex-Convicts Reform and Rebuild Their Lives.* Washington, DC: American Psychological Association, 2001.

Maruna, Shadd, T. P. LeBel, M. Naples, and N. Mitchell. "Looking-Glass Identity Transformation: Pygmalion and Golem in the Rehabilitation Process." In *How Offenders Transform Their Lives,* edited by B. M. Veysey, J. Christian, and D. J. Martinez, 30–55. Cullompton: Willan, 2009.

McAdams, Dan P. *Power, Intimacy, and the Life Story: Personological Inquiries into Identity.* New York: Guildford Press, 1985.

———. *The Stories We Live By: Personal Myths and the Making of the Self.* New York: Guildford Press, 1993.

McAdams, Dan P., Ruthellen Josselson, and Amia Lieblich, eds. *Identity and Story: Creating Self in Narrative.* Washington, DC: American Psychological Association, 2006.

Mead, George Herbert. *Mind, Self, and Society: From the Standpoint of a Social Behaviorist.* Chicago: University of Chicago Press, 1934.

Mills, C. Wright. *The Sociological Imagination.* 1959. Reprint, Oxford: Oxford University Press, 2000.

Muncie, John, and Mike Fitzgerald. "Humanizing the Deviant: Affinity and Affiliation Theories." In *Crime and Society: Readings in History and Theory,* ed. Mike Fitzgerald, Gregor McLennan, and Jennie Pawson, 337–58. London: Routledge, 1981.

Plummer, Ken. *Telling Sexual Stories: Power, Change, and Social Worlds.* New York: Routledge, Kegan Paul, 1995.

Porter Abbott, H. *The Cambridge Introduction to Narrative.* Cambridge: Cambridge University Press, 2008.

Pratt, John, David Brown, Mark Brown, Simon Hallsworth, and Wayne Morrison. *The New Punitiveness.* Cullompton: Willan, 2005.

Presser, Lois. "The Narratives of Offenders." *Theoretical Criminology* 13, no. 2 (2009): 177–200.

Raggatt, Peter T. F. "Multiplicity and Conflict in the Dialogical Self: A Life-Narrative Approach." In *Identity and Story: Creating Self in Narrative*, edited by Dan P. McAdams, Ruthellen Josselson, and Amia Licblich, 15–35. Washington, DC: American Psychological Association, 2006.

Sarbin, Theodore R., ed. *Narrative Psychology: The Storied Nature of Human Conduct*. New York: Praeger, 1990.

Schaffer, Kay, and Sidonie Smith. *Human Rights and Narrated Lives: The Ethics of Recognition*. Basingstoke: Palgrave Macmillan, 2004.

Simon, John. "The 'Society of Captives' in the Era of Hyper-Incarceration." *Theoretical Criminology* 4, no. 3 (2000): 285–308.

Sutherland, Edwin. *The Professional Thief*. Chicago: University of Chicago Press, 1937.

Tannenbaum, Frank. *Crime and the Community*. New York: Columbia University Press, 1938.

Wacquant, Loïc. "The Curious Eclipse of Prison Ethnography in the Age of Mass Incarceration." *Ethnography* 3, no. 4 (2002): 371–98.

Part Three

Representation

"I Hear
the Approaching Thunder"

The Lyric Voice and Human Rights

PATRICIA HAMPL

A strong case has been made for silence. *Nach Auschwitz ein Gedicht zu schreiben, ist barbarisch* (To write poetry after Auschwitz is barbaric). The German cultural critic Theodor Adorno made his famously severe judgment in 1949, barely four years after the killing camps of the Third Reich were opened to the world.

One of the aspects of the Nazi genocide that elicits the greatest repulsion has been the image of German officers listening, of an evening, to string quartets played by inmates of the camps in the smoldering shadows of the smokestacks. Something about the lyrical transparency of Mozart "appreciated" in this setting casts a pall on the music, as if it, too, were part of the horror. Against this image, the lyric impulse is indeed powerless, even hideously complicit, if exercised against its will. There is nothing to be said.

Paradoxically, horror of this magnitude shares with the transfiguring experience of divinity an instinct for silence—YAWEH is not to be named, only indicated, in rabbinic Judaism. When pestered to identify himself in the Bible, the Voice comes back (depending on the translation) slyly elusive, refusing to acknowledge much more than *I am what is*. Divinity as the tautology of being—I am what it is to exist.

It's as if YAWEH were shrugging off definition with a louche *whatever*. Go figure. Or rather—don't figure, don't think. And quit asking. Don't expect explanations (about God, about evil). These are the conundrums of existence, beyond voice.

Literature won't help—not in articulating the transfiguring experience of the sublime, and certainly not in speaking from the dismay that accompanies horror. "Witnessing" is essential; bringing perpetrators before tribunals is necessary. But poetry is "barbaric."

This injunction against lyricism may be ancient, a family fury directed against the phony paternal power of language in the face of evil's boot on the throat. But it is also distinctly modern, this infuriating betrayal of language. In *A Farewell to Arms*, a book that inaugurated the stern minimalism of modernist prose, Ernest Hemingway's war-broken narrator, Frederick Henry, addresses the problem of language with a biting contempt we recognize as contemporary.

> I was always embarrassed by the words *sacred, glorious,* and *sacrifice.* . . . There were many words that you could not stand to hear and finally only the names of places had dignity. Certain numbers were the same way and certain dates and these with the names of the places were all you could say and have them mean anything. Abstract words such as *glory, honor, courage* . . . were obscene beside the concrete names of villages, the numbers of roads, the names of rivers, the numbers of regiments and the dates.

Hemingway's "names of the places" would have been those of World War I— Yres, Verdun, Chateau-Thierry, and all the littler battles known only to those who fought them in mud and blood in Italy and France.

Lieutenant Henry's judgment is not only an echo of the primordial understanding of the reverence inherent in reticence. He anticipates, perhaps even more powerfully for us inheritors of yet another great war, "the places" of World War II when what was once simply a Bavarian town about eleven miles from Munich—Dachau—is ventriloquized into radical evil. The fact that today Dachau is a thriving suburban bedroom community for Munich does not affect this other use of the name, burned into history. Or, more to the point, burned into the mind.

Adorno does not say it is barbaric to write poetry "after the Holocaust" or "after the massacre of millions" or even "after the Shoah" (Catastrophe). He reaches, perhaps instinctively, for the lancing dart of detail. This is the lyric paradox: only the small is able to confront the vast. Adorno needs only to say the name of "the place" for it to ripple like a still pool at the touch of a sharp, flat stone skipped across its spreading surface. The fact that Auschwitz is only one of the (many) places in the network of genocide underscores the power inherent in a single, specific reference. It confirms Lieutenant Henry's point.

After all, even the "Holocaust" is abstract, a construction, a heroic labeling of colossal mayhem. "Auschwitz," on the other hand, is "concrete," as Hemingway's lieutenant requires of language not to be "obscene."

It is also that most literary form of language: by 1949 "Auschwitz" had become a metaphor. And so it remains, surely as long as any kind of memory remains of how Europe defaced itself in the last century. Poetry, it seems, gets the last word after all.

Does this mean that only the "names of the places" have the power to stop the heart—and perhaps (the frail hope) to move it from gagged horror to possible meaning? And beyond meaning to effect change that, in turn, might make "Auschwitz" if not impossible, at least less likely?

\(\ell\)

Well, of course not. Long after Auschwitz, "the names of the places" continue to pile up their stacks of bodies. Srebrenica, Rwanda. You have your own names to add to the list.

Still, the curious fact remains—the stunning power of metaphor, that lyric instrument. The destination, the achievement of lyricism, may be metaphor. But at its core lyricism is born of the intimate voice speaking not to the world but to itself as to another. This "other" is both oneself and yet paradoxically the absence of a personal self. It is the individual voice of awareness calling from the depth of chaos.

It has become the indispensable voice of the Holocaust, the genocide that, more than any other, haunts western consciousness.

"It's a wonder I haven't abandoned all my ideals, they seem so absurd and impractical. Yet I cling to them because I still believe, in spite of everything, that people are truly good at heart." This is the most quoted passage in Anne Frank's *Diary*. These lines, confirming human goodness, appall many discerning readers. Maybe she could write such a line in the relative safety of the secret annex, but would this acute writer have said such a thing as she lay dying of typhus in the fetid camp?

This line strikes me as less telling of her lyric genius than the meditation that follows it. "It's utterly impossible for me to build my life on a foundation of chaos, suffering and death," she writes. "I see the world being slowly transformed into a wilderness, I hear the approaching thunder that, one day, will destroy us too, I feel the suffering of millions. And yet, when I look up at the sky, I somehow feel that everything will change for the better, that this cruelty too shall end, that peace and tranquility will return once more. In the meantime, I must hold on to my ideals" (Saturday, July 14, 1944).

Less than a month later she was taken away.

This is the testament of a committed, already psychologically and spiritually mature writer, even a prophetic one. Her essential instrument is her lyricism, her capacity to see and render detail through the pulse of her individuality while still holding to her "ideals." Anne Frank was not simply a little girl who believed everybody was good at heart. She was a writer capable of naming her fate and the fate of the world she grieved for: "I hear the approaching thunder that, one day, will destroy us too, I feel the suffering of millions."

Knowing the fragility of life as it faces the brutality of racial hatred and rigid ideology, feeling the suffering of millions, intuiting one's own imminent destruction—this is what the frail first-person lyric carries on its back through the *Diary*. In writing her diary faithfully, Anne Frank wrote our history. We have discovered that we can trust no other voice as completely to express this reality. It isn't that she—or any lyric writer—has the facts. She is not a "witness" in the sense of the essential testimonies from those who describe *what happened*. This is not what makes her an indelible presence.

It comes as a shock to remember that, though writing in extraordinary circumstances, hidden in a spice warehouse in Amsterdam, Anne Frank had not yet experienced what we call the "Holocaust" when she wrote the book that made her its voice. It was not the evidence of her horrific experience that somehow made her the representative of the millions who shared her fate.

However sentimentalized her "image" may have been made by play or movie, her voice is not diluted by false sentiment even as she keeps solidarity with her essential self—which is to say with the lyrical sensibility that makes possible her sustaining faith in life.

She wrote roguish portraits of those around her; she touched the pulse of the days and seasons. Finally, in the privacy of her inner voice, she touched the metaphor that brought her to prophecy. She heard the approaching thunder and recognized it as the reality that is still resounding.

WORKS CITED

Adorno, Theodor. "An Essay on Cultural Criticism and Society." In *Prisms*, 34. Translated by Samuel Weber and Shierry Weber. Cambridge, MA: MIT Press, 1967.

Frank, Anne. *The Diary of a Young Girl: The Definitive Edition*. Translated and edited by Otto H. Frank and Mirjam Pressler. New York: Doubleday, 1995.

Hemingway, Ernest. *A Farewell to Arms*. New York: Scribner, 1929.

The Fictional Is Political

Forms of Appeal
in Autobiographical Fiction and Poetry

MEG JENSEN

Cathy Caruth has argued that trauma "is always the story of a wound that cries out, that addresses us in the attempt to tell us of a reality or truth that is not otherwise available."[1] Much of the work in this collection centers on how, and under what conditions, life stories of human rights violation are remembered, told, heard, and recognized and become justiciable. Caruth and others explain, however, that when such violations give rise to trauma, the victims' ability to process and contextualize their terrifying experiences is compromised, resulting in an inability to forge linear narratives. Trauma, that is, often renders its victims unable to convey their stories in a traditional, coherent manner.[2] Thus, when traumatized victims are called on to *tell* in legal, advocacy, and even therapeutic contexts, the result may be to retraumatize them, as they are forced to put into words that which is necessarily unmediated and unintelligible. In this essay, I will argue that, perhaps paradoxically, metaphoric and fictive modes of poetry and autobiography that are rooted in traumatic experience enable victims to speak and write of just such otherwise unutterable or inaccessible realities. These textual forms, as I will demonstrate, provide an effective, if unusual, method for accessing, mediating, and articulating the posttraumatic struggle between discursive practices and felt bodily experiences, both in personal and in sociopolitical contexts. Autobiographical fiction and poetry, therefore, constitute a unique and useful form of trauma testimony, not by telling the *story* of a trauma but as evidence of its ongoing personal and public aftermath.

Such texts also provide the opportunity to complete the *life cycle* of a human rights event, which typically begins with a person or community to which a violation of rights takes place. Testimony is then gathered from those victims by outsiders and *experts* with the important but limited goal of achieving justice, punishment, and/or legal, public recognition. Typically, in human rights discourse, such public justice is the end of the road. In order to complete the circle, however, it would surely be preferable for the final stage of these events to be the reinstatement of the figure of the whole, untraumatized person and/or community. As Molly Andrews argues in this volume, however, courtroom testimony does not tend to achieve this result. Metaphoric and fictive forms of posttraumatic autobiography can, on the other hand, offer just such an opportunity for victims and communities to begin the postjustice project of healing. Alongside the prevention of future rights violations, returning victims to bodily and psychic health must equally be the highest goal of human rights activism. These forms of posttraumatic autobiographical writing should be seen, therefore, as serving not only a valuable personal but also a vital political purpose, and one to which a great deal more time and interest on the part of scholars, activists, and therapists involved in posttraumatic interventions should be devoted.

The Limits of Autobiography

Many writers of autobiographical fiction and/or memoir that push the boundaries of what is truth and what is fiction have suffered trauma—often in childhood. Leigh Gilmore has examined a number of such works, including Dorothy Allison's *Bastard out of Carolina*, Mikal Gilmore's *Shot in the Heart,* Jamaica Kincaid's autobiographies, and Jeanette Winterson's *Written on the Body*, and argues that these texts test, and to some extent define, the "limits of autobiography."[3] They do so, Gilmore claims, by offering the posttraumatic writer "an alternative jurisdiction for self-representation in which writers relocate the grounds of judgment, install there a knowing subject . . . and produce an alternative jurisprudence about trauma, identity and the forms both may take."[4] Traditional autobiography, Gilmore explains, is concerned with the "literal and verifiable."[5] Posttraumatic autobiographical fictions that challenge the limits of autobiography, on the other hand, are often propelled by incomplete or inaccessible memories, raising questions rather than providing verifiable facts. In this sense they constitute not a presentation of traumatic experience but instead symptomatic evidence of its aftermath.

These texts may not be useful in achieving justice for, as Gilmore notes, they "offer histories of harm and the individual that differ from legal ones and which are . . . inadmissible as testimony."[6] They can, however, do what the law can't: enable the trauma victim to imagine. As Gregg Horowitz has noted, traumatic experience installs in its victims "annihilation anxiety" or fear of the "future." "And not," he argues, "because of any uncertainty about the future: to the contrary." Trauma survivors, he claims, "cannot be said to have a future, in the sense of fresh experiences, but rather only a past that recurs . . . over and again. When all futures are annihilating, it is certainty that terrifies."[7] Trauma is, moreover, an experience of the body, whether that body has been subject to violence of some kind or through the complex series of neurochemical events that occur in the wake of both physical and psychological terror.[8] The body is, to quote Judith Butler, "a social phenomenon . . . exposed to others, vulnerable by definition."[9] Works that challenge the limits of autobiography by interrogating the relations between body and text, and, as Gilmore claims, "concerned with the interpenetration of the private and the public, and how its impact is registered in personal, aesthetic and legal terms," may well provide the best possible textual space for posttraumatic writers exploring just those productive and sometimes terrifying tensions.

Concerns about the conflicts between public and private, personal and political are central not only to the texts Gilmore examines, of course, but to any number of historical and contemporary autobiographically based fictions, from *David Copperfield* to *A Heartbreaking Work of Staggering Genius*. In fact, one might say that a primary function of fictional autobiography is that it allows the writer to square the ethical dilemma of publicly exposing (and possibly betraying) not only their own private experience but those of the people closest to them, often in volume after volume.[10]

As Gilmore argues, the role of such genre-blurring, truth-and-fiction-eliding texts is precisely to trouble the limits of truth telling. By doing so, they call to mind the four questions Michel Foucault posed as central to any examination of *truth*: "who is able to tell the truth, about what, with what consequences, and with what relation to power?"[11] The hierarchical relations exposed by Foucault's interrogation of truth telling, moreover, give rise to tensions between speech and silence, vulnerability and power, in all acts of witnessing. These tensions, I would argue, are nowhere more deadly, and nowhere more productive, than in metaphoric and fictive renderings of traumatic autobiographical experience. As Gilmore states: "The conventions of truth telling . . . can be inimical to the ways in which some writers bring trauma stories into language. The portals are too narrow and . . . the risk of being accused of lying (or malingering, or inflating, or whining) threatens the writer into continued silence. In this scenario, the autobiographical project may swerve from the form of autobiography."[12] These "swerves" are varied and sometimes shocking, and they are governed by what Ian Hacking terms "memoro-politics" of "the secret, of the forgotten event that can be turned, if only by strange flashbacks, into something monumental."[13] The monuments of posttraumatic autobiographical writing enact the politics of memory within a context of multiple tensions. Here traumatic experience is figured as the secret glimpsed partially in strange flash-backs, couched often in gnomic, overburdened symbols, fragmented language, and hesitant, unreliable narrators.

In Judith Butler's recent study *Frames of War* (2009), she quotes from a number of poems that can be seen as enactments of posttraumatic "memoro-politics" collected in *Poems from Guantánamo: The Detainees Speak* (2007). She ex-amines, for example, the following lines from a poem by Sami al Haj, "who was tortured at U.S. prisons in Bagram and Kandahar before being transferred to Guantánamo."[14]

> I was humiliated in the shackles
> How can I now compose verses? How can I now write?
> After the shackles and the nights and the suffering and
> the Tears
> How can I write poetry?[15]

In their despair at the poet's inability to sublimate suffering and humiliation into verse, these lines recall Theodor Adorno's oft-cited claim that to "write poetry after Auschwitz is barbaric."[16] As Butler suggests, however, it is not only the tragic content of al Haj's poem that draws our attention, but also the manner in which it "enacts what al Haj cannot understand. He writes the poem, but the poem can do no more than only openly query the condition of its own possibility. How does a tortured body form such words?" As al Haj writes the poem he cannot write, Butler argues, "the forming of those words is linked with survival" and thus reminds us that traumatic experience is often the crossroads at which the personal and the political, public and private, emo-tional and legal are brought into confrontation and conflict.[17] Fictive and meta-phoric modes of posttraumatic autobiography, of which al Haj's poem and the works Gilmore examines are examples, may be seen to constitute a form of testimony that interrogates the nature of all remembrance constructed under conditions of ongoing suffering. The conditionality of such works as neither fully truth nor fully fiction reflects the insecurity of the posttraumatic memory at these complex crossroads, of which it is both the evidence and the symptom.

Personal and Political

Every moment of every day in every corner of the world there is a violation of human rights and a challenge to such violations. Testimonies from courtrooms to social networking sites attempt to capture and disseminate truth in the hope of recognition, justice in its multiple forms, and ultimately commemoration. As the Holocaust historian Simone Gigliotti has written, posttraumatic testimony is always "a mediation of experience, language and memory" and all such mediations take place in a sociohistorical, as well as personal, context.[18] Indeed, in Annette Wieviorka's examination of the emergence of survivor testimony in the public sphere, she notes that in principle, "[T]estimonies demonstrate that every individual, every life, every experience . . . is irreducibly unique." Nevertheless, those who testify "demonstrate this uniqueness using the language of the time in which they are delivered and in response to questions and expectations motivated by political and ideological concerns."[19] The contexts in which testimony is articulated and heard, that is, form what Judith Butler refers to as "interpretive frames," which "lead to an interpretive conclusion about the deed itself" on the part of speaker and listener, installing a politics on all forms of testimony.[20]

Carrie Doan's research suggests that a politics and hierarchical structure is always installed by the legal discourse around testimony, which, in cases of domestic and childhood sexual abuse, for example, privileges so-called expert testimony over that of the witness or victim. Moreover, as Doan explains, "in academic literature on the subject, it is often assumed that logico-scientific resources prove beneficial to survivors of abuse" as "forms of expertise serve to legitimize the claims of those whose testimony would otherwise be discounted."[21] As a result, Doan argues, such "expert testimony" exacerbates the victim's sense of powerlessness by mimicking the hegemonic structures that give rise to domestic violence.[22]

The historian Saul Friedlander suggests that such pressures on posttraumatic communication in all forms calls for an "aesthetics that remarks on its own limitations, its inability to provide external answers and stable meaning . . . that devotes itself primarily to the dilemmas of representation."[23] It is this very aesthetic, moreover, that I suggest is at work in much metaphoric, lyric, and fictive posttraumatic literature. As posttraumatic writers, like the poet al Haj, feel unable to offer the possibility of "external answers and stable meaning," their texts instead remark on their own limitations: the limits of autobiography in the face of traumatic experience. The result is a fictive and/or metaphoric traumatogenic narrative "primarily" concerned with "the dilemmas of representation," often fragmentary and intertextual in character.[24] The value of such an aesthetic, Friedlander suggests, is that it allows the writer to do what he or she must: "live without full understanding."[25]

As recent research into posttraumatic stress suggests, such an aesthetic is particularly suited to its sufferers: posttraumatic stress disorder (PTSD), it seems, has a traceable effect on its victims' relationship to language and meaning.

Psychoanalyst and critic Juliet Mitchell calls this effect "the pseudosymbolic language of post-trauma" in which words are "plagiaristic imitations or metaphors . . . expressions of feeling rather than of meaning."[26] Posttraumatic writers, therefore, may be attracted to autobiographical fiction and poetic metaphor as modes of life storytelling that allow them to express their feelings without being forced to attribute meaning to them.

In her essay "Trauma and the Impossibility of Experience," however, Idit Dobbs-Weinstein argues that any emphasis on linguistics and aesthetics blurs the truth of the traumatic experience. What is required, she claims, is to "make manifest" the "courage" of the writer or speaker "to resist the temptation of making the events intelligible," a language, that is, that "presents but does not seek or pretend to represent."[27] But is such a form possible? Butler's notion of "interpretive frames" suggests that all presentations of human experience, whether banal or terrifying, involve interpretive and therefore re-presentative acts. Moreover, testimonial acts must be understood to take place within a politics of multiple frames and interpretations, both public and private, and, indeed, in relation to the traumatized body's own "adaptive" response to traumatic injury.

Body as Witness: The Adaptive Speech of Trauma

Recently Kristen Brown Golden has made use of phenomenologist Maurice Merleau-Ponty's work to argue that traumatogenic narratives "register [bodily] adaptation, not representation." The *true story* of a traumatic experience called for in many posttrauma contexts, she argues, is "more precisely" a "paced eruption . . . of corporeal desire driven by the power of the traumatic wound but not representing it."[28] In her study, Brown Golden begins by revealing a number of startling similarities between the human body's adaptive responses to physical trauma, on one hand, and psychological trauma on the other.[29] A traumatogenic narrative in Brown Golden's account is an example of "adaptive speech" that constitutes the body's response to traumatic injury. In posttrauma, as Butler demonstrates, such speech must then be subject to interpretation, first by the body, and then, perhaps, by the outside world in legal, therapeutic, literary, or other interpersonal communications.

For Butler "the body is a social phenomenon," and therefore the interpretation of experience arises "not as the spontaneous act of a single mind, but as a consequence of a certain field of intelligibility that forms and frames our responses to the impinging world." Moreover, she argues, the "body does not belong to itself" but is "outside itself, in the world of others."[30] In the aftermath of trauma, however, the leap from bodily experience to intelligibility, interpretation, and social critique can be impossible to make. Nevertheless, as the work of both Brown Golden and Butler reminds us, the responsive, adaptive, social, and interpretative body is a key frame through which all forms of trauma testimony must be understood.

The manner in which bodies offer testimonies through these frames is examined in the work of historian Annette Wieviorka. In *The Era of the Witness*, she draws on Haim Gouri's account of the 1961 trial of Adolf Eichmann, architect of the Holocaust. As Gouri explains, the "witnesses," many of whom were concentration camp survivors, "served as faithful proxies of the Holocaust. They were the facts."[31] Wieviorka argues that during the course of this televised trial, the new identity of the "survivor" was created and "the witness became the embodiment of memory (*un homme-mémoire*)" through the act of testifying.[32] Like Butler, that is, she suggests that such an embodied identity, as well as the testimony it offers, arises within and is produced by the interpretive frame of the context of the telling. As Wieviorka puts it, "[T]he witness is the bearer of an experience that, albeit unique, does not exist on its own but only in the testimonial situation in which it takes place."[33] For Wieviorka, therefore, the Eichmann witnesses not only embodied their traumatic experiences in the Holocaust but their testimony in this context produced that experience and that identity. By testifying, then, to quote Butler, they "form an appeal" and attempt to "establish a social connection to the world, even when there is no concrete reason to think that any such connection is possible."[34]

Wieviorka also recounts the testimony at the same trial of Yehiel Dinor, who came to the stand calling himself Ka-tzetnik (a name that meant *prisoner* in the concentration camps). When asked about the name he replied:

> It is not a pen name. I do not regard myself as a writer and composer of literary material. This is a chronicle of the planet Auschwitz. I was there for about two years. Time there was not like it is here on earth. . . . And the inhabitants of this planet had no names, they had no parents nor did they have children. . . . They breathed according to different laws of nature; they did not live, nor did they die, according to the laws of this world. Their name was the number "Kazetnik."[35]

Dinor was hesitant, sweating, ill, and distracted throughout his testimony, and the officials found it difficult to question him. At one point, he was shown an inmate's uniform. He responded, "This is the garb of the planet called

Auschwitz. . . . I believe with perfect faith . . . that this planet of ashes, Auschwitz, stands in opposition to our planet earth, and influences it."[36] Dinor then recounts seeing the soon to be murdered prisoners lined up before him. "I was always left behind," he said. "I can still see them gazing at me." Soon after, Dinor began to exit the witness box, but then he returned, disoriented. The court officials said, "Can we ask you a few questions, please?" but Dinor ignored this, uttering, "I saw them in the queue" before falling from the stand in a faint. His limp body was dragged to the side of the courtroom as court officials attempted to revive him.

With the Eichmann trial, and its public show of the "alien," fainting body of "Ka-tzenik" in particular, the figure of the witness becomes literally, as Wieviorka argues, *un homme-mémoire*. Dinor's testimony, that is, embodies the traumatic experiences that can neither be accessed nor told in linear, logical form but only glimpsed in the hesitant, metaphoric, "adaptive speech" and the annihilated collapsed body of the renamed, or rather unnamed, "Kazetnik."

The Paradox of the *Homme-Mémoire*

Like Dinor's rendering of the alien ash planet of Auschwitz, where time and nature behaved differently, all posttraumatic discourse negotiates the paradox of how to make intelligible truth out of nonlinear, nondiscursive trauma. The question is not only "what is there to say" but also "who is there to talk?"[37] In *Forgetful Memory*, Michael Bernard-Donals argues that what is lost in the telling of trauma can be found in the gestures of the speaker. "The distance," he writes, "between what was seen and what can be said—is often wide and always palpable: not only in the witness statements but in the shrugged shoulders, the winces, the tears, and the silences that punctuate the oral testimonies." Such embodied testimony is evidence "not of memory but of forgetting, of what escapes."[38] In the aftermath of trauma, that is, a publicly and privately annihilated body and hesitant, dreamlike speech may themselves be the only reliable evidence of, and testimony to, a traumatic experience.

Doan likewise interrogates the frames through which we speak and hear posttraumatic discourse. Just as the social, public body provides a context through which to give witness to trauma, Doan argues that we must also be aware of the sociopolitical context in which trauma testimony, and indeed trauma itself, takes place. Historically, she explains, there has been a "theoretical debate" between the "value" of what she calls "logico-scientific" accounts of reality and "narrative accounts of reality" in cases of trauma.[39] For Doan "autobiographical accounts" of trauma, "such as those of Dorothy Allison and Maya Angelou, internally illuminate the contexts of inequality which perpetuate abuse and shape the lives of survivors, while discourses in legal institutions and popular media tend to reproduce hegemonic constructions."[40] The paradox of the *homme-mémoire*, therefore, is that to give witness to the past by speaking of it and embodying it reinscribes the terrifying personal and political power relations of trauma on the present and the future.

Gregg Horowitz has argued, in fact, that "the survivor of trauma . . . cannot be said to have a future." This, he suggests, is because traumatic suffering is "the appearance of something real in the place where phantasy ought to be."[41] Victims of trauma, that is, cannot fantasize about the future in any normal way as they are caught in an unmediated recurring past. "All one can do in the face of trauma," therefore, "is to speculate. . . . Speculation is thought unbound, a cognitive undergoing of experience that cannot find a place in the received patterns of conceptual knowing."[42] It is this "speculation" in the face of unmediated traumatic experience that I suggest both generates and is generated by metaphoric and fictive forms of posttraumatic life storytelling. By enabling this speculative relation between public and private, past and present, body and discourse, moreover, such work may even produce healing.

The Therapeutic Effects of Fictional Autobiography

According to Mitchell, post-traumatic stress disorder inscribes a particular and peculiar effect on its victims' relationship to language and meaning. Trauma, Mitchell argues, engenders "the pseudosymbolic language of post-trauma" in which words are "plagiaristic imitations or metaphors . . . [that] become expressions of feeling rather than of meaning, . . . plausible, perhaps" but "lying."[43] Like autobiographical fiction itself, that is, the language of posttrauma apes the codes of familiar forms yet is unable to attach or communicate clear meaning to those forms. Nevertheless, as Mitchell argues, "writing, as opposed to talking, gives the possibility of perspective . . . [and] the writer presents himself to another and thus sets up a position from which to perceive himself.[44] While attempts to speak *the truth* of traumatic experience may thus reinscribe the hegemonic power structures under which trauma took place, the act of writing enables some posttraumatic sufferers to carve out what Gilmore has called an "alternative jurisdiction," producing meaning, perspective, and a new, posttrauma identity position.[45]

In a recent work, "Therapeutic Effects of Fictional Autobiography," Celia Hunt uses neurophysiologist Antonio Damasio's two-part model of the unconscious self as a way to understand how fictive forms of life storytelling may increase the writer's "awareness of spontaneous bodily feelings and emotions, and a more reflexive relationship between different aspects of themselves."[46] For Damasio, as Hunt explains, a nonreflexive, innate, and wordless "core self" arises from the organism's bodily perceptions, producing a "bodily agency."[47] Damasio's second-level "autobiographical self" is produced by this "bodily felt self" as memories accumulate, and with the acquisition of language becomes, in Hunt's words, a "fully reflexive first person of consciousness," the "extended self." In their highest form, Hunt suggests, both the core and extended selves are "in process rather than fixed entities," with reflexive fluid movement between them. Threatening life experiences, however, can limit access to this bodily felt self, with the result that, in Hunt's account, "we may experience blocks to or stiffness in, cognitive processing."[48] And it is this much needed fluidity that Hunt suggests is increased by writing about one's life in fictive mode.

Writing fictional autobiographical narratives, Hunt argues, enables healing on the part of writers, as it "involves learning to trust the aesthetic of the writing process rooted in the felt body." The "deictic shift" such work enables, she claims, "eases psychic stuckness through facilitating the 'letting go' of familiar, sometimes inhibiting self-concepts, and the development of a stronger and more flexible sense of self rooted in the felt body."[49] This new self occurs as writers make "a sort of *autobiographical pact with themselves* that, as they are able, . . . will allow their material to fictionalize itself spontaneously," thus allowing "hidden or unknown aspects of the self" to be indirectly revealed. Such "fictions" make use of metaphors and rhythm to highlight emotional and corporeal aspects of self-experience, and by doing so, Hunt argues, they offer "a more fluid, open and multi-levelled mode of thinking than the everyday, a closer engagement with the body's felt perceptions and emotions and opportunities to . . . experiment with all of these possibilities."[50]

If, as Horowitz argues, trauma inscribes the "absolute assurance that the past, present and future cannot be mediated," Hunt's research suggests that the work of autobiographical fiction is precisely to interrogate this absolute by providing an opportunity for experimentation.[51] Thus, rather than attempting to "tell the truth" about trauma through logico-scientific narratives constructed in legal, nonfictional, or therapeutic contexts, fictive and metaphoric autobiographical writing may enable writers to enact a useful mediation of the past and present. In other words, by allowing access to new "conceptualizations of the self and others," such writing also provides possibilities for a new, posttraumatic politics of interaction with the world, apart from the perpetrator/victim hierarchy installed by trauma. These opportunities for "speculation," then, remove the absolute of annihilation from the posttrauma writer's view of the future and put in its place, as Horowitz puts it, the possibility of imagination.

Autobiographical Fiction as Insurgency

As Philippe Lejeune famously suggested, the reader and writer of autobiography forge an implicit "pact" between them, in which the writer endeavors to tell the truth to the best of his or her ability.[52] Hunt has shown, however, that when writers *consciously* use fictional and poetic techniques to tell their stories, they suspend the truth-telling intentions inherent in the "autobiographical pact" and this changes the "conceptual frame." Paradoxically, as Hunt notes, writers are thus provided with a "powerful tool for exploring 'truths' that lie beneath the surface of conscious self-knowledge."[53] This tool has enabled posttraumatic writers to return to the site of their inadequately processed experiences with curiosity and courage, gaining, perhaps, the healing that attends "an increased reflexivity of self."[54] Such flexible reflexivity, moreover, enables both the future fantasizing and the kind of "interpretation" and "social critique" that Butler argues is "a consequence of a certain field of intelligibility that forms and frames our responses to the impinging world." Metaphoric writings such as those Butler examines by the Guantánamo detainees, for example, "offer evidence of the kinds of utterance possible at the limits of grief, humiliation, longing and rage."[55] As the poetry of a writer/prisoner interrogates and enacts the conditionality of its own composition, it also asks, as Butler suggests, "how it can be that poetry can come from a tortured body." Thus, for Butler, "the overwhelming power of personal mourning, loss, and isolation becomes a political tool of insurgency—even a challenge to individual sovereignty," as "once the breath is made into words, the body is given over to another," thus becoming, like the collapsed figure of Ka-tzetnik, public and private, personal and legal, "evidence and appeal."[56]

In such work, the infinitely vulnerable "interconnectedness" and "precariousness" of all human beings is shown to enable "the condition of suffering" but also, Butler claims, "the condition of responsiveness," the "radical act of interpretation in the face of unwilled subjugation." She continues: "The very fact of being bound up with others establishes the possibility of being subjugated and exploited. . . . But it also establishes the possibility of being relieved of suffering, of knowing justice, and even love."[57] As such, metaphoric and fictive modes of testifying to traumatic experience may be seen to serve both a personal and a political purpose—embodying what Butler calls a "network of transitive affects." These modes of traumatogenic narrative work to combat authority, undermine expert testimony, and defy the logico-scientific demand to *stick to the facts*, as they give witness to the experience, desires, and terrors of the traumatized body and install the possibility for fantasies of past, present, and future. By doing so, they not only "ease psychic stuckness," as Hunt argues, enabling healing, but also perform what Butler sees as "critical acts of resistance, insurgent interpretations" that "live through the violence they oppose."[58]

Thus, the form of testimony enacted by posttraumatic autobiographical fiction counters Foucault's questions about the power relations and consequences inherent in any attempt at truth telling by giving witness to the victim's struggle between speech and silence, body and discourse, remembering and forgetting, seeking justice and avoiding self-incrimination. These generative, interrogative mediations, therefore, provide for alternative jurisdictions in which the aftermath of trauma, if not the experience of trauma itself, may be enabled to "form an appeal," and in that personal appeal achieve the highest political goal of human rights advocacy: the possibility for victims of violations to imagine their own futures.

NOTES

1. Cathy Caruth, *Unclaimed Experience: Trauma, Narrative, and History* (Baltimore: Johns Hopkins University Press, 1996), 4.

2. See, for example, Cathy Caruth, *Trauma: Explorations in Memory* (Baltimore: Johns Hopkins University Press, 1995); Juliet Mitchell, "Trauma, Recognition, and the Place of Language," *Diacritics* 28, no. 4 (1998): 121–33; and Paul John Eakin, *Living Autobiographically: How We Create Identity in Narrative* (Ithaca, NY: Cornell University Press, 2008).

3. Leigh Gilmore, *The Limits of Autobiography* (Ithaca, NY: Cornell University Press, 2001), 12.

4. Ibid., 143.

5. Ibid., 3.

6. Jamaica Kincaid once commented on the juridical place of her work: "Everything I say is true, and everything I say is not true. You couldn't admit any of it to a court of law. It would not be good evidence." Kay Bonetti, "An Interview with Jamaica Kincaid," *Missouri Review* 25, no. 2 (2002), accessed March 23, 2013, http://www.missourireview.com/archives/bbarticle/interview-with-jamaica-kincaid/.

7. Gregg Horowitz, "A Late Adventure of the Feelings: Loss, Trauma, and the Limits of Psychoanalysis," in *The Trauma Controversy: Philosophical and Interdisciplinary*

Dialogues, ed. Kristen Brown Golden and Bettina G. Borgo (Albany: State University of New York Press, 2009), 35.

8. For an introduction to the neurochemistry of memory in the aftermath of trauma, see Robert Strickgold, "EMDR: A Putative Neurobiological Mechanism of Action," *Journal of Clinical Psychology* 58, no. 1 (2002): 61–75.

9. Judith Butler, *Frames of War: When Is Life Grievable?* (New York: Verso, 2009), 33.

10. The serial form of fictional autobiography has been favored by numerous post-trauma writers, including Louisa May Alcott, Jack Kerouac, J. G. Ballard, Julia Alvarez, J. M. Coetzee, and Jamaica Kincaid.

11. Michel Foucault, *Fearless Speech*, ed. Joseph Pearson (Los Angeles: Semiotext[e], 2001), 170.

12. Gilmore, *The Limits of Autobiography*, 3.

13. Ian Hacking, *Rewriting the Soul: Multiple Personality and the Sciences of Memory* (Princeton, NJ: Princeton University Press, 1995), 214.

14. Butler, *Frames of War*, 55–56.

15. Ibid., 56.

16. Theodor Adorno, *Prisms*, trans. Samuel Weber and Shierry Weber, 6th ed. (Cambridge, MA: MIT Press, 1967), 34. Note, however, Adorno's expansion of this prohibition in his later work, in particular in "Elements of Anti-Semitism," in Theodor Adorno and Max Horkheimer, *Dialectic of Enlightenment*, trans. John Cumming (London: Verso, 1997), 168–208.

17. Butler, *Frames of War*, 55–56. Shoshana Felman argues that contemporary history is "crystallized around these two poles: the trial (law and justice) on the one hand, and trauma . . . on the other hand." Shoshana Felman, *The Juridical Unconscious: Trials and Traumas in the Twentieth Century* (Cambridge, MA: Harvard University Press, 2002), 3.

18. Simone Gigliotti, *The Train Journey: Transit, Captivity, and Witnessing in the Holocaust* (New York: Berghahn, 2009), 19.

19. Annette Wieviorka, *The Era of the Witness*, trans. Jared Stark (Ithaca, NY: Cornell University Press, 2006), xii.

20. Butler, *Frames of War*, 8.

21. Carrie Doan, "'Subversive Stories and Hegemonic Tales' of Child Sexual Abuse: From Expert Legal Testimony to Television Talk Shows," *International Journal of Law in Context* 1, no. 3 (2005): 296.

22. Doan argues that expert testimony in child sexual abuse cases "serves to frame the problem in depoliticizing, individualizing and medicalising discourses, and to assign epistemological authority to experts rather than survivors themselves." Ibid.

23. Saul Friedlander, *Memory, History, and the Extermination of the Jews in Europe* (Bloomington: Indiana University Press, 1993), 127–28.

24. On the genre blurring of autobiographical fiction, see Max Saunders, *Self-Impression: Life Writing, Autobiografiction, and the Forms of Modern Literature* (Oxford: Oxford University Press, 2010), 501–8. Suzette Henke first noted the fragmented forms of trauma

fiction in *Shattered Subjects: Trauma and Testimony in Women's Life Writing* (Basingstoke: Macmillan, 1998).

25. Friedlander, *Memory, History*, 127.

26. Mitchell, "Trauma, Recognition, and the Place of Language," 132.

27. Idit Dobbs-Weinstein, "Trauma and the Impossibility of Experience" in *The Trauma Controversy: Philosophical and Interdisciplinary Dialogues*, ed. Kristen Brown Golden and Bettina G. Borgo (Albany, NY: State University of New York Press, 2009), 100–101.

28. Kristen Brown Golden, "Trauma and Speech as Bodily Adaptation in Merleau-Ponty," in *The Trauma Controversy: Philosophical and Interdisciplinary Dialogues*, ed. Kristen Brown Golden and Bettina G. Borgo (Albany, NY: State University of New York Press, 2009), 83.

29. See, for example, Maurice Merleau-Ponty, *Nature: Course Note from the College de France*, trans. Robert Vallier (Evanston, IL: Northwestern University Press, 2003).

30. Butler, *Frames of War*, 59–60.

31. Haim Gouri, *Facing the Glass Booth: The Jerusalem Trial of Adolf Eichmann*, trans. Michael Swirsky (Detroit: Wayne State University Press, 2004), 269.

32. Wieviorka, *The Era of the Witness*, 88.

33. Ibid., 82.

34. Butler, *Frames of War*, 59–60.

35. This text is based on the English translation of Adolf Eichmann, *The Trial of Adolf Eichmann: Record of Proceedings in the District Court of Jerusalem*, 9 vols. (Jerusalem: Trust for the Publication of the Proceedings of the Eichmann Trial, 1992–1995). The testimony of Ka-tzenik appears at 1:324–26.

36. Wieviorka, *The Era of the Witness*, 80–81. Wieviorka's transcription of the scene stops at "influences it." What follows here is my version of the simultaneous translation of the testimony into English from *The Eichmann Trial, Session 68, 69*, accessed January 2, 2013, http://www.youtube.com/watch?v=m3-tXyYhd5U.

37. Roberta Culbertson, "Embodied Memory, Transcendence, and Telling: Recounting Trauma, Reestablishing the Self," *New Literary History* 26, no. 1 (1996): 191.

38. Michael Bernard-Donals, *Forgetful Memory: Representation and Remembrance in the Wake of the Holocaust* (Ithaca, NY: State University of New York Press, 2009), quoted from pages 11 and 77, respectively.

39. Doan, "Subversive Stories and Hegemonic Tales," 297.

40. Ibid., 295–96. Linda Alcoff and Laura Gray have similarly argued that, although "speaking out" is generally understood to be useful, in fact "bringing things into the realm of discourse works also to inscribe them into hegemonic structures." Linda Alcoff and Laura Gray, "Survivor Discourse: Transgression or Recuperation?," *Signs* 18, no. 2 (1993): 260.

41. Horowitz, "A Late Adventure of the Feelings," 35.

42. Ibid., 38–39.

43. Mitchell, "Trauma, Recognition, and the Place of Language," 130.

44. Ibid., 131.

45. Gilmore, *The Limits of Autobiography*, 143. Evidence of posttrauma writers making use of such alternative jurisdictions can be seen in the autobiographically derived characters of Virginia Woolf's Lily Briscoe, Charles Dickens's David Copperfield, Ballard's Jim, Kerouac's Sal Paradise, and Alvarez's Yo-Yo among numerous others. See Meg Jensen, "Why Write Sad Stories? Post-traumatic Writers and the Problems of Representational Modes of Narration in Autobiographical Fiction," *Journal of Literature and Trauma Studies* 3, no. 1 (2014).

46. Celia Hunt, "Therapeutic Effects of Writing Fictional Autobiography," *Life Writing* 7, no. 3 (2010): 232.

47. Antonio Damasio, *The Feeling of What Happens: Body, Emotion, and the Making of Consciousness* (London: Vintage, 2000).

48. Hunt, "Therapeutic Effects of Writing Fictional Autobiography," 232.

49. Ibid., 240.

50. Ibid., 234–35.

51. Horowitz, "A Late Adventure of Feelings," 35.

52. Philippe Lejeune, *On Autobiography* (Minneapolis: University of Minnesota Press, 1989).

53. Hunt, "Therapeutic Effects of Writing Fictional Autobiography," 234.

54. Ibid., 232.

55. Butler, *Frames of War*, 59.

56. Ibid., 59–60.

57. Ibid., 61.

58. Ibid., 62.

WORKS CITED

Adorno, Theodor. "Elements of Anti-Semitism." In Theodor Adorno and Max Horkheimer, *Dialectic of Enlightenment*, translated by John Cumming, 168–208. 1944. Reprint, London: Verso, 1997.

——. *Prisms*. Translated by Samuel Weber and Shierry Weber. 6th ed. Cambridge, MA: MIT Press, 1967.

Alcoff, Linda, and Laura Gray. "Survivor Discourse: Transgression or Recuperation?" *Signs* 18, no. 2 (1993): 260–90.

Bernard-Donals, Michael. *Forgetful Memory: Representation and Remembrance in the Wake of the Holocaust*. Ithaca, NY: State University of New York Press, 2009.

Bonetti, Kay. "An Interview with Jamaica Kincaid." *Missouri Review* 25, no. 2 (2002). Accessed March 23, 2013. http://www.missourireview.com/archives/bbarticle /interview-with-jamaica-kincaid/.

Brown Golden, Kristen. "Trauma and Speech as Bodily Adaptation in Merleau-Ponty." In *The Trauma Controversy: Philosophical and Interdisciplinary Dialogues*, edited by Kristen

156

Brown Golden and Bettina G. Borgo, 71–98. Albany: State University of New York Press, 2009.

Butler, Judith. *Frames of War: When Is Life Grievable?* New York: Verso, 2009.

Caruth, Cathy. *Trauma: Explorations in Memory.* Baltimore: Johns Hopkins University Press, 1995.

———. *Unclaimed Experience: Trauma, Narrative, and History.* Baltimore: Johns Hopkins University Press, 1996.

Culbertson, Roberta. "Embodied Memory, Transcendence, and Telling: Recounting Trauma, Reestablishing the Self." *New Literary History* 26, no. 1 (1996): 169–95.

Damasio, Antonio. *The Feeling of What Happens: Body, Emotion, and the Making of Consciousness.* London: Vintage, 2000.

Doan, Carrie. "'Subversive Stories and Hegemonic Tales' of Child Sexual Abuse: From Expert Legal Testimony to Television Talk Shows." *International Journal of Law in Context* 1, vol. 3 (2005): 295–309.

Dobbs-Weinstein, Idit. "Trauma and the Impossibility of Experience." In *The Trauma Controversy: Philosophical and Interdisciplinary Dialogues*, edited by Kristen Brown Golden and Bettina G. Borgo, 99–114. Albany, NY: State University of New York Press, 2009.

Eakin, Paul John. *Living Autobiographically: How We Create Identity in Narrative.* Ithaca, NY: Cornell University Press, 2008.

Eichmann, Adolf. *The Trial of Adolf Eichmann: Record of Proceedings in the District Court of Jerusalem.* 9 vols. Jerusalem: Trust for the Publication of the Proceedings of the Eichmann Trial, 1992–1995.

The Eichmann Trial, Session 68, 69. Accessed January 2, 2013. http://www.youtube.com/watch?v=m3-tXyYhd5U.

Falkoff, Mark, ed. *Poems from Guantánamo: The Detainees Speak.* Iowa City: University of Iowa Press, 2007.

Felman, Shoshana. *The Juridical Unconscious: Trials and Traumas in the Twentieth Century.* Cambridge, MA: Harvard University Press, 2002.

Foucault, Michel. *Fearless Speech.* Edited by Joseph Pearson. Los Angeles: Semiotext(e), 2001.

Friedlander, Saul. *Memory, History, and the Extermination of the Jews in Europe.* Bloomington: Indiana University Press, 1993.

Gigliotti, Simone. *The Train Journey: Transit, Captivity, and Witnessing in the Holocaust.* New York: Berghahn, 2009.

Gilmore, Leigh. *The Limits of Autobiography.* Ithaca, NY: Cornell University Press, 2001.

Gouri, Haim. *Facing the Glass Booth: The Jerusalem Trial of Adolf Eichmann.* Translated by Michael Swirsky. Detroit: Wayne State University Press, 2004.

Hacking, Ian. *Rewriting the Soul: Multiple Personality and the Sciences of Memory.* Princeton, NJ: Princeton University Press, 1995.

Henke, Suzette, *Shattered Subjects: Trauma and Testimony in Women's Life Writing.* Basingstoke: Macmillan, 1998.

Horowitz, Gregg. "A Late Adventure of the Feelings: Loss, Trauma, and the Limits of Psychoanalysis." In *The Trauma Controversy: Philosophical and Interdisciplinary Dialogues*, edited by Kristen Brown Golden and Bettina G. Borgo, 23–44. Albany: State University of New York Press, 2009.

Hunt, Celia. "Therapeutic Effects of Writing Fictional Autobiography." *Life Writing* 7, no. 3 (2010): 231–44.

Jensen, Meg. "Why Write Sad Stories? Post-traumatic Writers and the Problems of Representational Modes of Narration in Autobiographical Fiction." *Journal of Literature and Trauma Studies* 3, no. 1 (2014).

Lejeune, Philippe. *On Autobiography*. Minneapolis: University of Minnesota Press, 1989.

Merleau-Ponty, Maurice. *Nature: Course Note from the College de France*. Translated by Robert Vallier. Evanston, IL: Northwestern University Press, 2003.

Mitchell, Juliet. "Trauma, Recognition, and the Place of Language." *Diacritics* 28, no. 4 (1998): 121–33.

Saunders, Max. *Self-Impression: Life Writing, Autobiografiction, and the Forms of Modern Literature*. Oxford: Oxford University Press, 2010.

Strickgold, Robert. "EMDR. A Putative Neurobiological Mechanism of Action." *Journal of Clinical Psychology* 58, no. 1 (2002): 61–75.

Wieviorka, Annette. *The Era of the Witness*. Translated by Jared Stark. Ithaca, NY: Cornell University Press, 2006.

Enter the King

Martin Luther King Jr., "Human Rights Heroism," and Contemporary American Drama

BRIAN PHILLIPS

Human rights awareness-raising and promotion frequently rely on the inspirational life story to engage large audiences and mobilize supporters for campaigning and advocacy. Not surprisingly, the dramatic lives of commanding figures in what Makau Mutua has termed the "grand narrative" of human rights history have proved especially attractive to artists intent on producing portraits of heroic struggle and moral example.[1] Over the past several decades, the film industry has notably mined the lives of several of these giants with varying degrees of success—from *Gandhi* (1982) and *Sakharov* (1984) to the more recent *Invictus* (2009), featuring Morgan Freeman as Nelson Mandela, and *The Lady* (2011), which dramatized the life of Aung San Suu Kyi. In 2009, three decades after the first broadcast of an American television miniseries called simply *King* (with Paul Winfield in the role of Martin Luther King Jr.—and with King's actress daughter, Yolanda, playing Rosa Parks), Steven Spielberg's DreamWorks studio announced plans for another King biopic, a film that the company claimed would be "the first theatrical motion picture to be authorized by The King Estate to utilize the intellectual property of Dr. King to create the definitive portrait of his life."[2] The question arises as to whether works such as these ought to present "human rights heroes" as candidates for a kind of sainthood or as complex and at times even flawed figures.[3] Do the requirements of inspiration for activism always necessitate a measure of avoidance of problematic aspects of the hero's character or awkward chapters of his or her life story? Or can the honest depiction of human fallibility render such figures more accessible—and therefore perhaps more likely to inspire emulation? And in our hyperpopulist age of reality television and ubiquitous video-recording devices—where, as Amnesty International Ireland asserts on its website, "everyone who makes a special effort to defend victims of human rights abuse is a hero"—what distinctive pedagogical purpose do we wish dramatizations of the tales of rights-defending titans to serve?[4]

The consolidation of Martin Luther King Jr.'s identity as a "human rights hero" has been a process at least as bewildering as it has been enlightening.[5] The past several decades have seen the elevation of King to the pantheon of official American icons—a period during which, as Manning Marable has argued, his "image evolved from an anti-Vietnam protestor and controversial civil rights advocate into a defender of a color-blind America."[6] Following the inauguration of Martin Luther King, Jr. Day as a national holiday in 1988, this sequence of state commemorations reached something of a climax with the dedication of the Martin Luther King, Jr. Memorial in Washington, DC, in October 2011. The story of that memorial's creation and the debate over the precise message to be communicated by its presence on the near sacred ground of the National Mall provides a remarkable case study in the possibilities and perils of translating a many-faceted human life (quite literally) into stone.[7]

But who is this rather stern, granite King who now stands across the Tidal Basin from slaveholder Thomas Jefferson, resplendent in his own memorial? Is he the man we know from what Derrick P. Aldridge has called "the three master narratives" of his life as embedded in many American history textbooks— "King as messiah, King as the embodiment of the civil rights movement, and King as a moderate"?[8] Or is he the King who as late as 1983 (during the US Senate debate on the proposal to make his birthday a national holiday) could still be reviled by North Carolina senator Jesse Helms as a man whose "action-oriented Marxism, about which he was cautioned by the leaders of this country at the time, is not compatible with the concepts of this country"?[9] In this second decade of the twenty-first century, how does a man described by Aldridge as "one of America's most radical and controversial leaders" come to be chosen by a megacorporation like Walmart (itself a major donor to the King Memorial) to serve as its gentler public face?[10] Walmart now regularly celebrates King—and the company's declared relationship with his ideals—in television advertisements and its claim in promotional material that "Dr. King believed everyone should have the opportunity to live a better life; a belief Walmart associates bring to life each day through our three Basic Beliefs":[11] "respect for the individual; service to our customers; striving for excellence."[12] This embrace of King the apostle of nonviolence and the fierce critic of American capitalism and militarism sits rather oddly with the company's much-criticized labor practices and its hugely profitable gun and ammunition sales.[13] Is all of this proof of what biographer Marshall Frady has suggested is the virtual disappearance of the real Martin Luther King Jr. into "the cloudy shimmers of a pop beatification" and is that vanishing act now irreversible?[14]

The immense theatrical potential of King's life story has long been recognized by playwrights, actors, and musicians.[15] Given the impending arrival of Spielberg's film portrait of King, with its lofty promise of definitiveness, critical reflection on three especially thought-provoking American plays about King that appeared in 2008 and 2009 is warranted. Michael Murphy's *The Conscientious Objector* (2008), Tracey Scott Wilson's *The Good Negro* (2009), and Katori Hall's *The Mountaintop* (2009) all had their premieres while the King Memorial in Washington was moving from design to completion. What makes this trio of plays particularly worthy of attention is that each attempts to avoid the pitfalls of the standard King hagiography and offer a much subtler treatment of the life story of the "human rights hero" than this burgeoning genre usually affords. Each of the plays engages imaginatively with the superabundance of contemporary scholarship on King and the familiar civil rights campaigns in which he played such a profound part. The best of this more recent academic literature inserts the King narrative into the history of a much wider and lengthier American "black freedom struggle" (to use historian Clayborne Carson's more inclusive phrase), a shift that has necessarily complicated King's life story and freed the man from at least some of the dead weight of unthinking reverence.[16] Central to that literature has been a more balanced, nuanced appreciation of King's admittedly mighty but far from solitary historical contribution. This expansive body of work has launched a sustained assault on those distorted aspects of the "master narrative" of the movement that have inflated King's role as a *national* leader and traditionally given his Southern Christian Leadership Conference (SCLC) a misleading pride of place within the *multiplicity* of organizations, initiatives, and equally laudable individuals across the United States that actually enabled social and political progress throughout the country.

Especially noteworthy in this new historiography of the black freedom struggle has been the boom in local studies, resulting in a plethora of place-specific chronicles of activism and reaction that have enriched and diversified our understanding of African American resistance to Jim Crow in the South and likewise to the deep structural inequalities persisting in cities of the North and West.[17] Similarly, there has been a new emphasis in this black freedom struggle scholarship on "shifting the frame so that women become more central to our analysis, not just fuzzy objects on the periphery,"[18] providing overdue redress for the many women who were typically relegated to supporting roles in the classic civil rights blockbuster narrative that almost always gave Dr. King and his male colleagues top billing.[19]

Peniel E. Joseph has recently described the way in which what he terms "the heroic period" of the civil rights movement (1954–65) "has been strategically appropriated by the state to deliver sanitized images that extol the resilicncc of democratic liberalism."[20] Likewise, in the interests of establishing King as a conventionally patriotic hero whose greatness arises chiefly—if not exclusively—from his charismatic pastoral role in the Deep South during that tightly bounded period, American memorializing narratives about King often quite pointedly choose to ignore what Joseph calls his "subsequent leftward political metamorphosis." In Joseph's view, "the pervasive image of King in contemporary American popular culture is that of an African-American minister preaching from the steps of the nation's capital, exhorting the disenfranchised in attendance to dream of a truly democratic society."[21] To secure that reductive, more comfortable image of King the Great American, the notably more astringent, later chapters of King's witness against American militarism and economic injustice in the second half of the 1960s are therefore much less likely to be incorporated into these conveniently selective accounts of his life and work.

Michael Murphy's *The Conscientious Objector* casts a welcome spotlight on King's too-often-neglected critical stand on the Vietnam War. This finely crafted play charts King's opposition to America's anticommunist interventions in Southeast Asia as his views evolved and deepened during the last three years of his life. Murphy presents the two defining moments of King's provocative engagement with the tragic conflict—his 1965 foray into public criticism of the Johnson administration's escalating involvement in Indochina and then King's more comprehensive critique of American foreign policy and his open embrace of the antiwar movement in 1967. Coinciding with Johnson's careful shepherding of crucial civil rights bills through Congress, newly anointed Nobel Peace Prize laureate King's initial statements calling the wisdom of American involvement in Vietnam into question are met with painful rcbukes from the media, Washington politicians, and even members of King's own staff and the leaders of other African American organizations. As Murphy makes plain in the play, King is attacked vehemently for venturing into territory lying well beyond what are understood to be the parameters of the civil rights struggle and outside the boundaries of his theological authority. And as a wounded Johnson himself emphasizes in a key scene in the play's first half, King's harsh words about the administration's policies half a world away (which many, including some of King's colleagues, also think looks rather like ingratitude toward the man who had proved to be the movement's "best friend" in the White House) could very well put at serious risk the prospects for further legislation securing the rights of African Americans at home. Slapped down forcefully by all around him, King steps back from the Vietnam debate for a time.

But by the spring of 1967, King is compelled to give stronger voice to his fierce concern that an unwinnable conflict is becoming a relentless drain on resources for Johnson's stalling War on Poverty. King's mounting righteous anger propels him to speak more boldly about the fact that a disproportionate number of poor African American young men are being shipped out to fight a dubious war for freedoms they cannot yet be fully guaranteed at home. Grounded in his self-understanding as a witness to the Christian gospel of peace, King's still astonishing (and too little known and quoted) April 1967 speech at the Riverside Church in New York brings a dramatic end to his self-imposed reticence.[22] That prophetic address is swiftly followed by King's appearance at an antiwar rally held in front of the United Nations headquarters. There he shares a platform with the likes of Stokely Carmichael and others who articulate what is seen to be a patently revolutionary political agenda. King's Riverside address and demo speech strain his relationship with Johnson to a breaking point. "That goddam nigga preacher! Gonna get me thrown outta office," bellows Murphy's LBJ on the morning after the Riverside jeremiad. "And after all I done for his people"![23] King's no-holds-barred condemnation of the Johnson administration foreign policy further fuels FBI director J. Edgar Hoover's determination to unmask him as a wily communist sympathizer whose subversion must be stopped. A very public clash on Vietnam with Urban League executive director and erstwhile movement colleague Whitney Young underlines King's feelings of terrible isolation from those whose companionship and support he had counted on since his beginnings in Montgomery, Alabama, more than a decade before. In the play's searing final scene, Murphy conjures up a broken LBJ and an equally tormented King joining together in a prayer for forgiveness—the president for his multiplying failures in Vietnam and King for what he fears is the ultimate futility of his own quest for full political *and* social and economic rights for his African American brothers and sisters.

With regard to the frequently excised, more radical strands of King's trajectory through the later half of the 1960s, Murphy's engrossing play can be seen as a kind of restoration drama—determinedly bringing back into the heart of the life story line "the totality of the vision of a truly democratic, poverty-free and peaceful society that King vigorously called for during his later years."[24] Murphy is writing very much *against* the heroic grain here, and in that illuminating last episode of King and LBJ's mutual confession he returns to us something of the massively conflicted man who was wont to say near the end of his journey, "I am tired of demonstrating. I am tired of the threat of death. I want to live. I don't want to be a martyr. And there are moments when I doubt if I am going to make it through. . . . I don't march because I want to. I march because I must."[25]

During the past three decades, numerous studies of King and the SCLC have explored in precise and sometimes unsettling detail his hugely complicated relationship to women. These include discussions of King's deep-seated patriarchal views on marriage and family life, as well as examinations of the corrosive power dynamics within the wider black freedom movement—structures and strategies that frequently marginalized and routinely left underappreciated the very different movement leadership styles and vastly important contributions of the likes of Septima Clark and Ella Baker.[26] King's philandering (as well as that of others in his milieu) has been extensively discussed and debated by scholars seeking to grasp how he was "both tortured by his adultery and awkwardly comforted by its serial anonymities and episodic thrills."[27] The prevailing sexism in the black freedom movement of the 1950s and 1960s and the very male culture of King's surrounding circle of pastors—a fraternity given to viewing "sexual adventure as a natural condition of manhood, or of great preachers obsessed by love, or of success, or of Negroes otherwise constrained by the white world"—has now become an integral part of the story of King as a subject of scholarly scrutiny, if not of King as the monument on the National Mall.[28]

Both Tracey Scott Wilson and Katori Hall have chosen to tackle head-on this decidedly less than heroic dimension of King's life and work in their recent plays. In *The Good Negro*, Wilson's choice to fictionalize her exploration of the personality of a King-like figure and his band of close associates (including characters bearing a distinct likeness to Ralph Abernathy and Bayard Rustin) allows her the freedom to blend into one setting a range of historic debates, interpersonal conflicts, and organizational challenges with which King's SCLC was contending during the second half of the 1950s and the early 1960s. The play finds Wilson's King character, James Lawrence, floundering in a still segregated Birmingham, Alabama, in the movement's uncertain early days. The nonviolent campaign that Lawrence has been leading to break the city's entrenched discriminatory practices is running low on inspiration, energy, and visibility—much as the efforts of King and his lesser-known but essential local partner, Fred Shuttlesworth, had run into similar troubles in Birmingham in the spring of 1963.[29] The arrest and detention of a young mother, Claudette Sullivan, after she takes her four-year-old daughter into a "Whites Only" rest room in a downtown department store suddenly offer the moribund campaign a fresh and much sought for opportunity to mobilize public outrage at the quotidian indignities facing the city's African American residents. Furthermore, the unassailable respectability of this young mother appears to make this the perfect appeal case on which to hang the movement's broader agenda of achieving equality and dignity. Much as Rosa Parks had been deemed by the National Association for the Advancement of Colored People (NAACP) in Montgomery to be exactly the kind of upstanding citizen required to become the catalyst for the transformational 1955–56 bus boycott, Sullivan here is seen to embody the ideal of "the good Negro" of Wilson's title.[30] Nevertheless, suspicions about the "worthiness" of Claudette Sullivan's husband, Pelzie—and Pelzie's own reluctance to submit to the possible dangers involved in becoming the movement's "poster family"—threaten the plans of Lawrence and his front-line associates. When the Sullivans' daughter, Shelley, dies in a Ku Klux Klan firebomb attack on their home, the terrible costs of placing this family at the center of the movement's strategy for social change and the startling inadequacy of what Pelzie dismisses as "preacher talk" in the wake of unbearable loss are made agonizingly clear to Lawrence.[31] In an anguished appeal for Pelzie's understanding at the child's funeral, Lawrence laments, "The whole world is watching. They are waiting for us to fuck it up. They are waiting for us to talk wrong, walk wrong, be wrong and then they can say, 'See? Look at them niggers. No better than animals. No better. I told you so.'"[32]

What makes Wilson's script so compelling as a modern morality play is that at the same time that she underlines the movement leadership's painstaking efforts to run a carefully choreographed campaign grounded in impeccable integrity and right, she also puts onstage the FBI's simultaneous endeavors to discredit Lawrence and his circle through the surveillance and exposure of some of their less than admirable private activities. The wiretapping FBI agents in the play are suitably repulsive figures, to be sure. But Wilson jams our customary wish to see the "good guys" as uncompromising exemplars of the highest moral standards by making it very clear that the attraction Lawrence and his sidekick, Henry Evans (an Abernathy-like lieutenant), feel for the young Mrs. Sullivan is indeed more than just an appreciation of her virtue and her courageous stand against segregation—and that the eager pursuit of an opportunity to marry rights talk with a little roguishness is entirely characteristic of this ministerial duo.

In one of the play's most powerful scenes, mirroring the story of J. Edgar Hoover's obsession with exposing King as a "tomcat" through FBI tape recordings of some of his sexual indulgences,[33] Wilson has Lawrence's wife, Corinne

(Wilson's stand-in for Coretta Scott King), confront her husband with the ugly proof of his womanizing. After Corinne listens to a blistering mixed tape sent to her by agents bent on her husband's destruction, Lawrence pleads for his wife's recognition of the root causes of his straying. He begs Corinne to see that "sometimes I just can't think straight and I go with these other women. . . . I'm afraid I'll be alone when they take me, alone in my bed, some hotel somewhere. I don't want to die alone, Corinne."[34] But Wilson's Corinne refuses to play the all-forgiving helpmate here—heaping scorn on Lawrence's banal "but it's you I really love" proclamations and asking, "How am I going to get this out of my head, Jimmy? How am I going to go on now ignoring things? Pretending you're not a dog?" When Lawrence pleads, "don't let that tape destroy us . . . that's what they want. That's why they sent it," Corinne insists on her husband's primary responsibility for the crisis: "You're destroying us, Jimmy. You! Not anybody else. You! That's why this movement is all messed up, 'cause you all messed up. Screwing your congregation, rubbing up against anything that moves. Acting just like the coons they say we are." When an ever more desperate Lawrence tries to play the loneliness of the long distance campaigner card at the close of this riveting exchange, Corinne simply replies: "I got lonely, too, James. All the time. All the time. But there's no tape of me out there, is there?"[35]

On the evidence of this wonderfully unsparing and unresolved scene, neither an understanding of the formative influences of traditional, male, African American preacher culture nor even the excuse of a hunted civil rights crusader's very real fears of annihilation appear to cut much ice with Wilson. In writing so forthrightly about the sexual indiscretions of movement leaders, Wilson (herself the daughter of an African American minister) recalled in an interview having to wrestle herself free of the kind of unquestioned veneration of King that surrounded her during her childhood—and of the attendant taboo on discussing aspects of King's personality that might introduce disruptive contradictions into his biography. She said, "I was always told as a child that you don't air your dirty laundry. It was 'Don't throw it out there, because white people already think the worst of us.'" But in writing the play, Wilson talks of experiencing "a revelation that what these people did in the civil rights movement was extraordinary because they had all these flaws. They weren't these saints—they had trouble forgiving, they had trouble with their marriages, they had trouble with drinking—yet every day they made the decision to keep going. To me that's inspirational, so I hope I'm honoring them by showing that complexity. When you show them as saints, it just seems easy."

In another take on this tangled, unheroic narrative of side-by-side justice seeking and rakishness, Katori Hall's *The Mountaintop* recasts King's last night on earth in Room 306 of Memphis's Lorraine Motel as a tumultuous encounter between an exhausted, frightened King—pining for his children and wracked with doubts about his past and his future—and a blowtorch of a "beautiful young maid," whose delivery of a cup of coffee to the weary preacher sets in motion a series of spectacular cosmic events.[36] This woman, Camae, utterly disarming and candid to a fault, brings more than room service to a beleaguered Dr. King—a man desperate for the instant comforts of caffeine, cigarettes, and just possibly a bit of the illicit sex with a stranger, which torments him with guilt even as he seeks the momentary solace offered by the kind of woman who can "make a man forget about it all."[37] After a series of flirtations and fiery exchanges with King on everything from movement tactics to the allure of Malcolm X's incandescent rage, Camae is eventually revealed to be nothing less than the angel assigned to bring King to his heavenly rest after his immanent assassination on the motel's balcony. As the play begins, King has just returned from delivering his shattering "Promised Land" speech to striking Memphis sanitation workers and their supporters.[38] For King their cause provides something of a curtain raiser for his forthcoming Poor People's Campaign, a coalition of impoverished Americans that he intends to lead on a march to Washington in the months to come. But perpetual death threats and an unending barrage of criticism of his preferred strategies for nonviolent change have ground King down to the brink of physical and emotional collapse—his spirit as washed out as the tatty furnishings of the dreary motel room in which he will pass this final day. Once Camae reveals her true identity and discloses the fate that awaits him in the hours ahead, King begs for additional time to complete more of the worldly mission to which he feels he has been called. But Camae holds fast to the heavenly line set down by her employer—a God who turns out to be an all-powerful She—and insists that King must prepare to take his leave. As a parting gift, however, Camae and the Almighty She permit King a glimpse into the future, a last look from the mountaintop, as it were, so that he might view something of his earthly legacy and the complex, joyful-sorrowful unfolding of African American life in the decades following his death.

Hall's play certainly succeeds in providing another corrective to any lingering conceptions of King as a uniformly larger than life, well-nigh holy individual unshakably rooted in his rock-solid faith. At its strongest moments, *The Mountaintop* pushes us that much farther away from any vision of King as a man whose belief in the indisputable rightness of his cause meant that he was always sure of his next steps as the "father" of the movement—serenely progressing from one glorious conquest of hatred and inequality to another. As in Murphy's and Wilson's plays, King here is a haunted man whose aching awareness of his limitations in his role and constant reminders of his own mortality strike at the very core of his being. "Fear has become my companion, my lover," King tells Camae as she unfolds God's terrible plan for him in Memphis. "I know the touch of fear, even more than I know the touch of my own wife's" [*sic*].[39] Hall's skill at underlining King's vulnerability, his yearning to escape the sheer awfulness of martyrdom, is unquestionably moving here. Here, too, are the unreformed attitudes toward women and the habitual roving eye. King chides Coretta in a phone call for forgetting to pack his toothbrush, displays more than a little vanity as he frets over his looks ("My physical appearance is important. To the people"), and consults Camae on whether his manly appeal might be decreasing with age. And when Camae suggests that on her arrival at his motel room, "a blind man coulda seen't the way you was borin' holes through my clothes"—King can only acknowledge the accuracy of Camae's spot-on reading of that moment.[10] The previously discussed critique of the stranglehold placed on the black freedom movement by a dominant male leadership style also has its welcome place in the sparring between King and Camae. When a proud King beseeches Camae to postpone the next day's assassination on account of his self-declared indispensability to the movement and its crucial next phase ("There's just so much I gotta do. So much I haven't yet accomplished"), his blunt guardian angel comes back at him with ego-slashing words that might have come straight from the mouths of countless women left in the shadows of movement history: "It ain't all about you. You! You! Gosh, you men are so selfish. They always think it's 'bout them. . . . Well, let me tell you something, Preacher Kang. Let me tell you! Like most men, you ain't gone be able to finish what you started."[41]

But for all the apparent boldness of Hall's playful metaphysical aspirations in the play's second half—where Camae informs King that the God to whom she answers and to whom he prays is both a proud, beautiful black woman *and* "a fuuuunnny-ass muthafucka," *The Mountaintop* somehow lacks the real moral heft of Wilson's work as it pulses with life in gripping scenes like the one in which Corinne (Coretta) demands accountability from her wayward husband. Introducing celestial beings into any drama is always something of a risk—too often a cue either for an irritating jokiness about the nature of God, angels, and the Great Beyond (and Hall doesn't entirely escape that trap when King and Camae have a pillow fight and King gets to chat with God on her cell phone) or for a dose of the kind of inflated rhetoric (see also the weaker moments in Tony Kushner's *Angels in America*) that sometimes mistakes pomposity for insight. The poetic grandeur that Hall reaches for in the concluding moments of the play, as Camae narrates Martin's sneak preview of African American life at the close of the last century and the start of the Obama era, feels strained and self-consciously monumental—generating precisely that stifling commemorative quality ("The baton passes on / And on and on / Till the break of dawn / For the American song / We shall overcome") that in so many moments in the play Hall has worked so hard to avoid.[42]

In *The Mountaintop*, Hall obviously wants to shake audiences up by showing us King the monument live and uncut and unbuttoned—and in dangerously sexy dialogue with a "cussin', fussin', drankin' angel" like Camae.[43] But what is meant to be combustible in that meeting feels oddly familiar, even tame, somehow. Camae too often comes across as the cartoonish, stereotypical, feisty young black woman who calls things as she sees them—a figure we have met many times before in popular entertainment extending back at least as far as Flip Wilson's Geraldine character from late 1960s American television. The problem, then, is that Camae just isn't dangerous *enough* to really transport the play—and us—anywhere genuinely new. As the critic Ben Brantley has rightly suggested, this "is at heart a comfort play, a nursery room fable for grown-ups that seeks to reconcile us with a tragedy that tore the fabric of a nation."[44] At the play's eleventh hour, Hall gives Camae a last big monologue in which she suddenly shifts register—expressing to King her bitter regrets about her sordid earthly life as she recounts her violent death and subsequent cleansing by a merciful God the Mother. But this last-minute flare of real feeling comes too late in that long night in Room 306 to move us as it should. Despite the stark confession of sin and the harrowing tale of redemption told here, Camae remains a kind of cutout angel, a construct rather than an unnerving flesh and blood character who might have both liberated King from the bloodless confines of commemorative encasement *and* offered us something really revelatory about a man whose true greatness was inextricably linked to his vast and devouring fears.

Complementing the new historiography on King and the black freedom movement, these three plays add up to a significant artistic counterweight to a uniquely American instance of the "human rights heroism" phenomenon that has increasingly sealed up King in the sarcophagus of national myth—a space where, as Frady argues, "the man himself has been abstracted out of his swelteringly convoluted actuality into a kind of weightless and reverently laminated effigy of who he was."[45] But surely far from diminishing the man, recent scholarship and closely related plays such as these enable us to value anew King's galvanizing role in the struggle with an informed, more appropriate combination of praise *and* measure. As Charles Payne has written: "Insisting that the movement was larger than Dr. King does him no dishonor. . . . Perhaps the most important point to remember about King is not that he 'led' the movement but that the movement gave him a platform from which he could appeal to the long-slumbering angels of our better nature, which he did as well as any leader of his time, probably better. That is honor enough."[46] Excitingly, these three recent American plays about King allow us to track the ways in which the insights and imperatives of this new and richer historiography are now filtering through to cultural forms like theater—as one hopes they will in turn influence future film projects concerning the movement as well. The writing and performing of these plays undoubtedly help confound the official version of King's story. Murphy's and Wilson's exemplary works in particular (and even Hall's play with its many flaws) do not merely fortify scholarly efforts to rescue King from narratives that seek to make him "an icon for the status quo or a puppet of civil and social order."[47] For those involved in cultural production, they also point toward strategies for articulating more authentic life stories of "human rights heroism" that provide powerful narratives of commitment and personal sacrifice—and at the same time take seriously a responsibility for complex historical truths.

NOTES

1. Makau Mutua, *Human Rights: A Political and Cultural Critique* (Philadelphia: University of Pennsylvania Press, 2002), 15.

2. DreamWorks Studios, "Oscar Winner Ronald Harwood to Write Martin Luther King, Jr. Story for DreamWorks Studios," accessed January 17, 2013, http://www.dreamworksstudios.com/news/oscar-winner-ronald-harwood-to-write-martin-luther-king-jr-story-for-dreamworks-studios. See also DreamWorks Studios, "Martin Luther King, Jr. Bio Set for Big Screen," accessed February 3, 2013, http://www.dreamworksstudios.com/news/martin-luther-king-jr-bio-set-for-bigscreen.

3. While it may be impossible to discover the precise origin of the phrase "human rights hero," a simple web search reveals that it is now widely used as a category. Such a search reveals its use by, among others, Amnesty International USA, the Carter Center, the International Gay and Lesbian Human Rights Commission, the British nongovernmental organization Liberty, and the Robert F. Kennedy Center for Justice and Human Rights.

4. Amnesty International Ireland, "Amnesty International Ireland—Gallery of Human Rights Heroes," accessed January 28, 2013, http://www.amnesty.ie/node/1587.

5. For a stimulating overview of this process, see especially Michael Eric Dyson, *I May Not Get There with You: The True Martin Luther King, Jr.* (New York: Simon and Schuster, 2000).

6. Manning Marable, *Malcolm X: A Life of Reinvention* (New York: Viking, 2011), 483.

7. For the full story of the creation of the King Memorial, see chapter 19 in Clayborne Carson, *Martin's Dream: My Journey and the Legacy of Martin Luther King, Jr.* (New York: Palgrave Macmillan, 2013).

8. Derrick P. Aldridge, "The Limits of Master Narratives in History Textbooks: An Analysis of Representations of Martin Luther King, Jr.," *Teachers College Record* 108, no. 4 (2006): 664.

9. Helen Dewar, "Helms Stalls King's Day in Senate," *Washington Post*, October 4, 1983, accessed January 28, 2013, http://www.washingtonpost.com/wp-srv/opinions/articles/helms_stalls_kings_day.html.

10. Aldridge, "The Limits of Master Narratives," 680; "Walmart Supports Martin Luther King, Jr. National Memorial," accessed January 24, 2013, http://washingtondc.walmartcommunity.com/walmart-supports-martin-luther-king-jr-national-memorial.

11. "Walmart Supports Martin Luther King, Jr. National Memorial."

12. "Walmart Statement of Ethics: Our 3 Basic Beliefs," accessed January 28, 2013, http://ethics.walmartstores.com/StatementOfEthics/BasicBeliefs.aspx.

13. See, for example, Steven Greenhouse and Stephanie Clifford, "Protests Backed by Union Get Wal-Mart's Attention," *New York Times*, November 18, 2012, accessed February 3, 2013, http://www.nytimes.com/2012/11/19/business/wal-mart-files-with-nlrb-to-block-union-backed-protests.html?_r=0; and George Zornick, "How Walmart Helped Make the Newtown Shooter's AR-15 the Most Popular Assault Weapon in America," *The Nation*, December 19, 2012, accessed February 3, 2013, http://www.thenation.com/article/171808/how-walmart-helped-make-newtown-shooters-ar-15-most-popular-assault-weapon-america.

14. Marshall Frady, *Martin Luther King, Jr.* (New York: Viking, 2002), 6.

15. Theatrical presentations of King's life and work extend at least as far back as Billy Dee Williams playing him in a 1976 Broadway production (combining music and the spoken word) called *I Have A Dream*, and have continued through actor Craig Alan Edwards's one-man show about King, *The Man in Room 306* (performed off-Broadway in 2010). Elsewhere, King scholar Clayborne Carson's *Passages of Martin Luther King*—originally presented at Stanford University in 1993—has subsequently been staged at the National Theatre of China in Beijing (2007) and by Al Hakawati, the National Theatre of Palestine, in Jerusalem and the West Bank (2011). For a fascinating account of those Chinese and Palestinian productions, see chapters 20 and 21 in Carson, *Martin's Dream*. Less conventionally, in 2007 the New York–based performance group Waterwell mounted a musical exploration of the last year of King's life called *The/King/Operetta*—complete with a scene where King's archnemesis, Federal Bureau of Investigation (FBI) director J. Edgar Hoover, turns up as a drag act.

16. Clayborne Carson, quoted in Emilye Crosby, "The Politics of Writing and Teaching Movement History," in *Civil Rights History from the Ground Up: Local Struggles, a National Movement*, ed. Emilye Crosby (Athens: University of Georgia Press, 2011), 12.

17. See, for example, Steven F. Lawson and Charles Payne, *Debating the Civil Rights Movement, 1945–1968*, 2nd ed. (Lanham, MD: Rowman and Littlefield, 2006);Wesley C. Hogan, *Many Minds, One Heart: SNCC's Dream for a New America* (Chapel Hill: University of North Carolina Press, 2007); Emilye Crosby, ed., *Civil Rights History from the Ground Up: Local Struggles, a National Movement* (Athens: University of Georgia Press, 2011); and Manning Marable and Elizabeth Kai Hinton, eds., *The New Black History: Revisiting the Second Reconstruction* (New York: Palgrave Macmillan, 2011).

18. Crosby, "The Politics of Writing and Teaching Movement History," 25.

19. See, for example, Dyson, *I May Not Get There with You*, 155–74; Jeanne Theoharis, "Accidental Matriarchs and Beautiful Helpmates: Rosa Parks, Coretta Scott King, and the Memorialization of the Civil Rights Movement," in *Civil Rights History from the Ground Up: Local Struggles, a National Movement*, ed. Emilye Crosby (Athens: University of Georgia Press, 2011); Crosby, "The Politics of Teaching and Writing Movement History"; and Stephen Lazar, "Septima Clark: Organizing for Positive Freedom," in *The New Black History: Revisiting the Second Reconstruction*, ed. Manning Marable and Elizabeth Kai Hinton (New York: Palgrave Macmillan, 2011).

20. Peniel E. Joseph, "Waiting Till the Midnight Hour: Reconceptualizing the Heroic Period of the Civil Rights Movement, 1954–65," in *The New Black History: Revisiting the Second Reconstruction*, ed. Manning Marable and Elizabeth Kai Hinton (New York: Palgrave Macmillan, 2011), 158.

21. Ibid.

22. For the text of King's Riverside Church speech, see Martin Luther King Jr., "A Time to Break Silence," in *The Eyes on the Prize Civil Rights Reader*, ed. Clayborne Carson et al. (New York: Penguin Books, 1991), 387–92.

23. Michael Murphy, *The Conscientious Objector* (New York: Dramatists Play Service, 2009), 31.

24. Aldridge, "The Limits of Master Narratives," 679–80.

25. Frady, *Martin Luther King, Jr.*, 189–90.

26. See, for example, Dyson, *I May Not Get There with You*, 155–74; Theoharis, "Accidental Matriarchs and Beautiful Helpmates"; Crosby, "The Politics of Teaching and Writing Movement History"; Lazar, "Septima Clark"; and James H. Cone, *Martin and Malcolm and America: A Dream or a Nightmare* (Maryknoll, NY: Orbis Books, 2012), 272–87.

27. Dyson, *I May Not Get There with You*, 161. See also Taylor Branch, *Parting the Waters: America in the King Years, 1954–63* (New York: Simon and Schuster, 1988), 859–62; and Frady, *Martin Luther King, Jr.*, 62–67, 130–33.

28. Branch, *Parting the Waters*, 860.

29. Frady, *Martin Luther King, Jr.*, 98–118.

30. Branch, *Parting the Waters*, 120–36.

31. Tracey Scott Wilson, *The Good Negro* (New York: Dramatists Play Service, 2010), 80.

32. Ibid., 81.

33. Branch, *Parting the Waters*, 859–62; Dyson, *I May Not Get There with You*, 155–74; Frady, *Martin Luther King, Jr.*, 130–33.

34. Wilson, *The Good Negro*, 64.

35. Ibid., 65.

36. Katori Hall, *The Mountaintop* (London: Methuen Drama, 2011), 7.

37. Ibid., 31.

38. For a detailed history of this campaign, see Michael K. Honey, *Going Down Jericho Road: The Memphis Strike, Martin Luther King's Last Campaign* (New York: Norton, 2007).

39. Hall, *The Mountaintop*, 39.

40. Ibid., 15, 19.

41. Ibid., 44.

42. Ibid., 28.

43. Ibid., 37.

44. Ben Brantley, "April 3, 1968. Lorraine Motel. Evening," *New York Times*, October 13, 2011, accessed January 31, 2013, http://theater.nytimes.com/2011/10/14/theater /reviews/the-mountaintop-with-samuel-l-jackson-angela-bassett.html.

45. Frady, *Martin Luther King, Jr.*, 7.

46. Charles Payne, "Debating the Civil Rights Movement: The View from the Trenches," in *Debating the Civil Rights Movement, 1945–1968*, 2nd ed., ed. Steven F. Lawson and Charles Payne (Lanham, MD: Rowman and Littlefield, 2006), 154–55.

47. Dyson, *I May Not Get There with You*, 305.

WORKS CITED

Aldridge, Derek P. "The Limits of Master Narratives in History Textbooks: An Analysis of Representations of Martin Luther King, Jr." *Teachers College Record* 108, no. 4 (2006): 662–86.

Amnesty International Ireland. "Amnesty International Ireland—Gallery of Human Rights Heroes." Accessed January 28, 2013. http://www.amnesty.ie/node/1587.

Blankenship, Mark. "Civil Rights, and Wrongs, in Alabama." *New York Times*, March 1, 2009. Accessed January 17, 2013. http://theater.nytimes.com/2009/03/01/theater /01Blan.html?_r=0.

Branch, Taylor. *Parting the Waters: America in the King Years, 1954–63*. New York: Simon and Schuster, 1988.

Brantley, Ben. "April 3, 1968. Lorraine Motel. Evening." *New York Times*, October 13, 2011. Accessed January 31, 2013. http://theater.nytimes.com/2011/10/14/theater /reviews/the-mountaintop-with-samuel-l-jackson-angela-bassett.html.

Carson, Clayborne. *Martin's Dream: My Journey and the Legacy of Martin Luther King, Jr.* New York: Palgrave Macmillan, 2013.

Cone, James H. *Martin and Malcolm and America: A Dream or a Nightmare*. Maryknoll, NY: Orbis Books, 2012.

Crosby, Emilye, ed. *Civil Rights History from the Ground Up: Local Struggles, a National Movement*. Athens: University of Georgia Press, 2011.

———. "The Politics of Writing and Teaching Movement History." In *Civil Rights History from the Ground Up: Local Struggles, a National Movement*, edited by Emilye Crosby, 1–39. Athens: University of Georgia Press, 2011.

Dewar, Helen. "Helms Stalls King's Day in Senate." *Washington Post*, October 4, 1983. Accessed January 28, 2013. http://www.washingtonpost.com/wp-srv/opinions/articles/helms_stalls_kings_day.html.

DreamWorks Studios. "Martin Luther King, Jr. Bio Set for Big Screen." Accessed February 3, 2013. http://www.dreamworksstudios.com/news/martin-luther-king-jr-bio-set-for-bigscreen.

———. "Oscar Winner Ronald Harwood to Write Martin Luther King, Jr. Story for DreamWorks Studios." Accessed January 17, 2013. http://www.dreamworksstudios.com/news/oscar-winner-ronald-harwood-to-write-martin-luther-king-jr-story-for-dreamworks-studios.

Dyson, Michael Eric. *I May Not Get There with You: The True Martin Luther King, Jr.* New York: Simon and Schuster, 2000.

Frady, Marshall. *Martin Luther King, Jr.* New York: Viking, 2002.

Greenhouse, Steven, and Stephanie Clifford. "Protests Backed by Union Get Wal-Mart's Attention." *New York Times*, November 18, 2012. Accessed February 3, 2013. http://www.nytimes.com/2012/11/19/business/wal-mart-files-with-nlrb-to-block-union-backed-protests.html?_r=0.

Hall, Katori. *The Mountaintop*. London: Methuen Drama, 2011.

Hogan, Wesley C. *Many Minds, One Heart: SNCC's Dream for a New America*. Chapel Hill: University of North Carolina Press, 2007.

Honey, Michael K. *Going Down Jericho Road: The Memphis Strike, Martin Luther King's Last Campaign*. New York: Norton, 2007.

Joseph, Peniel E. "Waiting Till the Midnight Hour: Reconceptualizing the Heroic Period of the Civil Rights Movement, 1954–65." In *The New Black History: Revisiting the Second Reconstruction*, edited by Manning Marable and Elizabeth Kai Hinton, 157–68. New York: Palgrave Macmillan, 2011.

King, Martin Luther, Jr. "A Time to Break Silence." In *The Eyes on the Prize Civil Rights Reader*, edited by Clayborne Carson, David J. Garrow, Gerald Gill, Vincent Harding, and Darlene Clark Hine, 387–92. New York: Penguin Books, 1991.

Lawson, Steven F., and Charles Payne. *Debating the Civil Rights Movement, 1945–1968*, 2nd ed. Lanham, MD: Rowman and Littlefield, 2006.

Lazar, Stephen. "Septima Clark: Organizing for Positive Freedom." In *The New Black History: Revisiting the Second Reconstruction*, edited by Manning Marable and Elizabeth Kai Hinton, 231–41. New York: Palgrave Macmillan, 2011.

Marable, Manning. *Malcolm X: A Life of Reinvention*. New York: Viking, 2011.

Marable, Manning, and Elizabeth Kai Hinton, eds. *The New Black History: Revisiting the Second Reconstruction*. New York: Palgrave Macmillan, 2011.

Murphy, Michael. *The Conscientious Objector*. New York: Dramatists Play Service, 2009.

Mutua, Makau. *Human Rights: A Political and Cultural Critique*. Philadelphia: University of Pennsylvania Press, 2002.

Payne, Charles. "Debating the Civil Rights Movement: The View from the Trenches." In *Debating the Civil Rights Movement, 1945–1968*, 2nd ed., edited by Steven F. Lawson and Charles Payne, 99–138. Lanham, MD: Rowman and Littlefield, 2006.

Theoharis, Jeanne. "Accidental Matriarchs and Beautiful Helpmates: Rosa Parks, Coretta Scott King, and the Memorialization of the Civil Rights Movement." In *Civil Rights History from the Ground Up: Local Struggles, a National Movement*, edited by Emilye Crosby, 385–418. Athens: University of Georgia Press, 2011.

"Walmart Supports Martin Luther King, Jr. National Memorial." Accessed January 24, 2013. http://washingtondc.walmartcommunity.com/walmart-supports-martin-luther-king-jr-national-memorial.

"Walmart Statement of Ethics: Our 3 Basic Beliefs." Accessed January 28, 2013. http://ethics.walmartstores.com/StatementOfEthics/BasicBeliefs.aspx.

Wilson, Tracey Scott. *The Good Negro*. New York: Dramatists Play Service, 2010.

Zornick, George. "How Walmart Helped Make the Newtown Shooter's AR-15 the Most Popular Assault Weapon in America." *The Nation*, December 19, 2012. Accessed February 3, 2013. http://www.thenation.com/article/171808/how-walmart-helped-make-newtown-shooters-ar-15-most-popular-assault-weapon-america.

Témoignage and Responsibility in Photo/Graphic Narratives of Médecins Sans Frontières

ALEXANDRA SCHULTHEIS MOORE

Médecins Sans Frontières/Doctors without Borders (hereafter MSF) emerged in 1971 out of its founders' (both doctors and journalists) medical aid work on behalf of those caught in the Nigerian civil war and a major flood in what is now Bangladesh. A legacy of its founders, MSF's distinguishing feature, according to its mission statement, has been its dual commitment to provide medical care "to people whose survival is threatened by violence, neglect, or catastrophe, primarily due to armed conflicts, epidemics, malnutrition, exclusion from health care, or natural disasters" and to perform *témoignage*: a blend of witnessing and advocacy on behalf of egregious human suffering in the areas where MSF staff members are working. That combination of objectives raises an implicit question about the relationship between the kinds of representation and responsibility engendered by its different roles. Although MSF explicitly defines itself as a civil, as opposed to political, organization, it must nevertheless negotiate the political contexts framing its missions, particularly in "push[ing] the political to assume its inescapable responsibility."[1] The organization frames its own responsibility in the face of suffering as medical and moral—scientific and logistical on the one hand and overtly rhetorical on the other—both animated by the deep structure of crisis to which responsibility responds. Delineated according to both a "'minimalist' biopolitics" ("the temporary administration of survival within wider circumstances that do not favor it") and "the deeper humanitarian goal of reestablishing human dignity,"[2] crisis determines the targeted scope of medical relief, the moral claim of the witness, and whether that claim is directed toward political actors, aggressors, potential donors, or some broader citizenry.

Whereas MSF promotes *témoignage* on its website and through promotional materials to raise the profile of its missions and the circumstances they address, I am interested here in how *témoignage* becomes repurposed in photographic and graphic narratives of MSF missions that stand apart from the organization itself and extend beyond the crises in which the narratives began. Poised between advocacy and the aesthetic, three books—Salgado's *Sahel: The End of the Road* (2004), Haviv et al.'s *Forgotten War* (2005), and Guibert, Lefèvre, and Lemercier's *The Photographer: Into War-Torn Afghanistan with Doctors without Borders* (2009)—grew out of MSF-sponsored photographic campaigns to document and publicize its work. While some of the individual images in the books were published in news media when they were taken, the books circulate as aesthetic, journalistic, foreign affairs texts, and their range of visual and narrative styles offers multiple perspectives on how the spatial and temporal representation of crisis produces distinct narratives of humanitarian responsibility.[3] When news images of humanitarian crises work by depicting the presence and ostensible "*self-evidence* and *objectivity* of painful feeling, and [thus] . . . the nation's duty to eradicate it,"[4] they depend on structures of (mis)identification and a supposed universalization of emotion to generate the viewer's sense of immediate responsibility. I analyze the representation of space and time within the photo/graphic narratives of MSF for possible alternatives to such models of identification.

Témoignage and Responsibility

The material and rhetorical spheres of MSF action overlap to offer the protection of both bare life and human dignity as essential aims of humanitarian responsibility, making the question of how dignity is defined and represented all the more urgent.[5] In his Nobel Peace Prize acceptance speech on behalf of MSF in 1999, then president Dr. James Orbinski defines humanitarianism in universalizing terms of moral concern based on presumably shared and self-evident values of crisis, normalcy, dignity, rights, suffering, and action: "Humanitarian action . . . aims to build spaces of normalcy in the midst of what is abnormal. More than offering material assistance, we aim to enable individuals to regain their rights and dignity as human beings."[6] This rhetoric posits a common humanity predicated on shared values that transcend structural imbalances and cultural differences. At the same time, the story of what constitutes a crisis, against that universalized state of normalcy, depends on the different roles MSF might assume. Orbinski turns to the discourse of rights and dignity to bridge temporal and spatial disjunctions between immediate crisis and history, emergency and normalcy, and that discourse finds its rhetorical expression in *témoignage.*

Notwithstanding MSF's commitment to *témoignage*, ambiguity is inherent in its praxis: is it a moral position, inherent capacity (by virtue of being a member of the organization), or political action? Does it presume that those who are suffering are unable or unwilling to represent themselves? Implicit within the practice of *témoignage* are both the capacity of and the opportunity for MSF staff members to publicize injustice from multiple subject positions, as well as the belief that listeners—potential donors, sympathetic or shamed political actors, other professional organizations in the field—*ought* to heed and respond to their efforts. In effect MSF defines one facet of its responsibility as reminding others of theirs.

The tension between offering medical relief determined by a minimalist biopolitics and speaking out about the structural and political contexts of an emergency requires a continual balancing act of different temporal frames. When crisis becomes condition, and exceptionality generates other forms of normalcy, no matter how unconscionable, certain humanitarian appeals—such as those built around crisis as shock and sudden rupture—lose their efficacy in galvanizing the spectator, demanding other narrative forms in their stead. The relationship of *témoignage* to the spatial dimensions of responsibility works through a parallel paradox: much like the universalizing rhetoric of dignity it echoes, as well as MSFs pledge to work "without borders," *témoignage* is geopolitically engaged in that it "confronts the basic territorial logic of the nation-state; however, it also recalls the legacy of imperial expansion."[7] At the same time, *témoignage* implicitly contracts the distance between safety and suffering by calling on the relationship between them as a requirement to act.

The Structure of an Appeal

Whereas *témoignage* may be directed to a targeted audience, as in a letter-writing campaign or human rights report, humanitarian appeals typically address themselves as broadly as possible to shape public opinion and/or generate donations. Although the range of critical analyses of mediatized humanitarian appeals exceeds the space available even to summarize it here, two forms of appeal have particular bearing on the techniques employed by the photo/graphic narratives of MSF. One form works through documentary-style photography and personal, representative stories of victims. This approach certifies the crisis as real and immediate, while simultaneously establishing a distance between the potentially beneficent, ostensibly safe spectator and the obviously vulnerable subject that defines a unilateral humanitarian gesture at once possible and necessary. The humanitarian impulse in such efforts is quickened by the political legacy of "the articulation of justice with pity," a formulation Lilie Chouliaraki describes as circulating through discourses of "grand emotion" toward those who suffer.[8] Such appeals work primarily through structures of (mis)identification and aim to move the spectator from the position of voyeur to one of philanthropist.[9]

Chouliaraki identifies a second, "post-humanitarian" form of appeal, which focuses on the viewer rather than the sufferer of atrocity, the addressee of the appeal rather than its subject. "Drawing upon playful textualities," as opposed to realism, and embracing irony over pity, "this communicative structure challenges claims to 'common humanity,' characteristic of earlier humanitarian genres, and replaces solidarity as action on human suffering with artful stories that promise to make us better people." The "morality of irony" transforms potential solidarity "into self-centred consumerism, [and] ultimately reproduces rather than challenges the existing relations of power between the West and vulnerable others." The suffering are bracketed as viewers' identification with the humanitarian generates the force of the appeal. The two styles, based on photorealism and pity on the one hand and ironic, postmodern textual play on the other, "fail to sustain a legitimate appeal to action on vulnerable others," Chouliaraki argues, because neither one interrogates the structural imbalances that divide secure and vulnerable worlds or "construe[s] the world as 'common and shared' to all."[10] In neither case do the appeals move the spectator further along the spectrum from voyeur to philanthropist to protester, who might seek both relief and justice.

The question remains as to whether the photo/graphic narratives of MSF that adopt these representational strategies (through documentary photography, hand-drawn comics-style images, or both) can effect that final move, one that implies a higher degree of responsibility for the spectator's secondary witnessing of the images of suffering. Can they formulate responsibility *apart* from the viewer's (mis)identification with those suffering and/or MSF staff members, especially as partial by-products of the organization itself? This challenge, combined with the increasing scope of MSF missions, underscores the need defined by trauma theorist E. Ann Kaplan for active witnessing as that which involves understanding the "*structure* of an injustice" (my emphasis) as well as the avoidance of "empty empathy" generated by sentimental attachment to decontextualized images of suffering.[11]

How, then, do the photo/graphic narratives of MSF—particularly their efforts at once to show and tell of suffering—function rhetorically, aesthetically, and ethically as a form of active witnessing and *témoignage* that might galvanize the viewer/reader's engagement into some form of action? In Chouliaraki's terms, how might these photo/graphic narratives transform the recognition of shared responsibility to ameliorate suffering into a potential for solidarity through "'proper distance': the recognition that it is this very asymmetry of power that must become the principle of solidarity upon which we act toward vulnerable others" and that vulnerability itself is a political rather than universal "question of injustice"?[12]

Témoignage and Photo/Graphic Narrative

Photography plays a key and familiar role in both maintaining and disrupting these narratives of crisis and intervention, of vulnerable versus secure worlds. Many have commented on the politics of the objectifying, colonizing gaze inherent in photographic campaigns featuring shocking images, victims "deserving" of aid, and portrayals of abject helplessness. On the other hand, as simultaneously visual and literary media, whose narrative arcs emerge through the relationship among discretely framed moments, these books play with constructions of temporality and distance (moral, intersubjective, and geographic), which govern the terms on which humanitarian responsibility depends.

Sebastião Salgado is perhaps one of the most recognizable photographers documenting humanitarian and environmental degradation around the globe, and the photographic project *Sahel: Man in Distress*, later also published as *Sahel: The End of the Road*, is one of his earliest works. The product of a fifteen-month project in 1984–85 to photograph the effects of drought in parts of Chad, Ethiopia (including Tigray Province), Mali, and Sudan, the photographs were collected and published in different editions in France (1986) and Spain (1988) with the proceeds going to MSF. As Fred Ritchin writes in an introductory essay to the US edition of the book, only published in 2004, US coverage of the drought and famine at the time favored short-term engagements couched in the rhetoric of solidarity, charity, and pity: Hands across America, We Are the World, a *People* magazine story, a portfolio of Salgado's photos in the *New York Times*. The photographs gained more exposure in the United States in 1990 when they were included in a traveling retrospective (and exhibition book) of Salgado's work, *An Uncertain Grace*. As Ritchin notes:

[S]ince Salgado's work on the Sahel was rarely published in the U.S. press at the time, the photographs' engagement with the visceral reality of the famine and its aftermath was to some extent subverted, put off for another day. His images had to be labeled "art" in order to be widely exhibited in the United States; their artistry rather than their urgency then became the focus of the critique. The recorded fact of people dying (what Susan Sontag called the "footprint" of the photograph) and the concomitant issue of social responsibility—the stuff of the documentary—were short-circuited and made nearly irrelevant.[13]

Ritchin's critique underscores the importance of context in determining the legibility of the photographs. Those contexts may be multiple and conflicting: in keeping with the complex relationship between photojournalism and humanitarian work by nongovernmental organizations (NGOs), for example, Doctors without Borders announced the opening of its first office in the United States in conjunction with the New York exhibition of *An Uncertain Grace*. How, then, might we read the large format, beautifully printed volume *Sahel: The End of the Road*, published two decades after the event it documents, depicting suffering so grievous that it's nearly impossible to imagine that many of its sufferers have survived? In what temporal framework do the photos exist today? What kind of responsibility do they call forth on behalf of those distanced by time, space, and perhaps life itself?

In her analysis of television news reports of distant suffering, Chouliaraki offers a schema for analyzing the combined effects of visual and verbal reporting along a spectrum of possible outcomes for the spectator: the fascination and minimum pity of the voyeur to the charity of the philanthropist to the sense of indignation, outrage, injustice, or complicity that galvanizes the protester. Chouliaraki evaluates spatial representations according to how closely the subject and the subject's background are related, the level of uniqueness and differentiation of environments, and the relationship depicted between safe and dangerous spaces. Temporal dimensions receive parallel attention according to when the event is taking place; whether its past, present, or future seems most important; and whether the future, if it is invoked at all, looms far or near.[14] These criteria— with the important addition here of how MSF staff members are represented in relation to those they serve, as well as the environment—provide a framework for analyzing how both suffering and the responsibility for its amelioration are construed. Or, to build on Judith Butler's analysis of how grievable life is framed photographically, if the photograph extends the event, what is the field in which responsibility is newly constituted through Salgado's book?[15]

The separation of the visual and verbal elements in *Sahel: The End of the Road* (the captions are published in the back of the book, rendering it more legible as an art book whose images ostensibly stand apart from their contexts) makes specific locations difficult to pinpoint; however, even without the captions the photographs depict a varied geography with direct bearing on human suffering. Through Salgado's lens, the different regions of the Sahel range from an otherworldly depiction of a seemingly barren landscape, which spectral humans traverse with unknown purpose, to an apocalyptic take on the end of human civilization (a vulture hovering above a famine camp; silent, naked, waiting children; or a littered, depopulated landscape). Other depictions offer a larger social context, however precarious, through long and close shots of outdoor spaces (an encampment, a pathway lined with water jugs) and indoor spaces devoted to the minimal necessities of medical care, food, and shelter. Those indoor spaces appear only slightly less catastrophic than the outdoor ones, in that the necessities of bare life emerge in the carefully focalized mat, shawl, or bowl, yet these images are marked primarily by the failure of those few objects to sustain life and the inability to distinguish among some subjects the living from the dead. Salgado's movement across categories of "presumed, possible, or certain death" and the difficulty of distinguishing among them destabilize conventional ways of reading and demand considerable "interpretative work by the public to complete what is not shown."[16]

Depictions of MSF and other NGO staff members (and their limited equipment) offer similarly disturbing and unsettling conclusions. Pictured in iconic arrangements—in the operating room, hovering tenderly over a dying child—they are illuminated in relation to their patients yet seemingly unable to save their lives. The spectator has as little access to their interiority as to those suffering the famine, and all the images portray a deep silence. As spectators in the global north may more readily identify with the beneficent aid workers in the photos than with those wavering at the edge of life or who have already passed over it, those aid workers function pedagogically to model a charitable response. At the same time, and to work against radically othering processes, Salgado consistently renders the individuality and social bonds of the sufferers through gesture and proximity—the communal prayer, the sharing of water, a parent's hand on a child. The perspectives he offers on his subjects "begin at compassion and lead from there to further recognitions. One of the first is that starvation does *not* obliterate human dignity. . . . Salgado did not photograph passive victims, and pity does not suffice."[17] By paying close attention to these moments, viewers might recognize the compassionate gestures *among* sufferers as catalysts for engagement at least as powerful as those of the MSF staff.

In consistently making this argument through his photographs, states David Levi Strauss, Salgado redefines the responsibility of his field: "Eschewing the vaunted 'objectivity' of photojournalism, Salgado works in the realm of collective subjectivities, aspiring to that 'transcendence of the Self that makes possible the epiphany of the Other.'"[18] The language of transcendence and epiphany borrowed from Emmanuel Levinas also references the spiritual or sacred dimension of Salgado's aesthetic, one that, depending on one's point of view, removes suffering from the realm of the political or provides another, powerful vocabulary through which to articulate the terms of recognition of and responsibility to (rather than paternalistically for) those subjects. At its best, in Levinasian terms, this aesthetic fosters the recognition of one's responsibility *to* another that precedes identity and, thus, exceeds the terms of the encounter at hand and any singular gesture of beneficence. In Wendy S. Hesford's summary of this ethical relation, "the face-to-face encounter," which invokes humanity as a witness, "breaks the objectifying gaze and moves beyond narcissistic recognition," asking the viewer to look beyond himself or herself toward a larger ethical frame.[19]

Hesford insists on this ethical relation and the visual field in which it operates as socially mediated and historically contingent, rather than otherworldly or wholly abstract.[20] In their temporal dimensions, Salgado's preference for black-and-white photography contributes to the sacred aura of timelessness as the images seem to take place in an undetermined past or present, seemingly escapable only through death. The "'decisive moment'" of the photograph also exists, however, within a longer temporality that calls forth worldly responsibility.[21] The collection provides a visual and textual narrative of political failure and the insufficiency of humanitarian aid alone to compensate for it. Images of desperate migrations or a lone helicopter hovering in the background behind those suffering the famine aim to "'provoke a discussion' . . . [of] the issues *behind* the photographs."[22]

Salgado's iconic depictions of victims and aid workers and exquisite care with framing, focus, and formal arrangement give the images a hyperdramatic quality that has been critiqued for romanticizing and aestheticizing suffering. This danger, when "the image tends to bring forth the formal properties of suffering . . . and take attention away from the content of suffering as a painful reality for somebody out there in the world,"[23] decreases if we examine the narratives implicit in the arrangement of the photographs and even more so if verbal and visual texts are reunited. Taking the first third of the book as an example, the photographs move from stark images of sufferers against an unrelentingly desolate backdrop to the continuity of social bonds (men praying, children playing, a hand comforting the dying) in bare life in the camps to, finally, the importance of those bonds and their cultural expressions in death, visible in three women reading next to two shrouded corpses in an unmarked landscape.

The captions offer a richer context for the photos not only in their descriptive content—the form of narration that merely confirms the fact of suffering and aligns closely with the perceptual realism of the image itself—but also in what Chouliaraki terms their narrative and expository functions: including elements of storytelling (galvanizing emotion toward the suffering depicted) and argument or opinion in the pursuit of justice.[24] In the expository mode, for instance, the caption for the first photograph in the book, of two distant figures walking out of the frame across a desert landscape bare except for a distant mountain and a gigantic bush in the center of the photo, reads, "On the outskirts of Tokar. Before the drought of 1973, this region was perhaps the most prosperous in the Sudan. It was the chief supplier of cotton, the source of wealth for this delta population. Now the warehouses are empty and the villages deserted. Sudan, 1985."[25] The caption is noteworthy not only for its attention to history (thereby stretching the moment of the photograph) but also for its insistence on describing what the photograph does not show: a population, warehouses, a village. Another caption, for a photograph of the shrouded corpses of a parent and child on the ground, surrounded only by a few footprints, stones, and dead grass, expresses outrage at the political failure that both initiated the journey and led to this conclusion: "Welo province, Ethiopia. They have walked, crossing mountains, enduring hunger and cold. They have hidden and waited, clinging to hope, and have pressed onward. But why flee? Why walk so far and suffer so greatly only to end up like this? Ethiopia, 1984."[26] Here, too, the caption exceeds the precise limits of the photograph with its ambiguous temporality in verb tenses and distance between the speaker and the subjects, an ambiguity that allows the caption to describe others who have not (yet, perhaps) met the same end.

Chouliaraki combines the criteria for interpreting temporal and spatial representations into an overall chronotope of suffering that measures four attributes for determining a work's effectiveness in moving the spectator along the path from voyeur to protester:

> concreteness—"shows the concrete context of suffering as a physical space"
> multiplicity—"moves spectators through the multiple physical contexts of suffering"
> specificity—"shows the context of suffering as a singular space . . . or individualizes the sufferer"
> mobility—"which connects the contexts of safety and danger, suggesting a specific relationship of action between them."[27]

On first view as a photographic book, *Sahel: The End of the Road* at once seduces the spectator through the beauty of its images and insists on a limited voyeuristic responsibility for that view by anchoring it in specific subjects, spaces, and cultural practices. Mobility in the sense defined above increases when captions and images stand together and we put this content in the context of the front matter of the book with its critique of US publishers' earlier refusal of the material; however, mobility plays a scant role in proposing a course of action that attends to relief and repair, charity and justice. As noted above, the images "provoke a discussion" rather than outlining a response. Even the effort to cultivate philanthropy is limited by its only tenuous reminders of the project's link to MSF. While not proscriptive, Salgado's images consistently portray suffering as a form of injustice, and as his photographs "leave remarkably durable afterimages that reappear long after one walks away from them,"[28] they might foster deliberation in anticipation of a shared future. His visual language of epiphany and transcendence speaks at once to the radical humanity of the vulnerable, as well as to the enormity of the gap between recognizing that humanity and the political will to act on it.

Ron Haviv, Gary Knight, Antonin Kratochvil, Joachim Ladefoged, and James Nachtwey's *Forgotten War: Democratic Republic of the Congo* also underscores the power and importance of photographs as a form of remembering with both present and future implications. The book is a product of one of several collaborative projects between MSF and the VII photographic agency, the latter formed by an initial seven photojournalists in September 2001 "to produce an unflinching record of injustice and the people caught up in the events they depict."[29] The relationships MSF builds with the members of VII and other photojournalists take different forms, from paid assignments to "provid[ing] access and logistical support—including local transportation, meals, lodging, and information—to photographers who are working on issues or in regions where MSF is also working."[30] Both parties recognize the complexity of this relationship, especially when photojournalists gain access to stories with only limited obligations to MSF for the resulting images. From a photojournalistic perspective, as David Walker writes, "For nearly 40 years, Doctors Without Borders . . . has been a catalyst for world-class journalism from difficult places around the globe. And its role in bringing epidemics and humanitarian disaster to the world's attention is bound to expand as news organizations cut back their international coverage." Yet that access for photojournalists is also circumscribed by MSF security guidelines and priorities, as MSF representative Jason Cone explains in the same article: "'They can't just jump out of the car and shoot' wherever and whatever they want, Cone says. 'We're an NGO. We're not about independent journalism. We're up front with [photographers] about that. They have to be willing to accept that they might be held back in terms of their reporting.'"[31] *Forgotten War*, as a small format, limited run edition of five photographers' views of the Democratic Republic of Congo (DRC) in 2004, is neither strictly news reportage nor art, although many of the images draw attention to their own formal characteristics. It functions most clearly among the three books under consideration here as a form of *témoignage* in MSF's own terms. With a foreword by MSF executive director Nicolas de Torrenté, the volume aims to "make visible to the world" the cost of war, endemic disease, and sexual violence upon local populations in the DRC and to motivate the spectator's refusal of "a kind of normalization of the unacceptable" depicted in the images.[32] The introduction also instructs viewers to see both individuals and the larger context of war and disease in the images that follow.

Forgotten War uses rhetoric of *potential* temporal and spatial proximity. That the war has been "forgotten," for instance, implies that it was once known; that the reader will see how conditions of extremity can become "normal," as opposed to exceptional, implies a comparison with his or her own understanding of normalcy. The movement from immediate crisis to persistent need also clears space for deliberation of the very kinds of normalcy MSF cites as at the heart of its objectives. The decision of what to shoot and what to publish in this context reflects the photographers' vision of what ought to be different, determinations that can only be made in the context of evaluating what might count as "normal" and the structural inequalities that undergird those attributions. Their five portfolios within the book focus, in order, on internally displaced persons in different regions and camps; Bunia, with particular attention to its hospital; HIV/AIDS patients at an MSF clinic in Bukavu; sex workers in Kinshasa; and individual suffering caused by malnutrition, disease, and war in various districts of the DRC. Their arrangement offers an exposition of how the radical social disruptions (rather than the wounds of weaponry) inflicted on civilian populations in war lead to severe, chronic forms of suffering. The arrangement of the portfolios also situates the overtly medical, institutional work of MSF in the hospital and clinic within the larger project of witnessing extreme social upheaval and endemic suffering. The structure and themes of the book parallel, in other words, MSF's dual responsibility for medical aid and *témoignage*: pervasive and extreme need calls for broad responsibility.

The individual portfolios have distinct aesthetic perspectives on their subjects, which, taken together, offer high degrees of the concreteness, multiplicity, and specificity of suffering. Haviv's color photographs of internally displaced persons, for example, feature contrasting colors and striking lines that lead the eye to different corners of the images and create tension with whatever image of suffering lies at the center (an illuminated cross at a child's funeral, a woman framed by bed sheets in a hospital, a United Nations truck departing down a dusty road). These images contrast with the final black-and-white portfolio by Nachtwey, whose intimate perspective often focuses on the laying on of hands: a mother stretching her arms over her sick children, a wife comforting her husband, or MSF staff treating a patient. Significantly in these photos, Nachtwey shows only the hands of MSF workers, at once keeping the focus on the patients and inviting a philanthropic response.

Between these bookends, Kratochvil's portfolio of an MSF HIV/AIDS clinic features much more abstracted images, often with a body part of the fore-grounded human subject (a bent back, an X-ray, a head) blurred against a focalized background. His images thus bespeak their own limits and draw atten-tion to a situated perspective, as opposed to striving for any coherent, objective, totalizing, or unanchored view. Kratochvil's one direct, focused portrait of a female patient has a double-page spread in the book, and, although her face fills the page with only the suggestion of a clinic room behind her, the caption references the MSF staff omitted from the photo: "An AIDS patient being cared for by MSF doctors at a local hospital in Bukavu." This, too, reminds the spectator of the limits of what is visible. Knight's tilted and askance perspectives and Ladefoged's depictions of sex workers often juxtapose body parts of various subjects, refuting any suggestion of a complete or self-evident perspective.

In one image, Ladefoged's photograph of a patient on a gurney, lying beneath a poster of a pregnant woman's belly and being examined at the MSF sex worker clinic, underscores its own status as representation and plays with the question of visual address. Responsibility in the poster is defined by the pregnant woman's hands encircling her belly and the command "Proteger a seu bebé / contra a aids / é mais do que un dever / É un direita" (Protect your baby against AIDS / It is more than a right, it's a duty); however, in Ladefoged's photograph that message, and thus the scope and locus of responsibility, is also reflected in both the patient's and the doctor's hands, respectively exposing and examining the patient's abdomen. Rather than providing a clear portrait of injustice and responsibility, the photograph portrays complex and competing narratives. The poster with its white body, Portuguese text, paternalistic and imperative tone, and language of rights and duties offers an ironic reminder of the DRC's earliest European contacts and, perhaps, the centuries-long history of disastrous foreign involvement. The body in the poster (naked except for a partial sleeve) is marked primarily by biology (race and pregnancy), whereas the living subjects of the photograph—the doctor and the patient—are defined socially, highlighted with visual referents such as the doctor's white robe and the patient's silver-painted toenails. The ostensible "natural" everyday of maternal responsibility in the poster, which is apparently not so natural that it can avoid a stern reminder, contrasts vividly with the social contexts of the subjects. Finally, none of these three positions—poster, patient, or physician—invites the viewer's identification, instead deflecting it with the backs of the doctor's robe and patient's jacket. The proximity the camera provides to this semi-intimate scene can only be justified, then, through a consideration of the historical, political, and medical terms that make it possible.

Forgotten War ultimately serves as an injunction to remember and respond because the roots to the crisis are long, tangled, and transnational and its scope so pervasive, although, in terms of the mobility Chouliaraki outlines, it does not specify the terms through which viewers might feel interpellated. As opposed to the visual language of epiphany and transcendence of Salgado's work, these photographers underscore the impossibility of a full revelation of distant sufferers through off-kilter framing, the tension between focused and blurred subjects, and the insistence on partial perspectives. The depictions of ostensibly private moments, including the sense of intrusion the camera conveys when it reveals naked women in childbirth or family members mourning a dead child, provide concrete examples of just what the "normalization of the unacceptable" might include. Rather than a proximity of intimacy and immediacy, the images illuminate and demand recognition of that "asymmetry of power" between spectator and sufferer, that "proper distance" Chouliaraki argues is necessary for the pursuit of justice. The images do not circle back, so to speak, to remind the viewer to contribute to MSF's work so much as frame the scope of the crisis in large and complex terms that exceed the capacity of any single organization to respond to it.

Avoiding the privileged association between the obviousness of suffering and its immediate response and cultivating the conditions for deliberation are precisely the claims that supporters of the innovative potential of graphic narrative make for it. According to Hillary Chute, graphic narrative's formal characteristics, its overt attention to the structures of representation, produce the possibility for ethical engagement: "Its formal grammar rejects transparency and renders textualization conspicuous, inscribing the context in its graphic presentation."[33] As its title suggests, *The Photographer: Into War-Torn Afghanistan with Doctors without Borders*, approaches this task through a focus on Didier Lefèvre as both subject of his 1986 photographic assignment with MSF and witness to the medical team's work. These two roles are reflected in the multi-modal narratives that compose the book: Lefèvre's black-and-white photographs, Emmanuel Guibert's graphic narrative (based on Lefèvre's stories of his trip and undertaken thirteen years later), and Frédéric Lemercier's design

and coloring of the final product. These different modes of storytelling blend
into one another: the different forms are interwoven and interspersed to tell the
story, graphic narrative textual frames overlay some photographs, and an
earthy palette that, especially in a book of this length, which requires a sustained
reading, emphasizes the formal parallels between the graphic and photographic
story lines. The interaction of these modes of representation moves the reader
back and forth between what Lefèvre sees and how he reacts. The author-
witness thus serves at once as a surrogate and model for the more removed spectator (the reader), compressing the distance between them, as well as between
the viewer and the subjects of Lefèvre's work, even as it offers, accordion style,
to expand that distance by displacing concern for the victims onto that of the
witness.

The Photographer traces Lefèvre's journey from innocence and naïveté to
experience as he accompanies a small MSF group in a caravan into northern
Afghanistan to staff their small, remote clinics. Beginning and ending in Paris,
the book is divided into three parts, documenting his introduction to Pakistan,
Afghanistan, and MSF's work; the arduous trek across war zones, high passes,
and rivers and the work at the clinics; and Lefèvre's decision to leave the group
and return to Pakistan and then home on his own. Although the medical work
is at the literal center of the book and is portrayed with genuine admiration, the
narrative arc and dramatic tension depend on Lefèvre's direct, personal experiences, reaching their climax in his dangerous departure without the rest of
the MSF team and his near death. The visual centerpiece of the book, a double-
page spread of what he believes will be his last photo, follows an extended, gray-
scale, graphic narrative sequence of Lefèvre's guide abandoning him on a high
pass, his losing his temper at his exhausted horse, and his lying down in the
path to write his last diary entry and take his final photos: "I take out one of my
cameras. I choose a 20mm lens, a very wide angle, and shoot from the ground.
To let people know where I died. (Click.)"[34] Switching to Lefèvre's direct perspective, three large-format photographs of his horse on the rough rock and
snow path and against a stormy background lead to a panoramic view of the
forbidding, uninhabited pass and valley below. The progression in image size
and realism of the preceding images and poignant text that sets up this photograph enhance its emotional weight and invite the viewer's direct identification
with it. This dramatic image—devoid of signs of war, MSF, or Afghan people—
locates suffering solely within the photographer, who has left MSF to test himself
against the rigors of Afghanistan.

The focus on Lefèvre functions as a (successful, if the measure is the wide
circulation of *The Photographer*, especially compared with the other two books)

narrative device that provides a compelling point of identification for distant readers curious about MSF or Afghanistan, as well as an example of the "inequality of lives" inherent in humanitarianism.[35] As Didier Fassin, a former MSF board member, writes, such inequalities result not from "theoretical premises or from individual prejudices. They are structural aporias of humanitarianism which are grounded in the asymmetry of the objective risk of death and of the subjective relation of compassion."[36] *The Photographer* reinstantiates those asymmetries and makes them available for scrutiny. On the one hand, Lefèvre's photographs, dark in tone, dense in visual content, and large in number, appear in a small, sometimes tiny format that usually corresponds to the size of the much simpler graphic narrative frames yet makes the rich subject matter of individual photographs difficult to discern completely. On the other hand, the relationship between the two media provides multiple contexts through which to consider the position of Lefèvre in relation to the MSF team and those it treats. This interplay of graphic and photographic content establishes what Chute terms "an expanded *idiom of witness*, a manner of testifying that sets a visual language in motion with and against the verbal in order to embody individual and collective experience, to put contingent selves and histories into form."[37]

The "idiom of witness" of the graphic narrative has a pedagogic function as it reflects Lefèvre's admiration for the MSF team and his distress over the individualized and specific suffering of the Afghan people he witnesses. At the same time, it situates the photographs in specific cultural, gendered, geographic, and political contexts. The complex relationship between members of the MSF team—"those who have a moral involvement in the humanitarian project, who are called 'volunteers' but receive a regular salary"—and himself as one of "those who are not related to the humanitarian saga, since they are simply 'employed' by the organization" emerges, for instance, in his decision to return on his own.[38] Over sixteen frames, Lefèvre and team leader Juliette Fournot debate who has responsibility for his safety now that his specific task of documenting the work at the clinic has ended. Responsibility, as a product of asymmetry, becomes subject to trade as they negotiate their positions vis-à-vis one another: "So I'm handing back to you the responsibility that I have over you. You're a big boy. If you want to leave, leave," Juliette finally tells him. The gendered language works on multiple levels to situate responsibility in a larger context: it reflects Juliette's frustration with his insistence on leaving the group and denotes the limits of her responsibility over her mission, it features as a significant milepost in Lefèvre's own quest as hero in his own story "to be left to my own devices and have to manage," and it references an extensive portrayal

Frame from *The Photographer,* © 2009 by Emmanuel Guibert. Reprinted by permission of First Second Books, an imprint of Henry Holt & Company, LLC. All rights reserved.

earlier in the book of the cultural sensitivity of the MSF team, and Juliette in particular, to its responsibility to work responsibly in local contexts.[39] "Her role, and her immersion in Afghan society where she spent her teenage years," as Chris Hedges notes, "repeatedly shatters easy stereotypes about Afghan and Muslim culture."[40] Her language of acquiescence to his demand for independence also echoes the latent maternalism in humanitarian responsibility more broadly, invoking at once an ethics of care and the structural imbalance of parents and children.

The interplay of graphic narrative and photography provides a richer frame for the absence of any visual depiction of war as a direct conflict in the book. If graphic narratives as *témoignage* potentially "put pressure on dominant conceptions of trauma's unrepresentability,"[41] without masking their own representational strategies, here the two narrative strands reveal the war through "damage done to bodies and souls by shells, bullets, and iron fragments, and the frantic struggle to mend the broken."[42] Although the graphic narrative emphasizes the telling of Lefèvre's personal story, it also invites a deeper reading of the photographs by characterizing the photographer's emotional reaction to the suffering he captures on film. The photographs, meanwhile, emphasize proximity to their subjects and the proximity of those subjects to danger: the ground-level view of Lefèvre's shot on the pass, close-ups of the basic surgery available for wounds caused by shrapnel and household accidents, the view MSF staff members have from the porch of their rudimentary clinic. In terms of Chouliaraki's chronotope of suffering, then, *The Photographer* encompasses all four elements of concreteness, multiplicity, specificity, and mobility. The last of these, which, again, "connects the contexts of safety and danger, suggesting a specific relationship of action between them,"[43] is achieved through the dialogue of forms and enhanced by the profiles of key figures at the end of the text. Because the book functions as a posthumous tribute to Lefèvre and his attachment to Afghanistan, as well as to the dedication of humanitarian workers (and was published long after the Soviet invasion it documents), it reinforces MSF's broad mission of medical humanitarianism and *témoignage*, rather than a specific political goal, and enjoins the reader on the level of philanthropy.[44]

Conclusion

MSF's practice of *témoignage* is central to the organization's mission and its larger contribution to the broad understanding of humanitarianism as a project that entails both medical relief and the pursuit of justice. These discourses frame responsibility through the obviousness of suffering on the one hand and, in exhorting others to assume their responsibilities, through the dynamics of identification on the other.

As texts made possible by the sponsorship of MSF yet not beholden to it, the photo/graphic narratives construe responsibility in an expanded register of *témoignage*, which, at times, offers alternatives to models of responsibility that are based on identification with humanitarians (proximity), disidentification with those suffering (distance), or an abstracted universalism. The books' serious play with the chronotopes through which they structure the relationship between spectator and subject draw attention to representational self-reflexivity and the incongruences between perspectives and/or visual and verbal components. Notwithstanding their differences, all three books underscore the partiality of their own constructions, historical embeddedness, and aesthetic qualities, characteristics that ask for a reciprocal responsibility from readers. These books do not define concrete political goals or strategies; however, at best they may foster consideration of what Chouliaraki terms "agonistic solidarity," which is "neither about the sharing of the same humanity for all nor the sharing of our own feelings for distant others but about the communication of human vulnerability as a political question of injustice that can become the object of our collective reflection, empathetic emotion and transformative action."[45]

NOTES

This essay has been revised from an earlier version published in the *Journal of Human Rights* 12, no. 1 (2013): 87–102. Reprinted by permission.

    1. James Orbinski, "Médecins Sans Frontières—Nobel Lecture," Oslo, Norway, December 10, 1999, accessed March 1, 2012, http://nobelprize.org/peace/laureates/1999/msf-lecture.html.

    2. Peter Redfield, "Doctors, Borders, and Life in Crisis," *Cultural Anthropology* 20, no. 3 (2005): 344, 345.

    3. Substantial scholarly work attends to the distinct properties of human rights photography and graphic narrative (see, e.g., Ariella Azoulay, *The Civil Contract of Photography* [NY: Zone Books, 2008]; Wendy S. Hesford, *Spectacular Rhetorics: Human Rights Visions, Recognitions, Feminisms* [Durham, NC: Duke University Press, 2011]; Wendy Kozol, "Complicities of Witnessing in Joe Sacco's *Palestine*," in *Theoretical Perspectives on Human Rights and Literature*, ed. Elizabeth Swanson Goldberg and Alexandra Schultheis Moore [New York: Routledge, 2012], 165–79; Sharon Sliwinski, *Human Rights in Camera* [Chicago: University of Chicago Press, 2011]), and much more could be said about how those differences relate to the arguments herein. Rather than read each of the three texts discussed in this essay strictly within these two formal categories, a project that exceeds the present space available, I focus instead on the representation of *témoignage* across those differences.

    4. Lauren Berlant, "The Subject of True Feeling: Pain, Privacy, and Politics," in *Transformations: Thinking through Feminism*, ed. Sara Ahmed et al. (New York: Routledge, 2000). 35.

    5. As Dr. James Orbinski emphasizes, "MSF was born out of an understanding of the role humanitarians could play in shaping public opinion. It insisted on the responsibility not just to act but to speak out in solidarity against violations of human rights and international humanitarian law." James Orbinski, *An Imperfect Offering: Humanitarian Action for the Twenty-First Century* (New York: Walker, 2008), 69.

    6. Orbinski, "Médecins Sans Frontières—Nobel Lecture."

    7. Redfield, "Doctors, Borders, and Life in Crisis," 336.

    8. Lilie Chouliaraki, "Post-humanitarianism: Humanitarian Communication beyond a Politics of Pity," *International Journal of Cultural Studies* 13, no. 2 (2010): 109.

    9. I take these three positions, marking key points on a spectrum from passive to active engagement with representations of suffering and the conditions that underlie them, from Lilie Chouliaraki, *The Spectatorship of Suffering* (London: Sage, 2006), 145–46. Although Chouliaraki analyzes television news depictions of suffering, her focus on the chronotope of representation is particularly relevant to the kinds of texts I address here.

    10. Lilie Chouliaraki, "'Improper Distance': Towards a Critical Account of Solidarity as Irony," *International Journal of Cultural Studies* 14, no. 4 (2011): 364.

    11. E. Ann Kaplan, *Trauma Culture: The Politics of Terror and Loss in Media and Literature* (New Brunswick, NJ: Rutgers University Press, 2005), 23, 93.

    12. Chouliaraki, "Improper Distance," 364, 377.

    13. Fred Ritchin, "Introduction: Twenty Years Ago, and Later," in Sebastião Salgado, *Sahel: The End of the Road* (Berkeley: University of California Press, 2004), 4.

    14. Chouliaraki, *The Spectatorship of Suffering*, 86.

15. Judith Butler, *Frames of War: When Is Life Grievable?* (New York: Verso, 2010), 83.

16. Barbie Zelizer, *About to Die: How News Images Move the Public* (New York: Oxford University Press, 2010), 68.

17. David Levi Strauss, "Epiphany of the Other," *Artforum International* 29 (February 1991): 99.

18. Emmanuel Levinas, *L'Humanisme de l'autre homme* (Montpelier: Fata Morgana, 1972), quoted in Strauss, "Epiphany of the Other," 99.

19. Hesford, *Spectacular Rhetorics*, 50.

20. Ibid., 52.

21. Ritchin, "Introduction," 6.

22. Mev Puleo quotes Salgado's frequent claim, "I'm not showing these pictures to make anyone feel guilty, but to provoke a discussion." Mev Puleo, "The Prophetic Act of Bearing Witness: The Work of Sebastião Salgado," *ARTS* 11, no. 2 (1999): 10n1.

23. Chouliaraki, *The Spectatorship of Suffering*, 50.

24. Ibid., 77–78.

25. Salgado, *Sahel*, 125.

26. Ibid., 129.

27. Chouliaraki, *The Spectatorship of Suffering*, 87.

28. Strauss, "Epiphany of the Other," 96.

29. Ron Haviv et al., *Forgotten War: Democratic Republic of the Congo* (Millbrook, NY: de.Mo, 2005).

30. David Walker, "How NGOs Work with Photographers: Doctors without Borders," *Photo District News* (PDN), September 16, 2009, accessed March 1, 2012, http://www.pdnonline.com/pdn/index.shtml.

31. Ibid.

32. Nicolas de Torrenté, "Foreword," in Ron Haviv et al., *Forgotten War: Democratic Republic of the Congo* (Millbrook, NY: de.Mo, 2005), n.p.

33. Hillary Chute, "Comics as Literature? Reading Graphic Narrative," *PMLA* 123, no. 2 (2008): 457.

34. Emmanuel Guibert, Didier Lefèvre, and Frédéric Lemercier, *The Photographer: Into War-Torn Afghanistan with Doctors without Borders*, translated by Alexis Siegel (New York: First Second, 2009), 219.

35. Didier Fassin, "Inequalities of Lives, Hierarchies of Humanity: Moral Commitments and Ethical Dilemmas of Humanitarianism," in *In the Name of Humanity: The Government of Threat and Care*, ed. Ilana Feldman and Miriam Ticktin (Durham, NC: Duke University Press, 2010), 239.

36. Ibid., 255.

37. Hillary Chute, *Graphic Women: Life Narrative and Contemporary Comics* (New York: Columbia University Press, 2010), 3.

38. Fassin, "Inequalities of Lives, Hierarchies of Humanity," 248.

39. Guibert, Lefèvre, and Lemercier, *The Photographer*, 155, 154.

40. Chris Hedges, "What War Looks Like," review of *The Photographer: Into War-Torn Afghanistan with Doctors without Borders*, by Emmanuel Guibert, Didier Lefèvre, and Frédéric Lemercier, *New York Times*, May 20, 2009, http://www.nytimes.com/2009/05/24/books/review/Hedges-t.html.

41. Chute, *Graphic Women*, 182.

42. Hedges, "What War Looks Like."

43. Chouliaraki, *The Spectatorship of Suffering*, 87.

44. Lefèvre survived the 1986 mission to Afghanistan and later return visits but died of heart failure in 2007.

45. Chouliaraki, "'Improper Distance,'" 377.

WORKS CITED

Azoulay, Ariella. *The Civil Contract of Photography*. New York: Zone Books, 2008.

Berlant, Lauren. "The Subject of True Feeling: Pain, Privacy, and Politics." In *Transformations: Thinking through Feminism*, edited by Sara Ahmed, Jane Kilby, Celia Lury, Maureen McNeil, and Beverly Skeggs, 33–47. New York: Routledge, 2000.

Butler, Judith. *Frames of War: When Is Life Grievable?* New York: Verso, 2010.

Chouliaraki, Lilie. "'Improper Distance': Towards a Critical Account of Solidarity as Irony." *International Journal of Cultural Studies* 14, no. 4 (2011): 363–81.

———. "Post-humanitarianism: Humanitarian Communication beyond a Politics of Pity." *International Journal of Cultural Studies* 13, no. 2 (2010): 107–26.

———. *The Spectatorship of Suffering*. London: Sage, 2006.

Chute, Hillary. "Comics as Literature? Reading Graphic Narrative." *PMLA* 123, no. 2 (2008): 452–65.

———. *Graphic Women: Life Narrative and Contemporary Comics*. New York: Columbia University Press, 2010.

Fassin, Didier. "Inequalities of Lives, Hierarchies of Humanity: Moral Commitments and Ethical Dilemmas of Humanitarianism." In *In the Name of Humanity: The Government of Threat and Care*, edited by Ilana Feldman and Miriam Ticktin, 238–55. Durham, NC: Duke University Press, 2010.

Guibert, Emmanuel, Didier Lefèvre, and Frédéric Lemercier. *The Photographer: Into War-Torn Afghanistan with Doctors without Borders*. Translated by Alexis Siegel. New York: First Second, 2009.

Haviv, Ron, Gary Knight, Antonin Kratochvil, Joachim Ladefoged, and James Nachtwey. *Forgotten War: Democratic Republic of the Congo*. Millbrook, NY: de.Mo, 2005.

Hedges, Chris. "What War Looks Like." Review of *The Photographer: Into War-Torn Afghanistan with Doctors without Borders*, by Emmanuel Guibert, Didier Lefèvre, and Frédéric Lemercier. *New York Times*, May 20, 2009. http://www.nytimes.com/2009/05/24/books/review/Hedges-t.html.

Hesford, Wendy S. *Spectacular Rhetorics: Human Rights Visions, Recognitions, Feminisms*. Durham, NC: Duke University Press, 2011.

Kaplan, E. Ann. *Trauma Culture: The Politics of Terror and Loss in Media and Literature*. New Brunswick, NJ: Rutgers University Press, 2005.

Kozol, Wendy. "Complicities of Witnessing in Joe Sacco's *Palestine*." In *Theoretical Perspectives on Human Rights and Literature*, edited by Elizabeth Swanson Goldberg and Alexandra Schultheis Moore, 165–79. New York: Routledge, 2012.

Levinas, Emmanuel. *L'Humanisme de l'autre homme*. Montpelier: Fata Morgana, 1972.

Orbinski, James. *An Imperfect Offering: Humanitarian Action for the Twenty-First Century*. New York: Walker, 2008.

———. "Médecins Sans Frontières—Nobel Lecture." Oslo, Norway, December 10, 1999. http://nobelprize.org/peace/laureates/1999/msf-lecture.html.

Puleo, Mev. "The Prophetic Act of Bearing Witness: The Work of Sebastião Salgado." *ARTS* 11, no. 2 (1999): 7–12. First published in 1995.

Redfield, Peter. "Doctors, Borders, and Life in Crisis." *Cultural Anthropology* 20, no. 3 (2005): 328–61.

Ritchin, Fred. "Introduction: Twenty Years Ago, and Later." In Sebastião Salgado, *Sahel: The End of the Road*, 1–7. Berkeley: University of California Press, 2004.

Salgado, Sebastião. *Sahel: The End of the Road*. Berkeley: University of California Press, 2004. First published as *Sahel: Man in Distress* in 1986.

Sliwinski, Sharon. *Human Rights in Camera*. Chicago: University of Chicago Press, 2011.

Strauss, David Levi. "Epiphany of the Other." *Artforum International* 29 (February 1991): 96–99.

Torrenté, Nicolas de. "Foreword." In Ron Haviv, Gary Knight, Antonin Kratochvil, Joachim Ladefoged, and James Nachtwey, *Forgotten War: Democratic Republic of the Congo*, n.p. Millbrook, NY: de.Mo, 2005.

Walker, David. "How NGOs Work with Photographers: Doctors without Borders." *Photo District News* (PDN), September 16, 2009. http://www.pdnonline.com/pdn/index.shtml.

Zelizer, Barbie. *About to Die: How News Images Move the Public*. New York: Oxford University Press, 2010.

Representing
Human Rights Violations in
Multimedia Contexts

KATRINA M. POWELL

To understand the ways in which an individual life can illuminate systemic human rights violations, humanists have placed great value on the ways in which stories are told, represented, and re-presented in various genres. Whether these stories come in the form of interviews, films, memoirs, novels, news articles, or photographs, we feel that they will reveal some sort of truth about human rights violations occurring globally. In this essay, I examine the story of one woman, Mary Frances Corbin, represented through various mediated forms, to show how her private experience has been made public and in turn how that publicity has helped shape our understanding of the histories of US eminent domain law and human rights violations.[1] Mary Frances was removed from her home as a child and committed to a state hospital that routinely practiced sterilization, legal at the time under Virginia's 1924 Sterilization Act. Ultimately one woman's life story allows us to examine the manner in which the displaced are often constructed as passive victims responsible for their "out-of-placeness" from normative discourse, therefore inviting us to revisit these discourses in different ways.[2]

In order to examine a private life through public representations, I use a critical framework that combines analyses of vulnerabilities and notions of represented truth, precarity, and states of exception. Using those theoretical lenses combined, together with Wendy S. Hesford's explanation of a "crisis of witnessing," I turn to multimedia contexts in which Mary Frances's story has been represented. While I examine various media contexts, I focus on documentary film, and in particular use Paula Rabinowitz's analysis of documentary, the ethics of visual representation, and the ways in which "we come to understand that nothing we have heard or seen in this film is trustworthy. There will always be one more thing."[3]

In her introduction to *Frames of War,* Judith Butler discusses the normative discourses that render a subject's life worth living. She says, "Normative schemes are interrupted by one another, they emerge and fade depending on broader operations of power, and very often come up against spectral versions of what it is they claim to know: thus, there are 'subjects' who are not quite recognizable as subjects, and there are 'lives' that are not quite—or, indeed, are never—recognized as lives."[4] As in her previous work on the precarity of life, Butler's framing of subjectivity helps us to see how audiences "frame" or understand a particular life and the ways in which lives that are outside normative discourses, and therefore not recognizable, are particularly vulnerable. Her recent work extends this argument to the notion of dispossession, not only in terms of material possession but in terms of the ways in which bodies that stand up to their dispossession are particularly vulnerable (e.g., protesters).[5] When people stand in front of a camera, in what ways do they make themselves vulnerable? What rhetorical choices are they making and what control do they have over their choices? And furthermore, in what ways do viewers frame those choices in order to understand the story at hand?

The very concept of human rights and the laws surrounding those rights are bound by notions of sovereignty. The philosopher Giorgio Agamben explains that a consequence of the exclusionary language of human rights law is that hierarchical sets of decision-making processes about whose life is "worth" saving operate when others are witnessing human rights stories and violations. Agamben explains that the judicial power to make decisions about human life is paradoxically violent: both to constitute the law and to sustain it.[6]

Humanities scholars interested in human rights discourses are thus concerned about the ways in which vulnerability is mapped onto particular bodies, like those forcibly removed from their homes.[7] Dispossessed bodies take on the burden of representation in domestic and international politics and law. As Katharyne Mitchell argues, the dispossessed are "excluded exclusions, those for whom there exists no possibility of return. Legal abandonment is produced through all kinds of institutions and at multiple scales. But, in almost every case, the victim of banishment is represented as causing his or her own exile, torture and/or immiseration."[8]

The representation of vulnerable bodies, then, adds another layer to the implications of human rights discourses. Not only do we question the function of human rights laws and discourses themselves but we also question the notions of testimony and witnessing as we struggle to report on human rights violations.

In documenting stories like that of Mary Frances, we are cautioned to recognize the limits of human rights discourses yet also compelled to understand the ways in which the dispossessed are vulnerable as a politically induced condition.[9] Mary Frances's story asks us to consider who qualifies as a human rights subject and in what contexts, deepening our understanding of the struggles of the poor, women, and children for legal and cultural recognition.

However, in telling the stories of the dispossessed, we risk appropriation and additional trauma. Hesford warns that "in reliving the trauma, in the name of giving evidence, the witness and the viewer, perhaps unavoidably, are implicated in recreating the spectacle of trauma."[10] Creators of the various genres of testimony (such as film, memoir, magazine article, photograph) risk reappropriating the stories of the dispossessed and viewers of those genres, depending on how the narratives are constructed, are asked to consider their relation to that text and the subjects within. How one witnesses either one's own or someone else's human rights violation is paradoxical—the narrative structure of witnessing can direct certain kinds of responses. Hesford explains this "crisis of witnessing" as the "risks of representing trauma and violence, ruptures in identification, and the impossibility of empathetic merging between witness and testifier, listener and speaker."[11] Likewise, human rights rhetoric scholars Arabella Lyon and Lester C. Olson have noted that "protection" can be a euphemism for taking control.[12] Lyon and Olson also argue that attention to the rhetorical dimensions of witnessing can help us understand and hopefully prevent the potential harm in witnessing. Hesford similarly points out the "spectacle of trauma and oral testimonials as both empowering *and* voyeuristic, collective *and* individual. . . . To find testimonial narratives and images of suffering simultaneously empowering and voyeuristic is not, however, to remain undecided about their role, but rather to recognize their complex rhetorical dynamics."[13] In her analysis of Farm Security Administration (FSA) photography during the Depression era and its influence on newsreels, documentaries, and Hollywood films, Rabinowitz similarly highlights the tensions of witnessing present in these various media—providing the context in which my work with Mary Frances played out. Rabinowitz focuses on the photography of Dorothea Lange and the films of Pare Lorentz and others and suggests that Hollywood spoofed some of these overbearing truth-telling films. She says, however, that "for a time—and Lange and Lorentz perhaps best embody this—the practice of socially engaged image-making, 'art' as 'propaganda,' as political discourse, as historical fact, even historical agent implied seeking out privations, imaging need, and hoping those representations would produce actions. For the implicit meaning of documentary is not only to record but to change the world—to evince material effects through representation—and to do so through highly personal interventions into public life." She goes on to explain that Hollywood films borrowed from the "truth" of documentary even when documentary photography was posing subjects and staging shots; indeed, as Rabinowitz argues, Dorothea Lange "understood and manipulated, perhaps even fashioned, the semiotics of visual and textual interactions for a broad audience." So while the photographs were overly stylized, what Rabinowitz suggests is that there is "slippage among popular culture and people's culture and public culture, between extreme fantasy and harsh reality, between Busby Berkeley musicals and FSA photographs."[14] The public was used to seeing these tropes and they were present in both fictional and nonfiction genres.

Like his colleagues Dorothea Lange and Walker Evans, Arthur Rothstein took photographs documenting the Depression for the FSA. Most famous for his Dustbowl photographs, Rothstein also took a series of photographs in Shenandoah National Park, just before the people living there, many of them poor, were relocated as their land was transferred from Virginia to the federal government. Rothstein took photographs of several families, including many that were a part of Mary Frances's extended family.

My encounter with Mary Frances, her family, and their neighbors was deeply affected by the legacy of this original, problematic form of "witnessing," as will become apparent. However, before I turn to my research, it is important to explain the context in which their rights were arguably so abused. In Virginia during the 1930s, some five hundred families were forcibly removed from their homes through eminent domain law when Shenandoah National Park was formed under Virginia's Public Park Condemnation Act of 1928. In the United States, condemnation of private property for public use through federal eminent domain law has long been controversial. Indeed, government-sanctioned displacement holds a significant place in the country's history.[15] When the state of Virginia condemned the property of the five hundred families in the late 1920s in order to "donate" the land to form Shenandoah National Park, many moved on their own to find housing elsewhere. Many others, however, were in need of government assistance and applied for government loans that would allow them to move to resettlement housing. Those families went through an eligibility process whereby their finances were examined and it was determined whether they could repay a government loan for a "homestead." Families that were not able to qualify for the loans were placed under the care of the newly formed Department of Public Welfare.[16] Social workers found alternative housing for a few families, and in the park's archives, correspondence between park officials and social workers highlights the decision-making processes of government officials as they worked toward relocating families.[17]

In addition to correspondence between government officials, area social workers, and local magistrates, the park's archives contain a collection of letters written by some family members during the process of removal, between 1934 and 1938. The primary content of the letters includes requests from residents for assistance as they prepared to move, for permission to take building materials with them, and for access to their crops.[18] One of the letters, dated February 5, 1937, states:

> Dear Mr. Hoskins, I heard that you are going to move Fennel Corbin and Dicy Corbin to the Feble mind Colinly [sic] if you do please move me in that house as Mr. Smith that live there is my Brother and that house wold suit me I could get my mail every day and I could my food Brought to me and I wold have some Fruit and I wold Be on the road so a Dr could reach me whare I live it is 3 miles to the nears narber no road up the mountin Just a path and a Bad way I am 76 years old and if you can Please let me have that house and move me as soon as you take them a way Please see MrsHumrickhouse she was to see me some time a go and said she wold try to get me a Place off of this mountin your truly Mrs WA Nicholson.[19]

This letter, written by Barbara Nicholson to park ranger Taylor Hoskins, refers to Finnell Corbin and his daughter Dicey, who, together with her children, were forced to leave their home in the mountains to make way for the park. Finnell was the patriarch of a large extended family living in Corbin Hollow, one of the populated areas in the park. One of Finnell's sons was named Harrison, who was married to Sadie. They had several children, one of whom was Mary Frances. Finnell Corbin and many of his children, grandchildren, and extended family members were photographed by Arthur Rothstein.[20]

Finnell Corbin owned nineteen acres in the mountains of central Virginia before it became part of the park. The Corbins were a large family in the area, and well known by the officials in charge of the relocations. After being paid the "just compensation" of 530 dollars for his land,[21] Finnell was labeled "feeble-minded" and was sent to a state hospital in Staunton, Virginia. Various members of his family were also sent away, including his daughter-in-law Sadie and her five children, one of whom was Mary Frances, age seven. Mary spent sixteen years in the Virginia Colony for Epileptics and Feebleminded and was sterilized when she was eleven without her knowledge or consent. When she was released, she remained in the area and later married. She did not know until she was an adult that could not have children.

I first read Mrs. Nicholson's letter in 2002, while researching the displacement of families from the park. I was familiar with the Corbin family, both because many of the photographs of park families include members of the Corbin family and because it is widely known that the "Colvin" family in *Hollow Folk* (1933) is a thinly veiled pseudonym for the Corbin family. *Hollow Folk*, written by sociologists Mandel Sherman and Thomas Henry, was partly based on the research of Miriam Sizer, a schoolteacher and sociologist from the University of Virginia who lived among the families and "surveyed" them to determine their needs during the relocation process.[22] The written images in *Hollow Folk* have since been analyzed as monolithic, misguided, and reminiscent of eugenics field studies.[23] Similarly, Rothstein's and other FSA photographers' visual images have been critiqued for their highly stylized staging despite the fact that they purported to document "real" life and spontaneous situations.[24] The images of Mary Frances's extended family and other mountain families were widely publicized in the mid-1930s in Rothstein's project and in various news articles in the surrounding communities and Washington, DC (which is less than two hours from the park).

But it wasn't until 2009 that I examined more closely Mrs. Nicholson's phrase "febly mind colinly" and the connections between the removal of families from Shenandoah National Park and the Colony. My understanding was illuminated by pooling archival resources with filmmaker Richard Robinson, who was working on a documentary film about Arthur Rothstein's Shenandoah project. In 2009 and 2010, he photographed and filmed the places in the park where home sites had been, interviewed descendants of displaced residents, and retraced Rothstein's photographic steps of 1935 to understand his rationale for photographing particular families for his assignment.[25] During his search, Robinson found that reporter Mary Bishop had already made the connection. In her 1995 news article "Sterilization Survivors Speak Out," Bishop interviewed several people who were willing to speak about their experiences at the Colony. One of the people interviewed was Mary Frances Corbin—and when Robinson read her name, he sought Bishop's help in determining a connection between Mary Frances and the Corbins displaced from the park. At the same time, I revisited an archived letter from a prominent doctor to the national park service's director, recommending Miriam Sizer for a position, in which he stated that "arrangements [are] made for moving out and colonizing the worst of these people."[26] These combined facts suggested that more research was necessary to determine whether there were direct connections between the National Park Service and the eugenics movement, a connection Robinson hoped Mary Frances could make.

Bishop's news reporting in the 1990s had rekindled an interest in Virginia's history of promoting eugenics. "Feebleminded" was one of the categories used during the progressive era of social reform to label people with a range of mental disabilities. Commonly, the term was also used to judge those whose behavior (like "fits" or "hysteria") was considered distasteful at best and a menace to society at worst. There were several hospitals across the country in the late nineteenth and early twentieth centuries where the "feebleminded" were committed. One of the hospitals located in Lynchburg, approximately one hundred miles from Shenandoah National Park, the Colony was well known for its sterilization practices.[27] According to Bishop, more than sixty thousand Americans were rounded up, judged genetically inferior, held in government asylums, and sterilized against their will. Some were mentally retarded; many were not. Most were poor, uneducated country people — orphans, petty criminals, juvenile delinquents, epileptics, and sexually active single women. All were people that those in power, from social workers to legislators to judges, saw as threats to the nation's gene pool.[28]

Bishop's article represents Mary Frances as one of several survivors of sterilization who were willing to speak out. The article is carefully crafted, weaving Mary Frances's story with several others, including the history of eugenics in Virginia together with court records and commitment papers.[29] According to Bishop, Mary Frances, whose sterilization operation at the age of eleven left her in a coma for two weeks, "wasn't told the purpose of her operation. Many young women grew up believing they had appendectomies. . . . Decades later, [Mary Frances and other former patients] still talk as if the colony might reach across the river and capture them again if anyone questions their behavior."[30]

Bishop's story and our archival research about Rothstein and the park thus converged to suggest possible connections between the eugenics movement and the resettlement of families due to eminent domain. Together, Bishop, Robinson, and I interviewed Mary Frances in June 2010. It was more than ten years after Bishop's initial interview. Robinson was interested in knowing if Mary Frances remembered Rothstein photographing her family; I was interested in her memories of living in the mountains of Virginia and her family's reaction to Shenandoah National Park.

Before speaking to Mary Frances, I understood the displacement of families as a collective story, one in which nearly everyone I interviewed spoke of their parents' and grandparents' memories of losing their homes and their lasting

Mary Frances Corbin during an interview in June 2010. Photograph by Richard Knox Robinson.

sadness or bitterness because of their displacement. Mary Frances, however, told a different story. She did not have many memories of her childhood in the mountains as she was only seven when she was taken to the Colony. She responded, "I remember they took my brother and two sisters first . . . that's all I know. They said everybody was feebleminded. . . . My mama was taken away too." During our interview, we showed Mary Frances several photographs she had never seen of her extended family members. Her caretaker called a few days later to say that Mary had requested copies of the photographs. Robinson wrote of this request in his blog: "When I started going through Rothstein's archive to make [Mary Frances's] copies, it was then that I comprehended how closely related the majority of Rothstein's subjects were. Rothstein's archive on this assignment was essentially Mary Frances' family album. Most of Rothstein's photographs were of her family. This realization was all the more stunning since Mary Frances didn't have any family photographs in her home. Her life had been so disrupted, she hardly knew who her family was."[31] Mary Frances displayed great willingness to listen to our questions and to work toward answering them. We went to her asking for very specific information, hoping she could help us make connections because the archival records weren't clear. My memory and experience of interviewing Mary Frances give a different perspective than what one sees in the documentary film, where only brief portions of the interview are included. The audience hears my questions, and hears her answers through her absent dentures and a thick Appalachian dialect, but then viewers of the film can hear the filmmaker's voice-over while my hands can be seen moving Rothstein's photographs in and out of Mary's view. In one of my hands is a pen, at the ready to take notes about what Mary is telling me about the person in each picture. As I lay Rothstein's photographs of her family members in front of her, Mary Frances seemed to remember more, or at least was willing to reveal more. With some distance I see now that we really don't come to know Mary Frances in this film at all. Though sympathetic to her story, through this film, as through the newspaper articles and other coverage, we only see Mary Frances through the context of her life at the Colony. The circumstances of the history of the park are so complicated that even with Mary Frances's help it remains difficult to understand. However, her story illustrates that individual lives and the way they are narrated provide some measure of filling in the missing pieces.

Robinson says of his film, "To a large degree, Mary Frances is 'Rothstein's First Assignment's' central character. Though her appearance comes at the end of the film, it is her family that was [at] the center of [it]. . . . Mary Bishop . . . reported [that the] shame that comes with being labeled 'feebleminded' creates its own exile. Few are willing to talk about their experiences. Of the thousands of individuals who were sterilized in Virginia, only a handful have been willing to go on the record."[32] Mary Frances became the central figure because she was the link among the central family photographed by Rothstein, the Colony, and the filmmaker's response to this. His realization of these connections deeply impacted the way he edited the film so as to highlight the possibility of Rothstein's connection to eugenics field studies.

While making the film, Robinson was concerned with highlighting the staged nature of documentary film, photography, and storytelling, in obvious contrast to Rothstein and the photographers of the 1930s. *Rothstein's First Assignment: A Film about Documentary Truth* is an experimental documentary in which the pacing is slow, images are repeated for effect, and the narrative progression is confusing. Many characters are introduced but not explained, the plot is uncertain, and, while Robinson suggests a connection between eugenics field studies and the FSA, no direct conclusions are drawn. For some audiences, this is disconcerting. But for Robinson the unanswered questions are precisely what he wanted for his audience—and perhaps for the researchers too. Indeed, the process of researching and filming the documentary was a muddled one, and the final narrative of the film reflects this chaotic process.

As we moved from the texts of the letters to photographs of Mary Frances's ancestors, back to the text of Mary's commitment papers, and finally to the editing process of the film, we were aware of the implications of retelling portions of her story, and throughout the process attempted to be "mindful of how rhetorical acts of witnessing may function as new forms of international tourism and appropriation."[33] Documentary film has its history in legal interviewing, with the tradition of finding the so-called truth. In his experimental documentary, Robinson sought to expose the notion of truth, and the film highlights the mediated nature of the interviews by showing the staging of the interview, images of the interviewers, and the film and sound equipment and by juxtaposing Mary Frances's life with historical images of her family taken by a government-employed photographer.

The mediated nature of documentary film, in terms of both the filmmaker's editing decisions and audiences' responses to it, reflects the paradox of life narrative more generally, that despite its limitations it "plays a central role in the rights process."[34] That "testimony contains a lacuna" brings to the forefront the ways in which the truth can never be fully represented. In the case of *Rothstein's First Assignment* and the varied aspects of research contributing to that film, the role of the witness remains in question. According to Agamben, "the value of testimony lies essentially in what it lacks; at its center it contains something that cannot be borne witness to and that discharges the survivors of authority."[35]

The film created around Mary Frances's experience at the Colony asks audiences to reconsider a displacement narrative that "entails recognition of the ongoing state of and need for the call to action — a continual empathetic unsettlement predicated upon the inherent incompleteness of the present and the ungovernability of the past."[36] As the subtitle of his film suggests (*A Film about Documentary Truth*), Robinson was explicitly conscious of issues of form, of the way documentary is constructed, of the obtrusiveness of the camera, and of the role of the filmmaker and the interviewer in constructing a certain kind of narrative. *Rothstein's First Assignment* invites its audience to see the complexity of the story, the unanswered questions, Mary Frances as a witness, the film as a witness, and the unreliability of any of the witnessing occurring in the film. The film does not draw definitive conclusions and has been critiqued for that. But the filmmaker, in an attempt to question documentary film's ability to ever get at any so-called truth, purposefully leaves questions unanswered, narratives unfinished, and viewers uneasy. While this approach does not necessarily let us off the hook of reappropriating Mary Frances's life, it does bring to the fore the inability of ever fully understanding every twist and turn of either an individual's life or a historical event.

Understanding the complexities of displacement narratives challenges us to consider stories like Mary Frances's as offering counternarratives of the displaced as passive agents responsible for their "out-of-placeness."[37] Members of the Corbin family, described by Dr. Sexton as "the worst of these people," fell under the discourses (and literal violences) of eugenics because of their poverty. The individuals and agencies charged with the well-being of the families displaced from the park used the language of the eugenics movement to justify placing them in state-run facilities that ended their ability to bear children, most often without their knowledge or consent. Based on our individual work and our conversations with each other and Mary Frances, we have sought to connect her individual story with the geopolitical implications of human rights violations. When a displacement narrative conforms to expectations of victimhood, nostalgia, and subsequent "saving" by the state, the story remains one that we are used to reading and knowing. However, Mary Frances's willingness to "speak out" counters this narrative. The agency of the displaced as emphasized in narratives like Mary's is evident in what they *do*, enacting agency through the *active* writing of letters, refusing to move from their homes, requesting documents and photographs, and sharing the stories with reporters and filmmakers. Robinson's film examines the multiple rhetorical ways in which Rothstein's original photographs were used. While they were ostensibly taken to document the poor in the rural South and to raise awareness of the devastation of the Depression, they were at the same time used against individuals to prove their "unworthiness" as citizens and hide them away in asylums. Despite her vulnerability, Mary Frances has spoken out, to reporters and filmmakers, and she attended a public screening of the film near her home.

Mary Frances's story, as it has been presented in various media, including this essay, represents the making of a forcibly sterilized subject and the nationalizing of a particular kind of Virginia that elides decision making with the work of philanthropists, doctors, and social workers, all educated at prestigious places. The point, however, is not to vilify the places where eugenics was practiced or the people employed there—that's an easy narrative. Rather, Mary Frances's story points to the deep-seated discourses of normativity at play. While we know this history already through the work of various eugenics scholars, this discussion highlights the ways Mary Frances's story changes our view and adds "one more thing" to our understanding of a complicated history.

Until now, I had avoided writing individuals' stories—I understood the history of the park as a collective story. Mary Frances's story changes that view, takes us back to the archive, asks us to reexamine previously found documents, and helps us to make connections and change our perceptions of history.

Finally, our collaboration on this project and our many conversations about our individual and combined research revealed the "subtle variations" of different forms of media in representing Mary Frances's life.[38] The film and the various other representations of the story combine to make yet another version to add to the historiography of eminent domain, eugenics, and Virginia history. When states create literal and discursive boundaries, the implications for citizens can be profound, as they are placed in a precarious position, placed outside the law, and subsequently abandoned by the law. Mary Frances's story implicates us as we seek to understand these complicated connections. The forced naming of some of the park's residents as feebleminded, and thus subhuman, and their subjection to the dominant discourses of the state, resulted in violations of their human rights and thus connect Mary Frances's story to larger geopolitical concerns about human rights violations enacted through eminent domain law.[39] The removals and subsequent sterilizations of members of the Corbin family warrant great pause when considering issues of eminent domain and US government or state-sanctioned forced removals for the "public good."

The history of Shenandoah National Park has been fraught with tension from the beginning, and Mary Frances alters our understanding of both the ways in which eminent domain law can be enacted and the long-term human rights consequences of such enactments. In addition, the creation of Robinson's documentary challenges us to consider how "documenting human rights violations is paradoxical in that violence is often represented in order to resist it."[40] By retelling Mary's story, we do indeed reappropriate it, but we do so with a keen self-consciousness and self-reflection about the ethical dimensions of that retelling.

NOTES

1. The Fifth Amendment in the US Constitution states, "nor shall private property be taken for public use without just compensation." Individual state laws, such as Virginia's Public Park Condemnation Act, fall under the auspices of "eminent domain law," whereby a property owner's land can be "taken" for "public use" only if that property owner receives just compensation. The families who owned land within Shenandoah National Park were compensated a "fair market value" for their property. However, many residents were tenants and received no compensation for their relocations.

2. On "out-of-placeness," see cultural geographer Tim Cresswell's "Weeds, Plagues, and Bodily Secretions: A Geographical Interpretation of Metaphors of Displacement," *Annals of the Association of American Geographers* 87, no. 2 (1997): 330–45.

3. Paula Rabinowitz, *They Must Be Represented: The Politics of Documentary* (London: Verso, 1994), 216.

4. Judith Butler, *Frames of War: When Is Life Grievable?* (London: Verso, 2010), 4.

5. See Judith Butler and Athena Athanasiou's *Dispossession: The Performative in the Political* (London: Polity, 2013).

6. Here I draw from Agamben's explanation of the paradoxes of law, as understood through Walter Benjamin's discussion of the violence inherent in laws. See Giorgio Agamben, *Homo Sacer: Sovereign Power and Bare Life*, trans. Daniel Heller-Roazen (Stanford, CA: Stanford University Press, 1998).

7. See Kay Schaffer and Sidonie Smith's *Human Rights and Narrated Lives: The Ethics of Recognition* (New York: Palgrave, 2004) and Joseph R. Slaughter's *Human Rights Inc.: The World Novel, Narrative Form, and International Law* (New York: Fordham University Press, 2007) for examples of these recent discussions.

8. Katharyne Mitchell, "Geographies of Identity: The New Exceptionalism," *Progress in Human Geography* 30, no. 1 (2006): 102.

9. Judith Butler's turn toward the subject of human vulnerability in *Precarious Life* and *Frames of War* informs the analysis here.

10. Wendy S. Hesford, "Documenting Violations: Rhetorical Witnessing and the Spectacle of Distant Suffering," *Biography* 27, no. 1 (Winter 2004): 122.

11. Ibid., 107.

12. Arabella Lyon and Lester C. Olson, eds., " Human Rights Rhetoric: Traditions of Testifying and Witnessing," special issue, *Rhetoric Society Quarterly* 41, no. 3 (2011): 207.

13. Hesford, "Documenting Violations," 124.

14. Paula Rabinowitz, "People's Culture, Popular Culture, Public Culture: Hollywood, Newsreels, and FSA Films and Photographs," in Paula Rabinowitz, *They Must Be Represented: The Politics of Documentary* (London: Verso, 1994), 102, 103.

15. Examples include the 1830 Indian Removal Act and Executive Order 9066, which authorized the Japanese internments during World War II.

16. See Elna C. Green's work on the history of public welfare and Virginia's in particular. Elna C. Green, "Introduction," in *The New Deal and Beyond: Social Welfare in the South since 1930*, ed. Elna C. Green (Athens: University of Georgia Press, 2003); and *The Business of Relief: Confronting Poverty in a Southern City, 1740–1940* (Athens: University of Georgia Press, 2003).

17. The Shenandoah National Park Archives are located in Luray, Virginia, and include correspondence, land use maps, geographic surveys, and documentation of flora and fauna.

18. Many of the letters in the park's archives are published in Katrina M. Powell, ed., *"Answer at Once": Letters of Mountain Families in Shenandoah National Park, 1934–1938* (Charlottesville: University of Virginia Press, 2009). In Katrina M. Powell, *The Anguish of Displacement: The Politics of Literacy in the Letters of Mountain Families in Shenandoah National Park* (Charlottesville: University of Virginia Press, 2007), I analyze the rhetorical significance of the letters in documenting the history of displacement in order to form Shenandoah

National Park. See also "Small Stories, Public Impact: Archives, Film, and Collaboration," *Reflections: Public Rhetoric, Civic Writing, and Service Learning* 12, no. 1 (Fall 2012): 111–33, where I discuss the collaboration process of working with filmmaker Richard Robinson.

19. In *"Answer at Once,"* I transcribed the letters exactly as they appear, leaving in nonstandard spellings and grammar.

20. These photographs are archived at the Library of Congress. See Rothstein's FSA collection, accessed June 15, 2006, http://loc.gov/pictures/collection/fsa/ (search for Arthur Rothstein).

21. Darwin Lambert, *The Undying Past of Shenandoah National Park* (Lanham, MD: Roberts Rinehart, 1989), appendix 3, 292.

22. See Mandel Sherman and Thomas R. Henry's *Hollow Folk* (New York: Thomas Y. Crowell Company, 1933). Also, the University of Virginia played a significant role in advocating for eugenics practices. See the "Eugenics" online exhibit at the Claude Moore Health Sciences Library, accessed June 15, 2006, http://www.hsl.virginia.edu /historical/eugenics/. Miriam Sizer's extensive report, "Tabulations," systematically recorded the living conditions of the families in Corbin Hollow (among others). Sizer's report is steeped in eugenics discourse, attending to children's and their parents' hygiene, home conditions, and mental condition, in addition to providing an accounting of their personal property. See Miriam Sizer, "Tabulations" (Shenandoah National Park Papers, National Archives Satellite, College Park, MD, 1932). Sizer also appears in *A Trip to Shenandoah*, a newsreel or documentary-style film from 1936. In the film Sizer holds a malnourished child still for the camera, and in the next cut the same child appears well dressed and well fed. While there is no sound, the film's narrative suggests that taking the child from his parents and environment is what improved his condition. Rabinowitz's analysis of FSA documentaries suggests that this film about Shenandoah might have been similarly produced, although it is not clear from the film's credits.

23. See Stephen Fender, "Poor Whites and the Federal Writers Project: The Rhetoric of Eugenics in the Southern Life Histories," in *Popular Eugenics: National Efficiency and American Mass Culture in the 1930s*, ed. Christina Cogdell and Susan Currell (Athens: Ohio University Press, 2006); Jane S. Becker, *Selling Tradition: Appalachia and the Construction of an American Folk, 1930–1940* (Chapel Hill: University of North Carolina Press, 1998); and Audrey Horning, "Archaeological Considerations of 'Appalachian' Identity," in *The Archaeology of Communities: A New World Perspective*, ed. Marcello Canuto and Jason Yaeger (London: Routledge, 2000).

24. See Susan Currell, "Taking Out the (White) Trash: Eugenic National Housekeeping and New Deal Photography in the Great Depression" (unpublished essay, 2012); and James Curtis, *Mind's Eye, Mind's Truth: FSA Photography Reconsidered* (Philadelphia: Temple University Press, 1991).

25. Richard Robinson, "Mary Frances and The Colony," *Rothstein's First Assignment* (blog), January 7, 2011, accessed February 19, 2011, http://rothsteinsfirstassignment .blogspot.com/2011/02/mary-frances-and-colony.html.

26. Dr. Roy Sexton to Horace Albright, 1932, Shenandoah National Park Archives.

27. The Colony was where Carrie Buck was institutionalized and forcibly sterilized. She was the woman named in the 1927 US Supreme Court case *Buck v. Bell*, in which the court upheld Virginia's sterilization act.

28. Mary Bishop, "Sterilizations Survivors Speak Out," *Southern Exposure* 23, no. 2 (1995): 13. Virginia eugenicists sterilized about eight thousand people before the state's 1924 Eugenical Sterilization Act, also known as the Sterilization Act, was repealed (much later, in 1974). See also Pippa Holloway's *Sexuality, Politics, and Social Control in Virginia, 1920–1945* (Chapel Hill: University of North Carolina Press, 2006) and Paul Lombardo's *Three Generations, No Imbeciles: Eugenics, the Supreme Court, and "Buck v. Bell"* (Baltimore: Johns Hopkins University Press, 2010) for a history of eugenics in Virginia; and "Eugenics" at the Claude Moore Health Sciences Library's online historical exhibit at http://www.hsl.virginia.edu/historical/eugenics/.

29. Eugenics, since debunked as a pseudoscience, gained traction in the 1920s in the United States. It espoused that, since certain conditions were hereditary, compulsory sterilization should be practiced to keep the gene pool pure. These conditions not only included disease but also extended to issues such as poverty, sexual appetite, and "feeble-mindedness." It is well documented that the Nazis' sterilization laws were modeled after Virginia's. See Paul Lombardo's *Three Generations* and "From Better Babies to the Bunglers: Eugenics on Tobacco Road," in *A Century of Eugenics in America: From the Indiana Experiment to the Human Genome Era*, ed. Paul Lombardo (Bloomington: Indiana University Press, 2011), Edwin Black's *War Against the Weak: Eugenics and America's Campaign to Create a Master Race* (New York: Dialog Press, 2012), and Anne Maxwell's *Picture Imperfect: Photography and Eugenics, 1870–1940* (Eastbourne: Sussex Academic Press, 2010).

30. Bishop, "Sterilizations Survivors Speak Out," 15–16. Mary Frances also appears in the documentary film *The Lynchburg Story: Eugenic Sterilization in America*, directed by Stephen Trombley (Worldview Pictures, 2008). In the film Mary Frances and other former patients interviewed speak about the horrible living conditions at the Colony and the punishments they suffered for misbehavior or escape attempts.

31. Robinson, "Mary Frances and the Colony."

32. Richard Robinson, "More Historic Screenings," *Rothstein's First Assignment* (blog), November 12, 2011, accessed November 15, 2011, http://rothsteinsfirstassignment.blogspot.com/2011/11/more-historic-screenings.html.

33. Hesford, "Documenting Violations," 121. Wendy S. Hesford and Wendy Kozol also say in their introduction to *Just Advocacy*, "This dialogic process [of witnessing] is also a transnational and transcultural process whereby reading or seeing human rights violations locates the viewer, the reader, and the witness within local and global communities. Pedagogically speaking, we might ask whether or how representations prompt self-reflexivity about the politics of viewers' historical, cultural, and social locations?" Wendy S. Hesford and Wendy Kozol, "Introduction," in *Just Advocacy? Women's Human Rights, Transnational Feminisms, and the Politics of Representation*, ed. Wendy S. Hesford and Wendy Kozol (New Brunswick, NJ: Rutgers University Press, 2005), 11.

34. Margaretta Jolly, "Introduction: Life/Rights Narrative in Action," in this volume.

35. Giorgio Agamben, *Remnants of Auschwitz: The Witness and the Archive*, trans. Daniel Heller-Roazen (New York: Zone Books, 1992), 33, 34.

36. Hesford, "Documenting Violations," 130.

37. See Cresswell, "Weeds, Plagues, and Bodily Secretions."

38. Jolly, "Introduction."

39. As Hesford suggests, "The methodological challenge that has plagued historiographers and rhetorical critics alike lies not in the pursuit of an inclusive human rights history, but in our insufficient attention to distinctions of geopolitical scale and scope, distinctions between the rhetorical tactics of individuals and the momentum of a social movement, and the contradictory subjectivities that human rights law, and, more broadly, rights-talk compels." Wendy S. Hesford, "Human Rights Rhetoric of Recognition," *Rhetoric Society Quarterly* 41, no. 3 (2011): 289.

40. Hesford, "Documenting Violations," 107. See also Wendy S. Hesford, *Spectacular Rhetorics: Human Rights Visions, Recognitions, Feminisms* (Durham, NC: Duke University Press, 2011); Peter Nyers, *Rethinking Refugees: Beyond States of Emergency* (New York: Routledge, Taylor Francis Group, 2006); and Michael Ryan, "Destruction and Social Theory: The Case of Liberalism," in *Displacement: Derrida and After*, edited by Mark Krupnick (Bloomington: Indiana University Press, 1983).

WORKS CITED

Agamben, Giorgio. *Homo Sacer: Sovereign Power and Bare Life*. Translated by Daniel Heller-Roazen. Stanford, CA: Stanford University Press, 1998.

———. *Remnants of Auschwitz: The Witness and the Archive*. Translated by Daniel Heller-Roazen. New York: Zone Books, 1992.

Becker, Jane S. *Selling Tradition: Appalachia and the Construction of an American Folk, 1930–1940*. Chapel Hill: University of North Carolina Press, 1998.

Bishop, Mary. "Sterilizations Survivors Speak Out." *Southern Exposure* 23, no. 2 (1995): 12–17.

Black, Edwin. *War Against the Weak: Eugenics and America's Campaign to Create a Master Race*. New York: Dialog Press, 2012.

Butler, Judith. *Frames of War: When Is Life Grievable?* London: Verso, 2010.

Butler, Judith, and Athena Athanasiou. *Dispossession: The Performative in the Political*. London: Polity, 2013.

Cresswell, Tim. "Weeds, Plagues, and Bodily Secretions: A Geographical Interpretation of Metaphors of Displacement." *Annals of the Association of American Geographers* 87, no. 2 (1997): 330–45.

Currell, Susan. "Taking Out the (White) Trash: Eugenic National Housekeeping and New Deal Photography in the Great Depression." Unpublished essay, 2012.

Curtis, James. *Mind's Eye, Mind's Truth: FSA Photography Reconsidered*. Philadelphia: Temple University Press, 1991.

Felman, Shoshona, and Dori Laub. *Testimony: Crises of Witnessing in Literature, Psychoanalysis, and History*. New York: Routledge, 1992.

Fender, Stephen. "Poor Whites and the Federal Writers Project: The Rhetoric of Eugenics in the Southern Life Histories." In *Popular Eugenics: National Efficiency and American Mass Culture in the 1930s*, edited by Christina Cogdell and Susan Currell, 140–63. Athens: Ohio University Press, 2006.

Green, Elna C. *The Business of Relief: Confronting Poverty in a Southern City, 1740–1940*. Athens: University of Georgia Press, 2003.

——. "Introduction." In *The New Deal and Beyond: Social Welfare in the South since 1930*, edited by Elna. C. Green, vii–xix. Athens: University of Georgia Press, 2003.

Hesford, Wendy. S. "Documenting Violations: Rhetorical Witnessing and the Spectacle of Distant Suffering." *Biography* 27, no. 1 (Winter 2004): 104–44.

——. "Human Rights Rhetoric of Recognition." *Rhetoric Society Quarterly* 41, no. 3 (2011): 282–89.

——. *Spectacular Rhetorics: Human Rights Visions, Recognitions, Feminisms*. Durham, NC: Duke University Press, 2011.

Hesford, Wendy S., and Wendy Kozol. "Introduction." In *Just Advocacy? Women's Human Rights, Transnational Feminisms, and the Politics of Representation*, edited by Wendy S. Hesford and Wendy Kozol, 1–29. New Brunswick, NJ: Rutgers University Press, 2005.

Holloway, Pippa. *Sexuality, Politics, and Social Control in Virginia, 1920–1945*. Chapel Hill: University of North Carolina Press, 2006.

Horning, Audrey. "Archaeological Considerations of 'Appalachian' Identity." In *The Archaeology of Communities: A New World Perspective*, edited by Marcello Canuto and Jason Yaeger, 210–30. London: Routledge, 2000.

Lambert, Darwin. *The Undying Past of Shenandoah National Park*. Lanham, MD: Roberts Rinehart, 1989.

Lombardo, Paul A. "From Better Babies to the Bunglers: Eugenics on Tobacco Road." In *A Century of Eugenics in America: From the Indiana Experiment to the Human Genome Era*, edited by Paul Lombardo, 45–67. Bloomington: Indiana University Press, 2011.

——. *Three Generations, No Imbeciles: Eugenics, the Supreme Court, and "Buck v. Bell."* Baltimore: Johns Hopkins University Press, 2008.

Lyon, Arabella, and Lester C. Olson, eds. "Human Rights Rhetoric: Traditions of Testifying and Witnessing." Special issue, *Rhetoric Society Quarterly* 41 no. 3 (2011): 203–12.

Maxwell, Anne. "Building a Health Nation: Eugenic Images in the United States, 1890–1935." In Anne Maxwell, *Picture Imperfect: Photography and Eugenics, 1870–1940*, 108–46. Eastbourne: Sussex Academic Press, 2010.

Mitchell, Katharyne. "Geographies of Identity: The New Exceptionalism." *Progress in Human Geography* 30, no. 1 (2006): 95–106.

Nicholson, Mrs. W. A. (Barbara Allen Smith Nicholson, wife of William Aldridge Nicholson). Letter to Taylor Hoskins, Shenandoah National Park Ranger, February 5, 1937. Shenandoah National Park Archives, Luray, Virginia.

Nyers, Peter. *Rethinking Refugees: Beyond States of Emergency*. New York: Routledge, Taylor Francis Group, 2006.

Powell, Katrina. M. *The Anguish of Displacement: The Politics of Literacy in the Letters of Mountain Families in Shenandoah National Park*. Charlottesville: University of Virginia Press, 2007.

———, ed. *"Answer at Once": Letters of Mountain Families in Shenandoah National Park, 1934–1938*. Charlottesville: University of Virginia Press, 2009.

———. "Small Stories, Public Impact: Archives, Film, and Collaboration." *Reflections: Public Rhetoric, Civic Writing, and Service Learning* 12, no. 1 (Fall 2012): 111–33.

Rabinowitz, Paula. "People's Culture, Popular Culture, Public Culture: Hollywood, Newsreels, and FSA Films and Photographs." In Paula Rabinowitz, *They Must Be Represented: The Politics of Documentary*, 25–104. London: Verso, 1994.

Robinson, Richard K., dir. *The Beekeepers*. Ephratic Productions, 2008.

———. "Mary Frances and The Colony." *Rothstein's First Assignment* (blog). January 7, 2011. http://rothsteinsfirstassignment.blogspot.com/2011/02/mary-frances-and-colony.html.

———. "More Historic Screenings." *Rothstein's First Assignment* (blog). November 12, 2011. http://rothsteinsfirstassignment.blogspot.com/2011/11/more-historic-screenings.html.

———, dir. *Rothstein's First Assignment: A Film about Documentary Truth*. Ephratic Productions, 2010.

Rothstein, Arthur. U.S. Farm Security Administration/Office of War Information Black-and-White Negatives. Library of Congress Prints and Photographs Division, Washington, DC. http://loc.gov/pictures/collection/fsa/.

Ryan, Michael . "Deconstruction and Social Theory: The Case of Liberalism." In *Displacement: Derrida and After*, edited by Mark Krupnick, 154–68. Bloomington: Indiana University Press, 1983.

Schaffer, Kay, and Sidonie Smith. *Human Rights and Narrated Lives: The Ethics of Recognition*. New York: Palgrave, 2004.

Sherman, Mandel, and Thomas R. Henry. *Hollow Folk*. New York: Thomas Y. Crowell Company, 1933.

Sizer, Miriam. "Tabulations." Shenandoah National Park Papers, National Archives Satellite, College Park, MD, 1932.

Slaughter, Joseph. R. *Human Rights, Inc.: The World Novel, Narrative Form, and International Law*. New York: Fordham University Press, 2007.

Trombley, Stephen, dir. *The Lynchburg Story: Eugenic Sterilization in America*. Worldview Pictures, 2008.

Part Four

Justice

Sugar Daddies or Agents for Change?

Community Arts Workers and Justice for Girls
"Who Just Want to Go to School"

JULIA WATSON

Over the three decades in which I have read and written on life narratives by women, especially those in the Global South, no goal has been asserted more strongly by women writers—from Nafissatou Diallo and Ken Bugul in Senegal to Esmeralda Santiago and Maryse Condé in the Caribbean to the Sangtin collaborative of *Playing with Fire* in India—than women acquiring the education to enable them to work and live with dignity. As the recent autobiography *I Am Malala* of Malala Yousafzai, the fourteen-year-old Pakistani girl shot in the head by the Taliban in 2012 for campaigning for girls' education, compellingly suggests, educating girls is still perceived as a threat in many developing countries and countered with lethal measures.[1] Indeed, development professionals now call the effort to educate adolescent women "the girl effect" because it seems the surest means to achieving a long-term decrease in poverty and infant mortality throughout the world.[2] But what could an ordinary American scholar-activist such as myself contribute on the ground in this postsisterhood moment of sharp political and economic divisions and inequities of privilege between Global North and South? A few years ago I learned something about the possibilities and stakes of the struggle to enhance access to education for girls, and the barriers, both practical and ideological, that such efforts still confront.

In July 2010 my friend Janet, a community muralist and activist in New York City, persuaded me to attend an international conference on making community art in the Ashanti capital of Kumasi, Ghana, with her and three colleagues. This is clearly not my field; as a scholar of life writing I critique others' stories rather than enacting my own. But living and teaching for a year in Dakar, Senegal, when my son was young awakened me to human rights initiatives on behalf of women and children in West Africa. The Kumasi conference, sponsored by the Art Education Department of Kwame Nkrumah University and a foundation, had fourteen participants from European, North American, and African nations, including several Ghanaian artists and academics. What I had not understood was that, in addition to giving a conference paper, all participants were expected to create a community art project: one group planned to engage with a *zongo*, or Muslim settlement, with high levels of toxicity in Kumasi; others would create art about community issues in a village with which the foundation works. I wondered what kind of meaningful art I, as a life-writing scholar, could contribute.

Soon after arriving in Kumasi, we visited the outlying village of three hundred or so residents, which had been wired for electricity only a few months earlier. Its main form of subsistence is money earned from cultivating the forest of palm trees ringing the community's huts; they are cultivated for palm oil, which is sent to a larger neighboring village for refining. While the village was prosperous and friendly and its leaders sported cell phones, it lacked the accoutrements that westerners take for granted, from toilets and cookstoves to refrigerators and automobiles. Meals were prepared over an open fire, supplies chilled and stored in a communal locker, and visitors welcomed and business negotiated in open-air meetings. Because there was little guest space for sleeping, most of us stayed at a small hotel in an adjoining village eight kilometers away and commuted by bush taxi down a dusty red-dirt road.

While speculating about how to engage the villagers in a collaborative project with Paul, a Belgian theater director in the group who was also in search of a project, I mentioned a story I had just read, "Two Sisters," by Ama Ata Aidoo, Ghana's internationally acclaimed woman writer and former secretary for education. "Two Sisters" is a cautionary tale about how a governmental minister, a married but womanizing, pompous "sugar daddy," seduces an ambitious young woman in collusion with her brother-in-law, who hopes to improve his family's circumstances by brokering the girl. The question of the young woman's desires—duty or ambition and prosperity?—is a complex one. Because Aidoo was unknown to villagers and her story humorously revealed the cultural changes now confronting women, we decided to dramatize it as our community art contribution. Since actors could not be trained in the few days available, we agreed that I would narrate a condensed version of the story in English, and find a speaker proficient in Twi, the regional language, which none of us spoke, to tell it with a local flavor. As villagers were selected to mime the parts, we were thrilled to find Elizabeth, a Methodist minister to several local villages, who was a native Twi and fluent English speaker with a resonant voice and ready smile.

When the time for the evening performance arrived a few days later, the entire village assembled on the ground in the gathering dusk to hear the story, led by its tall, stately chief, who strolled in, sheltered by the umbrellas of his retinue. Elizabeth convened the event by speaking earnestly to the audience in Twi before the play began. The actors reveled in the roles of the young career-minded woman, her married sister with "a baby on her back and one in her front," her sly husband, and the swaggering sugar daddy played by Paul in Janet's red-striped caftan bedecked with gold necklaces. The seesawing fortunes of the young woman with the sugar daddy were received with hilarity, and a fine time was had by all.

But later I wondered how to interpret the evening. Was the audience enlightened by the drama's critique of a government sugar daddy as an exploitative, disease-carrying seducer who ruined young women? Or was it simply entertained by the racy narrative of sex in a car on a dark beach and how an enterprising single woman could tease glittering silks and heels out of an aged benefactor and build her rise on his ruin? And just how had Elizabeth, the Methodist minister, introduced the play—as a Ghanaian literary landmark asserting the need for girls to have rights and choices? Or as a cautionary tale about remaining chaste and virtuous?

I have no definitive answer to these questions. But in preparing for the play I learned not only about being a storyteller but about the desire of village women and girls for more education. The village's school compound only offered classes through the sixth grade; adolescent boys and girls who wanted to attend junior high had to commute to a larger village eight kilometers away. While several boys had bicycles and were allowed to leave the fields to attend school, parents were reluctant to send away their physically developed but emotionally immature and vulnerable adolescent females. The girls had to either make the long walk daily, since none had bicycles, or live near the junior high during the week. But when they had stayed in town, several of them, feeling alienated and lonely, found boyfriends and become pregnant during their first year, at age thirteen. When their babies arrived, typically their partners were unwilling to marry them. The young mothers had to return to the village to care for their infants and work in the fields again. With their opportunity for schooling curtailed, the girls could neither leave farm labor nor achieve higher status within the village. A fundamental right to education and self-determination was foreclosed by circumstances.

Our artists' group, impressed by the goodwill and evident need of the village, discussed what contribution we could make to helping it develop an additional classroom for the junior-high level as a complement to our community arts projects. On returning home, as good Euro-Americans, several of us dug deep into our pockets to send money for bricks, mortar, and supplies to the village's head teacher. And yes, we congratulated ourselves that this mutually rewarding collaboration would transform the lives of the girls in a salutary way. Yet a lingering doubt haunted a few of us. Had we ourselves performed as foreign "sugar daddies" whose only real contribution could be monetary aid, a perpetuation of neocolonial relations? Or, conversely, had this cross-cultural encounter intervened in the seemingly hopeless future of rural adolescent girls and dramatized how modest local change could transform young lives?

That question may be irresolvable. But what I discovered in Ghana was that conversations among women across boundaries of class and culture affirm the necessity of education as a human right still denied many young girls, even when schools exist. As the platform of the Fourth World Conference on Women in Beijing, 1995, asserted, achieving equity in access to education must be central in campaigns for women's and children's human rights.[3] And, as Sidonie Smith and I have discussed, women's life narratives still attest to the pressures of patriarchal families and governments that impede the equitable access of many girls to education and enfranchisement.[4] In the village we had seen how some schoolgirls' eyes shone when they spoke of their dream of a different life through education. We were in on the secret that Marie, the beautiful twenty-three-year-old woman who pounded cassava with a six-foot pestle for the meals she prepared and had taken the lead role in the play, was engaged to the schoolteacher and determined to leave domestic work. Various members of our group were actively committed to supporting educational goals. "Mama Linda," an American, lives in Kigali, where she conducts photography workshops with children orphaned in the Rwandan genocide. The muralists, some of whom teach community arts in New York schools, were "on the wall" of a cement-block compound for three weeks, painting, together with several villagers, a large mural celebrating the West African family and engaging with the three Ghanaian artists, Patrick, Ralitsa, and Rex. Above all, Elizabeth, the wonderfully expressive preacher narrating in Twi about the sugar daddy, told me her story of combining a ministry with raising five children after her husband abandoned them. That story opened my eyes to the challenges and possibilities for women in rural Ghana. And yet I had to wonder whether, in Elizabeth's eyes, our visit was helpful primarily in spreading her moral gospel. This mix of stories made clear that what soothes the consciences of Euro-Americans in the Global

North may obscure, rather than address, the needs of women and children in the Global South.

The school addition was completed within three months and held its first class of seventh graders. In photographs I've seen the faces of some of the girls we met, and I learned that about thirty adolescent girls continue to attend classes, two years later, and expect to graduate. But then I recall the remark of the elder sister in Aidoo's "Two Sisters": "It's just that women allow [men] to behave the way they do instead of seizing some freedom themselves."[5] And I still wonder: Did our play and contributions to the junior high school enhance the rights of young women? Or did we serve as another kind of sugar daddy on the scene? Perhaps only the collaboration of several kinds of actors—community artists, educators from North and South, writers and tellers of life stories, and girls "who just want to go to school"—across borders of language and privilege can enable a more just access to this fundamental right.

NOTES

Thanks to Janet Braun Reinitz, Elizabeth Abtei, Paul de Bruyne, Sidonie Smith, Meg Jensen, and particularly Margaretta Jolly for help in shaping this essay and expanding its personal framework.

1. Malala's widely praised, best-seller autobiography was published in late 2013, after this essay was completed. Assisted by Christina Lamb, a professional writer, it is based on her memories and the handwritten diary pages that brought her to international attention. *I Am Malala* is a combination of coming-of-age and human rights crisis narrative and includes the pages of color photos readers have come to expect from both survivor and celebrity life stories; like many crisis narratives it ends with an appeal to send contributions to the Malala Fund and join conversations on Facebook and Twitter. For information on the diary, see Basharat Peer, "The Girl Who Wanted to Go to School," *New Yorker*, October 10, 2012, accessed November 19, 2012, http://www.newyorker.com /online/blogs/newsdesk/2012/10/the-girl-who-wanted-to-go-to-school.html#ixzz2 ChsCKq00, for a fuller discussion of how "The Diary of a Pakistani School Girl" was handwritten in Urdu under the by-line Gul Makki. It was smuggled, over time, to Mirza Waheed, the former editor of the Urdu website of the BBC World Service and sometimes translated into English on the website. Mirza stated, "She was just the girl who wanted to go to school."

2. See Centre for Innovation and Research in Childhood and Youth, "The Revolution Will be Led by a 12 Year Old Girl: Girl Power and Global Biopolitics," accessed November 19, 2012, http://www.sussex.ac.uk/lps/newsandevents/events?id=16359, a lecture by Dr. Ofra Koffman delivered at the Centre for Innovation and Research in Childhood and Youth, Sussex University, November, 20, 2012. She asserts, "An alliance

of corporate bodies, charitable foundations and NGOs have been promoting the view that adolescent girls hold the key to ending world poverty and improving wellbeing in the developing world. Investment in adolescent girls, they argue, will unleash a force of financial growth that will put an end to the cycle of poverty: A girl that is better educated will marry later and have fewer children. As a result her health—as well as that of her children—will improve. This sequence of economic advancement and health improvement is termed 'The Girl Effect.'"

3. "Fourth World Conference on Women: Beijing Declaration," 1995, accessed November 15, 2012, http://www.un.org/womenwatch/daw/beijing/platform/declar .htm.

4. See Sidonie Smith and Julia Watson, *Reading Autobiography: A Guide for Interpreting Life Narratives*, 2nd ed. (Minneapolis: University of Minnesota Press, 2010), 131–38, for a discussion of testimonial narratives by women attesting to impediments to pursuing their rights.

5. Ama Ata Aidoo, "Two Sisters," in *No Sweetness Here* (London: Longman, 1988), reprinted in *Daughters of Africa*, ed. Margaret Busby (London: Jonathan Cape, 1992), 535.

WORKS CITED

Aidoo, Ama Ata. "Two Sisters." In *No Sweetness Here*. London: Longman, 1988. Reprinted in *Daughters of Africa*, edited by Margaret Busby, 532–42. London: Jonathan Cape, 1992.

Centre for Innovation and Research in Childhood and Youth. "The Revolution Will be Led by a 12 Year Old Girl: Girl Power and Global Biopolitics." Accessed November 19, 2012. http://www.sussex.ac.uk/lps/newsandevents/events?id=16359.

"Fourth World Conference on Women: Beijing Declaration." 1995. Accessed November 15, 2012. http://www.un.org/womenwatch/daw/beijing/platform/declar.htm.

Peer, Basharat. "The Girl Who Wanted to Go to School." *New Yorker*, October 10, 2012. Accessed November 19, 2012. http://www.newyorker.com/online/blogs/newsdesk /2012/10/the-girl-who-wanted-to-go-to-school.html#ixzz2ChsCKqoo.

Smith, Sidonie, and Julia Watson. *Reading Autobiography: A Guide for Interpreting Life Narratives*. 2nd ed. Minneapolis: University of Minnesota Press, 2010.

Yousafzai, Malala, with Christina Lamb. *I Am Malala: The Girl Who Stood Up for Education and Was Shot by the Taliban*. New York: Little, Brown, 2013.

E-witnessing in the Digital Age

KAY SCHAFFER and SIDONIE SMITH

Since we published *Human Rights and Narrated Lives* in 2004, the social and structural environments of human rights campaigns have changed significantly. The major change we take up in this essay concerns the use of technologies and their implications for personal storytelling in human rights campaigns. These technologies, when deployed in the pursuit of social justice, affect every dimension of political organization, including modes of transmission, breadth and speed of information flows, rhetorics of appeal, and cultures of reception in rights campaigns. Whereas traditional United Nations rights campaigns and commissions have relied primarily on recorded interviews, oral witnessing before truth commissions, and published victim/survivor narratives, the environments attached to the current array of digital technologies involves ensembles of device, code, platform, site protocol, network, generic template, and multiply positioned user. This dense digital environment now affects the forms of online and offline witnessing mobilized to register grievance and advance collective forms of recognition and redress.

Historically, the primary mode of putting a human face on suffering and activating a human rights claim has been through primary and secondary witness testimony. Personal witnessing has traditionally been advanced through professional journalism and human rights organizations (governmental and nongovernmental) and often circulated globally by publishers who reap substantial profits from sensational tales of suffering and survival. Activists and survivor advocates promote the chain of telling and listening that links witness storytelling to empathy, response, and action. This human rights grammar assumes the emotive power of the individual voice. The paradigm of individual witnessing here described persists and is robustly explored in this volume by Annette Kobak and Michio Miyasaka, and eloquently enacted in Hector Aristizábal's personal storytelling. It is, however, being overtaken by other forms of testimony and modes of witnessing made possible by the pervasive presence of technologies that alert a larger public to suffering and grievance. New modes of witnessing are being advanced by the global use of digital technology in various forms, such as netizen microactivism, digitally driven surveillance technologies, cyberhactivism and ever-expanding, sophisticated user expertise. This is not to suggest that the individual story no longer has salience; it is to suggest that now multiple avenues for and modes of witnessing exist alongside one another and that, as Mark Muller argues, new technologies enable different kinds of witness politics, a politics that may not depend on the tropes, plots, and rhetorics of victim narratives.[1]

Digital environments raise provocative questions about how to approach emergent acts and instances of witness. How might digital technologies transform notions of the witness, acts of witnessing, and the efficacy of witness claims in the global arena of human rights activism? How do forms of e-witnessing conjoin user, story, interface, and device? How does technology impact modalities of affect and efficacy in responding to situations of abuse and violence? What happens to the supposed centrality of personal storytelling in human rights campaigns? How are modes of e-witnessing implicated in the conjunction of late global capitalism and neoliberalism? These are complex questions that have only begun to emerge in human rights discourse. In what follows, we engage these questions in relation to two modes of digital activism—social networking and hacking—both of which extend possibilities for witnessing events, registering resistance, and mobilizing action. Then we turn to a case study of the use of digital technologies that advance human (or civil) rights in China.

Social Media

In 2004, the same year we published *Human Rights and Narrated Lives*, Web 2.0 was launched. Ten years later, social media are ubiquitous. By late 2013, Facebook reached 1.19 billion users per month. And this is only one of the platforms for constituting sociality and engendering politics today. Facebook, Twitter, and YouTube provide global sources of information and nodal transmitters in diverse networks that can link people and form virtual publics. As one Cairo activist explained in the lead-up to the protests at Tahrir Square in the summer of 2011, "We use Facebook to schedule our protests, Twitter to coordinate them, and YouTube to tell the world."[2] In 2014, the number of platforms available to activists includes as well a range of messaging and media sharing apps, such as iPhone's WhatsApp, Instagram, and, inside China, Tencent's Weixin and, outside China, Tencent's WeChat, all available through smart phones and tablets. In the not-too-distant future, platforms will include apps available through wearable technologies. This array of media available to activists highlights how platforms expand the accessibility to and interactivity of information flows, intensifying the repertoire of activist tactics even, or especially, for protesters living within authoritarian regimes. Concurrently, however, these technologies also enhance the possibilities for government surveillance and control. How these divergent tactics interact and to what effect remains a burning question.

Just as social media reorganize our lives, our identities, and our self-understandings, so, too, they reorganize human rights politics, as Brian Brivati observes in his contribution to this volume. Information, images, and stories of everyday acts of violence can reach secondary witnesses across the globe in an instant. The repertoire of social media enables immediate, immersive, and adaptable reportage and communication. Their instantaneity, reach, and flexibility connect people in diverse virtual communities in local, national, transnational, and global settings. Increasing digital literacy and access to technologies such as cell phones, as well as the proliferation of translation sites and the pervasiveness of multimedia modes of communication such as videos, music, animations, and comics, combine to enhance possibilities for linking acts of witnessing across geographic, linguistic, and political borders. This capacity for mobilization was pervasive among the Egyptian and Tunisian protesters in 2011 when they began to organize campaigns in an attempt to topple their respective governments. Tunisian activists made connections with people in Egypt who began to assemble data and information, expanding the Arab language blogosphere, and Egyptian bloggers developed a software aggregator to aid social networking, thereby making access to information more available to those without access to Facebook and other platforms.[3]

At a social level, new media create imagined realities of fluid, interactive social relations for protesters. By contrast, "at the technical and infrastructural level," Seb Franklin observes, "they are emblematic of the newest forms of exploitation and restriction."[4] As Evgeny Morozov argues in *The Net Delusion*, as much as the Internet can be mobilized for political action, it is also and more often used to entertain.[5] It perpetuates the illusion of individual agency while also serving the interests of corporations. When used as a vehicle for entertainment, it can offer opportunities for comfort, narcissism, pornography, and spectacle, potentially dumbing down the general population and inuring people to conditions of oppression.[6] Moreover, Big Data is aggregated not only for the purposes of advertising and corporate profits but also for government agencies tasked with surveillance, censorship, and repression of people and dissident movements.[7] And as online usage produces fodder for Big Data, the individual is quantified and aggregated to serve the needs of global capital. Effectively, then, the inherent fluidity of the transmission of information can be used simultaneously by different actors to both advance and retard political action on behalf of social justice. Here is a case in point. In 2009 Emin Milli and Adnan Hajizadeh, both Azeri youth activists and bloggers, were arrested and detained for expressing widely circulating dissident views, a situation Milli explores in this volume.[8] Outside Azerbaijan, activists saw the pair's blogging as a force with revolutionary potential. Inside the country, the government cleverly responded to protests prompted by the blogs by deploying a neoliberal economic measure aimed at diverting the people's anger away from government policies. It reduced the price of eggs in order to garner community support in opposition to Milli's cause and then stigmatized the bloggers as being mentally ill. Both bloggers were sent to prison, during which time Amnesty International, among other groups, took up their cause. After their release, both Emin and Adnan became John Smith Memorial Trust fellows, and Emin was awarded a Chevening scholarship to complete his master's degree at the School of Oriental and African Studies (SOAS), University of London.

This example suggests how multiple forces intersect as social media are mobilized to protest injustice and violence, obviating any easy judgments about the participatory potential of social media in the service of social change. Furthermore, once content is created, it can be circulated and republished online on various sites; and yet, as Rebecca MacKinnon suggests, those who provide information can lose control of their data, which can be manipulated by other users on Facebook, Twitter, and the like.[9] Another aspect of this openness to manipulation is that web pages might not be updated. As Tavia Nyong'o observes, information can get dispersed to float in cyberspace, and users can subsequently connect to sites long after information has been posted; thus, people can be responding inappropriately to calls for action that are out of date.[10]

Hacking

A second technological mode of activism is hacking. There are multiple players in the world of hacking: hactivists, cyber anarchists, renegade youths, patriotic pro-government hackers, vigilante hacker groups, media conglomerates, and state actors (as in Israel's hacking of Iranian nuclear facility computers). It is the case that states can mobilize hackers for their own purposes, increasing their control of the media through deep packet inspection (DPI), cell phone tracking, and censorship software. Indeed, censorship software manufactured in the United States and Europe is sold to authoritarian states, among them Iran, Pakistan, Saudi Arabia, United Arab Emirates, Kuwait, Yemen, and the

Sudan, to assist them in curtailing dissident Internet activity.[11] State-sponsored hacking is also used, with illegal intent, to strip people in dispersed global locations of identities and assets, limit free speech, and invade personal lives. In other words, in some contexts hacking itself becomes a human rights violation. These tactics, in turn, prompt further action within hacker countercultures in a play of centralized power and diffuse pockets of resistance.[12]

Other instances of hacking challenge both democratic and authoritarian modes of state power. Perhaps the most recognizable example of large-scale citizen hacking in recent times is WikiLeaks under the leadership of Julian Assange.[13] WikiLeaks uncovered and exposed the faults and flaws in the democratic transparency of state relations, releasing thousands of secret documents across the web to a global public. Hacking can be used subversively in small-scale antics that disrupt the everyday business of capital and government. The "freedom fighters" of Anonymous have hacked into the computers of international corporations, creating a "denial of service" to businesses that cut their ties to WikiLeaks.[14] Hacking is also deployed to expose the graft and corruption of corporations and state agents. For instance, hackers exposed the collusion between politicians and the Murdoch press in Britain in 2011, thereby challenging the whole concept of freedom of the press and advocacy through the media that has been taken for granted by human rights advocates over the last five decades.[15] The Chaos Computer Club, founded in Berlin in 1981 in anticipation of the worldwide impact of technology on people's lives, continues to expand its user base with the intent of activating utopian resistance to media censorship.[16]

Hacking is a feral, anarchic kind of activism. Hackers are not necessarily operating out of a political agenda. A particular hacker might claim to be acting in the name of transparency, but transparency for whom and for what often remains unclear. Nonetheless, hacking has implications for human rights activism. It exponentially expands potential sites for circulating stories. It challenges both democratic and authoritarian modes of state power. It increases demands on the United Nations for peacekeeping and the adjudication of claims. Ultimately, it functions, to paraphrase Carl von Clausewitz, as "a continuation of politics by other means."

E-witnessing

Social media and hacking are two capacities of a global Internet environment that are being deployed in the human rights arena. This environment exists alongside what we called in our book the human rights regime—the discourses, institutions, protocols, conventions, and practices that have linked human rights activists through NGO networks to state-based and United Nations interventions for the last half century. As W. Lance Bennett observes, "The current era of social justice activism still includes NGO policy networks . . . but they now operate in a more emergent movement environment of large-scale direct activism, multi-issue networks, and untidy 'permanent' campaigns with less clear goals and [less clear] political relationships with targets," like G7 summits, for instance.[17] In addition, these horizontal, nonhierarchical modes of communication and the playful, improvisational tactics of protest are foreign to earlier modes of advancing human rights.

Personal stories witnessing violence and suffering are less critical to these newer forms of activism. What happens on the Internet is not "I"-witness story-telling in the traditional sense—that is, extended transcriptions of oral interviews of victim/survivors or published narratives of survivors circulating transnationally. Within traditional human rights frameworks and campaigns, personal witnessing is often the product of an ensemble of actors, those publishers, activists, editors, and benefactors who co-construct the witness narrative with a victim/survivor.[18] It often unfolds in the aspirational grammar cited above: storytelling, empathy, response, action. In contrast, what happens in the emergent digital environment of virtual and viral networks is something else, what might be described as "e-witnessing."

E-witnessing to grievance or violation or violence or corruption involves a combination of texting, SMS (Short Message Service), blog posts, tweets, podcasting, digital photography, video streaming, linking, and the like. It is witnessing without a singular agent of narration. It is an accumulation of fragmented contributions from many sources and actors impelled by a diversity of motivations and desires.[19] By the nature of the media, the focus is diffuse and decentralized. Any individual contribution is placed in a constantly changing web of paratexts and surrounds, links, calls for action, information flows, and networks of reception. When organized through websites, its dynamic is less progressive than recursively interactive as users contribute more commentary, information, or photographic evidence of an event, situation, or grievance. When organized spontaneously and in real time by grassroots activists, its effectiveness is enhanced as users deploy diverse protocols and platforms for the dissemination of information, a style of activism that attempts to forestall government censorship.

In addition, net informatics differ from a politics that involves "the patient, retrospective, and time-consuming work of piecing together the full picture of a situation."[20] This suggests that when users participate in a mobilization via the Internet, such as signing a petition, they do not know to whom they are addressing their demands. Nor do they always know who the victim is. In this sense there is no origin of grievance, no symbolic victim/subject behind the campaign. There is no symbolic self, but rather the self becomes a nodal site of conjunction.[21]

Given that virtual audiences are themselves indefinable and fragmented, e-witnessing may or may not coalesce into a claim of collective identities or a sense of solidarity.[22] It may or may not flow into traditional human rights activism, through NGO-based institutions, networks, and protocols. It may or may not coalesce into forms of effective change. In other words, it can both become attached to the structures of human rights activism and also be effective through other channels. Or it can fizzle away, dispersed through the web or erased through the censors.

Nick Dyer-Witheford describes digitally organized social movements as "a diffuse coalescence of microactivisms contesting the macrologic of capitalist globalization."[23] For many social movement commentators, the problem of the cultures of reception for these constantly shifting microactivisms is how to establish solidarity in such a fluid and decentralized environment and how to determine what the outcome of an action can be. The multiplicity of media devices and tools and the unpredictable responses of and to e-witnessing can lead to fragmentation. That multiplicity can also lead to broader networks of efficacy and more inventive and flexible tactics.

So, what kind of e-witnessing occurs in an environment where there is no linearity of agenda, no prescribed narrative mode, no progressive syntax leading from injustice to redress grounded in the stable testimony of victims and secondary witnesses?

The Case of China and E-witnessing

We will attempt an answer to this question through a particular case study, here China. There are currently 585 million Internet users in China, 350 million of whom have their own microblogs,[24] a combination of a tweet and a blog that is limited to between 140 and 200 Chinese characters, images, and photographs. Although China heavily censors all forms of digital usage by monitoring the Internet, tracking cell phone usage, and barring the use of Facebook, You-Tube, and Google, it provides a multiplicity of venues for social networking, including Twitter, SMS messaging, and gaming. This access is designed to encourage public debate within an authoritarian society and to temper increasing social unrest, thereby promoting the "health and harmony" of the state.

The most popular form of social networking occurs on microblog Internet platforms.

Let's look at one example of a "hot issue" as it develops on Weibo—China's major Internet platform. On June 2, 2012, Feng Jianmei, a woman from Shaanxi province in her third term of pregnancy, was beaten and subjected to a forced abortion. Her sister was in the room when the baby was aborted. Angry and frustrated at the abusive treatment of her sister, she placed the baby on the bed beside the mother and took a photograph that she uploaded from her cell phone to the web. She also took a screen shot of her cell phone, which captured a conversation with family members through SMS messages alerting them that Mrs. Feng was having an abortion against her will that could have been avoided with a payment of 40,000 renminbi (6,350 US dollars) to "One Child Policy Bureau" officials, an amount the family could not raise. The incident went viral, garnering a million hits within the first few days and continuing to be a hot topic of concern, drawing ongoing comments by users. User interest led the mainstream media in Hong Kong to report on the incident. So, too, did Japanese and BBC journalists. Media and microbloggers thus brought attention to the failure of officials to follow their own policies, which made late-term abortions illegal, and their attempts to cover up the evidence. On July 10, the abortion once again became a hot issue on the Internet when the government announced that Mrs. Feng would receive a payment of 76,000 renminbi as recompense for personal suffering and the delay in recognition of a violation. Five officials received punishments, three were suspended, and provincial officials issued an apology.

Illegal abortions of this type occur regularly in China. What is different in this case is that the immediacy of digital media and their use at the time of violation put graphic evidence of the abuse and official cover-up before the public. Microbloggers and journalists in locations inside and outside China kept attention focused on the case. Bloggers' posts, numbering more than a million, included debates about the one-child policy, women's rights, the morality of hospital and government officials, the gap between rich and poor, and the abuse of this woman while at the same time the first woman astronaut from China was returning from outer space. This event also became an occasion for a backlash of nationalist sentiment as many bloggers blamed the woman for shaming China by allowing Japanese and British media access to the story. And, in terms of outcome, although the woman received an apology and compensation and several provincial officials were removed from office, the protests involved no direct critique of Chinese politics nor of the Chinese Communist Party (CCP), which took the high ground in reprimanding the offending local officials.

Here is an instance of e-witnessing of multiple kinds. The sister's initial posts, the journalists' news reports, and the millions of microblog responses put in motion several narratives about this powerless woman in rural China. They evolved out of fragments of texts, images, videos, and SMS messages. These actions and commentaries channeled affect into anger, outrage, empathy, and shame. They also prompted an investigation that resulted in an apology and compensation for the woman and punishment for the local officials. They circulated through an online environment in which other "hot issues" of rights abuse and government culpability come to public attention throughout the country on a regular basis. These instances reveal the evolution of a participatory public mobilizing multiple discourses around human rights issues that affect urban and rural populations, challenge unjust policies, and call the government to account in ways that have never before been possible in China.

The second example dates from June 3–4, 2012, the twenty-third anniversary of the massacre on Tiananmen Square. On that day, auspicious stock market reports appeared to be commemorating the event, about which there was a total ban. It was reported that the Chinese stock index for the day fell by 64.89 points—interpreted by Chinese bloggers as a reference to the Tiananmen anniversary: 6 for June, 4 for the date, and 89 for the year of the massacre. In another twist, the Shanghai composite index opened at 2,346.98, which could be interpreted as referencing the anniversary of June 4, 1989, backward. The government immediately censored the stock market numbers and closed down reporting on the exchange, but not before millions of Chinese microbloggers had defied censorship and sent the figures across the digital sphere.

The excitement about these messages added to a "wonderful event" that had happened in Beijing the day before. On June 3 around 4:00 p.m., about the same time that the government had sent tanks to Tiananmen Square twenty-three years earlier, the skies grew black and a violent storm rained hail on Beijing. Bloggers immediately began to allegorize the event in terms of a classic Chinese drama from the Yuan dynasty (1271–1368). In *A Midsummer Snow*, a popular play by Guan Han-ching, the protagonist, a young girl named Dou'er, suffers the injustice of being wrongly accused of murder and appeals to the people for support. Faced with disbelief in her innocence, she predicts that should she be condemned the people would see snow in June as a sign of her innocence. After her death, snow falls in June, a just judge acknowledges her grievances, and the people read the event as providential. Recalling the drama, one blogger posted the message "President Hu Jinto, please look out your window!" That post went viral as users forwarded it to millions of people. In this instance of e-witnessing, ludic play, combined with references to classic

Chinese drama and Confucian beliefs, carried the collective memory of Tiananmen through new channels of recovery and enabled a nonpolitical mode of expression for the people of China, who have not forgotten the events of June 4, 1989, nor forgiven the government. Blog posts suggest that people interpreted the storm as a sign that Heaven had spoken and justice would prevail.

It has since been revealed that the manipulation of the stock market figures was most likely the work of hackers clever in reading the mood of the people and eager to take advantage of their ability to undermine the restrictions of state censorship. This "diffuse coalescence of microactivisms" in the form of microblogs and hacking turned the stock market event and the freak storm in Beijing into a collective narrative of remembrance. That narrative has no "I," no consciousness, no psyche. It operates across a force field of intensities, the dispersed affects of thwarted desires and disruptive aspirations within an authoritarian environment.

This is not to suggest that the occasional success of netizen protests and the intensity of public discussions will lead to massive transformations of the government. In fact, some commentators suggest that increased Internet use may actually prolong CCP rule in China. They reason that as long as social protests are controlled, and claims of abuse and corruption handled by prosecuting officials at a local or provincial level of government, the authority of the CCP can be maintained. The rising middle and upper classes are likely to trade political liberty for economic prosperity and maintain allegiance to the party.[25] Even the most optimistic of China watchers believe that political change, if it does occur, will proceed in gradual waves of expansion and retardation of citizens' rights and the evolution of semi-democratic processes.[26]

The Tiananmen Square massacre and post-Tiananmen narratives were the focus of the final case study in *Human Rights and Narrated Lives*. We chose China because it provided an instance in which victims of abuse had no outlet for human rights activism and witnessing. We argued that remembrance and testimony could only be routed through coded representations and the writings of the Chinese diaspora. In that same year, the Chinese government introduced human rights protections into the constitution. China also pledged a campaign to crack down on government officials for human rights violations. Despite these constitutional changes, in the absence of the rule of law these protections have little force. As we know, those who actively petition in support of victimized citizens and against government corruption and official misconduct continue to face threats of intimidation, detention, arrest, and violence. Nonetheless, as the examples above demonstrate, the Internet is providing multiple platforms through which increasing numbers of people participate in public forums on behalf of rights advocacy. As Jonathan Benney argues in *Defending Rights in Contemporary China*, citizen rights defense campaigns, emerging in both rural and urban areas of China, variously advance and promote the rights of citizens and develop legal awareness.[27] In the process, the Internet shifts from being primarily a tool of state repression to being an effective medium for *weiquan* (rights defense).

Conclusion

The modes and means of action to confront injustice and register grievance have changed. Our case study of e-witnessing in China focuses on some promising features of expanding public networks of efficacy even in authoritarian states. There are, of course, similar examples of effective networking outside of China, evidenced by the wealth of critical commentary on the role of social media in the widespread protests in North Africa and the Middle East in 2011 and 2012. Nonetheless, it is easy enough to locate the factors contributing to a sense of thwarted efficacy. Critics such as Wendy Brown have argued that in a neo-liberal environment information is targeted not to the political arena but to consumer markets.[28] In all parts of the globe regulation and surveillance have intensified. Corporate and state power is so dispersed and the networks produced through digital affordances so complex that many people retreat into a narrowing view of the possibilities for change. Brown observes that the possibility for corporations and governments to manipulate the media and activist campaigns extends far beyond the technological regulation of aspects of peoples' lives imagined by Michel Foucault.[29] Further, the question of who or what has agency in this complex and expanding arena confounds easy analysis. In any given instance, there are multiple players, including the state, corporations, media, NGOs, and grassroots activists. In this sense there is no origin of grievance, no symbolic victim/subject behind any given campaign. As noted above, there is no direct witness to a humanistic, symbolic self; rather, "the self" functions as a nodal site of conjunction.

Individual actions and grassroots campaigns are embedded in global capitalist modes of communication, and the media they mobilize are controlled by capital. Thus, we cannot, as Tavia Nyong'o argues, "disconnect the democratic and humanist messages disseminated across networks from the hierarchical and anti-humanist infrastructure of capital-intensive information technology that carries them." Nor, he continues, can we collapse them into an analysis that only celebrates the democratic and resistant capacities of digital media and devices or only focuses on the dystopian aspects of capitalist informatics.[30]

Prior to the digital era of human rights advocacy, campaigns relied on the personal voice of witnesses and their stories. Many commentators of the Left decry the loss of that voice and that singularity of story. However, the voice of the witness and the efficacy of a victim/survivor story have never been straightforward or uncompromised, as we demonstrate in our case studies in *Human Rights and Narrated Lives*. The contexts and histories of violence and oppression taken up by human rights campaigns are invariably complex and often contradictory—characterized by multiple stories, multiple subject positions, multiple interests, multiple modernities, and multiple political, historical, economic, and communal constraints on "choice." And these stories circulate within the commodifying processes of activist organizations, publishers, editors, and marketers who are differently invested in the empathetic appeal that victim stories solicit. Stories of suffering and victimization continue to saturate the markets, online and offline, in newspapers, in movies, on cable television, on YouTube, and on sites such as Witness and Human Rights Watch. The saturation of the image of the suffering victim in this mediatized environment is such that violence and abuse can become empty signifiers. Trauma fatigue elicits increasingly sensationalized stories of exploitation and abuse. And the stories themselves often become soft weapons in ideological warfare.[31]

While recognizing the dystopian aspects of communicative capitalism that have become increasingly predominant in a digital (as well as nondigital) environment, this essay has attempted to foreground some of the enabling features of e-witnessing and to theorize how the subject of witness, the message of witness, and the infrastructure for witnessing are shifting. For these reasons, e-witnessing in a digital era challenges those of us working at the intersections of human rights, the humanities, and the law to shift our thinking and extend our interdisciplinary reach. In confronting the speed of change and the scale of online activity, from everyday practices of billions of people across the globe to the large political projects for advancing social justice and dignity, we need to react nimbly and humbly in our engagement with social media phenomena in the pursuit of justice. The multifaceted assemblages brought into play by digital technology may exceed our modes of analysis and intellectual grasp and deny the possibility of synthesis. Human rights scholars and activists will continue to experiment with innovative ways to make grievances public and engage netizens in social movements and social networks that have yet to be imagined. And scholars and activists will adapt new literacies for recognizing and responding to e-witnessing and new modes of cultural analysis to understand how social media intersect with social movement advocacy in the digital age.

NOTES

We thank Dr. Xianlin Song and Minghua Wu for their generous assistance in tracking information about Weibo and its current usage.

1. Mark Muller, "Comments," paper presented at the conference Life Writing and Human Rights: Genres of Testimony, University of Kingston, Kingston-on-Thames, United Kingdom, July 11–13, 2011.

2. Philip Howard, "The Arab Spring's Cascading Effects," *Pacific Standard*, February 23, 2011, accessed November 24, 2012, http://www.psmag.com/politics/the-cascading-effects-of-the-arab-spring-28575/

3. Rebecca MacKinnon, *Consent of the Networked: The Worldwide Struggle for Internet Freedom* (New York: Basic Books, 2012), 23, 225.

4. Seb Franklin, "Virality, Informatics, and Critique; or, Can There Be Such a Thing as Radical Computation?," *WSQ: Women's Studies Quarterly* 40, no. 1 (2012): 160.

5. It should be noted that his comments, though still relevant, were made before the evolution of the so called Arab Spring.

6. Evgeny Morozov, *The Net Delusion: The Dark Side of Internet Freedom* (New York: Public Affairs, 2011).

7. *Big Data* is shorthand for the proliferation of raw data generated through sensor networks, social networks, social data, Internet text and documents, Internet search indexing, scientific research, military surveillance, medical records, photography archives, video archives, and large-scale e-commerce.

8. See also Milli's current blog, http://eminmilli.posterous.com/.

9. MacKinnon, *Consent of the Networked*, 22.

10. Tavia Nyong'o, "Queer Africa and the Fantasy of Virtual Participation," *WSQ: Women's Studies Quarterly* 40, no. 1 (2012): 48–49.

11. MacKinnon, *Consent of the Networked*, 60.

12. Ibid., 232.

13. WikiLeaks is a not-for-profit media organization with a stated mission to collect and publish original documents that contain important information, particularly that related to government, in an attempt to create transparency and reduce corruption.

14. Anonymous is a loosely associated group of hacker-activists.

15. Employees of Rupert Murdoch's now-defunct *News of the World* were discovered to have hacked cell phones and bribed police officers in pursuit of stories. As of January 2014, eight employees are on trial for phone hacking, including former *News of the World* editors Rebekah Brooks and Andy Coulson.

16. On the Chaos Computer Club, see MacKinnon, *Consent of the Networked*, 232.

17. W. Lance Bennett, "Social Movements beyond Borders: Understanding Two Eras of Transnational Activism," in *Transnational Protest and Global Activism*, ed. Donatella della Porta and Sidney Tarrow (Lanham, MD: Rowman and Littlefield, 2005), 212.

18. See Sidonie Smith and Julia Watson, "Witness or False Witness? Metrics of Authenticity, Collective I-Formations and the Ethic of Verification in First-Person Testimony," *Biography* 35, no. 4 (Fall 2012): 590–626.

19. Natalie Fenton, "Mediating Solidarity," *Global Media and Communication* 4, no. 1 (2008): 38.

20. Nyong'o, "Queer Africa and the Fantasy of Virtual Participation," 51.

21. See Rosi Braidotti, "PostHuman, All Too Human: Toward a New Process Ontology," *Theory, Culture & Society* 23, nos. 7–8 (2006): 197–208.

22. Fenton, "Mediating Solidarity"; Mario Diani, "Social Movement Networks Virtual and Real," *Information, Communication & Society* 3, no. 3 (2000): 386–401.

23. Nick Dyer-Witheford, *Cyber-Marx: Cycles and Circuits of Struggle in High Technology Capitalism* (Champaign: University of Illinois Press, 1999), 50.

24. As reported by the Chinese Internet Network Information Center, July 14, 2012, accessed July 14, 2012, http://www.cnnic.cn/.

25. MacKinnon, *Consent of the Networked*, 50.

26. See Jianying Zha, *Red Tide: The Movers and Shakers of a Rising China* (New York: New Press, 2011), 217–26.

27. Jonathan Benney, *Defending Rights in Contemporary China* (New York: Routledge, 2012).

28. Wendy Brown, "At the Edge," *Political Theory* 30, no. 4 (2002): 556–76. Brown elaborates the current problem for the Left. Progressives used to hate capitalism, but now they yearn for the loathed object to which they were nonetheless attached because it was the mode through which change for a more just and equitable future could be pursued. The political identities of leftists were shaped by liberal democratic ideas and the humanist subject constituted through those values even as those values contributed to the erasure of asymmetries of power.

29. Ibid.

30. Nyong'o, "Queer Africa and the Fantasy of Virtual Participation," 42–43.

31. Gillian Whitlock, *Soft Weapons: Autobiography in Transit* (Chicago: University of Chicago Press, 2007), 3, 9. Whitlock describes autobiographical narratives as potential "soft weapons" that circulate between cultures in conflict, able to spur recognition of human lives that might otherwise be ignored but also vulnerable to co-optation as propaganda for coercive ends.

WORKS CITED

Bennett, W. Lance. "Social Movements beyond Borders: Understanding Two Eras of Transnational Activism." In *Transnational Protest and Global Activism*, edited by

Donatella della Porta and Sidney Tarrow, 203–26. Lanham, MD: Rowman and Littlefield, 2005.

Benney, Jonathan. *Defending Rights in Contemporary China.* New York: Routledge, 2012.

Braidotti, Rosi. "PostHuman, All Too Human: Toward a New Process Ontology." *Theory, Culture & Society* 23, nos. 7–8 (2006): 197–208.

Brown, Wendy. "At the Edge." *Political Theory* 30, no. 4 (2002): 556–76.

Chaos Computer Club. Accessed December 2, 2012. http://www.ccc.de/en/.

Chinese Internet Network Information Center. Accessed July 14, 2012. http://www.cnnic.cn/.

Diani, Mario. "Social Movement Networks Virtual and Real." *Information, Communication & Society* 3, no. 3 (2000): 386–401.

Dyer-Witheford, Nick. *Cyber-Marx: Cycles and Circuits of Struggle in High Technology Capitalism.* Champaign: University of Illinois Press, 1999.

Fenton, Natalie. "Mediating Solidarity." *Global Media and Communication* 4, no. 1 (2008): 37–57.

Franklin, Seb. "Virality, Informatics, and Critique; or, Can There Be Such a Thing as Radical Computation?" *WSQ: Women's Studies Quarterly* 40, no. 1 (2012): 153–70.

Howard, Philip. "The Arab Spring's Cascading Effects." *Pacific Standard,* February 23, 2011. Accessed November 24, 2012. http://www.psmag.com/politics/the-cascading-effects-of-the-arab-spring-28575/.

MacKinnon, Rebecca. *Consent of the Networked: The Worldwide Struggle for Internet Freedom.* New York: Basic Books, 2012.

Morozov, Evgeny. *The Net Delusion: The Dark Side of Internet Freedom.* New York: Public Affairs, 2011.

Muller, Mark. "Comments." Paper presented at the conference Life Writing and Human Rights: Genres of Testimony, University of Kingston, Kingston-on-Thames, United Kingdom, July 11–13, 2011.

Nyong'o, Tavia. "Queer Africa and the Fantasy of Virtual Participation." *WSQ: Women's Studies Quarterly* 40, no. 1 (2012): 40–63.

Schaffer, Kay, and Sidonie Smith. *Human Rights and Narrated Lives: The Ethics of Recognition.* New York: Palgrave Macmillan, 2004.

Smith, Sidonie, and Julia Watson. "Witness or False Witness? Metrics of Authenticity, Collective I-Formations and the Ethic of Verification in First-Person Testimony." *Biography* 35, no. 4 (Fall 2012): 590–626.

Whitlock, Gillian. *Soft Weapons: Autobiography in Transit.* Chicago: University of Chicago Press, 2007.

Zha, Jianying. *Tide Players: The Movers and Shakers of a Rising China.* New York: New Press, 2011.

"Facebook Is Like a Religion Around Here"

Voices from the "Arab Spring" and the Policy-Making Community

BRIAN BRIVATI

Human rights activist Emin Milli's view of the role of Facebook in the popular protest movements of our age—that social media is like a religion—provokes an obvious and important question that this essay sets out to explore: if the recent revolts in the Middle East and North Africa were mobilized through open social media, why did no significant actors in the foreign policy-making and security communities see them coming? The answer lies in the way in which these communities of analysts read the information in front of them. As most of that information is now presented via electronic media, the way in which policy makers read those sources is key to an understanding of what went wrong. This understanding will lead in turn to two contrasting ways in which the growth of electronic information sources, like the social media spaces of the Internet, can be viewed. Either these are the new variables that determine events and there has been a paradigm shift in the nature of the way human history is made, or they are merely the latest in a long line of mediums of communication through which the traditional variables that determine outcomes are communicated. Kay Schaffer and Sidonie Smith, in their essay in this volume, discuss the implications of these changes from a theoretical perspective and the perspective of the human rights industry. My concern here is that if there has been a paradigm shift then policy makers, most importantly those who run the foreign policy and security apparatuses of member states of the United Nations Security Council, need to learn the languages of the new paradigm in order to predict what will happen next. They currently cannot do this. They do not understand the importance of digital voice. If, on the other hand, all we are seeing is the development of new communications platforms and not new means of deciding outcomes, then this does not matter and the policy makers can continue to look at the world in traditional ways. In the end, that is, the outcome of events will be determined in the same way they always have. On balance, though, through my job as director of a human rights organization, and having worked with a range of actors in many countries engaged either directly in these events or as analysts of them, I have come to believe that there has indeed been a paradigm shift: we continue to look at the world in traditional ways at our peril. But this conclusion has arisen from a finely balanced argument, and I will attempt in what follows to give a clear account of both sides. Whichever extreme position might be truer, no one can deny that those who do not engage with the new means of communication are doomed, at the very least, to live in ignorance.

The last ten years have seen a momentous series of changes on the international scene. It is worth stopping for a moment to consider these events, the consequences of which are still unfolding. In Afghanistan and Iraq, coalition forces launched regime-changing operations. To justify these actions they deployed elaborate narratives. Part of these narratives was the national liberation of these countries from oppressive and terroristic regimes that had sponsored the mass murderers of 9/11 and run programs of weapons of mass destruction. In 2011 the liberation of Libya from the regime of Colonel Muammar Gaddafi was enabled by the deployment of air power, but ground forces were not used. Throughout 2012 and 2013 violence has continued in Syria and to date, except for the decommissioning of chemical weapons, no intervention has taken place. In between these events there were risings in Egypt and Tunisia and elsewhere across the Middle East and North Africa and down to the Persian Gulf region. In South Sudan a new country was born and descended into renewed civil war. Since 2008 we have also lived through the collapse of the global financial markets, the freezing of credit, and the beginning of the worst depression since the 1930s.

Many of these events were played out live and in real time on 24/7 news channels and over the Internet. In the case of Iraq, the intervention was based on eyewitness testimony that was later discounted. In the uprisings of the Arab Spring, the first many policy makers heard about the events was via online news sites. In all these cases policy makers and members of the public who wanted to know could get detailed information on what was occurring. Situation maps recorded individual instances of violence on Global Positioning System (GPS) websites that were constantly updated.[1] Facebook and other social media groups connected sometimes tens of thousands of people who were interested or involved in the events and kept them fully informed. There has never been a period in human history in which more people could know more about events as they unfolded and in which policy makers were aware of public opinion on key issues and also had information on all the divisions or unity of opinion among players on the ground. Moreover, the use of social media tools like Twitter in the mobilization and direction of protesters has added a new dynamic to the confrontation between governments and opponents. The veil of ignorance has been lifted. The question is: what difference has this made to the outcome of any of these events and why did the policy makers fail to see any of it coming?

The human rights industry devotes a huge amount of time and energy to the accumulation and dissemination of eyewitness accounts. This is a central plank in advocacy and campaigning. Yet the evidence of the last ten years from significant foreign policy decisions is that arguably this is a waste of time in terms of changing policy outcomes: policy makers routinely ignore, discount, and discredit eyewitness testimony of human rights abuse and testimony from people protesting against human rights violations. I am not suggesting that testimony in terms of judicial processes to bring judgment against governments on specific human rights violations is not important. Nor do I discount here the vital therapeutic role of testimony. What I am saying is that the individual account, often based on personal experience, is very often not recognized as significant evidence in the shaping of *policy*. It would, however, be naive to explain this as the result of the difficulty of gathering representative and reliable testimony. Rather, it is in part a contemporary reflection of what C. P. Snow called in his famous book *The Two Cultures* a divide between the social sciences and the humanities, of which I will say more shortly.[2] In part it is because most policy is ideologically led and not evidence based, and in part it is because of the role of dominant narratives in the internal discussions of politicians and their advisers. One proof of this lies in the exception, where personal narratives are treated as serious evidence. We can appreciate this in the case of Iraq, where the US-UK intervention was partly justified as based on eyewitness testimony by key émigré figures. Testimony in this case could mobilize the intelligence community because what it said fully accorded with the existing narrative of events and policy direction. In other words, the eyewitnesses said what the administration wanted to hear.[3] The irony is that we now live in the era of the mass eyewitness account, in which unmediated communications can make individual testimony global, and groups communicating via social media platforms can shake the foundations of governments on a much wider, and much more representative, scale.

The job of a policy analyst in an ideal world would be rooted in evidence-based policy making, and voice would constitute an important evidential tool. The reality is, of course, that policy advisers mostly exhibit an ideologically driven policy making, even as it is based on the normative application of social science methodology. This is in part because of the construction of most international relations curricula in the universities from which the policy makers are drawn. These curricula remain dominated by a realist view of international relations. This view privileges realist analysis over any other approach and promotes "hard" evidence over the skills of listening and reflecting on the multiple possible truths of the texts and events that we encounter. This view is then compounded by career structures in organizations like the British Foreign Office (FCO) and the American State Department in which institutional worldviews are either fixed by long-term precedent, as in the case of the FCO, or altered by the political color of each new presidential administration, in the case of the State Department. In both instances, a realist worldview prevails but with significant variation in tone and content on the extent to which western powers have agency to influence the flow of events unfolding as rational actors seek to maximize their power and status. The Iraq War is the worst recent example of the dangers of this ideological policy making—so much so that we could describe its approach as "hyperrealist." Weapons inspectors in the run-up to the invasion of Iraq warned that they needed more time to establish if there were weapons of mass destruction. Planners told the US defense secretary, Donald Rumsfeld, that he would need an army of 300,000 or more to invade and hold the country, that he would need to use the Iraqi army, and that it would take a decade to stabilize any new regime. Instead, Rumsfeld ordered an invasion with 150,000 troops and disbanded the Iraqi army.[4]

Opponents of the war displayed exactly the same characteristics and justified their positions through selective use of testimony that, for example, entirely ignored the position of the Iraqi Kurds and Marsh Arabs as the victims of Saddam Hussein's genocide and dismissed the many millions of Iraqis and other Arabs who initially welcomed the removal of Saddam's regime. Policy advisers and makers might be trained in the methodologies of political science, and especially international relations theory, but these methods are then used to underpin and support their ideological positions. The world and the events that are unfolding in that world are being made to fit the prism of ideology and not the other way around. When the individual voice, witnessing abuse, torture, or murder or organizing and mobilizing protest, does not fit the established position, it will be silenced or ignored. In turn, voices and debates that might support foreign interventions or defend practices that western activists dislike are routinely ignored and downplayed by the human rights industry. In both cases the digitizing of testimony produces a flow of inconvenient truths that makes complex the simple narratives of both the jingoist and the peacenik.

Nevertheless, as I stated at the outset, the argument is finely balanced. Recent events have shown that voice expressed through the platforms of new social media and mobile phone technology is now, in some circumstances, a variable equal in force to the traditionally understood sources of political power. The combined ability of digital technology to keep protesters one step ahead of the brute force of governments, to project images of protest globally, and to communicate techniques of mobilization from country to country makes voice a much more important variable than ever before. Voice does not determine outcome on its own. No single variable in the complex interplay of profound political events can, in my view, be given a determinant role. This was ever so, even though Marxists and the many variants of the realist approaches to change, that is, those who believe that actors always behave in the way that is most in their own interests, especially if they are states, would like us to believe differently. In a multivariable explanation of change, what matters is the weight we give to different variables in relation to each other. We understand change and map that understanding onto our worldview, and if we are in a position to, we frame it into policy advice that gives weight to one set of evidence over another. What has been remarkable in recent events is that the voice of protesters as they organized went unheard by policy makers until they had mobilized the protests and shaken and changed regimes. It was not that insufficient weight was given to voice as these events unfolded; it was that no weight was given to what was being said and done online until the global news media framed the Arab Spring as the Facebook revolution. By doing so, moreover, they implicitly challenged governments around the world and the ways in which they responded to these events. In turn, and not unnaturally, what has been striking since the uprisings is the growing resistance among many in the policy-making community to the idea that they may have missed something.[5]

In the first wave of reporting and analysis of the democratic movement that began in the Maghreb and spread across the rest of North Africa, the Middle East, and the Gulf, the voice of protesters expressed through social media was defined as central and enabling in the places in the region with a free press, such as Egypt, and in Europe and the United States.[6] If Iran in 2009 was seen as the Twitter revolt, this was the Facebook revolution. In the second wave of analysis, including that which appeared in *Foreign Affairs* in May/June 2011, the central role assigned to voice was challenged. One of the world's leading experts on revolutions and a leading realist, whose analysis is governed by the view that power and self-interest will determine outcomes, Jack A. Goldstone, for example, argued that these protests were formed from more traditional causes and their outcomes would be defined in traditional equations of power plays.[7] For Goldstone, that is, it did not matter exactly what the interplay of voice versus traditional power was. What mattered was the outcome. Nevertheless, the complete failure of the world's intelligence and foreign policy community to predict what was about to happen other than in a very vague way is intriguing, and the growing consensus against the role of voice in these events is fascinating to watch play out.

In January 2011 Syrian president Bashar al-Assad gave an interview to the *Wall Street Journal* in which he lectured other leaders on how to maintain their enlightened despotisms. By November 2011 he was killing hundreds of his own people in order to cling to power. Over and over again the operating narrative of the world's foreign policy community and mass media was challenged and overturned and should, logically, then have been redefined. But it wasn't. Through the first part of 2012 the pattern continued. To a significant extent, rather than the established narrative being redefined in the face of testimony from the voices of those shaping or witnessing events on the ground, the dominant narrative in the policy-making community, and its primary organs, *Foreign Affairs, Foreign Policy, International Affairs, Washington Institute for Near East Studies, The Atlantic Monthly,* and related publications, has set out to discount these individual voices. The foreign policy establishment has repudiated the nature and content of the revolts themselves and laid on them a version of events and an explanatory framework that sit comfortably with the working assumptions of communities trained in traditional political science and historical methodologies, as discussed above.

In May 2011 the Henry L. Stimson Center published a systematic and far-reaching report on the Arab Spring called *Seismic Shift: Understanding Change in the Middle East.*[8] The study shows that it was not simply the main publications of the foreign policy community that did not see the events coming but each of the different sectors whose job it is to inform the West of what is going on— academia, nongovernmental organizations (NGOs), think tanks, public opinion polls, and risk analysis companies. As these were protest movements coming from the "Arab street," one might have expected the myriad of international NGOs that lay special claim to knowing the region from a bottom-up perspective to have predicted what was to come. In fact no NGO predicted the timing, pace, or breadth of Arab world turmoil. While some did foresee the possibility of violent protest in individual countries, for example, in Egypt, none described the dynamic of the protest or the way in which it would spread across the region. They described in detail a confluence of mounting regime repression and growing popular agitation over a variety of political and socioeconomic issues. But the "dots were not connected."[9]

The journalists who are experts on the region also failed to see the regional significance of what was happening. Max Rodenbeck of the *Economist*, Robin Wright of the *Washington Post*, and David Gardner in the *Financial Times* all predicted revolts in Egypt but not in Tunisia, Libya, or Syria.[10] Likewise, the business of risk companies and consultants is to predict for their corporate clients the likelihood of political change. But the revolution from below was not anticipated by them, and they had not focused on Tunisia. The revolution from above—the decision of security forces to intervene against the regime—was not foreseen in Tunisia, but some firms did expect it in Egypt. In Libya and Bahrain, the regimes did essentially defend themselves, as most firms would have forecast. The regional conflagration and rapid spread of unrest were not anticipated because few were looking at the region as a single political, social, or economic space.[11] *Seismic Shift* provides compelling evidence of similar failures among professionals concerned with democracy promotion, and the Labour Movement: Middle East Research and Information Project predicted unrest in Egypt but missed it in Tunisia and Libya.[12]

There was one notable sociological study that predicted how revolts might develop but did not predict where or when: Asef Bayat's *Life as Politics: How Ordinary People Change the Middle East*. There Bayat argues for the importance of the "collective actions of non-collective actors; they embody shared practices of large numbers of ordinary people whose fragmented but similar activities trigger much social change. . . . When the opportunity presents itself, such non-movements could be mobilized for larger collective action."[13] But other academic approaches, most importantly the Arab authoritarianism model, failed.[14] Of the four main state vulnerability studies that compile indices to predict change, none provided particular insights that would have aided in predicting the December 2010 events.[15] The index that was constructed to pick up the risk of a popular uprising, generated by the Economist Intelligence Unit, rated Egypt, Tunisia, and Libya at lower risk levels than the remaining three indexes. Neither the Food and Agriculture Organization of the United Nations' publication *The State of Food Insecurity in the World* (2009) nor the US Department of Agriculture Economic Research Service's *Food Security Assessment* for 2010–20 indicated that any of the Mediterranean North African countries (Morocco, Algeria, Tunisia, Libya, and Egypt) were at risk.[16] *The Arab Barometer Survey* consistently showed support for democracy across the Arab World but offered no link between this and the probability of regime change.[17] Ellen Laipson's conclusions in *Seismic Shift* indicate the extent to which western institutions failed to understand and believe the messages that were emerging from the region.[18]

In fact we have been here many times before. Rudolf Vrba and Alfred Wetzler escaped from Auschwitz and delivered detailed reports of what was happening there to the British and American governments.[19] They were largely discounted and ignored. Governments in Europe and the United States knew within days that the genocide in Rwanda was taking place.[20] The UK government had been warned that genocide was being planned at the end of 1993, but did nothing for months while a million people were murdered. Many eyewitness accounts reached the British and American governments of gas attacks, the destruction of villages, and the mass murder of Kurds by Saddam Hussein at the end of the 1980s.[21] These reports were buried.

What is new today is that voice expressed through new media is a vital component of making change happen, and these voices were being heard in a number of individual countries in the region. Western Arab watchers entirely failed to link these signs together by mapping them across social media platforms from the region and to predict that once the event began in Tunisia the protests would spread. The question is: do we therefore have a new paradigm that changes everything or does it make no difference because the wrong people are in charge and they do not know how to listen? Let us begin by unpacking the first part of that question. The case for the new paradigm rests on an equation that would look something like this: the firsthand testimony of people on the ground when articulated through the new social media produces a change in policy.

For this to be the case there must have been a change in the nature of power. Joseph Stalin famously articulated a central nineteenth- and twentieth-century notion of power when Winston Churchill asked him to consider the views of the Vatican. Stalin retorted, "Why? How many divisions does the Pope of Rome have?" If you looked at power from the perspective of the state in the age of realpolitik, this was the only question that mattered. Even as this era reached its height with the rise of dictators like Stalin himself, however, the purely reductionist-realist perspective (everything in this view could be reduced to base maximization of the self-interest of all actors) was not enough to explain outcomes or evaluate the role of actors in determining who would win and who would lose in the struggle between democracy and dictatorship. In Spain, for example, during the Civil War, dictator Francisco Franco's victory was by no means assured: the Spanish—with so many interested outsiders—tried to influence who would and would not opt for the defense of democracy through the

Second Republic and who would instead choose between fascist and communist variants of dictatorship.[22] A great deal of this attempt to influence actors took place through propaganda. Arguably, it has always been the case that leaders need the minds of their followers as much as their bodies. By the middle of the twentieth century, however, it was impossible not to ask of any leader: how many minds has he got?

Are we then living through the logical consequence of this evolution in our post–Cold War, Internet-driven social and cultural context? We now have the ability to communicate instantly to millions across shared platforms and mobilize them to action without the state necessarily knowing. Rather than the rulers and political parties communicating through the media to form coalitions and shape events, the people themselves can speak to each other and then act.[23] So would Stalin's question to the Pope now be: how many friends does he have on Facebook? Is this the age of the social media revolutions?

There were obviously considerable sources of discontent across the Middle East–North Africa (MENA) region, and, as we have discussed, major events have multiple causes. The most obvious feature is the widespread inequality that characterizes the region. There is both the economic inequality of widespread unemployment, especially youth unemployment, and a lack of social mobility and political equality because access to power is often tightly controlled by a narrow social group. In much of the region inequality in access to power is also expressed through repression of freedom of expression. Moreover, this is in the context of large- and small-scale corruption, which results in many places in poor public services. Clearly, a relative lack of economic development can be a cause of poor social services, but the elite's control of resources and the clientism of their delivery also accentuate this underlying inequality and feed the visibility of a lack of social mobility. Underpinning this are forces that have created a generation more willing and able to articulate its discontent than in previous eras. For example, between 1960 and 1995 the rate of literacy doubled across MENA while over half the population in the region is now under the age of twenty-four (53 percent or 211.6 million people). All this has been happening in the context of the digital revolution. As the Center for International Media Assistance states in its report *Social Media in the Arab World*:

> Broadband high-speed internet is available in countries like Algeria, Tunisia, Morocco and Egypt, while 3G mobile services are already developed in the North African region, as well as countries like Sudan and Syria (Ghannam, 2011). The global penetration rate of simple mobile phones is currently over 70%. Just to quote few numbers, only in 2009 Saudi Arabia had a mobile penetration rate of 103%, Tunisia 87%, Egypt 72%, Syria 45%, Yemen 34% (Ghannam, 2011),

while the whole Middle East region has currently seen a total rate of 285 million mobile subscribers (Africa and Middle East telecom-week report, July 2011).[24]

What is clear in looking back on the revolts that have run their course and assessing those that are still ongoing is that profound change has taken place across the region. The question that concerns us is why the scale suddenly tipped toward revolution and what role the new social media played in it. And, again, why did the information professionals not see it coming?

Those who have analyzed these responses are not agreed on the answer to these questions. The answers existed before the events of recent years, but all that has taken place has been used by the partisans on both sides as evidence that their positions have been vindicated. On one side sit the cyberrealists, most clearly represented in the work of Evgeny Morozov in books like *The Net Delusion*.[25] The key claims of the cyberrealists, that is, those who believe that actors are still behaving in completely self-interested ways despite the information revolution, are that social media and other technologies are not inherently democratic or revolutionary and can be used by dictators just as much as by democracies. Repressive regimes can use propaganda, surveillance, censorship, and intelligence gathering about its own citizens and can even depoliticize those citizens by distracting them with cheap entertainment or social expenditure. The MENA protesters, the cyberrealists argue, were organized by their shared desire for change and not their social networks. As Morozov puts it, "What I want is for people to realize the seriousness of the situation—that the Web is not necessarily a tool of liberation, that it can be a tool of oppression as well, and that we should do everything possible in our power, those of us in the West, to minimize its oppressive potential."[26] The problem with Morozov and many of the other cyberrealists is that while what they say about the web is true, that governments can also use it, this does not actually address the question of the way in which the new social movements have used the technology. Nor, indeed, does the view that the outcomes of these events will be determined in traditional ways address the question of how we got to the point at which the people were challenging their governments consistently and powerfully over an extended period of time and in the face of significant violence being used against them.

Set against this cyberrealist position is the alternative view, which can be summed up as cyberutopianism, well argued in *Here Comes Everyone* by Clay Shirky.[27] The key claims of this position are that technology enables networks to be generated without hierarchies and the costs and constraints of hierarchical structures. Therefore, random people can be connected purely by what connects them and the technology they share, and so new networks are created that would not otherwise exist. As Shirky puts it, "Social tools can improve outcomes."[28] But those tools do not cause the outcomes. This is best understood by thinking of Walter Lippman's famous view, articulated in *Public Opinion* in 1922, that the media does not tell people what to think, but it does tell them what to think about.[29] Shirky claims, "The best reason to believe that social media can aid citizens in their struggle to make government more responsive is that both citizens and governments believe that."[30] The evidence from the Arab Spring is that revolts were encouraged across borders through the knowledge of what was taking place in other countries. The demonstrations themselves were better organized and replenished by the use of multiple kinds of mobile technology, and governments found it much harder to repress the revolts once they had begun. Powerful supporting evidence for my argument comes from the *Arab Social Media Report*, produced annually by the Dubai School of Government, which "is part of a larger research initiative focusing on social engagement through ICT for better policy in Arab states, which explores the use of social networking services in governance, social inclusion and economic development."[31] One interesting note in this report was that

> [g]overnment attempts to ban such sites ended up backfiring, the survey of Egyptians and Tunisians found. Just over a quarter of those polled (28 per cent in Egypt and 29 per cent in Tunisia) said the blocking of Facebook disrupted their efforts to organize and communicate. But more than half (56 per cent in Egypt and 59 per cent in Tunisia) said it had a positive effect, motivating them to press on and mobilizing newcomers. The authorities' efforts to block out information, the report said, ended up "spurring people to be more active, decisive and to find ways to be more creative about communicating and organizing."[32]

As the reform movement across MENA developed, so the debate on the role of social media intensified. Many from the policy-making community came back hard to argue that all that had been demonstrated was that realpolitik determines outcomes, that the side the military came down on decided the winner, and that each revolt and outcome had been different. This was most powerfully argued, with respect to Egypt, in the key US journal *Foreign Policy*, published by the *Washington Post*, in February 2011, as well as in *Foreign Affairs*.[33] They conceded that protesters have become smarter but argued that they are still not more powerful than tanks. Populations are divided, and not all minds are on the side of revolution. But in my view, the case for a paradigm shift remains. No government is entirely safe in the world of communication flows. Protest is regional as well as national, but it has a global audience, and therefore repression cannot be hidden even if it is tragically ignored. The case has been well summed up by the leading academic on the impact of digital technology on the Arab world, Philip N. Howard:

> Over the last decade, information and communication technologies have had consistent roles in the narrative for social mobilization:
>
> - Coordinating and publicizing massive mobilizations and nonviolent resistance tactics against pseudo-democratic regimes after stolen elections
> - Allowing foreign governments and diaspora communities to support local democratic movements through information, electronic financial transfers, off-shore logistics and moral encouragement
> - Organizing radical student movements to use unconventional protest tactics at sensitive moments for regimes, particularly during (rigged) elections, elite power struggles or diplomatic visits to undermine the appearance of regime popularity
> - Uniting opposition movements through social-networking applications, shared media portals for creating and distributing digital content, and online forums for debating political strategy and public policy options
> - Attracting international news media attention and diplomatic pressure through digital content such as photos taken "on the ground" by citizens, leaking videos and documents to foreign journalists, or by diplomats raising flags over human rights abuses, environmental disasters, electoral fraud, and political corruption
> - Transporting mobilization strategies from one country to another, sharing stories of success and failure, and building a sense of transnational grievance with national solutions.
>
> There certainly are other causal recipes. The classic understanding of social mobilization is that it depends on the appearance of collective identities, shared motivations and grievances, and ultimately a change in the opportunity structure for collective action. To greatly simplify one of the most important recipes for democratization over the past few centuries, we might say that well-educated elites leave urban centers, radicalize the communities across the countryside and return in force to seize power. But for the modern democratization recipe, digital media is a key ingredient.[34]

The genie of globally informed and regionally organized public opinion is out of the bottle and cannot be put back in. Whether or not you believe that politics is now being shaped in new ways, it is difficult to deny that the way in which social movements have used social media has reframed the way that events are narrated. Yet we need more policy makers who can read and understand their texts of revolution. So we return to the question of when and why, if the change we have seen has been about the explosion of data and the rise of a cacophony of voices telling the world what will happen, most policy makers either missed it at the time or have spent the period since rubbishing the new political processes in their in-house journals *Foreign Affairs*, *Foreign Policy*, *National Interest*, and *American Interest*. What has occurred here is a misreading of global texts on a massive scale. If these policy makers were poets, we might say that they are suffering from an anxiety of influence, to use Harold Bloom's term.[35] If these policy makers were scientists, we might use Thomas Kuhn's language and say they were resisting a scientific revolution.[36]

There is a sense in which the policy-making community is paralyzed in the face of change by a fear of stepping out of the established debates between realists and idealists. There are many Bloomian weak poets among those who watch the world of international politics. They fear to contradict or move beyond the dominant voices in their field, so entire regions continue to be viewed through prisms forged in the Cold War and riven with clichés founded on the core texts of international relations, political economy, political science, and the other social sciences. Bloom has argued that the influence of older, greater poets inspires a sense of anxiety in younger poets that renders them unable to speak with originality. Likewise, the influence of older, more ideological international relations theorists inspires a sense of anxiety in younger, post–Cold War analysts that renders them unimaginative. But it is in Kuhn that we perhaps find a more fitting analogy. He argues that "a scientific community cannot practice its trade without some set of received beliefs" that are the foundation of the "educational initiation that prepares and licenses the student for professional practice." These practices are embedded and ensure that the scientists know what the world is like. Therefore, he states, "[N]ormal science often suppresses fundamental novelties because they are necessarily subversive of its basic commitments." The arrival of new conditions or new paradigms, that is, necessitates the "reconstruction of prior assumptions" and a reevaluation of what we think we already know.[37] Such paradigm shifting is a very difficult thing to do, and so it is resisted for as long as the old worldview can stand up against the onslaught of the new.

What is needed in the wake of recent uprisings is an approach to policy making that is genuinely evidence based and a training of policy makers that embraces an awareness of the importance of voice and testimony expressed through social media. Howard, again, crystallizes the point:

> The State Department has a nascent strategy to encourage democratic movements by actively supporting civil society and for actively engaging social networks through digital media. This has been a forward thinking, innovative approach

to statecraft. This new State Department has treated civic networks as incongruent with traditional political parties, unions, or factions. That is good. Social movement theorists tell us that what makes a regime collapse is not urban poor rioting in the streets, but "elite defection." When a country's entrepreneurs, lawyers, doctors, teachers, students, and state bureaucrats switch allegiances, a dictator falls.

If, in the twenty-first century, regimes fall when there is elite defection rather than unrest from below, then, as Howard says, "We need the State Department to do some 21st century thinking."[38] How can we understand and respond to these new dynamics except by rethinking our theories of change and employing analysts who think differently? While more developments of this kind will not remove the ideological path dependency of policy actors, they will help to promote the evidence of people on the ground, close to events, to a more equal status and embed a more complex view of how change takes place. There is an urgent need for this development because new communications technologies have changed the way events happen. While not everything is different now, and sadly tanks still kill people, it is important for the policy-making community to understand that the paradigm has shifted: it is time to listen to the eyewitnesses telling us that the world is not flat.

NOTES

1. See, for example, "The Crisis Map: Where the World Stands Still," accessed June 2, 2012, http://libyacrisismap.net/.

2. C. P. Snow, *The Two Cultures* (Cambridge: Cambridge University Press, 1959).

3. A full and balanced account of this issue can be found in Joseph Cirincione, Jessica Tuchman Mathews, and George Perkovich, with Alexis Orton, "WMD in Iraq: Evidence and Implications," Carnegie Endowment for International Peace, January 8, 2004, accessed June 2, 2012, http://www.carnegieendowment.org/2004/01/08/wmd-in-iraq-evidence-and-implications/dm8.

4. Michael Gordon, "The Army Buried RAND Report," *New York Times*, February 11, 2008.

5. See, for example, *Foreign Affairs*, May/June 2011. There has also been growing resistance to the idea that Twitter played an important role in Iran; see "The Twitter Devolution," *Foreign Policy*, June 7, 2010, accessed June 1, 2012, http://www.foreignpolicy.com/articles/2010/06/07/the_twitter_revolution_that_wasnt. News mining has been used to try to map the role of social media; see Guan-Cheng Li, "Precursor to the Arab Spring, Evidence from the Social Media," May 7, 2012, accessed June 1, 2012, http://bid.berkeley.edu/cs294-1-spring12/images/8/8f/Cs294-1-Guan-Cheng_Li_Arab_spring.pdf. A good overview of the debate is Eva Bellini, "Reconsidering the Robustness

of Authoritarianism in the Middle East: Lessons from the Arab Spring," *Comparative Politics* 44, no. 2 (January 2012): 127–49.

6. See, for example, Abigail Hauslohner, "Is Egypt About to Have a Facebook Revolution?," *Time*, January 24, 2011, accessed June 2, 2012, http://www.time.com/time /world/article/0,8599,2044142,00.html.

7. Jack A. Goldstone, "Understanding the Revolutions of 2011," *Foreign Affairs*, May/June 2011, accessed January 2, 2014, http://www.foreignaffairs.com/articles /67694/jack-a-goldstone/understanding-the-revolutions-of-2011.

8. Ellen Laipson, *Seismic Shift: Understanding Change in the Middle East* (Washington, DC: Harold L. Stimson Center, 2012).

9. Ibid., 41–54.

10. Ibid., 83–94.

11. Ibid., 29–40.

12. Ibid., 14.

13. Asef Bayat, *Life as Politics: How Ordinary People Change the Middle East* (Stanford, CA: Stanford University Press, 2010), 75.

14. This academic approach can be broadly summarized as being based on the assumption that there is something in the Arab mentality that accepts authoritarian governance and does not want to embrace democracy. This is discussed in Laipson, *Seismic Shift*, 11–28.

15. The details of the four indexes are cited in Laipson as follows. Monty G. Marshall, Jack A. Goldstone, and Benjamin R. Cole, *State Fragility Index and Matrix* (Fairfax, VA: Center for Systemic Peace and Center for Global Policy, George Mason University, 2009). The State Fragility Index and Matrix (SFI) rates state effectiveness and legitimacy across four dimensions: security, governance, economic development, and social development. The SFI places states into six fragility categories: extreme (8 states in this category), high (20), serious (30), moderate (31), low (29), and little or no (43). Tunisia's fragility rating is "low," as is Libya's. Egypt is rated "serious." Fund for Peace, *The Failed State Index*, 2010, accessed June 2, 2012, http://www.fundforpeace.org/web/index.php?option =com_content&task=view&id=452&Itemid=900 (versions from 2005 to 2010 are available on this website). The Failed States Index (FSI) uses the Fund for Peace's Conflict Assessment System Tool to generate its index from twelve social, economic, and political indicators. In the 2010 FSI (Fund for Peace website version), both Tunisia and Egypt are placed in "warning," the second of four categories: alert, the most likely to experience an internal conflict (37 states in this category); warning, the next most conflict-likely group (92); moderate (35); and sustainable (13). The third index is detailed in Susan Rice and Stewart Patrick, *Index of State Weakness in the Developing World* (Washington, DC: Brookings Institution, 2008). The Index of State Weakness assesses 141 developing states according to measures of their performance on economic, political, security, and social welfare criteria, establishing composite scores on a scale from 0 (worst) to 10 (best). Egypt scored 6.50, ranking in the third quintile with marks higher than India (6.28) and China (6.41). Tunisia (7.61) ranked in the fourth quintile, together with countries such as Brazil

(7.22) and Turkey (7.18). The final index is Economist Intelligence Unit, *Political Instability Index* (London: The Economist, 2009), accessed June 2, 2012, http://viewswire.eiu.com /site_info.asp?info_name=social_unrest_table&page=noads&rf=0. The Political Instability Index combines three measures of economic distress—gross domestic product (GDP) growth, GDP per capita, and unemployment—together with a dozen indicators of underlying vulnerability, such as corruption and ethnic fragmentation, to score countries on a scale from 8.8 (most risk) to 1.2 (least risk) and classify each state as very high, high, moderate, or low risk. In 2009 Egypt scored 5.4, slightly safer than Spain (5.5) in the "moderate" risk category. Tunisia, also in the "moderate" category, scored 4.6, the same as Ireland and just above Singapore (4.7).

16. Food and Agriculture Organization of the United Nations, *The State of Food Insecurity in the World* (Rome: Food and Agriculture Organization of the United Nations, 2009), accessed January 2, 2014, http://www.fao.org/docrep/012/i0876e/i0876e00 .htm; US Department of Agriculture, Economic Research Service, *Food Security Assessment 2010–20* ([Washington, DC]: United States Department of Agriculture, Economic Research Service, 2010), accessed January 2, 2014, http://www.ers.usda.gov/publications /gfa-food-security-assessment-situation-and-outlook/gfa21.aspx#.UsViiluuR8E.

17. The Arab Barometer, accessed January 2, 2014, http://www.arabbarometer .org/.

18. Laipson, *Seismic Shift*, 35–40.

19. See John S. Conway, "The First Report about Auschwitz," Museum of Tolerance, Simon Wiesenthal Center, Annual 1, chapter 7 (n.d.), accessed June 1, 2012, http://motlc.wiesenthal.com/site/pp.asp?c=gvKVLcMVIuG&b=394983.

20. See Linda Melvern, *Conspiracy to Murder* (London: Verso, 2004).

21. See, for example, the eyewitness account published in *Le Monde*: "My eyes became heavy, I had pain breathing, I vomited 8 or 9 times. Each time I opened a door of a house, there were children, women, & men agonising & dying." Mohamad Azizi, "25 years," *Le Monde*, April 8, 1988.

22. See Gerard Alexander's classic study, *The Sources of Democratic Consolidation* (Ithaca, NY: Cornell University Press, 2002).

23. The work of Philip N. Howard is critical to understanding these developments. It is neatly summarized in Philip N. Howard, "The Arab's Spring's Cascading Effects," *Pacific Standard*, February 23, 2011, accessed January 2, 2014, http://www.psmag.com /politics/the-cascading-effects-of-the-arab-spring-28575/, and explored at much greater length in his groundbreaking book, *The Digital Origins of Dictatorship and Democracy: Information Technology and Political Islam* (Oxford: Oxford University Press, 2010).

24. Social Change through Education in the Middle East (SCEME), "Mobile Phones, Social Media and the Arab Spring," August 16, 2011, accessed June 2, 2012, http://www.credemus.org/images/stories/reports/mobile-phones-and-the-arab-spring.pdf, citing Jeffrey Ghannam, *Social Media in the Arab World: Leading up to the Uprisings of 2011*, Center for International Media Assistance, February 3, 2011, http://cima.ned .org/publications/social-media-arab-world-leading-uprisings-2011-0.

25. Evgeny Morozov, *The Net Delusion: The Dark Side of Internet Freedom* (New York: Public Affairs, 2010).

26. See Brian Lynch, "Q&A: Net Delusion Author Evgeny Morozov Says Dictators Are Learning to Love Social Networking," *Georgia Straight*, March 14, 2011, accessed June 2, 2012, http://www.straight.com/article-381541/vancouver/qa-net-delusion-author-evgeny-morozov-says-dictators-may-learn-love-social-networking.

27. Clay Shirky, *Here Comes Everyone* (London: Penguin, 2009).

28. Ibid., 33.

29. Lippman's full argument can be explored in Walter Lippman, *Public Opinion* (New York: Harcourt, Brace, 1922), available at http://www.gutenberg.org/ebooks /6456.

30. Shirky, *Here Comes Everyone*, 46–47.

31. Dubai School of Government, *Arab Social Media Report*, accessed June 1, 2012, http://www.dsg.ae/en/asmr3/index.aspx.

32. Carol Huang, "Facebook and Twitter Key to Arab Spring Uprisings: Report," *The National*, June 6, 2011, accessed June 2, 2012, http://www.thenational.ae/news/uae-news/facebook-and-twitter-key-to-arab-spring-uprisings-report.

33. *Foreign Policy*, February 14, 2011, accessed June 2, 2012, http://www.foreignpolicy .com/articles/2011/02/14/think_again_egypt; *Foreign Affairs*, May/June 2011.

34. Howard, "The Arab's Spring's Cascading Effects."

35. Harold Bloom, *The Anxiety of Influence* (Oxford: Oxford University Press, 1997).

36. Thomas Kuhn, *The Structure of Scientific Revolutions* (Chicago: University of Chicago Press, 1996).

37. Ibid., 10–22.

38. Philip N. Howard, "A State Department 2.0 Response to the Arab Spring," *Huffington Post*, February 9, 2011, accessed June 2, 2012, http://www.huffingtonpost.com /philip-n-howard/state-department-arab-spring_b_820458.html.

WORKS CITED

Alexander, Gerard. *The Sources of Democratic Consolidation*. Ithaca, NY: Cornell University Press, 2002.

Azizi, Mohamad. "25 years." *Le Monde*, April 8, 1988.

Bayat, Asef. *Life as Politics: How Ordinary People Change the Middle East*. Stanford, CA: Stanford University Press, 2010.

Bellini, Eva. "Reconsidering the Robustness of Authoritarianism in the Middle East: Lessons from the Arab Spring." *Comparative Politics* 44, no. 2 (January 2012): 127–49.

Bloom, Harold. *The Anxiety of Influence*. Oxford: Oxford University Press, 1997.

Cirincione, Joseph, Jessica Tuchman Mathews, and George Perkovich, with Alexis Orton. "WMD in Iraq: Evidence and Implications." Carnegie Endowment for International Peace, January 8, 2004. Accessed June 2, 2012. http://www.carnegie endowment.org/2004/01/08/wmd-in-iraq-evidence-and-implications/dm8.

Conway, John S. "The First Report about Auschwitz." Museum of Tolerance, Simon Wiesenthal Center, Annual 1, chapter 7 (n.d.). Accessed June 1, 2012. http://motlc .wiesenthal.com/site/pp.asp?c=gvKVLcMVIuG&b=394983.

Dubai School of Government. *Arab Social Media Report.* Accessed June 1, 2012. http:// www.dsg.ae/en/asmr3/index.aspx.

Economist Intelligence Unit. *Political Instability Index.* London: The Economist, 2009. Accessed June 2, 2012. http://www.economist.com/node/13349331.

Fund for Peace. *The Failed State Index*, 2010. Accessed June 2, 2012. http://ffp.statesindex .org/rankings-2010-sortable.

Ghannam, Jeffrey. *Social Media in the Arab World: Leading up to the Uprisings of 2011.* Center for International Media Assistance, February 3, 2011. Accessed June 2, 2012. http:// cima.ned.org/publications/social-media-arab-world-leading-uprisings-2011-0.

Goldstone, Jack A. "Understanding the Revolutions of 2011." *Foreign Affairs*, May/June 2011. Accessed January 2, 2014. http://www.foreignaffairs.com/articles/67694 /jack-a-goldstone/understanding-the-revolutions-of-2011.

Gordon, Michael. "The Army Buried RAND Report." *New York Times*, February 11, 2008.

Hauslohner, Abigail. "Is Egypt About to Have a Facebook Revolution?" *Time*, January 24, 2011. Accessed June 2, 2012. http.//www.time.com/time/world/article /0,8599,2044142,00.html.

Howard, Philip N. "The Arab's Spring's Cascading Effects." *Pacific Standard*, February 23, 2011. Accessed January 2, 2014. http://www.psmag.com/politics/the-cascading-effects-of-the-arab-spring-28575/.

———. *The Digital Origins of Dictatorship and Democracy: Information Technology and Political Islam.* Oxford: Oxford University Press, 2010.

Howard, Philip N. "A State Department 2.0 Response to the Arab Spring." *Huffington Post*, February 9, 2011. Accessed June 2, 2012. http://www.huffingtonpost.com/philip-n-howard/state-department-arab-spring_b_820458.html.

Kuhn, Thomas. *The Structure of Scientific Revolutions.* Chicago: University of Chicago Press, 1996.

Laipson, Ellen. *Seismic Shift: Understanding Change in the Middle East.* Washington, DC: Harold L. Stimson Center, 2012.

Li, Guan-Cheng. "Precursor to the Arab Spring, Evidence from the Social Media." May 7, 2012. Accessed June 1, 2012. http://bid.berkeley.edu/cs294-1-spring12 /images/8/8f/Cs294-1-Guan-Cheng_Li_Arab_spring.pdf.

Lippman, Walter. *Public Opinion.* New York: Harcourt, Brace, 1922. http://www.gutenberg .org/ebooks/6456.

Lynch, Brian. "Q&A: Net Delusion Author Evgeny Morozov Says Dictators Are Learning to Love Social Networking." *Georgia Straight*, March 14, 2011. Accessed June 2, 2012. http://www.straight.com/article-381541/vancouver/qa-net-delusion-author-evgeny-morozov-says-dictators-may-learn-love-social-networking.

Marshall, Monty G., Jack A. Goldstone, and Benjamin R. Cole. *State Fragility Index and Matrix.* Fairfax, VA: Center for Systemic Peace and Center for Global Policy, George Mason University, 2009.

Melvern, Linda. *Conspiracy to Murder.* London: Verso, 2004.

Morozov, Evgeny. *The Net Delusion: The Dark Side of Internet Freedom.* New York: Public Affairs, 2010.

Rice, Susan, and Stewart Patrick. *Index of State Weakness in the Developing World.* Washington, DC: Brookings Institution, 2008.

Shirky, Clay. *Here Comes Everyone.* London: Penguin, 2009.

Snow, C. P. *The Two Cultures.* London: Cambridge University Press, 1959.

"The Twitter Devolution." *Foreign Policy*, June 7, 2010. Accessed June 1, 2012. http://www.foreignpolicy.com/articles/2010/06/07/the_twitter_revolution_that_wasnt.

The Importance of Taking and Bearing Witness

Reflections on Twenty Years as a Human Rights Lawyer

MARK MULLER

For a long time I have been at the center of human rights discourse as a practicing Queen's Counsel, chairman of the Bar Human Rights Committee, and director of the Kurdish Human Rights Project (KHRP), the Delfina Foundation, and more recently Beyond Borders, a new Scottish initiative dedicated to small-nation dialogue and international cultural exchange. Yet it is only relatively recently that I have begun to fundamentally question the nature of much of this discourse. Do not misunderstand me: I remain a total supporter of human rights and the protection of human rights undertaken by human rights advocacy organizations like Amnesty International and the Bar Human Rights Committee. However, over the course of twenty years of human rights work I have come increasingly to understand the role that cultural exchange plays in that discourse, particularly when we are confronted by personal testimony and life narratives involving people from distant lands. If my experiences over twenty years have taught me anything, it is the value of listening to the many different kinds of personal voices and perspectives that are out there in society rather than to the gilded rhetorical speeches of those advocates who seek or claim to speak on their behalf—be it in the courtroom, Parliament, or the myriad of nongovernmental organizations (NGOs) that now make up the human rights community. For it is the power of real experience and testimony that tends to open up the mind and heart to the plight of other people's suffering rather than the momentary impact of the well-honed address of the advocate. I have been able to listen to the life narratives of exceptional people taking part in extraordinary events in person, and the stories I tell here are about that one-to-one experience. What matters most, however, is the life narrative, the place of these events in the life stories of individuals and peoples: what I advocate here is the centrality of the witness. The medium, whether in person, through the Internet, or in memoirs, does not matter as much as the message. What matters most is that the witnesses take voice, find voice, rather than others giving it to them and that having taken voice, the rest of the world listens and learns.

In fact, many human rights defenders often act as both advocate and witness when in the field. For my part I first cut my human rights teeth as a young lawyer in the early 1990s in Southeast Turkey. I used to regularly go out to the Kurdish areas to collect evidence in order to help the Bar Human Rights Committee and the KHRP submit cases to the European Court of Human Rights on behalf of Kurdish human rights victims. In those days there was hardly a fax machine let alone a mobile phone to be found in the region. Consequently, obtaining firsthand evidence from victims in outlying Kurdish villages was an extremely hazardous business. The idea of instantaneously blogging an account or uploading a video of a human rights atrocity would have been considered a pipe dream back then. Yet the very lack of a medium by which to technically capture personal testimony made my own firsthand experience of receiving it an intense and enduring experience. Being forced to listen to personal testimony in situ left an indelible mark on me as a human rights advocate. In particular, it taught me how the act of "witnessing" can—in and of itself—constitute an important act of accountability, healing, and reconciliation, not to say of cultural understanding. Permit me to illustrate this point by recalling two fraught human rights situations I encountered in the human rights field—one in Turkey in the early 1990s and the other in Benghazi, Libya, twenty years later. Both, I believe, speak to the importance of listening to and actually experiencing the travails of other peoples' lives.

Turkey in 1992–93

In early 1992 the Turkish government and security apparatus decided to adopt a scorched earth policy toward its conflict with the Kurdish Workers Party, the PKK, which had taken up arms in defense of Kurdish political and cultural rights a decade earlier. It became intent on smashing all forms of resistance in relation to the Kurdish issue by attempting to "drain the swamp." Turkish and Kurdish human rights organizations, bar associations, journalists, and democratic politicians consequently all found themselves coming under legal, extralegal, and physical attack. These indigenous organizations and individuals were crucial not only to the success of the KHRP's evidence collection program but also to the future existence of civic society in the Kurdish areas of Turkey. Without these fledgling institutions ordinary Kurdish villagers and peasants were cut loose with little or no protection or avenues of redress against the brutal iron fist policies of the security forces. This was a recipe for disaster for ordinary Kurds and Turks alike. State repression almost inevitably resulted in further polarization between the warring parties, forcing those caught in the middle to choose between one side and another. The response of Europe and the West as a whole was therefore crucial. Yet, while Europe's governments remained largely silent on this so-called dirty war, its civil society elected to heed the call.

Over the next few years groups like the KHRP, together with other human rights organizations, conducted numerous fact-finding missions to the region to investigate allegations of torture, extrajudicial killings, and interference with the right to freedom of association and expression. We also conducted sustained trial observations of various politicians, lawyers, human rights activists, writers, and politicians that found themselves in one way or another the subject of continued prosecution for merely speaking out. These trial observations helped hold judicial authorities to account and challenged the immunity of those that had perpetrated human rights violations. Over the next ten years the KHRP brought literally hundreds of test cases before the European Court, enlarging the jurisprudence on all major articles concerned with fundamental freedoms. Yet the KHRP was always more than just a litigation or human rights clearing-house. It represented a beacon of light to an unrecognized people hitherto shrouded in official darkness and silence from Baghdad to Ankara. It routinely came to the aid of numerous Kurdish intellectuals, journalists, human rights defenders, artists, and ordinary villagers whose rights had been violated in both professional and personal ways. It brought redress to thousands of people not only through its cases and the innovative public awareness and human rights defenders program, which extended beyond Turkey to Iraq, Iran, Syria, and the former Soviet Republics, but also through its personal networks in which testimony was collated and came to be heard. In doing these things, it helped transform the international community's understanding of the Kurds, in what is a complex region from any point of view. The publication of a series of ground-breaking reports concerning freedom of expression and association, especially in relation to minority cultural identity and rights, helped educate the wider public about the plight of Kurds not just in Turkey but also in Iraq, Iran, Syria, and the former Soviet Union. As such the KHRP was at the forefront in efforts to help states in the region voluntarily comply with their human rights, European

Union (EU), and international obligations. Elsewhere, it increased environmental consciousness by running innovative and popular campaigns, such as the Illusu Dam Campaign, which brought together human rights activists and environmentalists, such as the inspirational Nicholas Hiliyard of Cornerhouse, as well as comedians, such as Mark Thomas, from the broadcast sector to save a two-thousand-year-old village earmarked by the United Nations Educational, Scientific and Cultural Organization (UNESCO) along the banks of the Tigris.

Nevertheless, if I'm truthful, twenty years on, it is not the celebrity-endorsed campaigns or the eloquent judgments handed down by the great and the good in the courtrooms of Strasbourg that I remember. Nor is it the speeches I gave to international bodies. No—what is burned into my memory is hearing the news of our first applicant being shot dead by the authorities for not withdrawing his petition to the European Court after we failed to communicate the threat to his life quickly enough, witnessing my Kurdish driver being forced to kneel as an automatic rifle was placed in his mouth by soldiers in search of information at a desolate checkpoint, seeing a military colonel drive over a small Kurdish boy without so much as a look back, meeting twelve-year-old paperboys who had had their arms cut off for selling opposition papers, and recalling the utter fear of our legal colleagues in Diyarbakir in 1994 who refused to even look at me as they found themselves being dragged into the dock of the Turkish State Security Courts. They had endured days of gruesome detention for merely filing human rights claims in the European Court. These are the images I retain in my mind's eye. They are graphic images and have a photographic quality about them. But there are also other, less haunting images that I remember. I cannot forget the simple but gracious hospitality of Kurdish villagers I came across just after their isolated and poverty-stricken houses had been burned by the Turkish military in the summer of 1994. They had just lost some of their young menfolk, trampled to death by a passing tank, and were awaiting the return of others who had fled to hide in the fields. Yet as dusk dimmed the effect of the scorching summer sun and heralded the return of their loved ones, it was we not they who were fed with what meager rations they had left. "Tell the world what is happening here," they said. "It is a miracle you have come," said another.

These types of firsthand experiences change one's perspective about law, conflict, and the protection of human rights. They bind you to a region and people in ways that are scarcely imaginable to you at the outset. I can still recall meeting young dissident journalists in the back streets of Sultan Ahmet in old Istanbul in November 1994 for a late night meal after they had gotten the morning edition out. We had just missed the bombing by Turkish security forces of *Ozgur Gundem*'s building by some thirty minutes. *Ozgur Gundem* was a Kurdish nationalist newspaper whose prosecution I was observing. More than twenty-two journalists had gone missing over the previous two years. Some of their bodies were later found abandoned along lonely roadsides in Southeast Turkey riddled with bullet holes. All the journalists chain-smoked and looked nervously at the door as they ate their dinner, conscious that the knock and the midnight run to the security cell could happen at any time. But what I also recall was the laughter, the stolen glances of tenderness between them, and the collective recognition that pervaded the place: they would live for the moment, as one of their number might not be dining with them tomorrow. In a strange and very real sense they all seemed so totally alive. They were caught up in a history of their own making. They felt proud to be involved in the fight to convey their version of the truth—a version of the truth that every self-respecting sentient human being could permit in a normal pluralist society.

As a consequence of all of this work much has changed over the last fifteen years, including the breaking of taboos concerning public debate about the Kurdish question. In Turkey the Justice and Development Party (AKP) undertook a series of EU-orientated legal reforms to begin the process of constitutional and ideological reform. In Iraq a Kurd now sits where Saddam Hussein once did in the presidential palace in Baghdad, while the Kurdish regional government in northern Iraq grows each day in self-confidence and power. Nevertheless, it was only because of a sustained commitment to its counterparts in the region on the part of European civil society that the lot of ordinary Kurds finally improved.

The Arab Spring

It was this type of solidarity and commitment that I later experienced in Cairo and Benghazi during the Arab Spring of 2011. But Turkey is where I first realized that there is more to human rights campaigning than drafting, report writing, and court advocacy. In the end it is also about establishing a profound sense of human solidarity and shared experience with those undergoing oppression and fighting injustice—a solidarity in which cultures and identities are shared and experienced, tasted, and assimilated into one's own existence. To my mind the work of the KHRP, and other regionally centered organizations like it, represents a graphic illustration of what can be achieved when peoples from different cultures East and West come together to protect certain universal values and share the load of that struggle equally over a sustained period of time. At the heart of its work lay the personal testimony and accounts of ordinary Kurds, whose precarious existence had come to life through the communication of their own words and experiences.

It is precisely this type of solidarity and enduring commitment that is needed if like-minded people in the Middle East–North Africa (MENA) region are to win their democratic struggle to transform their societies and provide a better future for ordinary people. Yet it is this sort of integrated legal, political, and moral solidarity between different civil societies acting together across different continents that has partially dissipated in the advent of the "war on terror" years, as human rights lawyers concentrate on UK-based cases to the relative exclusion of those elsewhere. What these actions miss is the immediacy of testimony taken in situ within the relevant cultural and political setting. This is not to say that such test cases lack importance in holding governments to account. It is instead to observe that much of the testimony received by lawyers in these cases is done not in the field but in the safe confines of the interview room at some remove from the atrocity being investigated. The act of bearing witness to another person's testimony in situ is, I believe, vitally important not simply because of the moral support and personal comfort it offers to those that have suffered the violation but also because by being there one understands more readily the cultural and political nuances of the individual's plight and the wider human rights context of the violation that has taken place.

Today a debate rages about whether the West was right or prudent to back the no-fly zone in Benghazi in March 2011 and assist in the overthrow of Muammar Gaddafi, particularly given the chaos and confusion that now engulfs Libya. Detractors argue that we have kidded ourselves into believing that the Arab Spring could be the engine of progress for the people of the MENA region. It is a desperately difficult and finely balanced debate, particularly if one does not have firsthand experience of the region. So let me turn to my last illustration— Benghazi in April 2011. I wager that my understanding of and present commitment to the people of Benghazi would never have sustained themselves through all the democratic disappointments that have followed the initial euphoria of the Arab Spring were it not for my experience of their personal struggle for freedom and prosperity at close quarters. By bearing witness and listening to their personal testimony I transformed my own understanding and commitment to the struggle unfolding before me. When we got into the center of Benghazi, I met lawyers, architects, teachers, ordinary people manning the barricades or trying to re-create little media centers. There were young people trying to put together a newspaper for the first time, or a group of teenagers suddenly experimenting with rap music and traditional Arab music, and there was a house where all the graffiti was being produced. And everybody was talking about how all they wanted was just the freedom to be themselves. They hadn't even had a cinema in Benghazi for twenty years because Gaddafi hated the place so much. The people of Benghazi did not just testify to their woes but also to a set of political ideas and dreams that in the end drove and continues to drive their defiance. No doubt, just as in Turkey, it will take at least twenty years for their vision to come anywhere near fruition. But I for one am willing to side with those I met in Libya. I probably do so because of my experience of bearing witness to their personal testimony and, through them, my own. The reason why the reports and dispatches of journalists like my friend Marie Colvin are so important is because of their sense of immediacy and authenticity. What Colvin did was take you from the safe confines of your room and into that killing field. If this chapter is dedicated to anyone it is to her and all those other journalists and human rights defenders who have given up their lives so that others might read and listen to and finally come to understand the life stories of the victims of human rights abuse. As I said at the beginning of this essay, what matters is to listen to those who are brave enough to bear witness and to strive to understand that their lives are not defined by the evil that has been done to them and their communities but by their ability to transcend those events and pursue justice.

Marie Catherine Colvin was an award-winning American journalist who worked for the British newspaper the Sunday Times *from 1985 until her death. She died while covering the siege of Homs in Syria in 2012.*

Part Five

Learning

Using Life Narrative
to Explore Human Rights Themes
in the Classroom

BRIAN BRIVATI, MEG JENSEN, MARGARETTA JOLLY,
and ALEXANDRA SCHULTHEIS MOORE

This volume has explored the interface between life writing and human rights. It will, we hope, encourage further research and collaboration and conversation between these two fields. This connection reflects the coming together of two increasingly defining aspects of our age—the telling of the stories of ourselves and the campaigning for the rights of others. While we can be confident that research at this meeting point will continue, we would also like to bring the nexus of these two contemporary concerns firmly into the classroom. To provide some support for that process, above and beyond the ideas already presented and debated in this volume, we have set out in this chapter a series of suggested texts and discussions. While most of these will, we envision, be interesting for students working in their disciplines and crossing over to engage with life writing or human rights, it would also be a worthwhile experiment to, where possible, bring students from these different courses together sometimes in joint workshops. If the insights from one field are to continue to inform and extend the concerns of the other, then students of both fields must learn to be comfortable discussing their views together.

To frame our examples of teaching exercises we take two structures from human rights discourse and explore them each in turn through life-writing texts. The first framework comprises the idea of "generations of rights," and the second relates to the elements of Hilberg's triangle.[1] Most introductory texts used in the teaching of human rights suggest that there are three generations of

human rights: civil and political rights (e.g., the right to vote), economic and
social rights (e.g., the right to work), and cultural rights (e.g., the right to a language).[2] The content of each generation is contested, and there are debates
over which rights should be absolute and which relative. There are also debates
over what should constitute a civil or political right and whether second- and
third-generation rights should be called human rights at all.

In turn what we might term human rights events, the planning and carrying
out of acts of human rights abuse, have life cycles—from planning and perpetration to liberation and then judgment, punishment, and finally memory and
memorializing. Testimony and life narrative interact differently in each of these
contexts. While Raoul Hilberg's conceptionalizing of the Holocaust as a triangle
of victims, perpetrators, and bystanders is not the same as the life cycle of the
event, it is a useful tool for structuring classroom exercises. Hilberg contended
that without the presence of each point of the triangle the Holocaust could not
have taken place. The human beings who occupy these positions each have
stories of their own or positions that we need to understand if we are to understand the meaning of events. Designing a series of classes that explore an event
from the vantage point of each allows us to understand the event that sits in the
center of the triangle but also to explore the multifaceted moral ambiguities
between the points of that triangle, which Primo Levi called the "grey zone."[3]

It is important to consider the relationship between the testimony being examined and its specific educational context, as well as the human rights issues
within that testimony and the place where they occur in the life cycle of the
event. In offering some guides to teaching human rights issues through the use
of life narratives, we must be conscious all the time of the complexity of the
context. At the same time, these issues need to be made accessible and meaningful to students. To do so, we take each of the three generations of rights in
turn and offer ways in which they can be opened up through life narratives.
We suggest questions that might be raised, classroom exercises, and some texts
that are easily available on which to base classwork. We then suggest a similar
set of exercises and texts using the prism of Hilberg's triangle. Obviously, this
brief survey is not intended to be didactic but rather illustrative of possible
approaches.

Before considering each generation of rights in turn, the educator can consider the following general questions, perhaps sharing them with students in an
opening session in response to one shared life narrative. Beneath each of these
general questions, we offer ideas of further discussion threads to which they
may give rise.

Q. What different purposes might a life narrative serve at different stages in the life cycle of a human rights event?

Discussion Thread: Consider the differences between an initial witness report of an abuse, close to the event and for the purposes of gaining a police response, perhaps, or indeed recording the actions of police, and a memoir looking back on events that took place earlier in life. The time for reflection obviously makes a difference, but there is also a normative discussion of the value of different testimonies at different moments. Human rights students coming at this question from a legal background will probably feel more comfortable with the testimony than they will with the memoir. It would be interesting to challenge this. Literature and life-writing students, on the other hand, might find the reportage format of an eyewitness account to be less compelling or engaging than a carefully crafted memoir. These differing perspectives might lead, in turn, to questions concerning the "use" of testimony and, of course, the nature of a "truth."

Q. How was the text at hand initially positioned in the public sphere and how is it situated in a classroom context?

Discussion Thread: The human rights industry has tended historically to place more value on some kinds of texts—laws, treaties, conventions, and so on—than on others. Does that same hierarchy operate in the classroom or does it rather depend on which classroom we are discussing? The historian Lucy S. Dawidowicz, for example, was famously dismissive of the value of firsthand accounts.[1] Students may well bring an instinctive view of the relative value of different texts because of the status they are accorded in the public sphere, and these preconceived ideas might be discussed productively.

Q. Does/did the text serve as legal evidence, historical representation, or aesthetic representation, and is it intended to raise consciousness, cultivate empathy, or do something else?

Discussion Thread: Asking students what a text is for and what it does can elicit interesting debates around the relationship between form and content. A text that is in some sense officially "sanctioned" might carry more weight with some students than one that is trying to reach an inner feeling or response. Examining the presumed uses of different life narratives may enable discussions around ideas about the legibility of human rights in different settings or jurisdictions. Students might also consider how the role of the text within a given syllabus or course unit relates to the text's original or nonacademic purpose.

Q. Which analytical and affective lenses frame these different purposes? In other words, what do we read for when we read a text within one of these contexts?

Discussion Thread: Different disciplines are going to have varying responses to this kind of question. Indeed, one can imagine some students struggling to understand the question itself. The "self-evident" response that we read to collect evidence, construct a case, or present an argument can be usefully challenged here. In turn the nature of the text or the memoir might raise some troubling issues, such as why so many people are drawn to perpetrator memoirs and testimonies and have difficulty engaging with the silence of those victims who did not bear witness. Further discussions arising from this question might engage the idea of the stages of a rights story. At what point in the life cycle of such a narrative does the text at hand appear to have arisen? Is it a contemporary eye-witness account? Courtroom testimony a decade after the events narrated took place? The work of an archival historian written fifty years and five thousand miles away from the conflict region?

Q. In what way might testimony retraumatize the speaker?

Discussion Thread: Throughout the twentieth century therapists with a variety of backgrounds and clinical approaches increasingly came to believe that the ability to name our sufferings is integral to the process of mourning and acceptance. Thus, wherever victims sought private acceptance or legal justice, a form of words had to be found to name their trauma, however complex, unspeakable, or irretrievable that experience might have been. So, while public justice cannot be served unless an atrocity is named, identified, and finally narrated, the form of narration that may be useful in healing the victim is likely to be very different from what is of use to the state, and a discussion of these differences may arise from this question.

Q. Is there evidence of this trauma in the text, and are there particular strategies for avoiding retraumatization?

Discussion Thread: For most persons, self-narratives or "life stories" provide space for reflection on and processing of experience. But for many posttrauma sufferers, linear codes and conventions, and the facts and figures necessary to produce such narratives, are unrecuperable and/or inaccessible: factual, chronologically arranged narratives and trauma are often at cross-purposes. Students may be asked to examine a number of life narratives looking for evidence of discrepancies, discontinuities, repetitions, broken speech, gaps, and nonlinear moments in the text that might suggest its traumatic origins and provide an important context for interpreting its content.

Q. How do truth-telling conventions differ among genres of life narratives?

Discussion Thread: The "grey zone" that Primo Levi identifies between the fixed points of Hilberg's triangle is made up, to an extent, of truth telling that can take place between the position of the perpetrator and the position of the victim. This can be very troubling for students. In life writing and narrative study, "truth" and "historical accuracy" are routinely understood as fraught and contingent concepts. Cross-disciplinary discussions of contextual and narrative pressures on truth telling, and indeed definitions of *truth* itself in light of specific texts, can be helpful in guiding students toward a more engaged and self-conscious approach to reading life narratives.

Q. How does the narrative arc of the life story or testimony compare to that of the law or the desired action of a human rights organization?

Discussion Thread: This question can elicit a discussion of closure and purpose, which helps reflect back on the issue of why we write. If students see the value of a life story as intrinsic and the action of a human rights organization as extrinsic, then the discussion can force an examination of motive and purpose that should break down these categorical boundaries, both within and across disciplines.

Q. Are there "alternative jurisdictions" that human rights organizations can seek?

Discussion Thread: This question may provoke debates surrounding how best to achieve justice that can allow further reflection on closure but also on the broader and more complex issues of what constitutes the end of a human rights event. If justice has not been done through conventional means—if there has been no judgment and no punishment—can such an event be seen to be at an end? Could a judgment that was not judicial but influenced cultural norms (e.g., a universal acceptance that slavery is wrong) allow for closure even if no reparations are paid by the slaveholding nations to the descendants of victims? Is there an alternative jurisdiction in art and representation that can be equal to or even greater than the judgment of a court? An examination and comparison of human rights recognition and advancement attempted in films, novels, journalism, dance, and verbatim theater will be useful in this discussion.

Q. What kinds of literacies does the text invoke or require? Are there words, concepts, or experiences that defy translation?

Discussion Thread: The point of these questions is to enable reflection on the idea of the legibility and accessibility of stories of human rights violations and campaigns for rights advancement. To what audiences are various forms of rights narratives accessible? What audiences are excluded from such narratives? What can be done to ensure greater accessibility to rights stories?

Finally, there is also a key question to consider from the policy or legal perspective.

Q. What human rights are being violated or challenged in the text?

Discussion Thread: It would be productive here to compare a number of narratives that highlight rights abuse, some of which may evoke explicit, perhaps violent offenses, and others in which the rights violations may be less clear or in which a crime has taken place but not necessarily a rights violation. This discussion could be supported with a copy of the Universal Declaration of Human Rights and its key protocols. Students could consider which human rights, if any, had been abused in the cases being considered and whether the victims in these circumstances would seek redress through national law or international tribunals and courts. This analysis and comparison should generate a discussion about the place of rights within the legal system and may develop into a consideration of whether the victim is seeking legal redress and/or recognition that a rights violation has indeed taken place.

First-Generation Rights: Civil and Political Rights

The purpose of this exercise might be to interpret a text in relation to specific conventions, treaties, and cases that relate to a specific right or civil and political rights in general. This area represents the most obvious and probably the most accessible way to use testimony in the classroom. The range of evidential witness testimony generated in civil and political rights cases is immense.

Suggested Texts

The most famous "political" set pieces, such as the Nuremburg Trials of Nazi officials involved in starting World War II (the primary focus of the case) and committing genocide against the Jews and other groups (the secondary focus of the case) can be accessed through written and filmed materials to explore not only issues of selective memory and the defense offered by perpetrators that they were merely obeying orders but also the theater of the legal process itself. Nuremburg does not, however, provide any testimony from victims.[5] Twenty years later, when Adolf Eichmann was kidnapped and put on trial by the Israelis, one of the world's first global media events, the voices of the victims came to center stage.

The Eichmann trial testimony can be used to explore many key themes, such as the centrality of human rights abuse to the life stories of individuals, in this case, the role of trauma in their present lived experiences and the traumatic nature of the testimonial process itself. In turn the contrast between the reading of transcripts of expressed testimony and the experience of watching and listening can be explored through both trials. The life stories of perpetrators, as explored in Nuremburg for many members of the Nazi regime and at the Eichmann trial through just one, are difficult but important topics for the classroom.

The use of the memories of perpetrators can be a device for engaging with questions of agency and free will in the perpetration of human rights abuses but also for reflecting on the nature of memory and the role of the interviewer in constructing the narrative. In this case the work of Gitta Sereny, especially her book on Franz Stangl, the commandant of Treblinka, *Into That Darkness*, is an important resource and source for such exercises.[6]

Classroom Exercises and Further Questions for Discussion

Text: The final chapter of Gitta Sereny's *Into That Darkness*.

Actions: The group is asked to explore the text as evidence that might be presented in court, as a memoir reconstructed from interviews, as interviews as the basis for history, and finally as a psychological study of an individual. Divide the class into four teams and ask the members of each to defend the text from the others' perspectives and critique it from their own perspective with respect to the other views.

This exercise should help students to explore the classic dilemma that the person collecting the testimony has an influence on the way it is presented and also allow them to question the extent to which they are reading about Stangl and the "truth" he is seeking to tell or about Sereny and the "story" she is seeking to tell.

Alternatively, with this or any other text, ask the class to imagine a conversation with the narrator/author. Consider:

- What additional knowledge or experience would be helpful in having that conversation?
- Do research to help fill in some of the gaps.
- Draft a letter to him or her that responds to the life story or testimony.
- Consider the differences between responding to an individual and a situation.
- How do we, as readers, respond to silences and gaps in life writing?
- What are the ethical dimensions of our responses and engaging with these kinds of texts?

Second-Generation Rights: Social and Economic Rights

Social democratic critiques of established rights discourse led over time to the articulation of a set of economic and social rights known as second-generation rights. In part they were a product of the Cold War debate over the relative importance of political rights, for example, the right to vote in free and fair elections and the right to welfare and education above the behest of government.

Suggested Texts

When considering second-generation rights, firsthand life narratives of social and economic deprivations in addition to historical fiction, for example, John Steinbeck's *The Grapes of Wrath*, can be used to explore the debate over whether or not basic standards of health, economic well-being, education, and social mobility are also human rights.[7] And, if they are, do they constitute absolute or relative rights? One can imagine the use of life narrative texts being especially effective in exploring themes around relative versus absolute deprivation. The sorts of texts and life narratives that might be useful in these kinds of classes would be more concerned with descriptions of everyday life in different socio-economic contexts.

An excellent source for this kind of exercise is the Mass Observation Archive.[8] This archive contains thousands of firsthand accounts of economic conditions in different social contexts through observation reports and diaries of everyday life in Britain. As these reports are set in the context of the Great Depression, they can serve as the basis for both comparative analysis of social economic rights and the debate over whether they actually constitute human rights. Economic and social rights relate to ordinary life, the lived experience of individuals and communities. They can therefore be very good ways for students to consider their own responses to human rights issues.

Classroom Exercises and Further Questions for Debate

Exercises could include reading, watching, or listening to a Mass Observation rights-based narrative and asking students to consider:

- Their own responses to these life narratives.
- Whether they think they were the primary intended audience for the text.
- How does the text define its audience?
- Does the text call for a particular response?
- How do they respond to that call?
- How does the life narrative or testimony define a time scale for the development or preservation of a human right? Does it imply a sense of crisis or the long duration of structural inequality?

Third-Generation Rights:
Cultural or Group Rights

Cultural or third-generation rights are also an area that can be richly explored in a teaching context using life narratives. One central tenet of the original definition of *genocide* when it was first used by Raphael Lempkin in the 1930s was the crime of vandalism and barbarism against the language, institutions, and culture of a people.

Suggested Texts

There is no better way to explore the cultural rights of individuals than by exploring their changing life stories over time, especially the testimony of the life stories of indigenous peoples. The oral history movement in the United States has collected many thousands of life stories of Native Americans as they moved from reservation to reservation and campaigned to defend the cultural and linguistic basis of their identity. In turn there are rich and often literary-autobiographical sources in the life stories of slaves, slave owners, and freed slaves that can be used to explore issues raised by third-generation rights. Third-generation rights raise important questions about individual versus collective rights. These questions are also important in terms of testimony.

Classroom Exercises and Further Questions for Discussion

How do individual and collective testimonial life narratives differ from one another, and what are the stakes of those differences? How can singular stories represent collective claims to human rights? If we do read a life narrative synecdochically, who may be excluded from its frame of reference? What other human rights claimants does it not represent?

- Is the text describing the structural basis for the continuation of the abuse, that is, the economic context of deprivation or the political system in which the perpetrators operate?
- Is it about the aftermath of the event itself, the punishment or judgment of the perpetrators of the abuse, or the system that perpetuates the injustice?

The position of the life narrative and/or testimony in the life cycle of the human rights event, or events, being considered can be important in understanding third-generation rights cases because they often entail the denial of other rights to a group rather than an individual.

A useful initial exercise with students would be to use extracts from life narrative texts and other forms of witness testimony to explore the position of the events in terms of human rights discourse and the arc of the human rights event the text describes. Situating the text like this then opens a second stage of analyzing the role of the text in the meaning of the event either at a single moment in the arc of its unfolding or in the overall narrative of the event through the arc of its existence. The "it" will be different depending on what you are trying to achieve. It might be the text itself, if the primary educative purpose is to understand and situate it in human rights discourse. If the intent is to explore the multiplicity of truthful accounts that can be constructed around a single event, then a simple exercise can be done with students.

Play the group a piece of film incorporating individual testimony from a variety of filmed media describing something related to the same event or set of events. Ask the members of the group to work in pairs and to describe and recount everything they have just seen or heard and then repeat the exercise in fours and finally in eights or half the group; then compare the differences that emerge at each stage of the witnessing process. This exercise can be combined with one that explores different rhetorical strategies that speak to the different purposes of life narratives and testimony. Find passages in the text that correspond to the different purposes and label them. Once the narrative has been annotated in this way, consider whether it contains any surprises in its rhetorical approaches. To what extent is it possible to read the narrative as effective in multiple contexts?

Additional Exercises

- Read several different life narratives or testimonies related to a single topic. Discuss their intersections, parallels, and divergences. To what extent does reading multiple stories shift the focus from the individual narrator to the shared experience?
- Compare a digital and a print-based rights-based life narrative, considering the particular advantages and disadvantages of each in light of pursuing a campaign, spreading awareness, or achieving a therapeutic or aesthetic effect.
- Consider the differences between a classroom, a clinic, or a court in studying traumatic narratives, and try to teach or learn about such

narratives on the assumption that there may be someone present who
has experienced trauma.

• Consider all the different life stories and testimonies one receives on a
given day through different media. For each of them, document the
organization, basic biographical information about the subject, length
of the appeal, rhetorical approach, and desired outcome. Do any
appeals stand out among the rest? What makes an appeal effective in
generating a positive response?

Hilberg's Triangle:
Victims, Perpetrators, and Bystanders

The simple presentation of the triangle can form a good basis for a discussion of
the structure of a human rights event and the different voices, and silences, we
might encounter. Students can be asked to draw the triangle and label each of
the points with one of the terms. This picture can form the basis for discussion.

Suggested Texts

There are three texts that suggest themselves, in addition to a reading and
discussion of Primo Levi's "The Grey Zone," as a way to explore the idea of
Hilberg's triangle. Each of these texts relates to one of the three points but also
reflects on the relationships among the points and to the "grey zone" in between,
thus allowing for further exploration of these themes in the classroom. The first
text is Annette Wieviorka's *The Era of the Witness* and her consideration there of
the different versions of Elie Wiesel's *La Nuit* (*Night*) as a way of looking at the
victim's position on the triangle.[9] The role of perpetrators is subtly and productively examined in James Dawes's two volumes *That the World May Know: Bearing
Witness to Atrocity* and *Evil Men*.[10] Discussions of the often overlooked place of the
bystander can be encouraged by an examination of the title chapter in Norman
Geras's *The Contract of Mutual Indifference*.[11]

Classroom Exercises

Hilberg's triangle is a key theme, and it would be impossible to cover all these
texts in a single teaching session; however, if time allows, one method of engaging
with these difficult issues that would elicit responses from both a life writing and
a human rights perspective would be asking students to produce a personal

journal. In parallel with the normal teaching program and in the run-up to an extended session in which students are invited to read their work, they are asked to keep a daily reading journal split into two distinct sections.

In the first section they reflect as they read the texts outlined above. These texts will take them around the points of the triangle in turn. In considering Wieviorka and Wiesel the issues of the language in which a victim can bear witness will be confronted. The Yiddish version of *La Nuit* is much longer and much more heavily descriptive than the French. It was written for a Yiddish reading audience. Students may be asked to consider the effect of translation in such cases: while there are no factual differences between the two versions, might the Yiddish translation be "closer" to the "real voice" of Wiesel?

The voices of perpetrators echo in James Dawes's ears in his two volumes. Students should be asked to read the five questions outlined in the preface to *Evil Men* and reflect on their own answers to them. Students confront the central issue of whether we should listen to the voices of the perpetrators and, if so, how we should listen. Finally, the students should confront Geras and his disturbing and unsettling essay exploring the indifference of the bystander, especially the image of the woman watering her plants as a column of Jews are marched to their deaths below her balcony.

In the second section of the reading log students should attempt to chronicle any experience in which they find themselves in the role of bystander, whether by walking past a homeless person or ignoring a newspaper article or advertisement soliciting donations to charity. This sort of reflection should lead them to consider the moral ambiguity of the "grey zone." We would recommend, however, that discussions of the grey zone be left for the opening of a longer session in which students read extracts from bystander diaries. A semi-staged reading of the first few pages of Levi's "The Grey Zone" followed by student readings should bring these ideas into sharp focus. The educator should be prepared to find difficult issues surfacing in the context of the discussion. Students will often reflect on past crimes through this prism. With this in mind it is important that the aim of the log is to document the position of the bystander, that reading aloud is not compulsory, that rules and guidelines are circulated prior to the exercise, and that each student is given an equal and fixed amount of time in which to read. It is equally important that the issues raised in the readings are then fully discussed in a standard seminar format after the conclusion of the reading workshop. We would further advise that anyone teaching these topics consider the possible dynamics of both rights claims and trauma in the classroom itself. A useful discussion of how to teach life narrative reflexively in the contemporary classroom can be found in Leigh Gilmore's "What Do We Teach When We Teach Trauma?"[12]

On a concluding note, we would like to point to the vital role that we believe is served by engaging in such morally, politically, socially, and historically complex ideas not only in the classrooms of human rights degree students but also in life narrative seminars and creative writing workshops: shedding light on the grey zone.

NOTES

1. Raoul Hilberg, *Perpetrators Victims Bystanders: The Jewish Catastrophe, 1933–1945* (New York: Harper Perennial, 1993).

2. See Michael D. A. Freeman, *Human Rights: An Interdisciplinary Approach* (Oxford: Polity, 2002).

3. Primo Levi, "The Grey Zone," in *The Drowned and the Saved* (London: Abacus, 1989).

4. Lucy S. Dawidowicz, *The Holocaust and the Historians* (Cambridge, MA: Harvard University Press, 1981), 177.

5. The Nuremburg Trials testimony can be found at the Avalon Project, accessed October 9, 2013, http://avalon.law.yale.edu/subject_menus/witness.asp.

6. Gitta Sereny, *Into That Darkness: An Examination of Conscience* (New York: Vintage Books, 1983).

7. John Steinbeck, *The Grapes of Wrath*, Penguin Classics (New York: Penguin Books, 2006).

8. Mass Observation Archive, accessed April 24, 2013, http://www.massobs.org.uk/.

9. Annette Wieviorka, *The Era of the Witness* (Ithaca, NY: Cornell University Press, 1998); Elie Wiesel, *La Nuit (Night)*, translated by Stella Rodway (New York: Bantam, 1982).

10. James Dawes, *That the World May Know: Bearing Witness to Atrocity* (Cambridge, MA: Harvard University Press, 2007); James Dawes, *Evil Men* (Cambridge, MA: Harvard University Press, 2013).

11. Norman Geras, *The Contract of Mutual Indifference: Political Philosophy after the Holocaust* (London: Verso, 1998).

12. Leigh Gilmore, "What Do We Teach When We Teach Trauma?," in *Teaching Life Writing Texts*, ed. Miriam Fuchs, Craig Howes, and the Modern Language Association of America (New York: Modern Language Association of America, 2008).

WORKS CITED

Dawes, James. *Evil Men*. Cambridge, MA: Harvard University Press, 2013.
———. *That the World May Know: Bearing Witness to Atrocity*. Cambridge, MA: Harvard University Press, 2007.

Dawidowicz, Lucy S. *The Holocaust and the Historians.* Cambridge, MA: Harvard University
    Press, 1981.
Freeman, Michael D. A. *Human Rights: An Interdisciplinary Approach.* Oxford: Polity, 2002.
Geras, Norman. *The Contract of Mutual Indifference: Political Philosophy after the Holocaust.*
    London: Verso, 1998.
Gilmore, Leigh. "What Do We Teach When We Teach Trauma?" In *Teaching Life Writing
    Texts,* edited by Miriam Fuchs, Craig Howes, and the Modern Language Association
    of America, 367–74. New York: Modern Language Association of America, 2008.
Hilberg, Raoul. *Perpetrators Victims Bystanders: The Jewish Catastrophe, 1933–1945.* New
    York: Harper Perennial, 1993.
Levi, Primo. "The Grey Zone." In Primo Levi, *The Drowned and the Saved.* London: Abacus,
    1989.
Sereny, Gitta. *Into That Darkness: An Examination of Conscience.* New York: Vintage Books,
    1983. First published in 1974.
Steinbeck, John. *The Grapes of Wrath.* Penguin Classics. New York: Penguin Books,
    2006.
Wiesel, Elie. *La Nuit (Night).* Translated by Stella Rodway. New York: Bantam, 1982.
Wieviorka, Annette. *The Era of the Witness.* Ithaca, NY: Cornell University Press, 1998.

Contributors

MOLLY ANDREWS is a professor of political psychology and the codirector of the Centre for Narrative Research (www.uelac.uk/cnr/index.htm) at the University of East London. Her research interests include the psychological basis of political commitment, psychological challenges posed by societies in transition to democracy, patriotism, conversations between generations, gender and aging, and counternarratives. Her monographs include *Shaping History: Narratives of Political Change* (2007) and *Narrative Imagination and Everyday Life* (2014).

HECTOR ARISTIZÁBAL, the 2012 recipient of the Otto René Castillo Award for Political Theater, has decades of experience as an internationally known theater artist and psychotherapist. In his work with marginalized populations in the United States, as well as with ex-combatants in Colombia, Croatia, Israel/Palestine, and Northern Ireland, he uses theater arts for community building and reconciliation, inviting participants to tell their own stories, challenge the inevitability of violence, and use their imaginations to achieve a more just and joyous life for all people.

BRIAN BRIVATI is the director of the D Academy—an international training and development organization. He was a professor of contemporary history and human rights at Kingston University from 2001 to 2008 and director of the John Smith Memorial Trust, 2008–12. He has written or edited fourteen books and published over one hundred articles on contemporary political history. He currently works on training and development projects encompassing programs in Armenia, Azerbaijan, Bahrain, Georgia, Iraq, Jordan, Lebanon, Oman, Russia, Ukraine, and Zimbabwe.

FINOLA FARRANT is a senior lecturer in criminology at the University of Roehampton. She has undertaken extensive research on behalf of a number of government departments, as well as for local governments and nongovernmental organizations. Previous to working in academia, she was an active campaigner for prison reform and has conducted a number of research projects in this area. She was a member of the management board for the Restorative Justice Consortium for five years.

PATRICIA HAMPL first won recognition for *A Romantic Education* (1981), a Cold War memoir about her Czech heritage (reprinted in 1999 with a post–Cold War "Afterword").

Her many publications, including *The Florist's Daughter* (2007), *Blue Arabesque: A Search for the Sublime* (2006), *I Could Tell You Stories* (1999), *Virgin Time* (1992), and *Resort and Other Poems* (1983), have established her as an influential figure in the rise of autobiographical writing. In 1990 she was awarded a MacArthur Fellowship. She is Regents Professor and McKnight Distinguished Professor at the University of Minnesota, Minneapolis, and a member of the permanent faculty of the Prague Summer Writing Program.

EVA HOFFMAN is the author of seven books, including *Lost in Translation* (1989), *After Such Knowledge* (2003), *Illuminations* (2008), and *Time* (2010). She has worked as a senior editor at the *New York Times* and written and lectured internationally on issues of exile, memory, Polish-Jewish history, politics, and culture. She has presented numerous radio programs and taught at various universities, including the Massachusetts Institute of Technology and Hunter College. She now teaches creative writing at Kingston University and lives in London.

MEG JENSEN is an associate professor of English literature and creative writing and the director of the Centre for Life Narratives at Kingston University, and she publishes both creative writing and literary criticism. Her publications include "Something Beautiful for Mary," in *New Writing: The International Journal for the Practice and Theory of Creative Writing* (2012); "Moments of Being in Virginia Woolf's Major Novels," in *The Cambridge Companion to the Modernist Novel* (2007); and *The Open Book: Creative Misreading in the Works of Selected Modern Writers* (2002).

MARGARETTA JOLLY is a reader in cultural studies and director of the Centre for Life History and Life Writing Research at the University of Sussex. She is the editor of *The Encyclopedia of Life Writing* (2001), a winner of an Outstanding Reference Book Award from the American Libraries Association, and the author of *In Love and Struggle: Letters in Contemporary Feminism* (2008), winner of the Feminist and Women's Studies Association Book Prize, United Kingdom, in 2009.

ANNETTE KOBAK's memoir, *Joe's War: My Father Decoded* (2004), was Book of the Week on BBC Radio 4. Her biography of the traveler Isabelle Eberhardt is a Virago Classic and was the basis for a film in the BBC2 series *Great Journeys*. She also translated Eberhardt's novel *Vagabond*. She lives in London, is an associate of Kingston University's Centre for Life Narratives, and is writing a book about Madame de Staël and Napoleon.

DIANE LEFER's collaborations with Hector Aristizábal include the book *The Blessing Next to the Wound* (2010), the play *Nightwind* (2004), and the Theater of Witness production *We Are Here* (2013), in which survivors of torture presented their stories publicly for the first time. She is the author of the novels *The Fiery Alphabet* (2013), *Nobody Wakes Up Pretty* (2012), and *Radiant Hunger* (2001) and the short-story collection *California Transit* (2007), which was awarded the Mary McCarthy Prize. Her political essays and interviews are widely published.

EMIN MILLI is a writer and dissident from Azerbaijan, imprisoned in 2009 for his critical views about the government. He was conditionally released in November 2010, after serving sixteen months of his sentence, in part due to strong international pressure. He studied at the University of London's School of Oriental and African Studies, where he wrote his dissertation on new media and Arab revolutions. In 2013 he launched an independent media platform for free speech based in Berlin and Baku called Meydan TV (www.meydan.tv), of which he is currently the managing director.

MICHIO MIYASAKA is a professor of health care ethics at the School of Health Sciences, Niigata University. He received his PhD from the University of Tokyo in 1998. He has published three books in Japanese, including *The Records of Hansen's Disease Prison* (in Japanese, 2006) and *Methods in Health Care Ethics: Principles, Procedures, and Narratives* (in Japanese, 2011). He has published more than sixty journal articles and book chapters in both Japanese and English.

MARK MULLER is a senior barrister who was appointed to the rank of Queen's Counsel in 2006 and has won numerous international test cases and awards in the field of human rights. Since 2005 he has been a senior adviser to the Centre for Humanitarian Dialogue, Beyond Conflict, and InterMediate. Muller is currently chair of Rule of Law for the International Committee of the Bar Council of England and Wales, a member of the Attorney General's International Committee, and was formerly Chairman of the Bar Human Rights Committee (2006–12). He is the executive director of Beyond Borders, a Scottish not-for-profit dedicated to the small nation dialogue and international cultural exchange, and a fellow at Harvard Law School.

BRIAN PHILLIPS is the coeditor of the *Journal of Human Rights Practice*. He is an independent human rights consultant, most recently for Equitas, Amnesty International, the Medical Foundation for the Care of Victims of Torture, and the Coalition to Stop the Use of Child Soldiers. He was the campaign coordinator for Amnesty's Europe Regional Program from 1995 to 2001 and a Joseph Rowntree Quaker fellow. He was closely involved in the development of Quaker Peace and Social Witness's program in the post-Yugoslav region. He is based in Toronto.

KATRINA M. POWELL is an associate professor of English at the Virginia Polytechnic Institute and State University. She teaches courses in autobiography, research methods, and writing and directs the Women's and Gender Studies Program. In addition to several books, including *The Anguish of Displacement* (2007) and *"Answer at Once": Letters of Mountain Families in Shenandoah National Park, 1934–1938* (2009), she has published articles in *College English*, *Prose Studies*, and *Biography*.

MARY ROBINSON is president of the Mary Robinson Foundation—Climate Justice. She served as the president of Ireland from 1990 to 1997 and as United Nations High Commissioner for Human Rights from 1997 to 2002. She is a member of the Elders and the Club of Madrid and the recipient of numerous honors and awards, including the Presidential Medal of Freedom from the president of the United States, Barack Obama. Mrs. Robinson was president and founder of Realizing Rights: The Ethical Globalization Initiative from 2002 to 2010 and served as honorary president of Oxfam International from 2002 to 2012. In March 2013 she was appointed the UN secretary general's special envoy for the Great Lakes region of Africa.

NAZEEHA SAEED is a Bahraini journalist who works for France 24 and Monte Carlo Doualiya Radio, covering business, politics, society, and sports. Her coverage of the events in Bahrain during the uprising in 2011 led to her arrest and torture. She is currently working on the promotion and protection of the right to freedom of opinion and protecting journalists.

KAY SCHAFFER is an adjunct professor in gender, work, and social analysis at the School of Social Studies, University of Adelaide. The author of ten books, including *Human Rights and Narrated Lives* (with Sidonie Smith, 2004), and numerous articles, she researches at the intersections of gender, cultural, and literary studies. Her most recent book is *Women's Writing in Post Socialist China* (with Xianlin Song, 2013).

ALEXANDRA SCHULTHEIS MOORE is an associate professor of English at the University of North Carolina, Greensboro. In addition to essays on representations of human rights, she is the author of *Regenerative Fictions: Postcolonialism, Psychoanalysis, and the Nation as Family* (2004) and coeditor, with Elizabeth Swanson Goldberg, of *Theoretical Perspectives on Human Rights and Literature* (2012), *Teaching Human Rights in Literary and Cultural Studies* (forthcoming), and *Doubling the Voice: Survivors and Human Rights Workers Address Torture, Resistance, and Hope* (forthcoming).

SIDONIE SMITH is the Mary Fair Croushore Professor of the Humanities and director of the Institute for the Humanities at the University of Michigan. She is a past president of the Modern Language Association of America (2010). Her most recent books include the second, expanded edition of *Reading Autobiography: A Guide for Interpreting Life Narratives* (with Julia Watson, 2010) and *Human Rights and Narrated Lives: The Ethics of Recognition* (with Kay Schaffer, 2004).

JULIA WATSON is a professor of comparative studies at The Ohio State University. She and Sidonie Smith have cowritten *Reading Autobiography: A Guide for Interpreting Life Narratives* (2nd ed., 2010) and coedited *De/Colonizing the Subject* (1992); *Getting a Life* (1996); *Women, Autobiography, Theory* (1998); *Interfaces* (2001); and *Before They Could Vote* (2006). Their recent essays are on authenticity in testimony and on online life narrative. Watson has also recently published essays on graphic memoir, visual diary, and autoethnography in American ethnic narrative.

GILLIAN WHITLOCK is an Australian Research Council professorial fellow at the University of Queensland, where she is working on letters in the asylum seeker archives. Her book *Postcolonial Life Narrative* (forthcoming) focuses on postcolonial testimony, and she recently coedited (with Tom Couser) a special issue of *Biography*, "Posthuman Lives" (2012).

Index

Page numbers in italics indicate illustrations.

Wisconsin Studies in Autobiography

WILLIAM L. ANDREWS
Series Editor

Robert F. Sayre
The Examined Self: Benjamin Franklin, Henry Adams, Henry James

Daniel B. Shea
Spiritual Autobiography in Early America

Lois Mark Stalvey
The Education of a WASP

Margaret Sams
Forbidden Family: A Wartime Memoir of the Philippines, 1941–1945
Edited with an introduction by Lynn Z. Bloom

Charlotte Perkins Gilman
The Living of Charlotte Perkins Gilman: An Autobiography
Introduction by Ann J. Lane

Mark Twain
Mark Twain's Own Autobiography: The Chapters from the "North American Review"
Edited by Michael J. Kiskis

Journeys in New Worlds: Early American Women's Narratives
Edited by William L. Andrews, Sargent Bush, Jr., Annette Kolodny, Amy
    Schrager Lang, and Daniel B. Shea

American Autobiography: Retrospect and Prospect
Edited by Paul John Eakin

Caroline Seabury
The Diary of Caroline Seabury, 1854–1863
Edited with an introduction by Suzanne L. Bunkers

Cornelia Peake McDonald
A Woman's Civil War: A Diary with Reminiscences of the War, from March 1862
Edited with an introduction by Minrose C. Gwin

Marian Anderson
My Lord, What a Morning
Introduction by Nellie Y. McKay

American Women's Autobiography: Fea(s)ts of Memory
Edited with an introduction by Margo Culley

Frank Marshall Davis
Livin' the Blues: Memoirs of a Black Journalist and Poet
Edited with an introduction by John Edgar Tidwell

Joanne Jacobson
Authority and Alliance in the Letters of Henry Adams

Kamau Brathwaite
The Zea Mexican Diary: 7 September 1926–7 September 1986

Genaro M. Padilla
My History, Not Yours: The Formation of Mexican American Autobiography

Frances Smith Foster
Witnessing Slavery: The Development of Ante-bellum Slave Narratives

Native American Autobiography: An Anthology
Edited by Arnold Krupat

American Lives: An Anthology of Autobiographical Writing
Edited by Robert F. Sayre

Carol Holly
Intensely Family: The Inheritance of Family Shame and the Autobiographies of Henry James

People of the Book: Thirty Scholars Reflect on Their Jewish Identity
Edited by Jeffrey Rubin-Dorsky and Shelley Fisher Fishkin

G. Thomas Couser
Recovering Bodies: Illness, Disability, and Life Writing

John Downton Hazlett
My Generation: Collective Autobiography and Identity Politics

William Herrick
Jumping the Line: The Adventures and Misadventures of an American Radical

Women, Autobiography, Theory: A Reader
Edited by Sidonie Smith and Julia Watson

José Angel Gutiérrez
The Making of a Chicano Militant: Lessons from Cristal

Marie Hall Ets
Rosa: The Life of an Italian Immigrant

Carson McCullers
Illumination and Night Glare: The Unfinished Autobiography of Carson McCullers
Edited with an introduction by Carlos L. Dews

Yi-Fu Tuan
Who Am I? An Autobiography of Emotion, Mind, and Spirit

Henry Bibb
The Life and Adventures of Henry Bibb: An American Slave
Introduction by Charles J. Heglar

Diaries of Girls and Women: A Midwestern American Sampler
Edited by Suzanne L. Bunkers

Jim Lane
The Autobiographical Documentary in America

Sandra Pouchet Paquet
Caribbean Autobiography: Cultural Identity and Self-Representation

Mark O'Brien, with Gillian Kendall
How I Became a Human Being: A Disabled Man's Quest for Independence

Elizabeth L. Banks
*Campaigns of Curiosity: Journalistic Adventures of an American Girl
   in Late Victorian London*
Introduction by Mary Suzanne Schriber and Abbey L. Zink

Miriam Fuchs
The Text Is Myself: Women's Life Writing and Catastrophe

Jean M. Humez
Harriet Tubman: The Life and the Life Stories

Voices Made Flesh: Performing Women's Autobiography
Edited by Lynn C. Miller, Jacqueline Taylor, and M. Heather Carver

Loreta Janeta Velazquez
The Woman in Battle: The Civil War Narrative of Loreta Janeta Velazquez,
    Cuban Woman and Confederate Soldier
Introduction by Jesse Alemán

Cathryn Halverson
Maverick Autobiographies: Women Writers and the American West, 1900–1936

Jeffrey Brace
The Blind African Slave: Or Memoirs of Boyrereau Brinch, Nicknamed Jeffrey Brace
as told to Benjamin F. Prentiss, Esq.
Edited with an introduction by Kari J. Winter

Colette Inez
The Secret of M. Dulong: A Memoir

Before They Could Vote: American Women's Autobiographical Writing, 1819–1919
Edited by Sidonie Smith and Julia Watson

Bertram J. Cohler
Writing Desire: Sixty Years of Gay Autobiography

Philip Holden
Autobiography and Decolonization: Modernity, Masculinity, and the Nation-State

Jing M. Wang
When "I" Was Born: Women's Autobiography in Modern China

Conjoined Twins in Black and White: The Lives of Millie-Christine McKoy
    and Daisy and Violet Hilton
Edited by Linda Frost

Four Russian Serf Narratives
Translated, edited, and with an introduction by John MacKay

Mark Twain
Mark Twain's Own Autobiography: The Chapters from the "North American Review,"
   second edition
Edited by Michael J. Kiskis

Graphic Subjects: Critical Essays on Autobiography and Graphic Novels
Edited by Michael A. Chaney

Omar Ibn Said
A Muslim American Slave: The Life of Omar Ibn Said
Translated from the Arabic, edited, and with an introduction by Ala Alryyes

Sylvia Bell White and Jody LePage
Sister: An African American Life in Search of Justice

Identity Technologies: Constructing the Self Online
Edited by Anna Poletti and Julie Rak

Alfred Habegger
Masked: The Life of Anna Leonowens, Schoolmistress at the Court of Siam

We Shall Bear Witness: Life Narratives and Human Rights
Edited by Meg Jensen and Margaretta Jolly

Made in the USA
Middletown, DE
25 April 2021